WHENCE WE CAME, WHERE WE WENT

WHENCE WE CAME, WHERE WE WENT

From the Rhine to the Main to the Elbe,
from the Thames to the Hudson

WALTER ALBERT EBERSTADT

W.A.E.
BOOKS

NEW YORK

FIRST EDITION

Frontispiece photograph by Shonna Valeska.
All other photographs courtesy the author.

Library of Congress Control Number: 2002106151
ISBN 0-9651645-6-X

Published in the United States of America by
W. A. E. Books, New York
c/o Whitehurst & Clark
100 Newfield Avenue
Edison, New Jersey 08837
732-225-2727
wcbooks@aol.com

Printed in the United States of America

TO THE MEMORY OF

MY PARENTS

Contents

ACKNOWLEDGMENTS

The impetus to write a family history came from my sons, George and Michael. I am obliged to them because it became a rewarding and enjoyable task, which absorbed me, on and off, over the past decade.

Michael, a skilled writer, urged me, usually while we were sailing: "Dad, first make an outline of what you want to write." I wish I had heeded him. I can thank George for teaching me the rudiments of using a laptop. Even if this tested his patience and filial loyalty, without his tutoring the book could not have been written.

Nor would the book have been possible if we were not a family of hoarders of the written and printed word. Letters, diaries, newspaper clippings, and photographs, made their way from Germany to England and America. My mother's Swiss cousin, Willy Dreyfus, preserved the World War II correspondence of my mother's parents, which passed through his hands, and is perhaps the book's singular contribution to wartime history.

I received needed and welcome editorial help from Paul De Angelis and his wife Elisabeth Kaestner, who proved to be superb and sensitive editors. I would not have known them but for a kindly introduction by Cynthia Cannell, a literary agent and fifth generation descendant from Ferdinand Eberstadt, mayor of Worms in the 1840s.

Susan Hayes is responsible for the production; she turned my labors at a laptop into an elegant, tangible reality. Mimi Wlodarczyk, program co-ordinator in the photography department at the New School, helped me with the selection and reproduction of the pictures. She now knows more about who is who in our family than any living being.

My special thanks go to Christof Eberstadt of Erlangen, Germany, another fifth generation descendant of Ferdinand Eberstadt who has made family trees his avocation. With his blessing I have cribbed shamelessly from the results of his labors.

Last but not least I am truly grateful to two good friends who made helpful suggestions and, even more important, encouraged me to persevere. Jonathan Fanton, then president of New School University and now head of the MacArthur Foundation, read the manuscript with the eye of a teacher and the mindset of a historian. Bob Millard, one of those rare and enviable people who excel at whatever they do — in his case investment banking, architecture, piano playing, and piloting a jet, to name but a few — liked what he read and thought others would, too.

I am confident of my facts, but less so of my opinions.

Preface

When Hitler came to power in 1933, half a million Jews lived in Germany. For many, perhaps a majority, being German meant more than being Jewish. It had become so with the Eberstadts, my father's family, and the Flersheims, my mother's family. It lasted until Hitler ended it.

For families such as ours, life in the nineteenth century had become better with each generation. We prospered. We dreamed. If they had a Christmas tree, we had a Christmas tree. If they liked Wagner, we liked Wagner, even if he did not particularly like us. You cannot legislate against prejudice, but we enjoyed equal rights under the law until Hitler came to power in 1933.

Father's generation of German Jews had high expectations for success and fulfillment, provided they had ability, no matter the walk of life they chose. In the event, their hold on success under the political and economic conditions of the Weimar Republic proved tenuous. A lawyer by training, my father was an infantry officer in the First World War, became a prominent banker in unstable times, and in 1936 left Germany for England. It was late in life for a fresh start, and he was an almost penniless refugee. In common with many others, his parents had him baptized a Protestant, doubtless with this world more in mind than the next.

My maternal family, the Flersheims, had lived in Frankfurt since the eighteenth century. While many Eberstadts chose the professions, the Flersheims remained business people. Their firm was founded in 1790. It ceased being theirs when it was "Aryanized" in 1938.

This memoir straddles the First and Second World Wars, one on the German, the other on the Allied side. At the core of Imperial Germany was the military. Much has been written about its pivotal role in Germany, also in German-Jewish life. Peacetime military service was compulsory. University graduates generally became army reserve officers — provided their religion was not Jewish. To be a reserve officer opened social and professional doors. It was a reason to convert, even if a few Jews managed to slip unnoticed as officers into the more obscure regiments.

For many German Jews the point of military service was to demonstrate they were willing to risk their lives for the Fatherland. They considered the risks worthwhile if frontline service would earn the next generation a level playing field in a country that at best accepted them halfheartedly.

In old Frankfurt newspapers, I found two articles written in 1904 on the occasion of the hundredth anniversary celebration of Philanthropin, my grandfather Flersheim's Jewish high school. One is about its fervent if somewhat servile patriotism, and the other asks, in a manner well-meaning but patronizing, how German this "alien" tribe could ever become. The Eberstadts and Flersheims did not consider themselves an alien tribe. Evidently they were hopelessly mistaken.

After we went to England in 1936, Germany became our past. In England we certainly were an alien tribe, however much we tried to fit in. I came to worship England and the English, and for a while considered myself to have become one of them. In 1940, internment came as a rude reminder that I was after all an alien, an enemy alien at that. Never mind that the English let us join the army, which got us out from behind barbed wire. Since the morning the police came to arrest me at my parents' home, England has not been the same for me.

Mine is not a unique experience. There is nothing particularly remarkable about me or my life, but I have lived in remarkably interesting times in three countries: in Germany, first as a child and schoolboy, then as a British soldier; in England, at school, Oxford, internment, army, more Oxford, the beginnings of a career, initially as a financial journalist; then for fifty years in the United States as a banker, and as a husband, father, grandfather. After bumpy beginnings a fulfilled life.

If Amschel Löb Eberstadt set out at the end of the eighteenth century in Worms to make his family part of the mainstream, this great-great-grandson, still German-born, became part of it, but in America. It has been a long journey, from the Rhine to the Main, from the Main to the Elbe, from the Elbe to the Thames, from the Thames to the Hudson — but we are afloat!

For many of my generation who were fortunate enough to leave Germany or Austria as children, Hitler has been a blessing, if at times rather too well-disguised. Thanks to him we fought the war on the winning side. We did well academically. We made good careers, more so perhaps than we might had it all been handed to us on a silver platter, helped by well-established parents in our native lands.

Much commends dying where you are born, but had I not left my homeland I would have missed out on a wonderfully varied and interesting life. I have been able to draw on three countries, at various times home, both loved, and hated.

Most of us need and want to belong somewhere, but if you don't totally belong to any country or creed, you become gun-shy of too much nationalism and religion. Flags, national anthems, hymns, the emotions they stir — and the pain they can inflict! I am far from immune to their spell but try not to be swept off my feet.

When we face our maker He should ask not only what we have done, but also why we did it. By "why" more than "what" we stand or fall. I may squeak by on what, but if He does his job halfway thoroughly I shall be in trouble over why. Even if I have found myself on the "right" side of a few issues or events, I am in trouble over the why, but if the why troubles me, will He at least give me a little credit for being troubled?

Had we been Gentile rather than Jewish Germans, I have no reason to assume we would have belonged to the courageous minority of Nazi opponents. I like to think we would not have been attracted to dictatorships, but then, tolerance is probably as much a matter of glands and temperament as of character or principles. Those who seemingly on principle champion unpopular causes, or are against the government of the day, tend to be contrarians by temperament, bile, and disposition as much as reason. They are contrarians in the stock market and contrarians with their spouses.

Jews have every reason to abhor Nazis, maybe any German, but having had no choice, how much moral credit should we claim for having found ourselves on the right side? Be that as it may, I was born and raised for the first twelve years of my life in pre-Nazi Germany. I was a schoolboy in Germany for Hitler's first three years. I lined the streets with the rest of my class, but stood there silently while they cheered the Führer's first visit to Hamburg.

With the Nuremberg Laws of 1935 my parents saw the writing on the wall. They sent me to school in England; my sister followed a few months later. My English school, Oxford, and six years in the British army left more than an Anglicized veneer. To this day I feel at home in Britain, though my onetime almost passionate love for the British has long since given way to deep affection and respect for the United States.

No religion played a role at home, but I attended Protestant prayers at school in Hamburg, Anglican chapel every morning and twice on Sundays at school in England, Anglican cathedral at Oxford, Anglican field services in the army. It is the Christian ritual, its music and architecture, that I came to know. Its familiarity is comfortable and comforting, no more than the Jewish ritual might have become had I been raised that way.

I am not a historian, but much of what I am writing is based on books, articles, documents, and letters about or by our family, from the ghetto in

Worms on the Rhine — Germany's oldest ghetto, where many of our family members lived — to clandestine correspondence during World War II between my mother in England and her parents in German-occupied Holland.

This, then, is the background that shaped me. My sons, George and Michael, asked me to write about our family and myself. They had a good idea. It matters, whence you come. If I don't tell them, no one will.

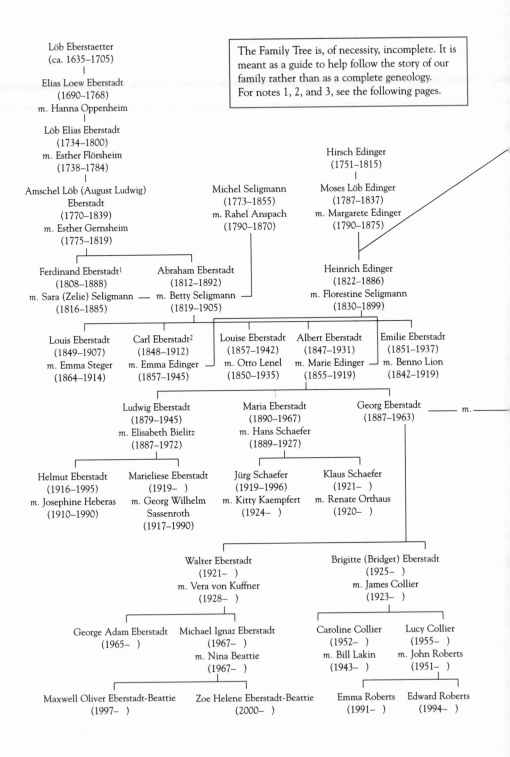

Löb Eberstaetter
(ca. 1635–1705)
|
Elias Loew Eberstadt
(1690–1768)
m. Hanna Oppenheim
|
Löb Elias Eberstadt
(1734–1800)
m. Esther Flörsheim
(1738–1784)
|

Hirsch Edinger
(1751–1815)
|

Amschel Löb (August Ludwig)
Eberstadt
(1770–1839)
m. Esther Gernsheim
(1775–1819)

Michel Seligmann
(1773–1855)
m. Rahel Anspach
(1790–1870)

Moses Löb Edinger
(1787–1837)
m. Margarete Edinger
(1790–1875)

The Family Tree is, of necessity, incomplete. It is meant as a guide to help follow the story of our family rather than as a complete geneology. For notes 1, 2, and 3, see the following pages.

Ferdinand Eberstadt[1]
(1808–1888)
m. Sara (Zelie) Seligmann
(1816–1885)

Abraham Eberstadt
(1812–1892)
m. Betty Seligmann
(1819–1905)

Heinrich Edinger
(1822–1886)
m. Florestine Seligmann
(1830–1899)

Louis Eberstadt
(1849–1907)
m. Emma Steger
(1864–1914)

Carl Eberstadt[2]
(1848–1912)
m. Emma Edinger
(1857–1945)

Louise Eberstadt
(1857–1942)
m. Otto Lenel
(1850–1935)

Albert Eberstadt
(1847–1931)
m. Marie Edinger
(1855–1919)

Emilie Eberstadt
(1851–1937)
m. Benno Lion
(1842–1919)

Ludwig Eberstadt
(1879–1945)
m. Elisabeth Bielitz
(1887–1972)

Maria Eberstadt
(1890–1967)
m. Hans Schaefer
(1889–1927)

Georg Eberstadt
(1887–1963)   m.

Helmut Eberstadt
(1916–1995)
m. Josephine Heberas
(1910–1990)

Marieliese Eberstadt
(1919–)
m. Georg Wilhelm
Sassenroth
(1917–1990)

Jürg Schaefer
(1919–1996)
m. Kitty Kaempfert
(1924–)

Klaus Schaefer
(1921–)
m. Renate Orthaus
(1920–)

Walter Eberstadt
(1921–)
m. Vera von Kuffner
(1928–)

Brigitte (Bridget) Eberstadt
(1925–)
m. James Collier
(1923–)

George Adam Eberstadt
(1965–)

Michael Ignaz Eberstadt
(1967–)
m. Nina Beattie
(1967–)

Caroline Collier
(1952–)
m. Bill Lakin
(1943–)

Lucy Collier
(1955–)
m. John Roberts
(1951–)

Maxwell Oliver Eberstadt-Beattie
(1997–)

Zoe Helene Eberstadt-Beattie
(2000–)

Emma Roberts
(1991–)

Edward Roberts
(1994–)

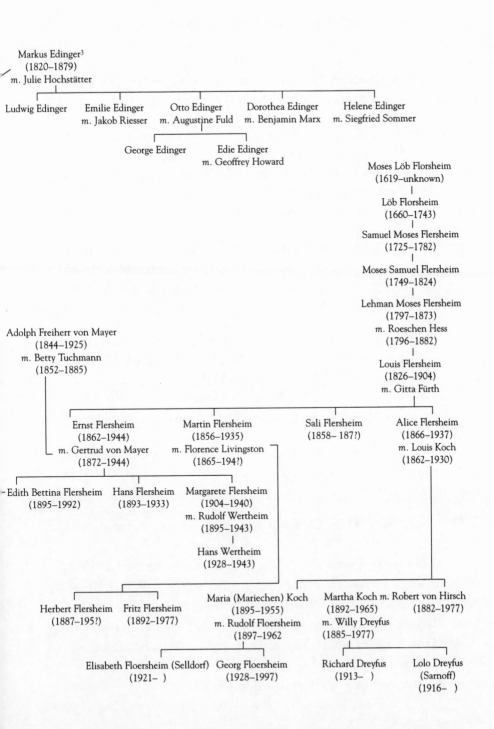

Markus Edinger[3]
(1820–1879)
m. Julie Hochstätter

Ludwig Edinger   Emilie Edinger   Otto Edinger   Dorothea Edinger   Helene Edinger
                 m. Jakob Riesser m. Augustine Fuld m. Benjamin Marx   m. Siegfried Sommer

George Edinger   Edie Edinger
                  m. Geoffrey Howard

Moses Löb Florsheim
(1619–unknown)

Löb Florsheim
(1660–1743)

Samuel Moses Flersheim
(1725–1782)

Moses Samuel Flersheim
(1749–1824)

Lehman Moses Flersheim
(1797–1873)
m. Roeschen Hess
(1796–1882)

Adolph Freiherr von Mayer
(1844–1925)
m. Betty Tuchmann
(1852–1885)

Louis Flersheim
(1826–1904)
m. Gitta Fürth

Ernst Flersheim   Martin Flersheim   Sali Flersheim   Alice Flersheim
(1862–1944)   (1856–1935)   (1858– 187?)   (1866–1937)
m. Gertrud von Mayer   m. Florence Livingston   m. Louis Koch
(1872–1944)   (1865–194?)   (1862–1930)

Edith Bettina Flersheim   Hans Flersheim   Margarete Flersheim
(1895–1992)   (1893–1933)   (1904–1940)
                                           m. Rudolf Wertheim
                                           (1895–1943)

                                           Hans Wertheim
                                           (1928–1943)

Herbert Flersheim   Fritz Flersheim   Maria (Mariechen) Koch   Martha Koch m. Robert von Hirsch
(1887–195?)   (1892–1977)   (1895–1955)   (1892–1965)   (1882–1977)
                                        m. Rudolf Floersheim   m. Willy Dreyfus
                                        (1897–1962   (1885–1977)

                          Elisabeth Floersheim (Selldorf) Georg Floersheim   Richard Dreyfus   Lolo Dreyfus
                          (1921–)   (1928–1997)   (1913–)   (Sarnoff)
                                                                                                  (1916–)

Notes on the Family Tree

1. Due to space limitations, five of the ten children of Ferdinand Eberstadt and Sara Seligmann are described in prose:

Eduard Ferdinand (Edward Frederick), born Worms 1843, emigrated to the U.S.A., American citizen in 1879. His descendants include: Edward Emory Eberstadt, born 1883, bookseller and collector of Americana; Ferdinand Eberstadt, born 1890, New York investment banker and World War II government official; Rudolph Eberstadt, born New Jersey 1896, industrialist.

Emma, born Worms 1840, married 1860 in Mannheim to Benedikt (Bernhard) Kahn, bed feather maker and banker. Their son, Otto H. Kahn, became senior partner in the New York investment banking house Kuhn Loeb and Co., as well as a leading figure in the New York cultural world.

Elisabeth (Betty), born Worms 1844, married 1867 to Sir George Lewis, senior partner of Lewis and Lewis, London solicitors whose clients included the Prince of Wales (later Edward VII).

Max, twin of Betty, became a banker in London.

Maria, born Worms 1845, married 1862 to David Joshua, London stockbroker.

Of the descendants who remained in Germany, some emigrated after 1933. Some survived in Germany. Some lost their lives in concentration camps.

2. The descendants of Carl Eberstadt and Emma Edinger included:

Otto Eberstadt, emigrated 1937 to England, where he died in 1975. His sons were: Professor *David Eversley* (died 1997), a WWII British Army Commando, a well-known urban planner, and a close friend of mine; *Heinrich (Heiner)*, who survived arrests and the war in Germany and died in 1968; *Gerhard*, board member Dresdner Bank, Frankfurt, who became a close personal and business friend; *Fritz*, a medical doctor, who emigrated to America in 1938 and died in 1973.

3. Other descendants of Markus Edinger:

His son Professor *Ludwig Edinger*, who was an early promiment neurologist, his granddaughter *Eva Sommer*, who married Victor Ehrenberg,
history professor at Prague University — their son Sir *Lewis Elton* became
Chichile Professor of Tudor History at Cambridge University, and one of
their great-grandsons is writer-comedian Ben Elton.

I am deeply indebted for the genealogic and other Eberstadt-Edinger
family data to Christof Eberstadt, great-grandson of Ferdinand and Zelie
Eberstadt, of Erlangen, Germany. His e-mail address is *cpa-eberstadt@
t-online.de*. His Eberstadt Web site is *www.crosswinds.net/~eberstadt/
eberstadt.htm*.

PART ONE

WHENCE WE CAME

1

The Worms Ghetto

It could not have been easy, let alone pleasant, to live in a ghetto, even be it Germany's oldest and most famed, at Worms on the Rhine. Located in one of Germany's most beautiful and historic regions, Worms, with its ancient diocese, was one of the oldest and most important cities in the Middle Ages. The well-established Jewish community had built a synagogue in 1175 and had one of the oldest and largest Jewish cemeteries (over two thousand graves) in all of Europe, dating back to the eleventh century. This is where our Eberstadt and Edinger ancestors had lived since the seventeenth century. Some were rabbis, the closest they could come to a scholarly life. Mostly they were in business, apparently relatively well off.

One hundred fifty-one years ago an Eberstadt became the first Jewish mayor of Worms. Few people, Jew or Gentile, know much about their forebears, but if they do, they consider themselves superior.

My great-great-grandfather Amschel Löb (August Ludwig) Eberstadt was born in 1770 and died in 1839. He was a textile merchant. His wife,

Esther Gernsheim, was born in 1775 and died in 1819. They had several children, one of whom was Ferdinand, who became mayor of Worms in 1849. Another was my great-grandfather Abraham. The parents of August Ludwig were Löb Eberstadt (d. 1800) and Esther Flörsheim (d. 1784). Löb's father was Elias who died in 1768. Elias's father was another Löb who was born around 1635 and died in 1705. His name first appeared on the Worms tax register in 1666. Esther Flürsheim's parents were Falck Gernsheim and Fränzchen Flürsheim. This makes me the seventh, and my grandchildren the ninth recorded generation.

In 1924, S. Rothschild, a teacher in the Worms public schools and secretary of the Worms Jewish community, described the life of the Worms Jews between 1563 and 1854 in two papers, the first about the financial burdens of life in the ghetto, and the second about the emancipation struggles. The ghetto population was constantly forced to make payments in cash or kind on the accession of a new ruler, to support wars, to obtain travel and work permits, to pay tolls of all kinds, while interest compounded on debts in arrears. In 1636, for instance, during the Thirty Years War (1618–1648), there was a letter from "the most humble, the most obedient and the most respectful but poor and common Jewish community in Worms to His most honored Excellency, the Count and Governor of Worms, . . . After supplying you with several hundredweight of grain, with wine and other victuals, with 10,000 thalers in cash for the support of the Florentine and Wedel regiments, instead of the promised and expected protection, further payments were extorted within one week, which are beyond our capacity, human or financial. If there is not some reasonable accommodation we will be forced to uproot ourselves and move away, God knows where." In response, the Elector of Mainz proposed that the tribute be limited to a more manageable sum and that the Jewish community be relieved of the compulsory billeting of troops. The relief did not endure long. A few years later the commanding general was implored to release two of the congregation's elders who had been imprisoned because payments were in arrears.

In 1716 the Jews were told to deliver to a local warehouse 8 beds and to pay 800 thalers of "Turkey tribute." (Local soldiers participated in wars against the Turkish Empire.) In 1734, on one day's notice, they were to provide the following morning 1,500 palisades, 4,000 bricks, and an unspecified quantity of large flagstones. If the latter were not supplied, the military would remove all grave markers from the Jewish cemetery.

Over the years there was a growing debt burden, endless arguments about paying, sometimes leading to forgiveness, funding at prohibitive interest rates (40 percent was not unusual in those days), and contributions from the better-off to help the community survive. But there were also loans from the Gentile aristocracy to fund overdue tributes. Repayment of these loans was guaranteed by better-off Jewish elders, among them in the 1780s various Eberstadts and Oettingers, forebears of the Edingers who later were to marry Eberstadts.

Another insight into the finances of the Jewish community appears in a letter headed Liberté Egalité, dated 8th Floreal, 6th year of the French Republic. The Gregorian calendar date was 1796, a time when Worms was under French rule. The Jewish elders addressed the letter to the president of the Worms municipality and signed it "with respectful and obedient greetings." Liabilities, it stated, exceeded assets twenty-five-fold. The debt amounted to 80,000 guilders. "The reasons for our paralysis, our total decay, the hopelessness to revive our conditions sufficiently so that we can one day satisfy our creditors are self-evident," Rothschild quoted in his account of the Worms Jews' financial condition. "We have been plundered in the various wars, there is a constant food shortage, there are horrendous restrictions imposed on us. We are without civil and human rights. We are restricted in the occupations we are allowed to practice. We have no property rights outside the ghetto, and are kept apart physically from the rest of society. The fiscal burden we have to bear is threefold that of our neighbors. We are segregated from our competitors and the rest of humanity."

The origins of the debt went back to the Thirty Years War, and it had grown further during the Seven Years War (1756–1763). The annual financial obligations of the Worms Jews in 1796 totaled about 11,500 guilders. Interest each year was 4,000 guilders. The magistrate had to be paid 1,800 guilders annually for "slave" money. Protection payments to the guilds and clergy amounted to 1,000 guilders annually. Each time a new emperor was installed (and there were four in short order), a tribute of 1,000 guilders was paid. Annual protection cost 100 guilders per capita. War subsidies took 4,000 guilders; 150 guilders were paid annually to Vienna; 1,500 guilders per year was paid to look after the inflow of "beggar Jews" from elsewhere.

Moneys owed by Jewish communities to Gentile creditors still accumulated substantial interest and, in 1820, the debt of the Worms ghetto, including interest in arrears since the 1750s, greatly exceeded the original loans. The Jewish community formed a committee of its wealthier members, including my great-great-grandfather Amschel Löb Eberstadt to raise money to settle these debts once and for all. Between 1824 and 1834 the community and individual members paid off 47,300 thalers, still leaving a debt of over 17,000 thalers in 1834. To raise this money, the community issued between 220 and 250 shares at 50 thalers each, repayable over fifteen to twenty years, bearing interest at 5 percent. The board invited the congregation to subscribe according to their means. There were nine subscribers who took ten shares each, among them A. L. Eberstadt; L. Edinger bought three shares.

When the issue of Jewish emancipation became more salient in the eighteenth century, Germany still consisted of innumerable countships, free cities, bishoprics, kingdoms or tiny states, each with its own history of "political" needs, dependencies, biases, prejudices, and competitive strivings for survival, power, or self-importance. These regions, each with their own societal structure and jurisdiction, had widely divergent "laws" pertaining to Jews, some upheld since the Middle Ages, and some striving to enact modern liberal views. The specific status of Jews in a given region greatly depended on pragmatic facts; that is, how necessary and useful the Jewish individual, family, or community was to the current rulers in power — in other words, whether or not the ruler had a particular need for money, foreign trade connections, or specific goods or knowledge a Jew could provide. The history of the Behrens bank (see chapter 5) where Georg Eberstadt was a partner in the 1920s, is an example. Prince Frederic of Waldeck, Count of Pyrmont, issued a letter of safe conduct and protection to Levy Behrens and his brothers to conduct business in 1780. The prince of Waldeck relied on Jewish business for access to money and goods and therefore granted privileges.

The struggle for the emancipation of the Jews in Worms and the other centers of Jewish communities in the Palatinate began in the eighteenth century and was facilitated by the French Revolution, which proclaimed equal rights and freedom to all people regardless of their origin or faith. In 1791, the French National Assembly granted full civil rights to all Jews in France. The Palatine communities, including Worms, were then under French rule, though only for a few years.

At the Congress of Vienna (1814–1815), when Europe was reorganized after Napoleon's rule, the parliament of the German Confederation (of thirty-nine politically independent regions) granted social and legal rights to Jews, though under significant protest from representatives who saw local regional interests threatened. The *Judenfleck* was abolished at long last. (At the end of the sixteenth century up until the eighteenth, a *Judentracht*, a coat with a round yellow patch and a pointy yellow hat, referred to as *pileum cornutum*, was required to be worn by Jews in certain areas of Germany.) Despite progress in certain areas, true equality was far from established.

In the 1830s various Jewish congregations in the Palatinate (including Mainz, Darmstadt, Offenbach, Giessen, Bingen, and Alzey) worked together to establish one central organization that negotiated with the government on matters such as properly organized teachers, uniform confirmations, or the religious and secular education of rabbis. In 1832 the association to attain the improvement of conditions of the Israelites in the Grand Duchy of Hesse was formed. Over time, the association's support decreased to the point that even the Hessian ministry, which wanted to effect changes, suggested they raise more money to increase their effectiveness. Subscriptions came in not only from Jews but also from numerous Gentiles, including public officials, clergy, army, and business. The individual amounts seem modest. A. L. Eberstadt, with 7 guilders, gave the largest sum. Mayor Renz of Worms gave 3 guilders.

Other areas of emancipation, besides the struggle to abolish the debt burdens, included the fight to abolish religion as a barrier to practicing any profession or to hold positions in public service. Jews were required to abide by the *Moralpatent*, a special certification for Jewish businessmen, and by the *More Judaico*, a special form of oath.

As Rothschild explains in his 1924 essay, the *Moralpatent* was an imperial decree of March 7, 1808, renewed in 1818. It required that any Jew in business had to obtain annually a patent from the elders in his community certifying that there was nothing in his character or conduct to be held against him. On the basis of this certification, the local mayor granted him permission, upon payment of a fee, to continue with his business.

Under the leadership of Dernburg, the head of the Mainz Jews, and in cooperation with the Jewish communities of other towns in Hesse, a deputation went to see a member of the Hesse parliament who was well disposed to the Jews. In 1836 they approached another public official, a Dr. Glaubrech, also open to the Jewish cause. Dernburg expressed complete confidence in Glaubrech. "To get to the point, our existence must not be dependent upon the rough and arbitrary powers exercised by a handful of village mayors. The jurisdiction of these mayors over our affairs, based upon a ministerial decree of Feb. 1, 1832, must terminate."

Four years later, however, on December 8, 1840, the Worms community, in a letter signed by Ferdinand Eberstadt, Heinrich Blüm, and Jakob Fulda II, wrote to the elders in Alzey, Mainz, and Bingen that "lately the 1808 decree is being enforced more severely than ever. The most law abiding of businessmen are unable to follow their trade without a morals patent. The complaints of our co-religionists are loud and clear and we feel it is our most urgent duty to take up this cause with vigor and perseverance. We must all work together to remonstrate how patently unfair and burdensome it is to have to prove every year one's honest conduct. It places an unfair and undeserved stigma on each of us. The vast majority of us is engaged in the honest pursuit of our occupations and in no way deserves to be singled out in this demeaning fashion. The decree was first issued by way of a mere ordinance and therefore could be revoked by another ordinance. We believe a large part of the government's subjects would be in favor of improving the situation of the Israelites."

A further letter from the Worms community in 1841, signed among others by Albert (Amschel) Eberstadt and S. Edinger, expresses the hope that "in keeping with the liberal spirit of the times, justice and humanity will in the end win out. We must not remain silent when it is our duty to speak out." In early 1845 there is correspondence between the Jewish community and Mayor Renz of Worms. The community asked that the patents not be issued as official documents requiring stamp duty; still, the request was denied.

Finally, on July 27, 1845, the heads of the Mainz community reported to Worms that Dr. Glaubrech's endeavors "met with approval in both chambers of the Hessian parliament, and the *Moralpatent* has been terminated." There was great rejoicing everywhere, also outside Hesse. Subscription lists were opened to collect money to present Dr. Glaubrech with a splendid silver trophy. Money given beyond the cost of the trophy was allocated to various charities. "Gratitude and charity have always been part of the Israelite tradition. Not even our worst enemies can deny this." The presentation to Dr. Glaubrech took place on August 1, 1847. He responded at length and promised continuing support. It was needed.

Another step toward equality was the abolition of the *more judaico*, imposed by Christian rule in the thirteenth century. If a Jew made a statement under oath, it was required to take place in a synagogue, in the presence of a rabbi, on the Torah. It was deemed deeply insulting that the oath should differ from any oath rendered by a Christian. Some regions even added grotesque requirements that were especially offensive and demeaning to Jews. In protest, during the 1840s, more and more rabbis refused to open the doors of the synagogue for oath-taking.

One such case occurred in February of 1843. Rabbi Bamberger of the Worms synagogue refused to administer an oath, stating he could not open the synagogue without the approval of its elders, and this they had refused. The Justice of the Peace in Worms consulted the state prosecutor of the divisional court at Alzey. They agreed, as indicated in correspondence, that nothing much could be done in such situations other than to file a memorandum to be passed to higher authority.

Those involved met in Rabbi Bamberger's home, in the presence of Jakob Fulda, president of the Worms congregation, who stated they would continue to refuse opening the doors of the synagogue for the administration of the *more judaico*. With the increase of liberalism and the March student uprisings of 1848, the first "German" National Parliament was elected and met in late 1848–1849 in Frankfurt. Influenced significantly by the French Revolution and the American Constitution, basic civil rights were granted to Jews in the German Federation. The *more judaico* ended formally, and from then on Jews, like anyone else, responded with "so help me God" when swearing an oath. To quote Rothschild, "Any still existing restrictions of civil or civic rights based on religion" ended. "Participation in communal or state legislatures, or the holding of public office of any kind, is not dependent upon any religious belief."

The question of legal and social rights of Jews in the German states was far from settled, however. Strong reactionary movements both within Prussian- and Austrian-ruled regions opposed the civil rights newly granted to Jews by the National Assembly of Frankfurt. Prejudice and de facto discrimination continued to flourish. At the same time, government positions could now be held by Jews in the Palatinate.

It is against this background that the Eberstadt ancestors need to be seen. More detailed knowledge about their lives begins with Amschel Löb, my great-great-grandfather, a textile merchant who was born in 1770 and died in 1839. He had several daughters and two sons, my great-grandfather Abraham and his brother Ferdinand. The brothers were partners in a textile and general soft goods business, and they married sisters, Betty and Sara (Zelie) Seligmann. Ferdinand was active in politics. He seems to have been the more important and interesting brother (see Fritz Reuter, *One Thousand Years of Jews in Worms*, published by the City of Worms, 1984).

In the years preceding the 1848 revolution there were two political factions in Worms. The republican progressives formed the Democratic union. Its followers were of the skilled artisan class and smaller tradesmen. J. P. Bandel, a vineyard owner, a doctor named Ferdinand von Loehr, and Ferdinand Eberstadt led the union. The other party was the pro-constitution pro-monarchy Bürgerverein, which drew its support from conservative elements among the professions, officialdom, and the business community. In the municipal elections of 1849 Ferdinand Eberstadt became mayor, even though he did not have the largest number of votes. Eberstadt supported many of the revolutionary notions of the time, such as raising a volunteer force of armed civilians. He favored an activist communal policy supporting industrial progress, which would bring employment to his artisan constituency. He was successful in business, well-read, and cultured but was said to have had a domineering, quarrelsome temper. The collecting of arms for the militia led to accusations of extortion and high treason. Though acquitted, he stepped down as mayor in 1852 and moved with his wife to Mannheim in the principality of Baden, which had for a long time a hospitable attitude toward Jews. Ferdinand's children married well and many of them moved on to more cosmopolitan cities.

Ferdinand Eberstadt's determination and that of other leading members of the Worms Jewish community to help the Worms Jews escape the ghetto and be accepted in all walks of life broke new ground for him and his fellow Jews. In 1847 he wrote to a sister that he was taken up with various public offices "which demonstrated the open-mindedness of his fellow citizens." Indeed, he became the first Jew to be sworn in as a juror at the Assizes in Mainz. He complained it was a costly honor — not counting time lost from his business, the costs associated with the position amounted to at least 100 guilders. But, he continued, "it is worth any personal sacrifice to break down old prejudices and do away with undeserved and illegal miserable impediments to equality of opportunity." No matter what the religious rites of a Jew, or his politics, it surely had to make them proud and happy to "live in a wonderful time, a time of progress, the modification and evolution of old institutions, a battle for truth and justice against prejudice and privilege. Step by step we are making headway, but we must not tire or give up because so much remains to be accomplished, especially for the Jews."

According to the book on Worms Jews, Ferdinand Eberstadt was considered a "tyrant" by his family, but with a strong sense of family loyalty. For example, the list of candidates for jury duty in Worms contained 23 names, of which 13 were Jews, and of these 5 were Eberstadts. The total population of Worms was 8,000, of whom 10 percent were Jews, yet as many as half of the jurors were Jewish.

Ferdinand Eberstadt also took part in the beginnings of the movement to reform religious practices. He wrote his sister, with apparent gratification, that at the past Passover celebrations he had been able to arrange for the synagogue service to be conducted in German rather than Hebrew, and that men and women could sit together. The orthodox in the congregation fought the changes. They went so far as to appeal to the government to prohibit the modernized ritual. The authorities, however, not only allowed the changes to stand but also ordered the orthodox to pay their share of the costs of the new form of services. Ferdinand reported to his sister that as soon as tempers calmed down the congregation would buy an organ for the musical part of the services.

In the nineteenth century Germany still consisted of innumerable independent cities and princely states competing for money and influence. It was a time of political upheaval, territorial wars, and fights for political and economic power, among others between Austria and Prussia. Despite continued prejudice and attempts to restrict the tenuous legal equality of Jews granted around 1848, the North German Bund, formed in 1866 after Prussia triumphed over Austria and consisting of seventeen states and free cities, continued to uphold civil rights for Jews.

The main themes in the debate among German Christians over the emancipation of Jews revolved around the questions of religious freedom and national identity. For some, religious freedom was easy to grant, while civic rights, they argued, needed to be restricted since Jews had their own nationality and could not be entrusted with German national interests. This argument supported restricting access to universities, guilds, land ownership, and the like. There were vast regional differences in the extent to which the rights of Jews were enforced, since the National Assembly was rather a theoretical and idealistic entity, without much political bite.

After German national unity was established, many Christian Germans still argued that Jews could not be considered German nationals because they belonged to the nation of Israel.

Equality of rights had been attained in the Palatinate, much to the satisfaction of those who had striven for it so long. It remained a constant struggle to achieve the employment of Jews, for example, as teachers or lawyers. It took the First World War to have Jewish army officers, and Rothschild concludes in his essay that a "chronicler's reticence prevents him from saying too much about the actual implementation of the constitutional changes." In 1921 he wrote, "A new form of anti-Semitism has replaced the old form of hating Jews." When legal equality was finally achieved, it remained a theoretical equal status.

Possibly because of the strong influence of the liberal thinking of the French Revolution in the Palatinate, Jews in Worms were integrated relatively early. This is demonstrated by another well-regarded, influential, and well-to-do Worms family, the Edingers, in-laws of the Eberstadts. Heinrich Edinger and his brother Markus (1820–1879) established the first mass manufacturing business for men's clothing in Germany. Heinrich's daughters Marie and Emma Edinger later married Abraham Eberstadt's sons, Carl and Albert (Albert was my grandfather). Markus's daughter Emilie married Jakob Riesser, who became prominent in the banking world of the Weimar Republic and had connections with my father, Georg Eberstadt, Albert Eberstadt's son.

Markus Edinger was a leading figure in Worms. He died on June 16, 1879, "of a stroke after many years of asthma." According to the *Wormser Zeitung* he died

> at the peak of his powers, an upright citizen, a true patriot, a precious human being . . . a child of Worms; by his own endeavors he worked his way up to a respected position in the business world.
>
> The honors bestowed on him . . . by electing him to local and state offices reflected the trust of his fellow citizens. . . . If no party could claim his sole allegiance, his name did belong to the causes

of liberty. In its ranks he marched all his life, untouched by prevailing fashions or the noises of some ephemeral one-day wonder. He was tolerant in the classic sense of the word, not seduced by success or broken by failure, respected all views or convictions, but in the end always abided by his own principles. Nothing hit him harder than the outbursts of the crassest political and social intolerance in our immediate vicinity as well as up and down the whole country. . . . These attacks led him eventually to resign his posts in public life and leave his native city. . . .

The life style of this admirable man was simple. He was born in 1820, educated at the Worms Gymnasium, and went into business. His public service began when he founded the still flourishing Vorschuss- und Credit-Verein, a co-operative savings and loan association. . . . Edinger was similarly engaged in the promotion of numerous other agencies based on the principle of self-help (. . . a mutual health insurance group . . . a workingmen's adult education association and the Jewish hospital). . . . He first stood for the Hesse Landtag [parliament] in 1862 but ceded his seat to the present ministerial counselor Finger. In 1866 he was elected unopposed and in 1872 he won a hotly contested re-election against a national-liberal candidate. . . . This is not the place to recount what Edinger meant for the poor and suffering, for family and friends. . . . May he rest in peace.

The *Neue Wormser Zeitung*, politically his opponent, wrote on June 18, 1879, "Yesterday afternoon a funeral procession of several hundred men from all religions and political parties paid the last respects." In his tribute, Julius Nett said, "In a few minutes the earth will cover a heart which beat warmly for Worms, for Hesse and for our beautiful German fatherland. You, often misunderstood and opposed, can rest peacefully. Members of all parties stand here mourning you. . . . Farewell."

Justice, liberty, and Fatherland were ideals of the liberal movement of the times, and were often evoked as the highest values that Jews striving for emancipation and integration could follow. Albert Eberstadt was one who wanted his children to prosper as Germans. His kin achieved prominence and he wanted the same for his children.

Memories of ghetto life, Ferdinand Eberstadt's struggle for equal civil rights, and the Edingers' prominence in public life may have influenced subsequent Eberstadts and their relatives, who included the Riessers, Bambergers, Sommers, and Lenels — all of them families noteworthy in politics, public service, the academic world, and medicine. Gabriel Riesser (1806–1863), uncle of Jakob Riesser, was an eloquent and courageous political leader who spoke in favor of the moral and political necessity of the emancipation of Jews, first in the Baden parliament and later in the National Assembly in Frankfurt. Widely published and highly influential, he became famous as the first Jew to successfully declare the need for basic civil rights, irrespective of religious creed, and to define Jewish identity as religious, not national. He opposed baptism as a means of gaining civic rights. Like most liberals, he shared in the German nationalist sentiment of the time and ardently supported its cause.

Early on, many influential Jewish families were baptized and sanctioned mixed marriages. They sought the professions, law, medicine, public service, politics — walks of life that appeared all the more desirable because they were the first generation for whom these doors were open. The doors were more easily opened if they abandoned the Jewish faith.

In 1862, a decade after Ferdinand Eberstadt moved from Worms to Mannheim, he and his brother Abraham Eberstadt formally ended the partnership in the textile firm founded by their father Amschel Löb Eberstadt. In 1867 Abraham, my great-grandfather, moved our branch of the Eberstadts from Worms to Frankfurt. Here he founded a general merchandising business. Abraham's three sons — my grandfather Albert and his two brothers, Carl and Louis, worked for their father.

In 1878 the business wound down, and in 1881 the four founded a weaving and finishing company in Frankfurt and in Konradsreuth, near Hof, in Bavaria. In 1888 it became the Mechanische Buntweberei with its own mills, exporting to North and South America and other markets, which previously had been the preserve of the British. Abraham and his three sons lived in Frankfurt. At first non-family employees ran the Hof mills. The sales office was in Frankfurt. Abraham became a limited partner and died in 1892. His three sons, Albert, Carl, and Louis, carried on. Louis died in 1907 and Carl in 1912, which left my grandfather the sole survivor of his generation.

2

Albert Eberstadt

About the time my grandfather Albert Eberstadt (b. April 13, 1847, Worms; d. March 27, 1931, Frankfurt) was born, Germany became a country of many emigrants. The ambitious on the way up, the poor, the misfits, the ne'er-do-wells, Jew or Gentile, were tempted or forced to seek greener pastures, make fresh starts, migrate from village to town, from the Old World to the New.

Thanks to the Rothschilds, the Bethmanns, and other banking families, Frankfurt had early become a financial center. By the middle of the nineteenth century, however, Frankfurt was beginning to be eclipsed as the crossroads of commerce and politics in places such as London, Paris, and New York, fertile territory for the ambitious young seeking fame and fortune, or at least fortune. The wine merchants, cattle dealers, horse traders, and grain merchants in rural southern Germany, predominantly Jewish, were in effect bankers of sorts; they advanced money against future produce. They belonged to a religious and cultural minority, at best tolerated, certainly not loved. They might no longer live in the ghetto, but they still remained outsiders. These small-time merchants, stock traders, or clerks, were lured by stories of success and tolerance in London or New York. They read about Jacob Schiff of Kuhn Loeb in New York, the Lehmans in Alabama, the Goldmans and the Sachses in New York, the Hellmans and Schwabachers in San Francisco, Cassel and Speyer in London, all barely a couple of generations away from the ghetto when they left Germany. They might still be outsiders where they had gone, but they had become part of larger, more confident, and prospering minorities.

Ferdinand's offspring went to the United States and England; Abraham's stayed in Germany. My grandfather Albert and his two brothers, Carl and Louis, worked for their father. Abraham had moved the family from Worms and founded a wholesale business in Frankfurt. Abraham became a limited partner and died in 1892. His three sons carried on. Albert and Carl married two Edinger sisters. On April 14, 1878, Albert married Marie Edinger. They had three children — Ludwig, my father Georg, and Maria. Albert's brother Carl married Emma Edinger, and their children were Otto, Heiner, and Fritz. Marie and Emma Edinger were daughters of Heinrich Edinger, brother of the prominent Markus Edinger of Worms.

I know little about my maternal grandmother, Marie Edinger, or the role she played in the family. She died in 1919. In photos she looks attractive.

Her brother, Max Edinger, was a popular figure, a small-town lawyer in Witzenhausen in the state of Hesse. He lived too well in his youth and exhausted his inheritance with horses, carriages, and drink. Still he enjoyed social standing in Witzenhausen, though he married "beneath his station"— the daughter of a well-to-do local butcher. He survived the Nazis, thanks to a courageous (second) wife. At the end of the Second World War in 1945 the American occupation authorities made him a *Landrat,* a kind of rural district magistrate. He retired in the late 1940s. I paid him a visit while in the occupation army and was impressed by his bearing.

Emma Edinger, sister of Marie and Max, married Albert Eberstadt's brother Carl, who managed the family textile business in Hof, Bavaria. Of their three sons Fritz was a doctor, first in Frankfurt and later in the

United States, and Otto ran the family textile business with his brother Heiner (Otto was in Frankfurt and Heiner in Hof). Otto and Heiner worked first with their father Carl and, after his death, with my grandfather. My grandfather retired in 1914, though he had withdrawn from day-to-day business several years before.

In the Nazi years, my father's cousin Otto Eberstadt emigrated to England. He had two sons, one of whom, David Eversley, became a well-known urban planner and, in his later years, an interesting friend of mine. Heiner Eberstadt, thanks largely to a courageous non-Jewish wife, survived the Nazi years in Germany. One son, Gerhard, is on the board of Dresdner Bank in Frankfurt. We are friends and have done some interesting transactions together.

My grandfather Albert was more scholar than businessman, fluent in Latin and Greek, though members of his generation rarely attended university. According to my father, his father did not care particularly for his brothers, nephews, or the business itself. He sold them his interest in the business before the first war. He believed he could further his children's careers more effectively as a rentier than as a businessman. My own father seemed to have inherited this coolness toward his textile-business cousins; for as long as we lived in Germany he paid them little heed and I rarely heard a complimentary word about them.

Albert Eberstadt concentrated his ambitions on his children rather than on himself. He wanted them to prosper as Germans. His kin had achieved prominence in public life and he wanted the same for his own children.

By the end of the nineteenth century, all walks of life, with the exception of the officer corps, had been opened de jure to the Jews. De facto, however, it was a great deal easier to enter public service or the professions if one had converted to the Christian faith. Many did, not only in Germany but throughout western Europe. It is easy, in retrospect, to dismiss such conversions as merely opportunistic, but there was much more than opportunism to this wave of Jewish baptism. They were shedding what they considered the shackles of atavistic rituals. I cannot imagine that my grandfather Albert Eberstadt, who had his three children baptized, did so because he had concluded the Christian God was "truer" than the Jewish.

Perhaps he wished to seem less sectarian, less secretive, and more accommodating to the mores and customs of the second half of the nineteenth century. Be that as it may, it must have been a baptism with this world more than the next in mind. Father never appeared to have embraced the Christian creed with great conviction, but he became, like Felix Mendelssohn and many others, attracted to its ethics and its aesthetics, be they music, architecture, art, or ceremonial.

In this regard the words of Felix Mendelssohn's father, Abraham Mendelssohn, seem pertinent. They were written for his daughter's confirmation:

> The form of your religious instruction was historical and changeable, like all human pronouncements. Some few thousand years ago the Jewish form predominated, then the pagan, now it is the Christian. Your mother and I were born and brought up as Jews by our parents and have known how to follow our conscience and the godly within us without having to modify this form. You and your brothers and sisters we have brought up as Christians, since it is the form of belief of most civilized people and contains nothing that will lead you from goodness, rather much that should point you toward love, obedience, patience, and resignation (humility) if only through the example of its originator, known by the few and followed by the even fewer.

Albert was probably a little disappointed in two of his three children. They did not fulfill his expectations for them. Ludwig, the oldest (born in 1879), became a lower court judge in Cologne, a respectable but modestly paid position. He married into an impecunious army family, whose chief virtue in Ludwig's eyes may have been that they were not Jewish. His wife proved loyal and courageous in the Nazi years. They had two children, Helmut Eberstadt and Marielise Sassenroth, first cousins of mine who with their mother survived Hitler in Germany. Though it seemed as if he would be spared, Ludwig died in 1945 in Theresienstadt, the "model" concentration camp. His family believe he was shot attempting to escape.

Maria, born in 1890, the youngest, tiny in stature, was enormously well liked. My parents were close and devoted to her. In her youth she played championship tennis. In the Great War she had nursed a wounded soldier, Hans Schaefer, decent if not particularly noteworthy, whom she married in 1919. Albert Eberstadt secured a minor position for him in Lazard Speyer Ellisen, a respectable though no longer important Frankfurt private bank. He died in 1927 and left his wife without means. From then on, with some help from my parents, she supported herself taking in lodgers. Her two sons, Jürg and Klaus, almost my exact contemporaries, were like brothers to me. They became perhaps my closest friends. Every year at Eastertime we went to visit the Frankfurt family, and the Schaefers came to stay with us in Hamburg during fall school vacation.

World War II kept us apart, but within weeks of the Armistice in 1945, we took up where we had left off a decade earlier as if nothing much had occurred in between. The Schaefers survived Hitler by the skin of their teeth. They got some protection from the Nazi racial laws on account of their father's World War I record. Maria Schaefer died in Frankfurt in 1967, two blocks away from where she was born — in a different world — seventy-five years before.

Georg, my father, the middle child, was born in 1887. Head of his class in school, lawyer by training, banker by profession, he did what Albert Eberstadt aspired to for all his children. What a blessing that Iron Crosses and baptismal waters did not lull him into thinking he could survive under National Socialism!

My grandfather Albert's ambitions for his children were in part motivated by a desire to keep up with his Mannheim cousins. His uncle Ferdinand Eberstadt had been the mayor of Worms. He probably had more money than the Frankfurt branch of the family. He had numerous children, some of whom emigrated to the United States, where they attained wealth and standing as bankers, public servants, and collectors of Americana. He also had three daughters, considered in their day to be great beauties and intelligent. One daughter married a Mannheim bed feather merchant and their son, Otto H. Kahn, emigrated via England to the United States. Kahn married a Loeb whose father was a partner in

Kuhn Loeb and Co., the most prestigious Jewish Wall Street firm of its day, and became himself a partner in the firm. His Loeb father-in-law had, a generation earlier, obtained legal permission from Mayor Eberstadt to emigrate from Worms to the United States. Kahn became a major figure in Kuhn Loeb, chair of the Metropolitan Opera, a notable art collector, and one of the first Jews to be accepted socially by the non-Jewish New York upper crust.

Two of Ferdinand's daughters married in England, one to the solicitor Sir George Lewis, then the leading society lawyer in Edwardian England, Edward VII's confidant and lawyer, patron of Sir Edward Burne-Jones, the painter, and other prominent figures of the era. Two sons emigrated to the United States where they and their descendants achieved recognition in diverse walks of life: finance, government, rare books, and academe.

Besides the Mannheim Eberstadts who married well and went to England, one Edinger cousin went to London. There he founded Edinger and Asch, which became a leading stockbrokerage in the South African mining share market. His partner was Wilhelm Asch, who had run the London branch of Deutsche Bank.

The young Paul Wallich, later a colleague of my father's, had contact with Edinger and Asch while training in London in 1907. He described them as socially ambitious, Asch as kind and helpful, but Otto Edinger as hard to get on with. Wallich had numerous stories about Edinger; for instance, about him dissolving in tears at the coffin of his good client Sir Alfred Beit, the mining magnate. Moneymaking was second only to the pleasure it gave Edinger to annoy his wife. Like her husband she had become *plus royal que le roi*. In August 1914, shortly after the outbreak of the Great War when all things German, especially speaking the language in public, were taboo in London, the pair was walking in Hyde Park. When they encountered a group of young British Guards officers, supposedly Edinger said to his wife at the top of his voice in German — this when dachshunds were stoned in the streets and German waiters suspected of espionage — "Ach, *Liebchen, ganz wie in Potsdam.*" "Look, dear, just like Potsdam" — the heart and soul of Prussian militarism.

Otto Edinger's firm did not survive the First World War. The German-born members of the London Stock Exchange, who were largely Jewish, were forced to resign from the exchange, even if they had become British subjects. Edinger's Berlin-born nephew, Alfred Marx, partner in his firm, served in the British army in the war. Though naturalized he could serve in only one regiment, a battalion of the King's Own — promptly nick-named the Kaiser's Own. Spy mania and anti-German sentiments were widespread.

Edinger's eccentric son George became an influential columnist in Lord Beaverbrook's *Sunday* and *Daily Express* group of newspapers. A tal-ented but unkempt journalist, he never quite fulfilled the early promise of a brilliant Balliol undergraduate career at Oxford. His daughter Edie mar-ried Geoffrey Howard, member of an old West Country Quaker family. The Howards developed the use of quinine as the first effective antidote against malaria. They were warm and supportive when their refugee kin arrived in England. Their three sons became good friends of mine. Michael, now Sir Michael, Howard, at one time the Chichile Professor of Military History at Oxford, is England's preeminent military historian.

Albert Eberstadt was closest to his sister Louise. Rather less attention was paid to Emilie, a sister who married a certain Karl Lion, of whom little is known. Louise, on the other hand, was married to Otto Lenel, professor of Roman jurisprudence at Freiburg University, and to this day is considered Germany's leading scholar in his field.

Otto Lenel, baptized at birth, died at the age of eighty-five in 1935, two years into Hitler's Germany. By then one needed courage to attend — let alone speak — at the funeral of a Jew; yet his fellow professor Baron von Bieberstein had glowing words to say. Bieberstein recounted how five years before Lenel's death, academics from over one hundred universities from twenty different countries had come to honor him. Bieberstein described Lenel as a leader for an entire generation of scholars, as "even-tempered, incorruptible in his opinions, fair, generous, and courageous if someone was attacked unjustly. He was a passionate patriot, fought as a volunteer in the war of 1870–1871 in the Baden Dragoon Guards, stood guard outside the palace of Versailles during the proclamation of Wilhelm I as German Kaiser, lost one son in the first war killed in action as an infantry captain in 1918. Events in the last two years of his life broke his heart. He feared for Germany, for the role of Roman law, the future of the Freiburg University, and the future of his (half-Jewish) grandchildren."

Lenel's successor in Freiburg, Professor Pringsheim, was no less generous in his praise. At the end of a lecture he spoke of Lenel's concerns about the Weimar constitution's weaknesses, in particular the inadequate authority accorded to the Reichspresident's position. He emphasized Lenel's place on the right of the political spectrum, and his "passionate love for truth and justice. . . . His modesty was disarming, but he fought fanatically for a worthwhile cause or against any sort of injustice. The National Socialist revolution, which threatened to deprive his grandchildren of their rights as Germans, broke his heart."

Only seven years later Albert's sister Louise Lenel died at Gurs, a concentration camp in southern France. Her daughter, who had become a Lutheran nun, survived, was liberated in 1945 and returned to Freiburg where my father visited her from time to time in a pleasant convent in the shadow of the cathedral. I am friends with Lenel grandchildren, several of whom have had distinguished careers in their respective walks of life.

Albert lost most of his money in the German inflation that followed World War I. In the end his only significant asset was a substantial home in Frankfurt's Westend, one of its better residential districts.

The above mentioned do not remotely represent all relatives on my Eberstadt-Edinger side. Some I know well. About many I have little more than snippets of knowledge. All interest me, and I hope the feeling is mutual. Few had significant wealth but none, to the best of my knowledge, went to jail. That, in a large family, is also worth something. Many did sufficiently well in their walks of life to command respect in their chosen métier, but I don't know that they made many front pages. As it is with most families, they were fairly ordinary, reasonably competent, occasionally made a footnote in history.

3

The Flersheims

My mother's family, the Flersheims, had lived in Frankfurt since the middle of the eighteenth century. Moses Samuel Flersheim (1749–1829) founded the Flersheim firm in 1790, hawking walking sticks on his back. By the beginning of the twentieth century he had become a world leader dealing in horn, ivory, bamboo, cane, mother-of-pearl, and tortoiseshell.

My great-grandfather Louis Flersheim (1826–1904), was active in the firm from 1856 to 1892, when his sons Martin and Ernst, my grandfather, took over. Martin's son Herbert and Ernst's son Hans joined their fathers' business before the First World War. Hans died in 1933 and Martin in 1935. Herbert fled Germany in 1935 and Ernst in 1936, both to live in Holland. In 1938 Flersheim-Hess was "Aryanized" and sold to some employees for one-third of its book value. The proceeds later were confiscated by the Gestapo.

In 1939 my grandfather Ernst Flersheim dictated some business and personal memoirs to his son-in-law Rudolf Wertheim. Following are excerpts from his memoirs:

> Our firm was started in the late eighteenth century by Moses Samuel Flersheim. His son, Samuel Moses, continued the business and passed it on to his two sons. In 1838 they parted company. My grandfather Lehmann Flersheim carried on under the name of Flersheim-Hess, his wife's maiden name. His brother competed as S. M. Flersheim and Son until he liquidated his business in the 1850s or '60s.
>
> My father Louis and his father were partners for many years. The older employees liked to reminisce about some of my grandfather's quirks. Supposedly it irritated him that the staff spent too much time washing their hands. A distant relative by the name of Abraham Hess busied himself duplicating letters with a handpress and feeding the cats. Everyone teased him, myself included. If this became too much he would go around announcing he had just called the boss's son a louse.
>
> I arrived by 7 A.M. to open the office. For lunch we went home. At night we worked till 7 P.M. After work I took French, English, and Italian classes. Generally I did not get home until 9 or 10 P.M. Toward the end of the day my father went to the warehouse to sort the horn inventory.
>
> I used to enjoy greatly the theatre (standing room). It started at 6:30 P.M. and I disappeared unnoticed while my father was in the warehouse. Theatre and opera were excellent. The well-known Meiningen Theatre Company often gave guest performances. I recall productions of Julius Caesar and Kaethchen von Heilbronn. In the early '80s we went to the gala opening of the new opera house, in the presence of the Emperor William I.
>
> My brother Sali died of diabetes in 1886. He had worked with the finished goods. My brother Martin and I were more interested in the raw materials. Around 1879 I went to Nuremberg on my first business trip. Soon thereafter I was allowed to go with one of

our salesmen to Berlin. Also around that time my father took me to Amsterdam for a bamboo auction. He gave me time off to go on a short side trip to Scheveningen where for the first time I saw the ocean.

In 1881 I went to Amsterdam to sort a consignment of buffalo horns of which part was shipped to a customer in Paris. As he had some complaints about the shipment I had to go to Paris where I met some school friends. We all went to the Grand Prix, which was won for the first time by an American horse.

In October of 1883 I joined the Bockenheim Hussars to do my one-year service. Before joining I learnt to ride horseback. Just before Christmas 1883 I fell with my horse in the barracks. I broke a collarbone and tore some muscles. As a result I was invalided out of the army. Until World War I was paid a monthly pension of 6 marks. Until war broke out in 1914, I continued riding most mornings between 6 and 8 A.M. before work.

In 1882 I went on my first trip to Italy. This journey came about because my father would not let me come to Mainz where at Whitsun each year my mother's siblings met for a family reunion and a two-day boat ride down the Rhine. My father made me stay behind to mind the shop. Half in jest to make up for it, I asked him to let me go to Italy through the Gotthard Tunnel, which had just been opened. My father took me up on my suggestion to combine a holiday with exploratory business calls. Three days after the tunnel opened, I started off, not knowing a word of Italian. I traveled to Milan, Turin, Genoa, Bologna, Venice, and Verona. With the help of an interpreter I called on potential customers. It became evident we could do worthwhile business in Italy. My father, who did not spoil his sons with praise, wrote me a highly complimentary letter. As soon as I came home I started learning Italian. Six months later I took a second trip, this time as far south as Florence, Rome and Naples. I was able to develop a sizable business in tortoiseshell. Until I married I went to Italy twice a year. Aside from business I spent a lot of time in museums and developed my taste for art, which later was to give me so much pleasure.

A Milan customer owed us a substantial sum of money, which I came to collect. In his office they said he was out of town, but the concierge let on he was at home, where I found him lying in bed. As I demanded payment he suddenly jumped out of bed and went for me with a long knife. "*Oggi ho gia ammazzato due, voi siete il terzo!*" (I have already killed two people today; you are going to be the third!). Soon after he was certified and sent to an asylum. A few days later my parents cabled to ask was I all right. He had telegraphed he had killed me: "*Non puo essere stato suo figlio ma sicuramente suo bastardo*" (It couldn't have been your son, it must have been your bastard).

Since 1838 our office was at #17, Toengesgasse, a seventeenth- or eighteenth-century patrician house in the old quarters of Frankfurt. It had a handsome facade and a rococo cast-iron staircase. In the 1870s my father bought the building. In the ground-floor storefront we wholesaled combs and brushes. In the courtyard at the back we kept our walking stick inventory, and also stored other raw materials. All the horns were kept in the large basement.

The actual office was a small room shared by my brother, two bookkeepers, and myself. My father worked at a standing desk in a small dark room facing the courtyard. He never sat down at work. There was one cane chair for visitors. In this room my father kept the books. Sunday mornings before lunch he struck a trial balance. Generally the cash balances were off and we helped him find the difference. If we did not find the error we wrote it off.

The cane warehouse together with the necessary washing facilities was at Praunheim, a suburb of Frankfurt. The cane was shipped by barge up the river Main, was unloaded and brought by horse van to the warehouse. To fill cane orders it had to be brought to the Toengesgasse, a laborious, costly process. The horns were sawn off by hand, also a cumbersome procedure. Finally, in the late '70s, we started using a power saw.

Eventually we took over an additional floor for our retail inventory and general office space. My father moved into a smaller office. My brother Martin and I shared a rather larger room next to his. The courtyard in which we kept some of our horn inventory was covered with a glass roof. The remodeling was done by the first Jewish architect in Frankfurt, a Mr. Kutznitzky. Around that time we obtained our first telephone.

In 1892 we gave up the retail business. We handed it over to two of our salesmen, Messrs. Silberhorn and Simon. We provided them with office space. They stayed in business for many more years. In the same year my father retired. My brother and I became the sole proprietors.

We concentrated on a handful of commodities: horns from overseas, cane for chairs, bamboo cane, ivory, tortoiseshell, and mother-of-pearl. My brother looked primarily after ivory and tortoiseshell while I concentrated on horn, cane, and mother-of-pearl. We, of course, kept each other posted. Our respective sons divided the work similarly. Each commodity had one senior employee in charge under our supervision.

In 1899 we bought land in the Mainzerlandstrasse, which was connected by a spur to the main railway line. We built something designed specifically for our business needs. The cane inventory was moved from Praunheim. Receiving as well as dispatching was speeded and simplified greatly by the rail link. Until the war there were daily incoming shipments. Horn and saws were in the basement, cane on the ground floor and in a shed behind the main building. Ivory storage and cutting facilities were on the ground floor, tortoiseshell and mother-of-pearl one flight up. The partner's room for the four of us was on the ground floor, as was the correspondence secretariat. The bookkeepers were one flight up.

It may interest my grandchildren for whom I am writing these notes to learn a bit more about our product lines. The horn imported from overseas was from steers and buffaloes. Initially we bought at various European ports as well as in Paris. In later years we imported the steer horns from South America and South Africa and the buffalo horn from the East Indies. The hollowed-out part of a horn was used to make combs, buttons, and salad serving spoons and forks. The solid tips were used to make smoking pipes, door handles, buttons, and knife handles. Our customers were in Germany, France, Austria, and Bohemia. In the days of the corset, buffalo horn was often used in lieu of whalebone. The corsets were manufactured predominantly in France. In 1908 we made arrangements with a competing firm in Cologne and one in Paris to cooperate and not compete in the purchase of all buffalo horn. The purpose of the agreement was to force the French manufacturers to buy from us and not to import on their own. In these negotiations I represented our firm. Due to insufficient demand we had to inventory a large part of our horn imports which we were not able to sell until the outbreak of the war. During the war we were cut off from our overseas sources. Instead we purchased domestic horns at the slaughterhouses and resold them for uniform buttons.

We had a good system of unloading from the railroad freight cars into a storage area from where the horn was dropped down to a dozen or so electric power saws. The strength of our horn business lay in sorting the horns to suit the specific needs of our customers.

Cane comes from the Netherlands East Indies — Celebes, Borneo, and Sumatra — and originally we bought at auctions run in Holland by the Nederlandsche Handelsmatschappij. In later years we bought directly in the East Indies and in Singapore. Cane is used for chairs, baskets, riding crops, walking sticks, and umbrella handles. The demand for riding crops has declined with the growing importance of the automobile, that for walking sticks by changing fashions. To begin with we sold mainly in Germany, but later on our customers were all over Europe. We kept some inventory in major European ports such as Hamburg, Amsterdam, Antwerp, Genoa, and Le Havre to supply the local markets.

Early in the century we started doing business in the United States of America. We financed a young man called Emil Miltenberg to go to America as our representative. Previously he had worked for a horse and riding crop maker in Germany. On the American East Coast there were numerous crop manufacturers in the town of Westwood, New Jersey, and they became customers of ours. With the rise of the automobile most of them went out of business, but for a while Miltenberg was able to sell cane to American furniture makers. He also sold for us other products, in particular mother-of-pearl to the American button trade. During the war Miltenberg started a firm of his own and became a well-to-do man. He did, however, continue to take care of our interests.

After the war my son Hans considerably enlarged the cane market for us in France and Spain. Italy continued as one of our most important markets. The basis for our Scandinavian business goes back to my holidays in the Nordic countries. In the war the artillery used cane for munitions baskets. The Dutch were not permitted to sell us cane as they had made an agreement with all the belligerents not to supply them with arms-related products. At the beginning of the war we were able to obtain one last shipment by going via New York and another by importing through Italy. Afterward with the full approval of the German government we had dummy companies in Holland buy cane on our behalf and ship it through Germany to neutral Switzerland. While it traveled through Germany the Army confiscated it. I went to Holland quite frequently to facilitate these transactions.

Bamboo comes from Japan and China. For us it became an important product once we began toward the end of the century to import directly from the producer countries. Bamboo is used for sporting goods such as fishing rods, ski poles, high-jump vaulting poles, and arrow shooting. It is also used in flower gardens. The root, the so-called yellow bamboo, is used widely for walking and riding sticks. Our market is throughout Europe.

Ivory comes from East and West Africa, in particular the Belgian Congo. We bought at the quarterly auctions in London and Antwerp, and, later, in the overseas countries. We cut the ivory vertically or horizontally with different saws, and turned billiard balls on two lathes. Other uses were piano keys, carvings, knife handles, combs and other toiletry articles, etc. Before the war Russia was an important market for billiard balls, but with the arrival of synthetics demand everywhere declined. Bombay was important as the Indian center for bangle production. The Japanese and Chinese used ivory for many different purposes including chopsticks and carving knives. In Germany our main customers were in the Odenwald region, not far from Frankfurt, where there was an old established craftsmen trade for carving figures, necklaces, bangles, and so on. Other customers were in France, Belgium, Italy, Austria, and Spain. Turkey was an old market for ivory turned into combs. There was a big market for piano keyboards in the United States, but the American piano manufacturers got a lot of their ivory from the countries of origin or the auctions.

We bought tortoiseshell at bimonthly auctions in London, and at one time in Singapore and Malaga. More recently we went to suppliers in the West Indies. The main uses nowadays are for spectacle frames and all kinds of toiletry articles. At one time tortoiseshell was used for women's fans and hair decoration, but fashions have changed and there is little demand left. Our customers were all over Europe, including Germany, Vienna, France, and England, and especially Naples, where since the Middle Ages there are innumerable small and miniscule processors of tortoiseshell.

From some of the above it becomes self-evident that synthetic materials and changing fashions have cost us a lot of business.

Mother-of-pearl was, originally, of no great importance to us.

Around 1910 we began to develop an interest in this product and soon became a leading factor in the trade. We made our purchases at the six auctions which took place in London each year or from the original source countries, mainly Australia, the Dutch East Indies, Persia, and Egypt. There is a great variety of shells in these countries. In recent years we began importing freshwater shells out of the Mississippi and various South American rivers. The main use is for buttons and knife handles, and the main markets are Bohemia, Germany, France, Spain, and Italy. England was a good market, but hard to break into as there was strong local competition.

There was a time when we dealt in woods but gave up, as we had no competitive edge. In a modest way we dealt in some minor commodities such as coconut shells, for which there was a market in France and Turkey, mainly for rosaries.

When I joined the firm our staff was quite small. Eventually it grew to about 70 employees — blue and white collar. From the '90s on we enjoyed sustained growth. Just prior to the war we reached an annual turnover of six million marks. The war and all it brought with it — confiscation of our foreign warehouses, foreign accounts receivable, and the severing of most links abroad — hit our business hard. The inflation initially wiped out our mark balances, although in the end we survived the inflation relatively well by starting early on to keep our books based on gold, an idea that came from my nephew Herbert. Business revived well in the years before the depression in 1930. The younger generation, Herbert and my son Hans, were largely responsible for this revival.

Our real trading advantage came from a strong balance sheet. We did not require credit, other than acceptance credits for shipments from overseas, but were in a position to extend longer-term advances to our customers.

With my brother Martin I worked in complete harmony for nearly 60 years. I do not recall a single serious disagreement. We worked in the same spirit with the next generation. Until we were

"Aryanized" in 1938 we were for six generations truly a family business. Many of our workmen and staff spent their entire working lives with us. Herr Rompel, our senior employee who had full power of attorney for the firm, was with us for 40 years. There was a harmonious relationship of mutual confidence between the entire staff and the family.

To counteract the increasingly competitive postwar conditions we made various mutual assistance agreements with other firms in the horn, ivory, and tortoiseshell trades. In the horn trade we agreed with two competitors in Cologne that each would continue to trade in their own name as heretofore, but we agreed on a three-way split of profits. We made a similar arrangement with an ivory house in Amsterdam.

For tortoiseshell, three firms — ourselves, one in Cologne, and one in London — formed three separate trading firms which were merged into a holding company named Tortosia, which is owned by the three of us.

The last few paragraphs of Ernst Flersheim's memoirs about his business life I will save for the end of this section. Meanwhile I will continue with a few extracts of his memoirs about himself and his family. First a little background: Ernst Flersheim was born during the last decade of the Germanic Confederation or Bund (1815–1866), which consisted of about thirty-five separate "states," German only because of their language and cultural heritage. After the defeat of Napoleon, who had conquered central Europe in several wars, the rulers, now freed of French dominance, negotiated their own territorial and political advantages at the Congress of Vienna (1814–1816), during which central Europe was reorganized. More than two hundred larger or smaller sovereign "states," governed by dukes, counts, princes, archdukes, noblemen, landgraves, bishops, or kings, had helped to defeat Napoleon and were now ready to solidify their local powers. Power was inherited and negotiated and traded through marriages and treaties.

When Ernst Flersheim refers to "Ernst" the Duke of Sachsen-Coburg-

Gotha, his namesake, we can see the importance of the potentate of the unimportant small dukedom made larger through family ties between the houses of Sachsen, Coburg, and Gotha. The war of 1866 was the so-called German War in which Prussia and Austria fought for dominance over each other. Frankfurt, Hesse, and nearby Baden fought for the cause of Austria — which lost to Prussia. This might explain why Ernst and his brothers and parents escaped from Frankfurt before the Prussian occupation, and why Ernst Flersheim's father would refuse to go to Berlin for business. After all, Frankfurt was assigned to Prussia, along with parts of Hesse. In the peace treaty that resulted, the North German Federation was formed under the leadership of Prussia, excluding Austria. Bismarck, Prussia's chancellor, took advantage of popular sentiment in favor of German unity and used his proverbial diplomatic finesse to have the reluctant King Wilhelm I of Prussia accept the crown of the new German Empire in 1871.

Here then is another excerpt from the personal memoirs of Ernst Flersheim:

I was born on July 13, 1862, at #35, Seilerstrasse, in Frankfurt on Main. It happened to be the day of the first marksman champion shooting of the German Bund. I was named Ernst, after the Duke of Sachsen-Coburg-Gotha, who was patron of the festivities.

My first recollections go back to the year 1866. We lived next to an orphanage, which during the war of 1866 had been turned into an army hospital. I recall seeing the wounded. My brother Martin saw the Prussians march in. I saw the withdrawal of the Austrians. We were watching from the balcony of my grandmother Fürth's house next to the old Hanau railway station. I still recall the white jackets and blue pants of the Austrian troops. Before the occupation by the Prussians my two older brothers, my parents, and myself escaped in a horse carriage to Bad Homburg.

At the beginning of 1867 we moved to #2, Hanauer Landstrasse, at the corner of Obermainanlage. The house belonged to my grandparents Fürth. We lived two floors up. My brothers slept in the attic. The apartment was far superior to the old one. We did have gaslight, but there were as yet no water mains. Water was pumped from the garden into a bin in the kitchen. Baths were ordered from an establishment called "The Little Red Man." They sent a tub with several barrels of heated water. The water in the kitchen was used only for cooking and washing. As a small boy I was taken by my father from time to time to the river Main where we bathed in so-called box baths. These were cabins from which one descended a few steps until the water reached your neck.

Easter of 1868, aged 5¾ years, I started school at the Philanthropin, in the Rechneigrabenstrasse. The school enjoyed a good reputation under its principal Herr Hermann Baerwald. I was among the better students in my class. From the time I was 10 years old my parents sent me after school in the afternoon to a teacher by the name of Wertheim. We were about 12 of us, did our homework and went for walks. Wertheim was a pleasant man with whom I was on good terms. We went plant collecting. I started a herbarium and an aquarium.

The Philanthropin was the Jewish high school in Frankfurt. In addition to the Jewish teachers there were a number of Christians. With one of the latter we put on classical plays in the senior grade. I played Wilhelm Tell when he shot the apple and the sergeant in Schiller's *Wallenstein*. Some of the older Jewish teachers were quite eccentric. Our handwriting teacher, Herr Allenberger, known as Oli, had to put up with a lot of teasing. He often pulled me by the ear and said my mother, Gitta, had been a better student than I was.

After junior high school there was a change of writing teachers, with more emphasis on calligraphy. Herr Mueller, a Christian teacher, replaced Oli. I recall Herr Blumenthal, our natural history teacher. On the side he ran a nursing home for needy people. Every week we brought him a kreuzer, as a small contribution. In return, at the beginning of class, he gave us a rambling account of what he had done with the money. I enjoyed swimming but did not care for ice-skating. On the skating rink there was a lot of fighting with the kids from Bornheim, frequently provoked by their anti-Semitic taunting.

At the age of 13 I took Hebrew class with Herr Lehmann Michel, cantor in Willy von Rothschild's private synagogue. I was confirmed in the Kompostellhof. I recited from the Torah. I was still so little that I had to stand on a stool to reach up to the Torah. The best part of my *barmitzvah* was the presents. I kept the books I was given until we left Germany.

I recall with pleasure the way of life in the homes of both my grandparents, different though it was. The household of my Flersheim grandparents was orthodox. They ate kosher and observed the Sabbath. For Passover they kept a special set of china. At Easter the whole family came together to celebrate Seder. On holidays my grandmother dressed beautifully. She wore a white cap with flowers and a silk jacket. My father read prayers. All present were handed small, illustrated prayer books. The younger group at our end of the table did not take the celebrations too seriously. I don't think for any of us the religious ceremonies had deep meaning.

My grandfather Flersheim died in 1873. His wife had a large circle of friends. She was well liked and respected. She was an intelligent woman who one day said to me that as three brothers, one of us should live in Frankfurt, one in London, and one in Paris. It made me think of Gudula Rothschild's advice to her sons.

My grandmother Fürth came from a far more liberal religious tradition. She had been widowed young. Until she died all of her family celebrated New Year's Eve at her home. We improvised theatricals and played charades. My aunt Lust, sister of my grandmother Fürth, celebrated Christmas with a tree as far back as the 1870s. All of the family were invited to her house and received generous presents. My father did not care for her Christmas and only arrived once the celebration was over.

My grandparents Flersheim vacationed every summer for a

few weeks at Bad Soden in the nearby Taunus hills. They always rented the same rooms in the house of a Jewish family named Meyer. Every Sunday my parents took all of us to visit them. Later in life my grandmother Flersheim spent the summer in a furnished garden apartment in the Eschersheimer Landstrasse. My grandparents Fürth had had since their younger days a summer apartment in the Friedberger Landstrasse. My mother liked to reminisce that in 1848 two parliamentary deputies, Lichnowsky and Auerswald, were chased by the mob past her house and later murdered.

There were four of us — my brother Martin born 1856, Sali born 1858, my sister Alice born 1866, and myself, born 1862. During the Franco-Prussian War [1870–1871] on one occasion Sali went around Frankfurt with some French prisoners to show them the town, and acted as their interpreter. He let me keep him company. The French prisoner-of-war camp was on the Pfingstweide, which later became the Zoo. I pinned little flags on a map to follow the war. I recall vividly the peace celebrations. My parents took me at night to look at the illuminated town. At the signing of the peace treaty in May 1871 at the Hotel Schwan I saw Bismarck and the Kaiser in the streets.

In the '70s and '80s my parents had a weekly evening family get-together with their siblings and their respective children. In the summer they rented a coach. There would be 15 to 20 of us and all were in high spirits. Lunch usually was at the Schützenhof at Oberursel [in the Taunus hills], which had a bowling alley. A great treat was to be taken out by my parents to dinner in a restaurant. My parents were fond of Schwagers Felsenkeller on the Röderberg or Bärs Felsenkeller in Sachsenhausen [a suburb of Frankfurt].

I left school with a good report card and qualified for the one-year volunteer army service. Easter 1877 I started as a trainee in my father's firm. I learned about all parts of the business, which included frequent errands to the post office and the bank.

My father went twice a year on a buying trip to Paris. He stayed several weeks. He loved Paris, but as a native Frankfurter he could not get himself to go to Prussian Berlin. As early as the 1840s he used to travel by mail coach to Paris. There was only a handful of railway lines, and he rented a horse wagon to travel with his samples all over Germany. Buyers from central and southern Germany and also some from abroad came to the various trade fairs in Frankfurt.

In 1887 my brother Martin married Florence Livingstone. She became a much-liked sister-in-law. After his marriage I took over most of my brother's business travels, in particular attending the Leipzig fair, and trips to Berlin and Vienna. On several occasions I had to go to Budapest. In England I went to London and on one occasion to Sheffield. I loved going to Vienna, which in the 1880s had enormous charm. I went to the theatre a lot — still in the old Burg. The leading actors were Baumeister, Sonnenthal, Thimig, and Wolter. I spent a good deal of time at the races in Freudenau. In fact, all my life I have enjoyed the races and was one of the earliest members of the Frankfurt Jockey Club.

When in Berlin I used to enjoy at noontime standing in front of the old Kaiser's palace. After a while he appeared in the corner window of the palace, the so-called historic window, to watch the changing of the guard.

Every summer I traveled with friends. One year we went to Pontresina in the Swiss Alps. Another year we went to the Dolomites. In the spring of 1892 I traveled to Scandinavia. From Copenhagen and Christiania (now Oslo) we went in two little two-wheel horse-drawn carts (carioles) to Odde, Stahlheim, and Bergen. The journey took several days and involved frequent changes of horses. From Bergen we went by ship to Molde and Trondheim, and from there back to Stockholm by train. I went with a cousin of my future wife's; I became engaged to her a few months later. We sent her one postcard jointly. To do more would have been considered improper.

I became engaged on Oct. 30, 1892. The engagement took place at #46, Liebigstrasse, the home of my parents-in-law to be. The wedding and reception took place on Dec. 28, 1892, at the Frankfurter Hof. Numerous out-of-town family members came for the occasion. We were about 60 for the wedding dinner. As was the custom there was a special wedding newspaper, songs written by various friends, and short one-acters.

My wife, Gertrud von Mayer, came from a Coburg family. At the age of 13 she lost her mother. Soon thereafter my father-in-law moved to Frankfurt. His second wife, Flora, née Boehm, became a devoted mother to us all. For our own children she was not only a grandmother but also a good friend to whom they brought their problems, big or small. My wife had two brothers, Martin and Ernst, who was only three years old when we married.

My father-in-law's business, first in Coburg and later in Frankfurt, was trading in yeast. He had an uncomplicated, happy disposition and was a popular figure with many friends. He was a keen and accomplished shot. He was at ease equally with the Duke of Sachsen-Coburg-Gotha — who in 1886 had ennobled him — as he was with any workingman or cabby. It is a funny coincidence that I was named after the same Archduke Ernst who had granted my father-in-law his title. Up to his death he was on the board of the Henninger brewery in Frankfurt.

The first few days of our honeymoon we spent at Heidelberg. From there we went for several wonderful weeks to Monte Carlo. My dear wife was not particularly enthusiastic about going to the Casino. But one evening I won enough to pay for a carriage to Nice.

At the beginning of February we came back to Frankfurt and took an apartment on the ground floor at #46, Westendstrasse, where we spent the early and happy years of our marriage. Our son Hans was born there in 1893, and our daughter Edith in 1895.

In 1897 we moved to #32, Myliusstrasse. Clara Schumann had lived there until her death, a short while before we bought

the house. In later years quite a number of people, in particular
from England, asked to see the house. They wanted to see the
place where not only Clara Schumann had lived but where
Brahms and the famous violinist Joachim had been frequent visitors. We had a large garden, which extended back to the next
street. In the summer we spent noon and evenings on the veranda
overlooking the garden in which our children played a great deal.

Sundays and sometimes during the week we went to dinner at
my parents', together with my brother and sister. My parents had
bought in 1880 #47, Feuerbachstrasse, a house on a lovely open
grounds opposite the palace of the last Duke of Nassau. New
Year's Eve used to be spent in their home, always a happy occasion
with lots of family. At midnight, dressed up in costumes, we came
down the wide flight of stairs to wish my parents a happy New
Year.

My father personified hard work and a sense of duty. He ran
the business along old established, traditional lines. It was not
simple for us to persuade him to modernize and adapt our methods to changing market conditions. He retired at the age of 66.
Instead of living for his work, he came to enjoy his comfortable
home, play with his grandchildren, or go to the opera. In the summer they visited my sister at her pretty Baden-Baden house. He
had a satisfying and enjoyable old age.

My mother was an intelligent, energetic lady. We all heeded
her advice gladly. Until her death she was at the center not only
of her immediate but also our wider family. She was loved and
respected by all. Nothing gave her more pleasure than to be
surrounded by her children and grandchildren. The grandchildren
enjoyed being with their cousins in the grandparental home.
From time to time my grandparents took a grandchild to the
opera. My son Hans used to recall how much he enjoyed being
taken by his grandfather as a small boy to see *Zar und Zimmermann*
[a popular German operetta by Lortzing].

Wednesday evenings we had dinner at my parents-in-law's

Liebigstrasse house. Generally we also went there for Sunday afternoon tea where some of the more distant relatives were invited. A regular guest was my mother-in-law's brother, our physician and close friend Dr. Henry Boehm. My father-in-law, Henry Boehm, I, and sometimes my son Hans played Skat [a card game] — not too seriously but with lots of laughter.

In the first couple of decades of our marriage there was a good deal of socializing and dinner parties with befriended families. Food and wine were generally quite excellent. After dinner the men withdrew to the library until brought back to the ladies by the hostess. Especially when some of the younger generation had been invited there was dancing — waltzing, the polka, mazurka, and quadrille (français). There was hardly ever a public ball. The most popular was the annual carnival masked ball, which took place on Shrove Tuesday at the zoological garden. In the early years of our marriage we used to go a few times. Otherwise our social life centered on the theatre, concerts, lectures, or other cultural and artistic activities. The Friday night Museumsgesellschaft concerts to which we went regularly were both an artistic and a social event. Duse and Caruso gave performances. The latter I also heard at Covent Garden.

Soon after my marriage we started to collect paintings. My wife, too, developed an active interest in art. We developed a liking in particular for contemporary German painters. Several, such as Steinhausen and Trübner, we came to know personally. We became good friends with Jacob Nussbaum, a Frankfurt artist. We met many artists at the home of my brother Martin. He had an important collection and ran a hospitable home. Since marrying I had devoted myself to my family, my business, and, during my leisure hours, to art. Most of my reading had to do with art.

My morning routine was to leave the house at 8 o'clock and walk to work. On the way I often picked up my brother who lived nearby. In very recent years I had myself driven to the office. Midday I came home for a couple of hours. Work ended at 7 o'clock, more recently at 6 o'clock. While my mother was alive my brother and I visited her on our way home every evening. In 1904 our youngest daughter Margarete was born.

After I was married I went on business trips only if there was a special reason. My wife came along quite often. In the first years of our marriage we went on our summer holidays without our children. The first summer, before our son was born, we holidayed in a villa at Bad Homburg. The following summers we spent walking in the Tyrol and in Switzerland. One summer we walked from Kandersteg over the Gemmi to Leuk, and took a train to Zermatt where we walked up the Gornergrat.

As the children began to grow up we took them along with us. Several summers we spent at the Villa Germania on the Ölmühlweg in Königstein or on the Tegernsee near Munich. Other holidays were spent at Engelberg in Switzerland, the Odenwald and Lac de Joux, in the Swiss Jura Mountains.

Between 1905 and 1911 we went several times to Domburg, a seaside resort on the isle of Walcheren in Holland. We went to Domburg at the suggestion of Jan Toorop, a Dutch artist we had come to know in Frankfurt. He was an important painter and a fascinating person, kind, generous, and deeply religious.

Toorop was highly musical and would sit at the piano improvising. My frequent evening walks with him left a deep impression on me. He would philosophize about the world and open my eyes to the beauty of nature. He was born in the Dutch East Indies, part Malay, part Dutch. His wife and daughter also came to Domburg. The latter became a well-known artist in her own right and we are friends with her to this day. I acquired numerous paintings of his, among them a crayon drawing of Edith at the age of 10, and one of me aged 50 or thereabouts. We also owned a number of sketches of Domburg, its surroundings, and the people met on our walks. We returned once after the war in 1930 with our children and grandchildren and again enjoyed Domburg greatly.

Again and again I went back to Italy and its art, either with my wife or one of my daughters. Once I went to Sicily, on my own. With my wife I went frequently to Coburg, her hometown, for which she maintained great affection. Other times we went to Paris and London, the latter in connection with taking Edith to boarding school at Eastbourne, where she spent a year in 1912.

In Paris we saw our first film, very soon after film had been invented. On another occasion in Paris the well-known painter Zuloaga, with whom we had become good friends at my brother's house, took us to meet Rodin at his studio. He received us warmly and showed us both his own works and his collection. Zuloaga took my wife and myself as well as my brother and his wife to Colmar to see the Isenheim altar, a picture that left a deep and lasting impression on me. One particularly enjoyable journey was with my daughter Margarete to Provence. We hired a driver in Avignon, and ended in Marseilles.

In 1903 we went to Vienna for my brother-in-law Martin von Mayer's wedding to Leonie Jordan, who came to be greatly liked by all of us. My 50th birthday coincided with the 50th anniversary celebrations of the marksmen's championship. My wife arranged a surprise garden party where everyone wore marksmen-related costumes. There were maybe 50 guests. A nephew of my brother-in-law Louis Koch turned up on "Scheckel," the horse I used to ride in the mornings before work. The horse carried a large sign marked "Congratulations."

In 1913 we remodeled our house, which in many respects was in need of modernizing. We enlarged the living room, which faced the street, and we created a much larger dining room, facing the garden. These were the rooms in which my pictures were hung and I much enjoyed showing them to guests interested in art. Both our daughters were married in these rooms. We also added a veranda overlooking the garden, which could be opened up in the summer. It adjoined a large terrace on which we had dinner outdoors on summer evenings.

Christmas was a happy holiday for the children. We lit a tree and there were presents for family and household staff. My parents used to come, as did my in-laws, brother, sister, and their families. A great success one Christmas was a dachshund named Waldi. He was around for many years. Part of our household, and really of our family, was Fräulein Lauber. She came in 1900, to begin with as children's nurse, and she stayed with us until we left Germany in 1938. Once the children were grown up she helped my wife run the household. In 1927 we purchased our first car. Our chauffeur, Nikolaus Mueller, was an exceptional person we liked greatly. He remained a loyal friend until we left Germany, and after that we arranged for him to work for my old firm.

Hans attended the Goethe Gymnasium. He graduated in 1912 when he entered our business as a trainee. In October 1913 he joined the Baden Dragoons in Bruchsal for his one-year voluntary army service. On August 1, 1914, he was called up for active duty. We spent the evening before they moved to the front with him in Bruchsal to say good-bye. I recall vividly the tension and excitement in Bruchsal as everyone reported for duty. Hans took part in the advance into France as far as the Marne, where he went on a number of mounted patrols. Subsequently they fell back to Belgium, where his regiment was transferred to the Russian front. On their way east through Germany we met him in Berlin and were allowed to travel on the troop train as far as Küstrin. His unit participated in General Litzmann's breakthrough at Brzezani. He had been promoted to staff sergeant. He was captured by the Russians but managed to escape and make his way back to his unit. He was reported missing, which caused us great worries, but four weeks later we finally heard from him that he was alive and well. In the course of retreating from Poland to East Prussia his unit was taken prisoner by the Russians. They were sent via Moscow to the notorious P.O.W. camp at Kattakurgan in Turkestan where numerous prisoners died from the murderous climate.

After a while he was moved to Omsk and then to Solotaia

Orda where on the strength of his rank he managed to get into an
officers' camp. The climate was not as bad as in Kattakurgan, but
it was equally hot and the prisoners slept out in the open. In 1918
he went on leave to Tashkent where he obtained a forged passport
as a Czech legionnaire. Together with his servant and an Austrian
officer they traveled for two weeks under the most arduous and
dangerous conditions until they reached the German lines in
Poland. On the way he suffered an attack of malaria, which he
had contracted in camp. The only place for him to lie down was
in a luggage rack. He was first put in quarantine in Warsaw and
then released to headquarters in Berlin to give a report on his
escape. He was able to telephone from Warsaw — and you can
imagine our joy and relief at hearing his voice. His heart was
affected somewhat by the malaria attack and he went with my wife
to convalesce a few weeks in Bad Nauheim. He could have stayed
in Germany on medical grounds but insisted on going back to
active frontline service. He was posted to an antiaircraft unit in
Belgium, where he was demobilized in mid-November 1918.

Frankfurt was a frequent target for air raids. One bomb landed
so close to our house that a number of windows were shattered.
One morning while walking to the office my brother and I saw a
red flag flying from the roof of the railway headquarter offices in
the Victoria Allee. The building was guarded by troops. The revolution had broken out the previous night. At the beginning of the
war my brother-in-law Martin von Mayer had turned his house
into a military hospital. My wife and my daughter Edith took
courses in nursing and served in his hospital.

During the war, in 1917, we celebrated our silver wedding.
We went to Munich and Garmisch with our daughters. Edith
illustrated a charming poem about our married life. Margarete put
together a collection of photographs. It was a bitterly cold winter
but for our daughters their first opportunity to ski.

Our daughter Edith, who had considerable talent for painting, went to art school after the war and in 1920 became engaged to Dr. Georg Eberstadt, at the time general counsel of I. Dreyfus and Co., bankers, then a partner in the Hamburg banking firm of L. Behrens and Sons, and later director of Dresdner Bank in Hamburg until they left Germany in 1936.

Margarete graduated from the Victoria School in 1923, studied literature at Heidelberg and Frankfurt and married Dr. Rudolf Wertheim, a lawyer, in 1927. Also in 1927 we bought an automobile. We enjoyed trips in the surroundings of Frankfurt, the Rhine, and Taunus. A favorite area was the Spessart Mountains. Trips farther afield took us to Paris, via Luxembourg and Rheims, to the Loire chateaux and Nancy, and on another occasion to Switzerland.

My 70th birthday we celebrated on the Tegernsee with our children and grandchildren. There were sketches and poems and illustrations by Edith. The weather was perfect, the atmosphere harmonious. In the light of subsequent events it was perhaps the last truly happy occasion in my life when we were all together without real worries and concerns.

To commemorate my birthday I donated to the Städel Museum in Frankfurt a large painting by Lovis Corinth [1858–1925] of Christ's Crucifixion. Newspaper articles described it as one of Corinth's most important works. The board of the museum expressed its appreciation by adding my name to the list of donors. I question that my name has remained on this tablet.

In the course of my life I have witnessed many inventions which have changed our entire way of life but are by now taken for granted. To mention a few: I recall the first electric streetlamps and the first telephone. I recall in 1887 the transmission by telephone of an opera from Munich. I have already mentioned my first experience with the cinema. In 1909 at the International Air Show in Frankfurt I saw the first attempts by a German pilot named Euler to fly an airplane. It barely got off the ground. I watched greatly admired exhibition flights by the French pilot Bleriot. Unforgettable was the first sight of a zeppelin, with the old Count [von Zeppelin] as pilot in the gondola.

Ernst Flersheim's account of his and his family's later life, after Hitler came to power, will continue in chapter 7.

The Frankfurt Philanthropin

Not long ago I found, in of all places the archives of the Lazard Frères firm in New York, two articles from Frankfurt newspapers written in 1904 on the occasion of the hundredth anniversary celebrations of the Philanthropin, the Jewish school in Frankfurt that Ernst Flersheim attended. The articles, one written by a certain Dr. Hammeran who appears not to be Jewish, show how the Germans felt about their Jews, and how the Jews felt about themselves and their Germans. Before I quote from them extensively, however, a word about the origins of the school.

Around the turn of the century, Jewish families throughout Germany had largely become integrated into the life of the predominantly Christian population. This was true especially for the well-educated, professional, and business families, most of whom had lived in Germany for several generations. Many families that wished for better opportunities for their offspring to become assimilated into mainstream German life preferred sending their children to secular schools instead of traditional Jewish schools emphasizing Talmudic studies. In the early 1800s several new *Freischulen*, free schools, had been established that subscribed to modern educational principles based on eighteenth-century Enlightenment ideals — schools no longer centered around religion. Gentile as well as Jewish students were admitted. The Philanthropin in Frankfurt that Ernst Flersheim attended was one such school.

"This coming spring," Dr. A. Hammeran wrote in the *Frankfurter Zeitung* of February 17, 1904, "the Jewish community in Frankfurt will celebrate the 100th anniversary of its school, the Philanthropin. It has a distinguished past. Bit by bit the talents of this large community have been forged. From the surrounding villages of the Rhineland elements have come together, which matured here. If I am not mistaken there is a traditional and a contemporary vein in the cultural roots of Judaism. The traditional vein is the devout orthodox Jewish family, righteous but narrowly focused as depicted by the ghetto painter Oppenheim. It has Old Testament grandeur. More contemporary is the drive to expand, its Americanized philosophy, a certain elbow logic."

Throughout his article Hammeran's feelings about his Jewish fellow Germans reveal a certain ambivalence. "There is," he writes, "something likeable, familiar, simple in the history of these Jews, namely how in the olden days they lived alongside the German farmers in the local villages." He draws on Bogunil Goltz and his deep, psychologically grounded comprehension of the Jews in West Prussia and in Poland, his understanding of their spirit and the worth of the race. Hammeran reflects on the "almost proverbial superior brainpower of the village Jew over even the cleverest peasant. The Jew is just plain smarter." — And for Hammeran the explanation is obvious: "At the root is an anthropological, not a social reason, which holds the secret of the superior place of the Jew in German life. In his baggage the Semite carries a culture going back thousands of years, whereas German culture has a mere two thousand–year history, no more than infancy as the history of races goes. The brain stores the experience, education, and wisdom of generations and its bearer is the custodian of an ancient store of worldly wisdom acquired over the ages. We Germans can be proud that notwithstanding our brief history we have successfully harbored an alien minority. The minority in our midst indeed has given us two princes of the mind — Spinoza and Heinrich Heine. In the political sphere there is the shining light of Johann Jacoby. They are close to the German spirit. Indeed it is surprising how close to the German spirit the Jewish mind is, much closer than to the Slav or Roman. Admittedly the Jews cannot come up with a Goethe, Beethoven, or Bismarck. For masterly achievements such as theirs, you need roots and to be part of a national tradition which the Jewish race does not possess. There is a limit to the potential of any race. But the downtrodden exile can certainly look to considerable accomplishments.

"Before my eyes," Hammeran continues, "appears an image in the German landscape, which generally tends to leave a viewer cold: a Jewish cemetery, out there, forlorn, in the middle of an open field. It is hard to think of anything more gripping than these exiled oriental tombstones on German soil, even in death alien to their surroundings. Outside their villages, they are forced to bury their dead. They can't cope with bright daylight. But how beautifully this picturesque messiness, these patriarchal stones appear at midnight in the summer, or before the sun rises, as one walks through these villages in Hesse or in the Main River valley and suddenly comes upon one of these cemeteries. The streets are empty and silent, and there it is, this burial place for an alien congregation, without a wall around it, set in the midst of our beautiful German land. A strange fear of death keeps the survivors away from their dead. They are left to themselves. There are no flowers to decorate a tombstone. Yet each stone is marked with the Star of David to establish its identity, separate and apart from its actual setting. The small handful of Jews who live in the village dig their own graves and bury their dead."

Hammeran goes on to describe the origins of the Philanthropin, first in the Frankfurt ghetto. He describes the opposition the school faced from the strictly sectarian traditionalists who were against the secular teaching and in particular the German culture being taught there. After the Napoleonic era Frankfurt became an independent city-state, which led to the loss of equal rights granted the Jews under Napoleon. Contributions from the city of Frankfurt to the Philanthropin were terminated. The board of the congregation and the school board did not see eye to eye. They wanted to revive the primacy of the Talmud. But the school survived. In 1868 Hermann Baerwald was appointed headmaster. He led the school for thirty-one years. He integrated it into the official German school system as a full-fledged *Gymnasium,* but one that ended at the tenth grade, in part because the majority of parents were opposed to schooling that continued to the age of eighteen.

Hermann Baerwald attracted first-class teachers. Alumni from his years attained prominence in many walks of life. His son Paul went to the

United States and eventually became senior partner at Lazard Frères in New York and a prominent figure as the head of the European Relief Commission after the First World War.

Hammeran had high praise for many of the faculty and alumni. For the highest praise he singled out Theodor Ceizenach as "unforgettable, for having raised the literary life of Frankfurt through his spirit and knowledge to a level not attained since."

The actual centennial celebration is described in the *Frankfurter General-Anzeiger* of April 13, 1904: "The great hall is packed with a huge and festive public. School board, faculty, and school choir are seated amidst a forest of palm trees on the dais. In the front row of the audience are the special guests, Excellency von Stülpnagel, commanding general of the Frankfurt military district, police president Scherenberg, state railway president Thome, state supreme court president Dr. Hagens, Lord Mayor Dr. Adickes, etc. Herr Fritz Auerbach, chair of the central Jewish committee, greeted the guests in opening words. For one century now, he said, the Philanthropin has kept faith with its motto 'for enlightenment and humanity.'"

The essence of Jewish hopes and ambitions seems contained in the commemorative address by the headmaster, Dr. Adler. He speaks of Sigismund Geisenheim, the founder, one hundred years ago:

> In his days the ideal that all are equal before the law proceeded victoriously through the land. Enlightenment and humanity are the motto of the times. Poet and thinker propound the rights of the individual as a human being, regardless of origin or religion. Love of mankind encompasses mind and spirit, enriching all forms of human endeavor. This spirit holds a special place in the education of the young. This is the spirit of Philantropinist thinking, which will help the individual to find happiness, fulfillment and contentment. The educated classes received it warmly. It was taken up enthusiastically in the Jewish ghettos of our German towns and villages. For the Jewish young, who hitherto had grown

up in an educational environment which limited itself to rigid methods and thinking to do only with narrowly based learning, the new methods came like a divine revelation.

Admittedly, Philanthropinism reached only the young of the better-off families, be it in the ghettos or outside. The majority of the Jewish population remained untouched by the new ideas. Its leaders continued to consider any form of learning not directly involving the Talmud a denial of the true faith and would not have anything to do with the contemporary German language. Instead, they continued to teach the traditional Yiddish, a mishmash of medieval German, Hebrew, and various Slavic dialects. The prospectus of the founders of the school called for an enlightened curriculum to make the children, especially the underprivileged co-religionists, useful members of society at large, the great and noble goals of mankind in general. Much of the Philanthropin's methods and thinking were modeled on Pestallozzi. In appearance the school body, similarly, followed those precepts, be it clothing, or wall tablets with names and ranking such as *signa deligentiae* or *notae pigritiae*. There were a code of a morals jury, graduation ceremonies, and festive graduation dinners. Religion, history, and German literature were taught under the aegis of enlightenment and humanity. Religious instruction becomes self-defeating if it emphasizes what separates rather than what unites different creeds. Religious teaching in the lower grades dealt with morals and ethics. Religious Jewish teaching was left for the senior classes and taught as part of Jewish history, rather than pure religion. What a momentous change it was in the mentality and teachings of onetime ghetto inhabitants. The different way of looking at religion, in turn requires fundamental changes in the form of religious services. Hebrew liturgy was replaced by music sung in German, accompanied by an organ. The rabbi's sermon was replaced by a sermon on morality. The nature of the teaching precluded religious segregation, and the admission of children of Christian background was welcomed.

The point is made that philanthropistic ethics run counter to religious segregation. Its early teachings were ahead of their time, and a more traditional and conventional approach to religious instruction got the upper hand. Sunday assembly again became a more traditional Sabbath service, though traditional Jewish music is sung in German rather than Hebrew, alongside religious hymns of German writers and composers. Outstanding contemporary Jewish theologians who are able to keep alive interest in religion among the well-educated congregation, which is their audience, spread the word of God. One Michael Creizenach was a teacher blessed with a liberal mind and great rhetorical skills. His annual confirmation address left a far-reaching mark. Two teachers of outstanding ability, Marcus Jost and Jacob Auerbach, took his place later. Their modern teachings raised the place of the Jewish religion to great heights and respect in our German fatherland. They were able to bridge the supposedly unbridgeable gulf between religion and the natural sciences. Similarly, new political ideas evolved. The Jewish population accepted enthusiastically the equality of man's nature and the irrelevance of what one's origins chanced to be. This was the fundament of world citizenship whose only objective is a sensible government, which has little respect for a nation-state or nationalism. To make them into citizens of the world is the educational goal of the Philanthropin for its Jewish pupils and of other schools for the whole population. It does not bother them that the German name at the time is in disrepute.

Attitudes changed in the Napoleonic era. There were the beginnings of a German genius, even if initially cosmopolitan. More and more, though, a special German culture took hold, from which stemmed the glorious national ideal. More and more this became the foundation of all German education, and the Philanthropin prided itself to be party to this development. The school prides itself that it is a German school, part of German culture and German traditions. Hess, the same school principal who only a few years previously had idealized world citizenship, now considered it his goal to educate at the Philanthropin virtuous and truly religious citizens of the Fatherland. In the dark years of reaction when it was considered high treason to profess belief in things German, Hess's successor, Sigismund Stern, a prominent member of the Gotha party and the Nationalverein, a firm believer in the unification of the German states, a prominent speaker on behalf of these causes at meetings of the German teachers' association, used every occasion, such as the 100th anniversary of Schiller's birth and the death of the poet Ludwig Uhland to imbue his Philanthropin pupils with ardent patriotism and Fatherland love.

To serve the Fatherland was also at all times the pride and goal of my immediate predecessor [Hermann Baerwald], who by the grace of God is able to be with us today. This faithfulness, this love of our German fatherland, or, better still, now we are able to say, this love for our Kaiser and the German empire, has never faltered, no matter the volatile and changeable political conditions after the wars of liberation. The Philanthropin has indeed earned its equal standing with all schools in Frankfurt and the Fatherland. Our earnest sense of duty and obligation best will serve to break down any barriers which are still in our path and open the doors for us to participate wherever the talents of the individual can best be employed for the common good and benefit of our Fatherland. In this unshakable confidence the school looks forward to its second century. There can't be another school in our Fatherland whose alumni have been more supportive of faculty and pupils. And we have never deviated from Jewish teachings and services in a manner suitable and fitting of the times we live in.

There were numerous speeches in the same vein. In the name of the Kaiser, the chairman of the school trustees, Town Councilor Horkheimer, was awarded the Royal Crown Order, Fourth Class, as was his deputy, Max Dann. The school principal, Dr. Adler, received the Red Eagle Order, Fourth Class, and numerous other awards were handed out. Fear of god and love of fatherland were repeated themes. Telegrams were read from many, including the minister of education, president of the province Count Zedlitz-Trutzschler, his deputy, the district military commander General von Lindequist, and so forth. The centennial anniversary fund reported contributions from more than one thousand alumni, some from places as far away as New York and San Francisco. The fund already exceeded 100,000 Reichsmark. The ceremonies closed with a rousing hip-hip-hurray for the Kaiser and enthusiastic singing by all present of the national anthem.

Only thirty years after hip-hip-hurrays for the Kaiser and "Deutschland Über Alles," Hermann Baerwald's son Paul, by then retired from Lazard Frères, was helping Jewish refugees to flee Nazi Germany. The son of Dr. Auerbach had become an insurance broker in New York. Supposedly he obtained the passenger lists of transatlantic liners in order to sell insurance to arriving refugees, virtually as they stepped off the boats. The Eberstadts had fled to England, the Flersheims to Holland and a concentration camp death, the Wertheims to Belgium and death.

4

My Father, Georg Eberstadt

My father, Georg Eberstadt, son of Albert and Marie Eberstadt, was born in Frankfurt on Main, Germany, on July 28, 1887. He died in London on the eleventh of December, 1963, at the age of seventy-six. During most of his life the tide did not run with him. By the time he qualifed as a lawyer, the First World War had broken out. He survived two years of infantry in the trenches, first as a sergeant, later as an officer. The last year and a half of the war he served as a divisional staff officer. In 1919 he started in banking as general counsel of I. Dreyfus and Co., a well-regarded Frankfurt private bank. In 1920, aged thirty-three, he married Edith Bettina Flersheim, my mother. Born in Frankfurt in 1895, she was the older daughter and second child of Ernst Flersheim and Gertrud von Mayer.

Although Mother must have been a foot smaller, in every sense she looked up to her husband, unduly so in many respects, because she had a far better mind than she gave herself credit for. Her temperament, like her mother's, was volatile, which caused her needless grief, yet still she was enormously well liked. She had a gift for friendship because she was genuinely interested in her friends and their lives, especially if they were family, however distantly, of hers or her husband's. Her constant need to communicate expressed itself in lengthy and frequent telephone conversations — before the telephone was taken for granted — and in writing long letters of twenty or thirty pages.

Her education at Steimer, a private girls' school in Frankfurt of social more than academic distinction, was skimpy, yet she was truly educated, remarkably well read, fluent in French and English when it ended at the age of seventeen. She was passionate about Ibsen, Strindberg, Shaw, the Russian novelists, and identified with their causes and polemics. She was a gifted artist but so much a wife that she did not pursue a real talent professionally. Letters written for special occasions were illustrated, wooden boxes charmingly decorated. Pictures, especially of fairy tales, hung in our nursery. Before her marriage she did anatomical drawings for the Senckenberg Natural History Museum in Frankfurt.

She had her father's love for art but her taste was more daring than his. If her husband had let her, she would have collected the German Expressionists. She would have bought them before they had become fashionable, but he considered "that kind of art" inappropriate in a conservative banker's home. Much later he came to like it, but by then it was unaffordable.

In 1924 Father became a partner in L. Behrens und Söhne, then one of the two leading private banks in Hamburg. The other was M. M. Warburg and Co. Both were Jewish houses. In 1931 he joined Dresdner Bank as cohead of the Hamburg branch.

From 1924 to 1929 politics and business finally took a turn for the better in Germany. At least on the surface, Germany was making a comeback. But for these five years in his working life, and even these were not without setbacks, Father and his generation had to buck the tides. Right after he joined Behrens in 1924, the firm suffered a major credit loss, and the next years were good. By 1929 all was over, first the Wall Street Crash, followed by the German banking crisis in which his firm, with many others, went more or less under; next came the Great Depression, Hitler, and emigration to England at a time when even well-established bankers barely made a living, and the Second World War. When it ended in 1945, he was fifty-eight, too old for major new ventures. Neither he nor England were in the best of health. Yet he built up G. Eberstadt and Co., a small banking business which enjoyed a good reputation. It provided him with no great work satisfaction, but a comfortable living till he died.

Those are the bare bones of his life. It was lived in adverse but unbelievably interesting decades. He had the ambition and ability to go a long way. For a while he succeeded. Some people, what a menace, have ambition but lack ability. Others, what a waste, have ability but lack ambition. A tougher man might have made it notwithstanding the obstacles, but he was more concerned with standing than money. Nor did he come from a particularly money-oriented family. His father, who had not cared greatly for his business or the brothers he owned it with, had retired young and was more ambitious for his children rather than himself.

I know too little about Father's childhood or adolescence. He was close to his father and his favorite child. He did well in school. Aged seven in 1894 at the Wöhler Elementary School in Frankfurt, his marks were "good" in behavior, attention, diligence, religion, German, mathematics, and handwriting. He was not once late for school but missed fifty classes owing to sickness. In the fourth grade in 1896 at Wöhler he got a "good" in behavior, "excellent" in attention and diligence, "excellent" in religion, German, mathematics, and handwriting, "good" in singing, "adequate" in sports.

In 1897 he entered the Goethe Gymnasium, Frankfurt's preeminent humanistic secondary and high school. In his first year at that school, in fifth grade, he was at the top of his class, first out of forty-two students.

In subsequent years he continued to be among the top five students. Athletics was clearly not his strong point; he was repeatedly given a grade of "deficient" or "inadequate." His first year of Latin in eighth grade earned him a "very good." Traditionally, German schools also graded Attention and Diligence, and Father's were noted as "adequate" yet "uneven." In twelfth grade, when he was seventeen or eighteen, his grading in Diligence sank to "poor, does not try hard enough." Important in those days was also the quality and care of handwriting; Father's was graded as "poor." Over the years, class size decreased to twenty-one students, suggesting that many students could not keep up with the rigorous curriculum and had to quit.

Relatively effortlessly he did well, but was he outgoing, did he have his friends, did he flirt (at least a little), dance, drink once in a while? He was good friends at school with Mother's first cousin Herbert Flersheim, whose parents Martin and Florence Flersheim lived around the corner from the Albert Eberstadts. He was a frequent guest at their Sunday poker evenings with the Frankfurt art world. He himself avoided cards because the stakes were too high. Another first cousin, Rudolf Lenel, a medical student, son of Otto and Louise Lenel (née Eberstadt) in Freiburg, was another friend. They climbed in the Alps, especially in the southern Tyrol. Rudolf Lenel became an army doctor in the First World War and married a doctor. He died young in the 1920s.

Where, other than in the Engadine, did the family vacation? ("Take a deep breath," Marie Eberstadt supposedly told her husband, "the air is very expensive here.") Did he have sufficient pocket money? I suspect he did not. It seems a fairly conventional childhood. He kept a few school-boy treasures such as a collection of butterflies and pressed flowers until we left Germany. A zoological atlas with pasted bird pictures is in my New York library. He played the violin and piano, both well. The Eberstadts, like the Flersheims, subscribed to the Friday night Museums-Konzert series. The saying went: "Are you a subscriber or are you here for pleasure?" Albert Eberstadt had a good voice and sang in the St. Cecilia choir.

After graduation from the *Gymnasium* in 1905, Father read law at university level (unlike the United States, there is no undergraduate college in Germany). Students would also change universities, often in order to study with particular professors of their choice. Father went first to Marburg University, then to Freiburg in the Rhine Valley close to the Black Forest and then to Strasbourg in the Alsace. In 1907 the Leipzig military district granted him the status of a one-year service volunteer (*Einjährig Freiwilliger*) with deferral until 1910 on medical grounds. In the event of a general mobilization, he was to report immediately for duty.

Studies of law at the university were formally completed with the First State Exam, a verbal examination administered by senior members of a State Court of Law rather than by the law school. Passing this exam qualified the student to enter the applied part of legal training. Positions were full-time, supervised, with full responsibilities within the state court system or state administration. The official title of Referendar given to all such positions came with no pay or a puny stipend, typical for positions of academics in training.

Father was summoned to his First State Exam on July 14, 1909, at nine in the morning before the Supreme Court of Hesse at Cassel. The bureaucratic nature of the court is best illustrated by the document informing Father of the examination, abbreviated here: "Should the candidate, on account of illness or for some other — to be precisely described — reason, be unable to appear on the appointed date, in order not to be disqualified under paragraph 9, subsection 6 of the examination regulations published as part of the General Regulations dated March 30, 1908, on page 186, the reasons had to be submitted, properly attested, prior to the date set for the examination. To avoid delaying the document certifying the successful passing of the examination, the candidate should have with him Mark 1.50 for stamp duty payable to the court clerk on duty." The certificate would be mailed promptly thereafter.

Having passed his first law exam, Father became a Referendar at the Rüdesheim court for nine months. It was a dream appointment, in the midst of the Rhine's best vineyards, though without pay. Two years later, in July 1911, the Frankfurt Oberstaatsanwalt (Public Prosecutor) made him a deputizing district attorney, without remuneration, for the month of August.

In 1914, he passed his second and final law exam, earning the title of Assessor, the next stage of his legal career. His thesis on *"Die Unechten Gesamtschulden"* (The Inauthentic General Debt), dedicated to his parents, earned him a doctorate. His orals were held in Berlin and began February 28, 1914.

On March 9, 1914, the Minister of Justice, #65, Wilhelmstrasse, Berlin, informed Referendar Dr. jur. Georg Eberstadt that having been

graded *"Gut"* in his finals, he was appointed a Gerichtsassessor with seniority as of March 4, 1914. This appointment was gazetted in the *Justiz-
Ministerial-Blatt* of Friday March 13, 1914. It is interesting to see how
the times were reflected in this publication, which documented changed
regulations and laws. For example, in the issue gazetting Father's appointment it gave notice of an impending amendment to regulations issued in
1897 and 1908 governing food provisioning in civil prisons, effective
April 1, 1914. Monthly price fixing of rye (in prisons holding more than
ten inmates) was ended. The price of flour and bread would no longer
be based on the price changes of medium-quality rye but negotiated independently of any fluctuations. "For further details read paragraph 24
section B1 of the regulations governing the feeding of prisoners." Lots
more paragraphs, sections, and subsections follow. The proceeds from this
quasi-official publication supported justice department widows.

Father received his letters patent and instructions to report to the
President of the State Supreme Court of Hesse within a week, for assignment to a court as Assessor, without pay. If he did not want court service he
could work in the state prosecutor's office. In the name of the King, by the
Minister of Justice, sealed by the King of Prussia, Elector of Brandenburg
and member of the House of Hohenzollern, he became Assessor.

An application for an appointment as Assessor in Königstein or
Höchst (both close to his home in Frankfurt) was denied, but he was
given leave to take law courses in England from March to September 1914.
His mother's cousin Otto Edinger owned Edinger and Asch, a London
stockbroking firm (see chapter 3). Another cousin, Alfred Marx, with
whom he shared an apartment, worked at Edinger. He had a good time in
London, went to the races and half contemplated settling in England. But
in August of 1914, after England had declared war against Germany, he
took one of the last trains home. He joined the German army right after
his return. Had he stayed in England he would have been interned as
an enemy alien and spent the war behind barbed wire or eventually been
exchanged for British nationals of military age interned in Germany.
However, it proved a blessing that Father, and later Mother, spent some
time in England before we went there to live in 1936.

On August 11, 1914, one week after the outbreak of the war, Father was assigned to the Frankfurt courts, an appointment he never took up because he joined the army.

He joined the army on October 7, 1914. He was posted to the 118th Landwehr Infantry Regiment on September 21, 1915. The regiment saw much fighting. It was engaged in the line west of the Argonnes from September 22, 1915, until November 3, 1915. It fought in the autumn battles in the Champagne from November 4, 1915, until July 14, 1916. There was more fighting in the same area from July 15 to September 2, 1916, from September 3 to November 27, 1916, and from November 28, 1916, to March 4, 1917. At various times in 1917 and 1918 the regiment was engaged at Verdun, in the Argonnes, the Champagne, more Argonnes, an attack on the Marne in July 1918, defensive rear-guard fighting in the Champagne and on the Maas. From the beginning of November till Armistice Day on November 11 the regiment fought on the Aisne and Avre fronts, and between the rivers Aisne and Maas. He was spared further frontline service after August 1917 when he was posted to the 9th Landwehr divisional staff as education and recreation officer. In July 1918 he was put in charge of divisional headquarters. He deputized regularly for the divisional judge-advocate and served as ADC (Ordonnanzoffizier) to the divisional commanding general. He bet his general that he would not notice the difference between horse meat and beef. There must have been a severe meat shortage for horse flesh to be on the divisional headquarters menu.

Soon after call-up Father was made a corporal. By the time he passed the exam and interview at Döberitz on June 12, 1915, for admission to an officers' training course he had become a Vizefeldwebel (staff sergeant).

Father served at the front for two years. He was lucky to survive without a scratch. In the Second World War I lasted barely two months before I was wounded. He was fond of quoting the refrain of a French curé on whom he was billeted: "La guerre, quelle malheur, pour nous, pour vous, pour toute le monde."

On January 27, 1916, he was awarded an Iron Cross, Second Class. The Mayor of Frankfurt congratulated him:

Herd und Heimat zu schirmen, zogt mutig hinaus Ihr zum Streite.
Botet in Waffen und Wehr trutzig dem Feinde die Stirn.
Herrlich ziert Euch die Brust des Kreuzes eisernes Zeichen.
Ruhmvoll zum Ritter geprägt hat Euch die eigene Tat,
Eisernem Ringen ward würdigster Lohn.
Der Gott unsrer Väter schütz Euch im Kampf ums Recht:
So unser täglich Gebet.

To protect hearth and native land, you bravely went off to war.

Doggedly confronted the enemy, facing him, armed to fight.

Magnificently your chest is decorated with the cross of iron.

Your own deeds have gloriously made a knight of you,

Iron struggles earned you your reward.

May the God of our fathers protect you while fighting for our Right:

That is our daily prayer.

On August 26, 1916, Ernst Ludwig, by the Grace of God Grandduke of Hesse, awarded to Lieutenant Eberstadt, 118th Landwehr Regiment, the Grand-ducal, "For Valor" medal.

On July 25, 1918, the Third Army Command presented him with a silver-handled ivory letter opener in recognition of his succesful endeavours on behalf of the 8th War Loan.

On October 26, 1918, he was awarded by the King's Commission for Royal Prussian Orders, the *Verdienstkreuz für Kriegshilfe* (Merit Order for War Services).

Less than a month before the war ended (the Armistice was signed on November 11, 1918) he was awarded the Iron Cross, First Class. It was late in the day for acts of valor, late for anyone in his senses to risk his neck. Most minds by then must have been on the future rather than heroics. With defeat and peace self-evident, he may have asked his general to give him the much coveted medal before all was over. The citatation is handwritten, signed by a captain, adjutant of the 9th Landwehr Infantry Division, bearing the divisional stamp.

He stayed with the 118th Landwehr Infantry Regiment until December 9, 1918, when he was hospitalized with jaundice. On January 2, 1919, he got his discharge from the army. Ironically, on February 5, 1919, after an entire world war, he was notified that his legal seniority forfeited while he was in England had been reinstated.

Father rarely spoke about the war. There are photos of him in uniform on horseback and there are manuals from his officers' training school. In 1932 he obtained an abstract of his war record from the War Ministry, hoping it might protect him under the Nazis. It was notarized in Hamburg on April 28, 1933, three months after Hitler had come to power, by Dr. Eduard Cadmus, a lawyer who later purchased our home when we left Germany in 1936.

A couple of years before Father died, his service as a staff officer became the subject of a heated correspondence with his cousin Hans Riesser. The latter had been in the German Foreign Office in the early 1930s. As a Jew, though baptized, he was forced to retire under Hitler. In 1945 he became the first postwar German Consul General in New York, a tactful appointment when, to Jewish New York, every German was an S.S. man. (I met Riesser on several occasions in New York. Given a chance, he would have made a good Nazi.) Riesser in his memoirs claimed he had retired from the Nazi German Foreign Office on political grounds. Come on, Father wrote back, you were dismissed because you were Jewish. Though himself baptized, father went on, he had only once made any bones about his origins. That was while on the staff of the 9th Landwehr Division in 1917, after two years in the trenches, when having a staff job probably saved his life. At one point his General had made disparaging remarks about Father's (Jewish) predecessor, saying that the man had been sent back to the trenches because he had become "more than the General could bear." That was the only reason, father wrote his cousin, that he had once avoided the subject of his own background.

My father got greatly worked up over this correspondence. Letters went back and forth. He evidently relished the argument, but the underlying issue mattered to him.

5

A Banker in the
Weimar Republic

After the war, Father was set on banking rather than the law. Through a connection of his father he trained for five months, from May to October 1919, at S. Merzbach, an old, established, and well-regarded firm in Offenbach, a small town adjoining Frankfurt. Merzbach liked Father. He gave him a glowing send-off: "Exceptionally quick grasp, pleasant personality, glad to expose him to all sides of the business, became a dear friend," and so on. The Merzbach bank was founded in 1832; it had several telephone lines, including the single-digit 3 — which must have been a prestigious number — as well as 337 and 338. It had a steel vault and rented out safe-deposit boxes. In World War II I served for a while in the Pioneer Corps with one of the Merzbachs, a likeable man who had reached England on the eve of war penniless.[1]

---

1. The Merzbach bank was taken over in 1938 by a non-Jewish employee named Friedrich Hengst. He made a great deal of money after World War II and took decent care financially of the Merzbach survivors. Hengst moved to Frankfurt in 1945 and bought the

In 1919 Father explored a number of jobs. He took counsel with his prominent and influential (Edinger) relative Jakob Riesser, economist, banker, Reichstag member, Vice President, Geheimer Justizrat (a juridical title of uncommon distinction), etc., etc. Riesser introduced him to Hans Arnhold of Gebrüder Arnhold, an up-and-coming Dresden bank which had recently opened a Berlin office. They had several meetings, but in the end Father declined Arnhold's offer and stayed with an earlier proposal from I. Dreyfus in Frankfurt. In light of my friendship with Hans Arnhold's nephew Henry Arnhold, Riesser's letter to Father is for me not without interest. He laid out the pros and cons. Arnhold offered better money than Dreyfus, even taking into account Berlin's higher living costs; there were fewer partners, which should have made it easier to get ahead. Dreyfus had six, which Riesser thought might hamper advancement — though nowadays it's hardly a daunting number. But Riesser also wrote that Dreyfus had a better reputation than Arnhold; it was "much more highly regarded."

When Father turned down Hans Arnhold, the latter wrote back, on November 8, 1919: "Sehr geehrter Herr Dr. Eberstadt, I have received your esteemed letter of November 8th. The friendly warm tenor in which you couch your negative response occasions me also to express regret from my side that our working together is not possible. On the other hand, I hope that in the future, even as we go our separate ways, we may find an opportunity for working together. It is taken for granted that our conversations remain confidential and I extend my greetings to you with highest respect, Hans Arnhold." Fax and e-mail have put an end to elegant language.

In hindsight, one wonders about Father's choice. The Arnhold firm flourished in the 1920s, more so than did Dreyfus or Behrens. Like a German version of Lehman Brothers, with a Bear Stearns flavor, Arnhold

---

bombed-out site of my great-grandparents Flersheims' home at #47, Feuerbachstrasse. His strikingly beautiful, blond socialite daughter married Count Ferdinand von Galen, senior partner of what had become Schröder Münchmeyer Hengst. He and the bank got into trouble in the 1970s. Galen went to prison; his wife stuck by him. I knew Galen in business and socially. Failing aristocratic financiers have a tendency to resort to desperate, often illegal, but rarely successful maneuvers.

had a knack for backing new industries. Father and Hans Arnhold, whom I came to know and like in New York, might have made an excellent team, to the advantage of both.

At Dreyfus Father got on well with Willy Dreyfus, the senior partner who had recently moved from Frankfurt to Berlin which had become the bank's main seat. Already in October 1920, only one year after he had joined the firm, J. Dreyfus and Co. notified its clients that their general counsel, Herr Gerichtsassessor a. D. Dr. jur. Georg Eberstadt, had been authorized to sign singly.

Willy's wife, Martha, the elder daughter of the Frankfurt jeweler and art collector Louis Koch, was a cousin of Mother's. The remaining resident partner in Frankfurt, Fritz Flersheim, was also a cousin of Mother's. Father was on adequate rather than close terms with him. Fritz Flersheim, by temperament a pessimist, was by no stretch of imagination a moneymaker or business-getter. He had a doctorate in economics and was well versed in monetary and banking theory. He had a rank-conscious, finicky personality and was a stickler for protocol and detail.

Father thought his nemesis at Dreyfus ultimately would become Paul Wallich, a Berlin partner who considered him a competitor. I never knew Wallich, but I have read his father's and his own biographies, published in English and German by well-intentioned but mistaken sons. Paul Wallich comes across as cultured but vain, and not wise. Before World War I Wallich had been a partner in the prestigious Berliner Handelsgesellschaft, a creation of the successful but difficult Carl Fürstenberg, who did not take him back after the war. Instead he joined Willy Dreyfus, who was probably attracted to Wallich's vivid personality, seeming credentials, and previous experience. Maybe the Dreyfus partnership was only moderately talented at moneymaking. Wallich's description of his own business role is unimpressive. He had spent time before 1914 at Goldman Sachs in New York and prided himself on connections that led to nothing more than occasional and minor sub-underwriting participations. He had business in eastern Germany and Poland that amounted to nothing much. He was Jewish by birth but not creed and went to considerable lengths to ignore his roots. He had been an officer in World War I and was an ardent

German nationalist. He married the daughter of a commanding general of the Potsdam officers cadet school, bought a landed estate, collected books, and coauthored some. The advent of the Nazis destroyed him. He sent his children and his wife abroad. He himself could not face emigration. By 1938 it had become hopeless to stay on and he jumped into the Rhine.

In any event, my father stayed only three years at Dreyfus. He had become unsure about a partnership. In January 1924, Dreyfus notified its clients that Dr. Eberstadt was leaving the firm on friendly terms to devote himself to new activities. In the same circular they announced that Herr Dr. Alfred Rosenfeld was granted single signature. Much later, Rosenfeld became a good friend and client of mine in New York. By then, he was Alfred Romney, a well-to-do investor, somewhat of a socialite, and an intelligent, interesting person.

Father survived the German inflation in the early 1920s relatively well, in part because his profit participation at Dreyfus was fixed in gold. He joined L. Behrens und Söhne in Hamburg on January 1, 1924, the same day that Eduard L. Behrens retired from the firm, "to their great regret but in view of his age and health." This left Eduard's son George as the senior member. The other partners were Eduard Hamberg and his son Percy; Felix Haase, who had worked with Father at Dreyfus and introduced him to George Behrens; and Walter Cahn, previously a manager in the firm. The partnership agreement provides an insight into family banking at the time. The retired Eduard Behrens kept 10 percent of annual profits without exposure to losses. His wife and a female Behrens relative were also provided for. All partners were liable with their own — and if marital property was owned jointly, their wives' — entire liquid capital as well as future capital accretions, whether earned or inherited. This proved a costly clause. Father had little money of his own. Mother's dowry was joint property. Already in his first year at Behrens the dowry was lost — to be replaced by Mother's parents.

The six partners received annual salaries: RM 77,000 for George Behrens; RM 25,000 for Eduard Hamberg; RM 38,000 for Percy Hamberg and Felix Haase; RM 31,000 for Walter Cahn and Father. Capital earned 5 percent. After deduction of all expenses and bonuses George Behrens came out with 29.5 percent in profits or losses, the older Hamberg had 12.5 percent, his son and Haase each had 16 percent, Cahn and Father had 13 percent each. On Eduard's death, the agreement stipulated that Father and Cahn would be raised to 15 percent profits and losses.

A Behrens partner was allowed to withdraw up to 10,000 goldmarks annually for each percentage point in the profit and loss account. The partners were forbidden to "speculate" for their own account or to borrow money. Directors' fees went to the firm. They were prohibited from engaging in any non-firm business activities. If a partner wished to withdraw more money than his entitlement, it required the approval of all other partners, excepting Eduard Behrens who required only George's consent. Two partners were needed to enter into commitments beyond the routine daily business. Any one partner had veto powers over a transaction. If firm earnings were insufficient for a partner to live *standesgemäss* — the style appropriate to his station in life — he could withdraw the necessary funds from the firm. There were stringent conditions attached to withdrawal of capital on leaving or retirement. The initial contract was for seven years. On the one hand, it was more restrictive than a modern partnership agreement. On the other, it permitted withhdrawals, which under adverse conditions must have been dangerous. Today an agreement that permits withdrawals regardless of profits to "support a lifestyle in keeping with one's station in life" is inconceivable.

Behrens has an interesting and distinguished history. The firm was founded in 1780 in Pyrmont, capital of the Duchy of Waldeck, by Levy Herz and Nathan Behrens. In 1780 Prince Frederic of Waldeck, Count of Pyrmont and Rappoltstein, etc., issued a letter of safe conduct and protection to Levy Behrens, and in 1788 to his two brothers. These letters were the foundation of their business and enabled them to establish themselves in Hamburg in 1796, after Napoleonic laws had granted rights to Jews in Hamburg and other areas.

To begin with, the business consisted chiefly of importing cloth from Manchester, England. This could be done more effectively from the northern Germany port city of Hamburg than from Pyrmont. Moreover, Herz Behrens had married the daughter of Moses Hertz, a well-established

Hamburg banker. During the Continental Blockade in 1806, trade with Great Britain was made difficult. Behrens became blockade runners but that was not sufficient. To offset the effects of the blockade, they built up a domestic textile business. They purchased goods in Saxony and sold them in northwest Germany. They also became forwarding and insurance agents, which led them into banking.

After the Continental Blockade was lifted in 1812, Salomon Levy Behrens moved to Manchester where he founded S. L. Behrens and Co. (Manchester Goods) which still exists. In 1832 Nathan Behrens sent his youngest son, Jacob, to Leeds to straighten out differences with suppliers. He founded his own firm and flourished as a leading mill owner, headed the Bradford chamber of commerce, and was knighted. The firm became Sir Jacob Behrens and Sons, Bradford, Manchester, London, Calcutta, and Bombay.[2]

The trading links with the English houses remained important, but increasingly the Hamburg firm developed its banking business. When Levy Behrens died in 1834, Wolf Levy (Wilhelm Leopold upon baptism) became the sole proprietor. The Hamburg firm owned ships which exported Manchester goods to many parts of the world and returned with spices and other colonial produce. By 1844 its capital was 10 million marks, a significant sum in those days. From 1853 to 1924, Wilhelm Leopold Behrens' son Eduard Ludwig was sole proprietor. Under him the bank grew greatly in significance. It joined the ranks of Germany's leading private banks. It continued the commodity business but withdrew from Manchester Goods.

Nathan Meyer Rothschild (1777–1836), founder of the London firm, sent his son Nathan to be trained at Manchester Goods, according to Lady Battersea's memoirs, published in 1922 (she was a granddaughter of Nathan Rothschild and cousin of Lady Charlotta Louise Rothschild-Behrens). This opened friendly relations with the Hamburg Behrens house. The

2. His son Gustav joined the firm. Another son, Sir Charles Behrens, became Lord Mayor of Manchester and married a daughter of the first Lord Rothschild. A nephew, Edward Beddington Behrens, founded Edward de Stein, a succesful investment banking firm in London which ultimately merged with Lazard Brothers.

Rothschilds saw to it that in joint dealings of theirs with S. Bleichroeder in Berlin, Behrens was taken along. Thanks to the Rothschild connection, after the 1870–1871 war between France and Germany, Behrens handled part of the French reparation payments to Germany. The large deposits Rothschild maintained at Behrens and their own resources enabled the firm to play a leading role in supplying liquidity to the Hamburg business community during the crisis of 1876, a series of economic repercussions created by Austro-Russian conflicts in the Balkans.

In the 1880s and 1890s Behrens were syndicate co-managers for Nordic government and municipal underwritings, Chinese bond issues, and equity offerings on behalf of foreign railroads and plantations. From 1879 to 1924 they handled the Hamburg state lottery jointly with two other Hamburg houses, as well as the Danish colonial, Bulgarian, and Romanian lotteries. They became a major acceptance house. They played a leading role in the Hamburg sugar, coffee, rubber, cotton, and metals futures markets. They acted for the Austro-Hungarian sugar producers as their main dealer in sugar futures. They were active in investment management, arbitrage, and futures. They were the Hamburg correspondents of numerous leading European banks. Around the turn of the twentieth century the coffee department became the European agents of leading Brazilian houses. The annual volume was over one million sacks of coffee.

After the war, the firm's importance diminished. There was far less of the business that had made Behrens wealthy. The pre-1914 German colonial empire was placed under League of Nations mandates. The shipowners had their finest vessels seized as reparations. The Hamburg merchants had lost much of their capital during the inflation. World trade and Hamburg's importance declined.

By 1924, M. M. Warburg probably had overtaken Behrens. George Behrens came from a family that considered the Warburgs newcomers. The drive and personality of Max Warburg, however, overshadowed that of the somewhat reticent Anglophile George Behrens. Max Warburg's links to New York through his brother Felix's strategic marriage to Frieda Schiff, the daughter of Jacob Schiff, the wealthy and influential senior partner of Kuhn Loeb and Co., must have been more useful than the Behrens connections with London, interrupted and poisoned by the First World War, not long ended.

In addition to their importance as bankers, by the 1880s the Behrens family had attained social acceptance in Hamburg. Many of the wives came from old, established (non-Jewish) Hamburg families. There was an O'swald wife, a Petersen, a Sloman. Daughters married into titled families. Wilhelm Leopold Behrens became honorary Belgian consul-general in 1879. In this post he was succeeded by his nephew Eduard Ludwig in 1883. The senior Eduard Ludwig was not only a prominent banker but a major collector of paintings of the Barbizon School and Meissen, Frankenthal, Ludwigsburg, and Fürstenberg porcelain.

George Behrens, senior partner in Father's day, had a non-Jewish mother who survived the Nazi and war years in Hamburg. As a soldier after World War II, I brought her CARE packages from relatives outside Germany.

It cannot have been easy to head a private banking firm in the 1920s. War and inflation impaired the bank's capital. Pre-1914 connections had to be reestablished or replaced. For example, during the first years after the war, it was almost impossible for a German to show his face in the City of London, not even for George Behrens with generations of English family links. Father went back to London for the first time in 1924. He made a wide circle around the Edith Cavell statue at the edge of Trafalgar Square because a German-speaking tourist had recently been stoned there. Cavell, an English nurse, had been matron since 1907 of a medical institute in Brussels, which in 1914 became a Red Cross hospital. She assisted about two hundred English, French, and Belgian soldiers to escape to the Dutch border between November 1914 and July 1915. She was arrested by the Germans, court-martialed, and condemned to death, an act which contributed to the German "Hun" ethos of the First World War. When we came to England in the 1930s, men passing the Cavell statue still raised their hats.

After the First World War the business of any Hamburg bank, historically based on foreign trade, had to adapt to different conditions. Banks dealt in financial securities and currencies rather than discounting bills based on merchandise transactions. In the First World War George Behrens had been in Belgium as a member of the German control commission overseeing the Belgian banks. Its head was Dr. Schacht, later president of the Reichsbank. Willy Dreyfus was another member. Both made friends with Schacht, which proved useful after the war. The Dreyfus bank became members of the Reichsbank government bond underwriting groups, a prestigious and profitable syndicate to which few of the Jewish private banks belonged. Through the Schacht connection, Behrens made friends with the Reichs Kredit Gesellschaft, the long-term credit arm of the Reichsbank. Father cultivated this important relationship, especially with Edgar Landauer, who later became one of his closest business friends in England.

Behrens still had a sizeable but probably increasingly risky commodity business. Their importance in the sugar market continued. They handled the export of German sugar as reparation payments to France. Jointly with British banks they financed the sale of Polish sugar. They had an active stock exchange, foreign currency trading, and arbitrage business. Unfortunately, they also had large credits outstanding in the traditional commodities and metals trades, which were the cause of serious losses even before the banking crisis of the 1930s. As stock and bond underwriters they were syndicate participants rather than originators. The major issues typically were handled by the Berlin head offices of Deutsche or Dresdner Bank, or Berlin-based private banks such as Berliner Handelsgesellschaft, Mendelssohn, and S. Bleichroeder.

Father was responsible for the investment business at Behrens. He invested firm capital in the German market and on Wall Street. A former Behrens employee once told me he considered Father the only intelligent partner at Behrens (this was Paul Levy, who later in London was known as Paul Langdon and was in charge of stock trading at Ullman and Co., a midsized London merchant bank which in 1974, as Keyser Ullman, all but went under). According to Levy-Langdon, if Father took positions in a stock, they were big. Some apparently worked out very well. The German market, fueled by cheap money, boomed in 1926, though it was followed by a severe bear market. Markets elsewhere, in particular on Wall Street, were booming. Father was making significant money for the firm. On one occasion, according to Mother, they went to Denmark for a weekend. Father had been told about a pending deal — nowadays it would probably be considered inside information — but something seemingly was going wrong. On the pretext of a social visit they went to see Father's source in Copenhagen. I don't know the outcome. Our stockbroker cousin Alfred Marx used to quote an old London stock exchange adage: "Information — Ruination."

When Father joined Behrens at the end of the inflation, savings institutions gained large inflows of funds for the first time since the war. Capital markets were reviving. Father was responsible for underwritings at Behrens. He recognized the change and arranged the first post-inflation bond issue in Germany by a utility company. When Behrens was invited by Deutsche Bank into a Kreuger and Toll underwriting, perhaps the most glamorous company of the inter-war years, involving Swedish Match, Father could not make sense of the prospectus. He made a special trip to the bank's Berlin head office to decline the invitation. A few years later in 1931 Swedish Match went bankrupt and brought down leading banks in the United States and Europe including Lee Higginson of Boston.

In my own business life I once turned down a "hot," highly lucrative underwriting. Model Roland and Co., where I worked from 1953 to 1969, had been invited by Guinness Mahon, N. M. Rothschild, Pierson, Heldring and Pierson, and other leading houses into the initial public offering of IOS (Investors Overseas Services), Bernie Kornfeld's Fund of Funds advisory company, a stockbroker's dream client. I had taken an intense dislike to the man and his methods. Fortunately Leo Model backed me, though some of our younger colleagues were furious. For a year or so after the offering I felt foolish. Kornfeld's growth continued. His stock boomed. He had taken us off his broker list. But it did not take long for IOS to become an embarrassment for the blue-blooded names who lent their reputation to sponsor Kornfeld. It was gratifying to have been among the minority who had not been blinded by Kornfeld's money. He later wrote a book, *Do You Sincerely Want To Be Rich?* I did not read it, but the title is thought-provoking.

No one wants to be poor. Most of us want to have money, maybe even quite a lot. But very, very few sincerely want to be really rich. We may pay lip service to the goal, but to achieve it requires the subordination of one's entire life to making money. Few act accordingly. Two in my own business life sincerely wanted to be rich — and succeeded. Leo Model was one, and the other, on a grander scale, Andre Meyer. Robert Lehman and Michel David-Weill were different. They wanted wealth but had it to start with. They came from families that had experienced and survived wars and depressions. They added skillfully but cautiously to their inherited wealth, though as they got older neither Robert Lehman nor Michel David-Weill kept sufficient control over their partners. Lehman Brothers fell apart and Lazard is not having an easy time. Both remained wealthy and seemed able to combine financial success with manifold other interests.

I started my own working life in the belief that the post-1945 world would be equalitarian and that there was little point in trying to make more than a decent living. I was over thirty before capital became important to me. Once I had some money, my appetite for more grew, but never, for better or worse, became gargantuan. I don't believe it matters greatly how much money one has while young. The better and less well-off among one's friends still have similar spending patterns. A little more or a little less is not of importance. In one's thirties, lives and friendships begin to diverge with differing incomes.

When Father joined the Behrens firm in 1924, the partnership was small. Individual percentages of profits as well as losses were correspondingly large. For Haase, Cahn, and Father, who were impecunious, the opportunities but also the risks were huge. Between 1927 and 1929 Father made very substantial money. He once alluded to me about his ups and downs and spoke of an "if only" scenario. In mid-1929 when he found himself wealthy he almost retired. He had the financial independence to enter public life. A 15 percent profit participation is wonderful when all goes well, but obviously hugely risky if you have little capital to tide over bad times. A credit balance could become a debit overnight. When this happened in 1930, Father, Haase, and Cahn lost their money.

Again the Flersheims helped Father to pay the debt incurred by his share of losses when he withdrew from Behrens. Haase and Cahn walked away from their obligations to Behrens. After the war, when Father and George Behrens met, he owed him nothing and they met as equals, a lesson not lost on me. At Lazard at one time, a real estate deal in which I was a limited partner went wrong. There was no legal obligation to put up additional capital, but there was a moral commitment. Unlike some, I paid my share, a decision that later stood me in good stead.

Hamburg, where we had lived since January 1924, ushered in years of business and social advancement for my parents. Willistrasse #7 became our greatly loved home, for me from the age of three till my fourteenth year. My mother recorded all her household expenses in a book, a practice she had learned from her father. She also wrote down every book she read, play she saw, where she had traveled, who came to dinner or stayed as a house guest. She started a travel and a theatre book for me, which I have kept up.

The years in Hamburg were happy years notwithstanding the ups and downs. Almost needless to say, Mother was, politically, to the left of Father. She voted left-of-center for the Deutsche Staatspartei, the party of Brüning, and he voted for and actively supported Stresemann's right-of-center Deutsche Volkspartei. Her party flew the black-red-gold colors of the Weimar Republic, his the black-white-red of the Kaiser's Germany. Her bookshelves were about literature and fairy tales of the world, his about history and biographies. He wanted a social life that furthered his career, she a circle of friends with a mixed background and family. It was hard for a family person such as herself to move away from Frankfurt, but Hamburg soon made her happy and fullfilled her marriage.

My sister Brigitte (Bridget) was born on Willistrasse. A lovely garden backed on one of the canals that connected with the Alster lake. The house survived the war. The way into Hamburg from the airport goes past it. I always ask the cab driver to slow down when we go past number 7.

In a birthday letter in 1924, a few months after he had started at Behrens, my grandfather Albert Eberstadt wished his son success and contentment in his new firm, happiness with his wife — whom Albert Eberstadt adored — and in his new house and with his son Walter: "All things in life repeat themselves, thus also that I seem nearly always to celebrate your birthday without you. . . . Better than elsewhere they know in Hamburg that the trader's ship sails the oceans in uncertain weather. Time-tested business principles need not always be sufficient to avoid risks and ensure safe arrival at distant destinations. So far in your life your talents have stood you in good stead. You have succeeded at whatever you have done. Now you will also need good luck on your side." Albert Eberstadt's premonitions were well founded.

Father was like most of us: we want to be comfortable, but lack that burning urge to accumulate major wealth. His ambitions went beyond a partnership in a prestigious but, as it turned out, financially unsound bank. Mother believed he should have been a lawyer. He, however, always eyed a financial position in the public sector or a major bank.

Little more than a year after he had joined Behrens, Father became bored and disillusioned with their business. In an early October 1925 letter to his father he complained that my sister Brigitte's birth was a week overdue and that he had time on hand and thus no excuse not to write more frequently. Behrens must have too little business, he wrote tongue-in-cheek to his father — otherwise they'd be involved in more bankruptcies. Almost with a sigh of relief he told his father confidentially of a bankruptcy of an Amsterdam firm named Siegmund Strauss Jr. in which the bank would — sooner or later — be involved. Fortunately, it would not cause Behrens much concern as they held a first mortgage on the Strauss office building. If the Strausses did not want all their assets eaten up by interest and losses, they should get it over with.

In another letter to his father (written on October 14, three days before Brigitte's birth), he hoped she might be born the following day which would have been Marie Eberstadt's seventieth birthday. ("She died less than seven years ago; think how much has happened in that short period of time in our small family circle and how much she would have enjoyed being part of it all.") Again he said he had plenty of time on hand. To divert mother from an overdue baby he was taking her to the movies in the afternoon. At night they played a newly acquired phonograph ("not the most highbrow way of listening to music"). He had two Caruso records, "the like of whom we shall never hear again." He asked his father if there wasn't something unseemly about enjoying the voice of a dead person in the comforts of one's home.

Father liked George Behrens but considered him somewhat weak and not a particularly hard worker. They remained friends, even though Father lost his money when the bank suffered in 1930. Father left at the end of that year to join Dresdner Bank. With improving business conditions Behrens recovered somewhat. It did not last long.

Father had already put out feelers for change in 1926. In that year he had confided to Eugen Oppenheim, senior partner of Jacob S. H. Stern, one of the oldest Frankfurt private banks, that he did not feel "comfortable" at Behrens. In a letter in May of that year, Oppenheim advised Father that their "mutual friends" (identified in a penciled margin note by Father as Norddeutsche Bank) were not looking for a new head, contrary to what Father had heard. The Oppenheims were well acquainted with his in-laws, the Flersheims. The two families had just spent "pleasant hours together over Whitsun in the surroundings of Frankfurt." The Flersheims had recently acquired a Mercedes-Benz and a chauffeur. They loved taking friends and family for Sunday outings.

In a letter from London on May 25, 1927, George Behrens reported to my father a lunch conversation with Arthur Guinness of Guinness Mahon about reorganizing S. Bleichroeder, the Berlin bank that had come to international prominence in Bismarck's Germany. Evidently, Bleichroeder was in difficulties in 1927. They would have failed in 1931 had they not been taken over (at the instigation of Dr. Hjalmar Schacht, president of the German Reichsbank), by Gebrüder Arnhold of Dresden and Berlin — now Arnhold and S. Bleichroeder in New York. In any case, in 1927 Arthur Guinness wanted to form a syndicate with Behrens and Ladenburg Thalmann of New York to refinance and reorganize Bleichroeder. Guinness wanted Father for the job and Dr. Rudolph

Brinckmann of M. M. Warburg as his number two. Behrens wrote to Father, "Since I will lose you sooner or later to Deutsche Bank or to Discontogesellschaft, I'd rather lose you to an allied and friendly firm." He told Guinness that Father would have to be a partner with dictatorial authority and have a salary of at least ten thousand pounds a year."

Behrens doubted that anything would come of the idea, especially as he had tried it once before and failed. Still, he asked if Father would see Arthur Guinness and Rosenthal (later Walter Rosen) of Ladenburg Thalmann, who would both be in Berlin the following weekend. Nothing came of it, but apparently Father was making important connections and a name for himself.

Many years later Arthur Guinness, Walter Rosen, and Rudolph Brinckmann played a role in my life. Brinckmann and I became close in 1945. He was then senior partner of Brinckmann Wirtz and Co., the successor firm of M. M. Warburg. I was a British army officer in Hamburg. Later in 1948, Guinness was chairman of the International Chamber of Commerce in London when I came down from Oxford to see him. I was exploring career opportunities, and he offered me a position as his personal assistant in the ICC. It might have been a good stepping-stone. The Chamber was then more important than it is nowadays. I would have met interesting people and made useful connections. But I turned it down. The work was not challenging.

When I moved to New York Guinness and I developed a business relationship and I am still friends with his son. Guinness introduced me to Walter Rosen who offered me a position at Ladenburg Thalmann (known to this day as "L.T."). I quickly realized that L.T. had become a shadow of its former self. Guinness also introduced me to Francis Callery, formerly of L.T. but by then an important Lehman partner. Callery was an immensely likeable handsome man, in charge of Lehman's oil ventures. He was enjoying a string of major wildcatting successes. We hit it off, which together with Siegmund Warburg's introduction to Ed Kapp, manager of their "industrial department," got me into Lehman Brothers.

6

The Congress in Cologne

In a sense, the year 1928 was the high point in Father's business life. He had just turned forty. He had made money. The Eberstadts had been accepted into Hamburg society. Father owned a Mercedes-Benz SSK supercharged convertible. The chauffeur, Heckemüller, turned out to have been an early Nazi. (The car registration number was HH 18113. Other numbers from my childhood: home phone, 523601; Father's office number at Dresdner Bank, 361003.) We spent a four-week summer holiday in 1928 at the Park Hotel, Gunten, on Lake Thun in the Bernese Oberland, together with my grandfather Albert Eberstadt and my aunt Maria Schaefer and her two children.

Father was one of the keynote speakers at the Seventh German Bankers Congress in Cologne on Sept 9 to 11, 1928. The Central Association of German Banks were the hosts. Its board chairman — Geh. Justizrat Prof. Dr. jur., Dr. rer. pol. h.c. Riesser — presided. (Titles were crucial in those days, and to omit any one of them was a grave mistake. Translated, these titles amounted to "Honorable Judicial Counsel,

Professor and Doctor of Law, Doctor of Political Sciences Honoris Causae"
and would be used in their entirety on letterheads and in introductions to
speeches; in personal address they were reduced to the most distinguished
one or two titles.)

The participants were a who's who of 1928 Germany. The congress, a
major annual event to this day, carries more cachet than the ABA (American Bankers Association) or IBA (Investment Bankers Association)
conventions in the United States. From the most prominent politicians
to distinguished government representatives, from the most influential
journalists to economic leaders, everyone was represented. Non-bankers
attended as invited guests, bankers as participants.

Konrad Adenauer, at the time Lord Mayor of Cologne and twenty
years later the first German chancellor, greeted the participants, over
1,500 altogether, not counting wives. President von Hindenburg cabled
greetings. Representatives of many federal and state government ministries attended, such as the treasury, justice department, or agricultural
ministry. National and regional government offices, wholesale and retail
trade organizations, professional or industrial associations, unions — too
many to name — were represented, including seventeen different stock
exchanges from within Germany alone.[1]

Everyone who was anybody in German banking attended, from Hjalmar
Schacht, Reichsbankpräsident, on down. In addition to its chairman

---

1. Also listed as participants were the post office, the department for the occupied territories, the Reich commissar for the occupied Rhineland, senior Reichsbank staff, Reichsbank
governors (among them Max Warburg), the department for war damage compensation,
the Reich statistical department, government research organizations, the Cologne con-
sular corps, 12 members of the upper Reichstag, 26 from the lower chamber, 26 members
of the provisional Reich business advisory board, 9 Prussian ministries, Saxon, Bavarian,
and Hanseatic ministers and senators, the wholesale and retail trades, manufacturing and
extractive industries, agriculture and landowners, the legal profession represented by forty
different associations, universities, conference board organizations, chambers of commerce,
the stock exchanges of Augsburg, Berlin, Bremen, Breslau, Chemnitz, Dresden, Düsseldorf, Essen, Frankfurt-Main, Halle, Hamburg, Hannover, Cologne, Königsberg, Leipzig,
Munich, Stuttgart, the Prussian, Bavarian, Braunschweig, Oldenburg, Saxony, Thuringia,
and Danzig state banks. There were seventy German and ten foreign journalists.

Jacob Riesser, the board of the Central Association of German Banks was composed of the leading bankers of the time. Present were Salomonsohn of Disconto Gesellschaft, Walther Frisch of Dresdner Bank, Max Warburg, Oscar Wassermann of Deutsche Bank, to name a few. Members of the Association present were, among others, Hans Arnhold, George Behrens, Cornelius von Berenberg-Gossler, Albert Hahn, Alexander Hauck, Paul von Mendelssohn-Bartholdy, Leopold Merzbach, and Robert Pferdmenges.

There were thirteen representatives from the association of — mostly Jewish — Berlin banks, including Gebrüder Arnhold and Carl Cahn and Co., whose partner Heinz Cahn became Father's closest friend.

Many additional then well-known Berlin financial firms attended[2] as well as mortgage bankers, the Reich Association of Bank Managers, and many regional bank associations.[3] Many non-German banks from neighboring countries sent representatives, as well as American houses active in German-American finance in the 1920s.[4]

Frankfurt's oldest but no longer wealthiest bank, Grunelius and Co. was represented. (A Frankfurt Rothschild, once asked how much he was worth personally, responded, "On a good day one Grunelius more, on not-so-good days one Grunelius less.") Father's partner Felix Haase attended, as did Albert Hahn—the prominent monetary theorist, sarcastic wit, clever speculator, board member of his family's Deutsche Effekten und Wechselbank in Frankfurt. (I once asked him how he weathered bear markets: "Wear two pairs of underpants. In bull markets, you should not be buying but have bought.") Alex Hauck of Georg Hauck in Frankfurt was there, school friend of Fritz Flersheim's, father of my friend and client

2. Marcus Nelken; Arthur Hirschfeld; Martin Schiff; S. Schoenberger, Königsberger and Lichtenheim; Schwarz, Goldschmidt and Wassermann.
3. The Lower Weser River Bankers Association, the Silesian bankers, the Dresden bankers, three separate associations from Frankfurt, associations from the Rhineland and Westphalia, Munich, Württemberg, Saarbrücken, and Memel.
4. Represented were, among others, Denmark, Italy (the Confederazione Generale Bancaria Fascista), France, Latvia, Austria, Poland, Sweden, Switzerland, the Kingdom of S.H.S (Zagreb) and Hungary. American firms included Equitable Trust of New York, Lawrence Stern of Chicago, and Strupp and Co. of New York.

Michael Hauck. Georg Hirschland represented Gebrüder Hirschland in Essen, which in the United States on a reduced scale carried on as New York Hanseatic Corporation. Anton Hübbe, old-line Hamburg family, and after 1931 Father's colleague at Dresdner Bank, also attended.

Another keynote speaker, Louis Hagen of Sal. Oppenheim talked about the German economy in general, Hans Fürstenberg of Berliner Handelsgesellschaft spoke about the comeback of Germany's private banks.

A panel discussion was held on Germany's Finances at the Beginning of the Fifth Year of the Dawes Plan. (Charles Gates Dawes, lawyer and financier who became vice president of the United States from 1925 to 1929 and was co-recipient in 1925 with Sir Austin Chamberlain of the Nobel Peace Prize, surveyed the German economy in 1923. From this report evolved the Dawes Plan, which suspended German reparations payments between 1923 and 1928. The plan went into effect on September 1, 1924).

Father spoke on the management of public sector funds by the Central Bank (Reichsbank). Opinions, apparently, were divided on how the public monies should be administered. Schacht (president of the Reichsbank, 1924–1929) believed the Reichsbank should be unilaterally responsible for their management.

In his speech, Father was largely in agreement with Schacht. He was in favor of public monies being held by the Reichsbank, however, he insisted that short-term capital, especially that of private insurance companies, continue to be on deposit with private sector banks.

Father's position appealed to the largely private sector audience who believed Schacht went beyond seeking control over public funds. Father welcomed Schacht's concept that public monies be deposited with the Reichsbank, free of interest. "Gradually it will become a matter of principle and pride, as anyhow it is interest-free, to get along in the public sector with the smallest float possible."

The concentration of public funds at the Reichsbank met with opposition from anti-centralists. They conjured up the "monster of a monolithic government" — something of which Father was not fearful. "Why should we bankers see in a centralized authority the black bogeyman who scares children? But let there be no misunderstanding, lest anyone accuses me of being a fanatic about centralization. . . . I speak, of course, only about the money market. In this as in other discussions, short- and long-term capital markets get mixed up. There is no need for the latter to be centralized." He complimented the British system, which vested great power and authority in the Bank of England. He concluded with a patriotic appeal, elevating public over self-interest: "We private bankers must keep our own house in order. We must accumulate sufficient reserves to be independent of central banking bailouts. Even the Reichsbank resources are not boundless. Private banking crises and the likes must become once and for all financial history. The more openly and transparently we handle ourselves without sacrificing any of our legitimate private interests, insist that business best executed by the private sector is not interfered with, but still subordinate our own concerns to the good of the entire German economy, the better we will serve society and, at the same time, ourselves." Was Father giving Dr. Schacht a signal that he would like to work for him?

The opportunity to speak at this convention gave Father tremendous exposure. President Geheimrat Prof. Dr. Jacob Riesser, Father's cousin, must have had something to do with the selection of him as a speaker. Riesser congratulated him and said he had proven to have been the "right man" for the topic. "I thank you and am particularly pleased that speeches such as yours show we have a new generation of bankers which will unhesitatingly act as we all must to further the best interests of our beloved Fatherland." (Bravo!)

Hans Fürstenberg, son of Carl Fürstenberg, founder of Berliner Handelsgesellschaft, traced the economic, fiscal, and financial developments since the war. He reminded the audience that not only Germany but France, England, and other European countries were suffering from the aftermath of 1914–1918. He showed some sympathy for the conservatives' arch villain Erzberger and his left-wing reforms. (Matthias Erzberger, controversial first finance minister after World War I, introduced radical property and income tax reforms and was accused of abusing power for personal financial gain.) While conscious of Germany's heavy foreign debt, Fürstenberg did not consider it unmanageable. He was proud that the private banking system had recovered its reputation and strength to act as conduit for foreign loans made to the German economy.

Keynote speaker Jakob Goldschmidt, head of Darmstädter and Nationalbank (Danatbank), and then at the peak of his career, made by far the most interesting presentation — provocative, imaginative, and witty. He was not, he said, much for speech making; he felt, like one Rabbi Ben Akiba, that "there is nothing that has not been said before." At a breath-taking pace he discussed private versus public enterprise, capital versus labor, the privileges and obligations of wealth, the threat to private initiative from needless controls and intervention while accepting that state and government play an essential role in society. In brief he asked questions that are asked to this day:

> If a case were made to exchange capitalism for a supposedly more efficient, more humane system, it still needs someone with sufficient courage and energy actually to lead the change. The moment for radical changes might have been immediately after the war; the moment went by. On reflection the planners gave up on their ideas. They concluded they were neither workable nor an improvement over the existing system. . . . If you compare the Russian system with the American, or even compare ours to Russia which found itself in more or less our situation in 1918, it gives you the shivers to see the mess made by government controls and planning. . . . The American society where people depend on their wages, rather than government support, for their living standard, is preferable; it forces each individual to think about his contribution and makes him responsible for his own life. . . . Ladies and Gentlemen! Socialism is no more capable of achieving a fairer division of property or its enjoyment than the medical profession is able to cure all disease, let alone overcome death.

On more immediate issues Goldschmidt stressed the need for capital formation and savings, which in turn depended on adequate profits. He was in favor of foreign borrowing as long as it was put to productive use and not to support an otherwise unsustainable standard of living. He concluded by challenging the politicians who thought life was "about nothing more than a (moderately) comfortable standard of living for everybody." They might get away with it for a while, but in the long run such a nation would be "overrun by young societies for whom life is not about rest and leisure but striving and progress" (tempestous sustained applause from all sides). A few years later Goldschmidt was vilified, pilloried as a "Jew banker," charged with ruining his bank and precipitating the German banking crisis and robbing the German economy. Goldschmidt escaped to New York soon after Hitler came to power. The auctioning of Goldschmidt's collection of French Impressionist paintings in the 1950s made the reputation of Peter Wilson as Sotheby's preeminent auctioneer.

Back in 1928, the hundreds of participants at the Cologne Congress were still working together on behalf of Germany. In hindsight, one wonders who of those who attended the Congress was already a Nazi or soon to become one. Who among the Jewish bankers survived, how and where? Which of them became Holocaust victims?

Cornelius von Berenberg-Gossler became an adamant Hitler opponent (see chapter 7). Paul Brändi was the father of Fred Brändi, senior partner of Dillon Read; Carl Deichmann's old, established Cologne bank fell a victim to the Depression; a Deichmann son, also Carl, helped Leo Model flee Holland ahead of the Germans in 1940 and as a thank-you worked at the Model firm after the war; a Deichmann daughter married Hellmuth von Moltke who was killed after the July 20, 1944, plot against Hitler. Dreyfus partners Willy Dreyfus and Fritz Flersheim, both Mother's cousins, attended — and both emigrated before too long.

Fritz Jessen of Norddeutsche Bank, Hamburg, was at the Congress — a family friend who remained a staunch anti-Nazi and was the father of Rolf James (Jessen) with whom I served in the British army; he was later finance chief of Siemens. Paul Kempner of Mendelssohn and Co. in Berlin was there; his wife was a descendant of Felix Mendelssohn and their son Max became a respected lawyer in New York and a good friend of mine. Albert von Metzler of B. Metzler in Frankfurt, the Flersheims' main banking connection, never became a Nazi. Though he was not young in 1939, he was drafted into the army, captured on the Russian front, and kept prisoner for over five years after the war's end because he was a banker. Hans Pilder, Father's predecessor at Dresdner Bank in Hamburg later became a Nazi. Jack A. Schwarzschild of J. A. Schwarzschild in Frankfurt, reputed to be less than generous, had a son, Boris Shields, who later served in the army with me. Otto Stürcken of Huth, Willinck in Hamburg, another friend of Father's who attended the Congress, stood firm and never gave in to the Nazis.

More attendants at the Congress later resurfaced in our lives. Paul Bergmann of Cahn and Co. had a daughter Irene who eventually became a New York stockbroker. The Cahns later became my parents' closest friends in England; Heinz Cahn made his office at G. Eberstadt and Co. Gebrüder Heyman was represented by Otto Eskeles, and Bernd Heymann linked up with Father in London in 1937. Heyman's nickname was *"Stationsvorsteher"* (stationmaster) on account of his bright red hair. He husbanded his considerable pennies carefully and always found reasons not to spend money.

Dr. Fritz Georg Steiner of Dillon Read's Paris office was later known as Frederic Steiner of Lazard Frères in New York; he was a knowledgeable but pedantic, harrassed, miniscule figure. The success of his brilliant scholar son George Steiner made amends for the father's stunted business life. W. E. von Marx of the long gone International Germanic Trust Company of Berlin, a stuffy man, reincarnated as Alla van Marx — I came across him later in New York. He had "Netherlandized" himself on the back of his particularly nice Dutch wife, a member of the Lippmann Rosenthal banking family in Amsterdam. His rather nicer brother Herbert von Marx, originally a partner in Bass and Herz of Frankfurt, became associated with G. Eberstadt in London after the war.

Swiss Bank Corporation was represented by Armand Dreyfus, a relative of my wife Vera; during the Second World War he looked after his bank's interests in the United States. Robert Lichtschein, then of the shrewd but speculative Vienna firm of Reitler and Co., later in New York became Robert Lambert-Lichtschein, and a substantial client of the

Model firm. Previously an avid hunter in Austria, he later shot polar bears in Alaska. My wife's Viennese family looked down on him.

Few in 1928 realized how fleeting was their moment in the sun. Father hoped he could build on the name he had made for himself at the Congress. On September 14, Albert Eberstadt wrote, "Dear Children, Already last night I told you how happy I was for you that you had such enjoyable days in Cologne and how proud I am of you, Georg, for the apparently really major success the event was for you. There must be many different opinions about such a complicated subject. You must expect newspaper attacks, some no doubt spiteful if the author disagrees. That is the price you pay for being in the limelight. I wish I had an opinion. My mind just does not seem up to it. I think where I come out is that the issue is less one of banking theory but that it comes down to people. Who is more competent to do the best job with administring the public funds: the central or the private bankers? . . . All good wishes for tomorrow" (their eighth wedding anniversary).

Soon after the Cologne Congress Father went to New York. It was his first journey across the Atlantic. He did not come back until he visited me in New York in 1956. Transatlantic travel in 1928 was not the everyday event it has become in our times. For one thing it took seven days at sea, not seven hours in the air. He went on September 18 on the *Resolute,* a 20,000-ton, three-smokestack, triple-screw vessel of the Hamburg Amerika Line. Germany had surrendered its pre-1914 passenger liners as reparation payments to the Allies. Under the Versailles Treaty its fleet was limited to maximum 20,000-ton vessels. *Resolute* was purchased from the United American Lines, which had named her after the yacht *Resolute,* a Herreshoff design built in 1914.

Mother and I saw Father off from Cuxhaven at the mouth of the Elbe where first-class passengers boarded to save the slow journey down the river from Hamburg. I was given the day off from school. We were allowed aboard. From that visit stems my fascination with ocean liners. As a hobby I began collecting brochures of ships from lines all over the world. I had the deck plans and knew the price of any cabin on the Hamburg America Line, North German Lloyd, Hamburg South America Line,

Cunard Steamship and White Star, French, Italian, Dutch, and Scandinavian lines. I knew whether they had one, two, three, or four smokestacks. (The fourth and at times even the third were dummies.) I could quote the cost of a cabin, single or double, inside or outside, with or without bath, on promenade, A B C deck, steerage in the bowels over the propellers, in season or off, knew how many pounds of caviar they took aboard, how many sides of beef, cases of wine and champagne. I felt sorry for anyone who did not travel first class. I knew the meal times and menus in second class, or worse still, steerage! Later I became interested in hotels: rooms with or without view, balcony, private bath, winter or summer prices, pre, post, or high season, *en pension* or breakfast only.

As the ship pulled out of Cuxhaven and blew its horn, the deck band played the traditional farewell: "*Muss ich denn, muss ich denn, zum Städelein hinaus.*" A few years later we left Germany for good to the same tune. Ashore, mother and I waved and waved. An empty boat train took us back to Hamburg.

In New York Father stayed at the Ritz Carlton. He also went to Chicago and Boston. In New York he called on Otto H. Kahn, whose mother, daughter of Ferdinand Eberstadt, was a cousin. Kahn was then at the height of his career at Kuhn Loeb and Co. Kahn received Father in a friendly fashion and also had him to dinner at home. Albert Eberstadt was "very pleased" with what his son wrote about his Kahn visits. Mrs. Kahn's maiden name, according to Albert Eberstadt, was Seligman. She came from Frankfurt, and her parents had lived across the street from the Eberstadts. Mrs. Kahn had a brother who became a lawyer in New York. Her mother had gone to school with Albert Eberstadt in Worms. She had been very pretty, and most of Grandfather's class had a crush on her. Albert Eberstadt would not say whether he had been one of her admirers. Later in Frankfurt the Seligmans and Eberstadts were friendly neighbors.

In New York Father visited Bache and Co., more prestigious and important than in recent years. Jules Bache was close to Walter Chrysler and told Father the stock was cheap. He called on American Metals where he knew Ludwig Vogelstein. He attended a lunch of the German American Chamber of Commerce in honor of Dr. Hugo Eckener, captain of the *Graf*

Zeppelin which had just completed its maiden voyage across the Atlantic. Perhaps he went to Lehman Brothers to see Paul Mazur, then a young partner. In my Lehman days Mazur had become a senior partner, greatly respected and admired by me. Mazur was an early product of the Harvard Business School. He believed in New Era economics, the then "New Economy." In 1929 Mazur called on Behrens with that message. It so scared Father that he liquidated the balance of the firm's holdings on Wall Street. In fact, he came back from the United States frightened by the speculative fever that had gripped Wall Street. According to Behrens trader Paul Langdon-Levy, the firm had no significant Wall Street commitment at the time of the Wall Street crash.

In Chicago Father visited the stockyards and had the obligatory steak dinner. Chicago and other parts of the Midwest were an important market for German securities. The leading internationally oriented Chicago firm was A. G. Becker. They had a Berlin office, and sold German stocks and bonds to midwestern farmers of German origin. Becker went all but under in the Depression. Three of its employees founded Stein, Roe and Farnham and became highly regarded investment counselors. In the 1950s they were clients of mine. A. G. Becker made a comeback. In the 1970s they were acquired by S. G. Warburg.

On November 10, 1928, Father began his journey home via Cherbourg on RMS *Homeric*, a twin-screw, 34,000-ton White Star liner originally owned by Germany. Mother met him in Paris at the Hotel Westminster at 4 P.M. on November 17. Among his fellow passengers were Theodore Roosevelt, his wife, and their son Kermit.[5]

Other fellow passengers were Stanley Resor, a famous early figure in advertising, his son Stanley who served with me on the board of the American Council on Germany, and J. A. Falconer of Martin Currie in Edinburgh, father of Keith Falconer, senior partner of the firm in my day.

As a result of the Cologne Congress Father came into demand as a

5. Kermit Roosevelt was a brigadier general in the American infantry in World War II. He was among the first to land at Omaha beach on D-Day in 1944. He had a serious heart condition from which he died the following day.

speaker at business and political functions in Hamburg. He was active in Gustav Stresemann's Deutsche Volkspartei (German People's Party). He considered running for the Reichstag. By the time we lived in England he must have felt a bit sheepish about his more jingoistic moments. The Volkspartei was right of center, to the right of Brüning's Centrum party and the Deutsche Staatspartei (German State Party), which was Mother's. It was left, though, of Hugenberg's Deutsch-Nationale Partei (German National Party), which had the backing of the landowners and heavy industry. Its party badge was a World War I steel helmet. Many of its members were war veterans. The political crucible was the flag. The official colors of the Weimar Republic were black-red-gold. The pre-1918 Imperial colors were black-white-red. Mother's party flew the Weimar colors. From the Volkspartei rightward, the colors were black-white-red.

At a Volkspartei dinner on February 28, 1929, Father spoke on current banking and finance issues. The Owen Young Committee was meeting in Paris to amend the Dawes Plan. The Young Loan, an outcome of the conference, was floated to raise dollars for German reparation payments. Young, a prominent Boston lawyer, at various times held high government posts. Twice he served as chairman of General Electric. The Paris agenda was about the magnitude and transferability of the reparations. Father thought it inappropriate during the negotiations to come up with his own estimate of what Germany could afford to pay: "For the entire German nation and its economy, there is no issue more vital to resolve than the oppressive load of the reparations payments under which we all suffer. . . . Suffice it to say, that any payments imposed beyond a burden we can tolerate not only under present conditions but in the future, would be for us a tragedy, and for our creditors, to put it mildly, the height of folly." He quoted Andrew Mellon, the new U.S. Secretary of the Treasury, who in "an examplary fashion" defined the capacity for reparation and interallied debt payments: "The debtors should not be pushed to the limit of their present or estimated future resources. They must be able to maintain and even improve their economies and living standards, balance their budgets, keep sound finances and strong currencies. No agreement which is oppressive and delays the recovery or future growth of the foreign debtor is in the interest of the United States or Europe."

Bankers and economists discussed incessantly the impact on the value of the mark of converting reparations payments into the currencies of the victor nations. The Dawes Plan was meant to provide "transfer protection." According to Father "everybody was talking and writing about transfer protection without knowing what exactly it meant." The Young conference debated whether to maintain or do away with it. There were those who said it was essential for the protection of the mark to keep transfer protection. Others thought it was an artificial prop and as such counterproductive. Father assured his audience he was "aware that already in the days of the biblical prophets prophesies were a thankless task." On balance, he thought, rigid adherence to transfer protection might no longer be necessary. Removal or at least modification might well be interpreted as a sign of strength and confidence that Germany had recovered sufficiently to handle the payments without transfer protection. He suggested that doing away with the controls was worth the risks. It might, and as it turned out, did attract greater amounts of foreign capital into Germany which was promptly recycled to meet reparation payments. The inflow and outflow initially equalled each other, until the eventual repayment of the borrowed money.

Father, at another political dinner in 1929, called for policies to lower the cost of foreign borrowing. Confidence in the mark was tenuous, as confidence is in the currency of any debtor nation. Foreign demand for mark-denominated bonds was limited, and the cost well above sterling or dollar interest rates. Today's objectives are no different from the Reichsbank's: keep interest rates as low as compatible with a stable currency and stable purchasing power. Another topic then, still around today, was a withholding tax on interest payable to foreigners. "You cannot ram it home hard enough into the heads of government and parliament that a withholding tax is nothing other than an import duty on borrowing costs."

Of public expenditures he said: "The way in which Reich, state, and local governments throw money out of the window must lead to a catastrophe if no end is put to it. Any economist, irrespective of his politics, knows perfectly well the government wastes money on a huge scale, but few are willing to speak up. The private sector cannot tolerate the pyramid of spending and spending, of hiring and hiring, by the government. This is not a partisan evening. It is not playing party politics to draw attention to the huge dangers inherent in the willingness of members of all parties to go along with this spending spree, even worse, to initiate much of it. It is a paradox of history that parliamentary government which evolved to rein in the oppressive expenditures of absolute monarchs, has itself become an uncontrolled master. Members fall over each other to approve, worse still initiate, enormous expenditures. It would be well to recognize these conditions are viewed with growing ill humor by influential entrepreneurial circles whose mentality normally abhors summoning strong men to clean out a political mess. There is a growing belief that parliament as now constituted is incapable of dealing with pressing fiscal and administrative issues. Nothing is further removed from my mind. . . . Still, the business community, and least of all we bankers, cannot afford not to think about these undercurrents, let alone pretend they do not exist."

About his profession he said: "We bankers do not set out to win popularity contests but can take some comfort that at the moment there is less than the traditional griping about us. Some grumbling goes with the trade, as long as there are periodic interest-rate hikes. Our popularity has not risen as much as it deserves." He described the tensions in the international monetary system reflected in a weakening mark and rising pound sterling exchange rate. The German long-term capital market remained tight (even though a handful of recent municipal bond issues had gone relatively well). The German money market had become increasingly liquid in contrast to London and New York where short-term rates were rising. America was enjoying a late-stage business boom, however; the money market was drained of liquidity by the Wall Street speculation. Overnight money was dearer in the rich United States than in impoverished Germany. British money market rates were low and the high New

York rates were draining money from London. This triggered an outflow of gold from London which in turn forced the Bank of England, notwithstanding plentiful money and a poor economy, to raise its discount rate by a full percentage point. The issue was Wall Street speculators and how, if, and when the Federal Reserve was going to fight them.

Father hoped his audience appreciated the dilemma of a German banker. To have the right *Fingerspitzengefühl* (touch) was an art, not a science. "I don't believe those supposedly all-knowing, all-wise demigods, the central bankers, understand things more clearly than we poor wretches, the private bankers."

Father spoke of the relatively minor role of the German stock market in the international arena. What the Federal Reserve might or might not do about the New York stock market speculation influenced the German money market, but otherwise was of limited concern because the stock market did not matter greatly in Germany. Though two years earlier the Reichsbank had put the brakes on excessive speculation in Germany, no brakes were needed at present: "There is no doubt in my mind that, if anything, too little interest is taken in our market. . . . The stock market fullfills an important economic function. . . . Both the public and the banking community should give it more attention. The general public is by no means anti-stock market. Little love or understanding, though, exists for it in the upper ranks of bank management. Few of the prominent Berlin bankers — and they are the ones that set the tone — ever bothered to go on the floor of the exchange. By their mere presence even leading bankers cannot turn bad times into good prices, but by their lack of involvement they can make poor markets out of good times." It was overdue to examine the role of stock exchange business in the banks.

Lastly he turned to the economy: "I am not going to moan and groan in typical banker fashion. We cannot afford to be prophets of gloom and doom. We are professionally condemned to be cheerleaders. The optimist is not frivolous, anymore than the skeptic should be written off as a pessimist. The banker who plies his careworn trade with a dose of optimistic skepticism must see much that is troubling. It requires no special genius to be aware that large parts of the economy are not doing particularly well, but neither am I aware of storm warnings foreshadowing an impending crisis. The economy has been declining for nine months and the decline has not yet run its course. We have been spared major debacles, and I don't believe any are on the horizon. We have witnessed increased business failures, but by and large the failed businesses were barely viable to begin with. The economy merely hastened their inevitable eventual demise."

Father did not think particularly well of prevailing business ethics. Aside from the failures which had long been coming, there had been, of late, numerous, regrettably shady bankruptcies. Banks had extended credits against forged documents, or documents pledged twice. Father advocated independent audits by British-type chartered accountants, and the tightening and unifying of bankruptcy laws to prevent the bankrupted from walking away from their obligations.

He closed on a patriotic upbeat note, confident of Germany's future, thanks to its hardworking efficient people. To the business community he appealed to uphold the standards of the Ehrbare Kaufmann, the guild of honorable Hanseatic merchants.

On September 23, 1929, just weeks before Black Friday on Wall Street, he addressed the Hamburg retailers' chamber of commerce on currency and credit questions. Unless they were exceptionally sophisticated retailers he must have spoken above their heads. Perhaps he was really addressing a wider audience, including his friends at the Reichsbank. Personally I learnt a lot I did not know, for instance that the post-inflation Reichsmark was fully backed by gold and foreign exchange.

On the recommendation of the Dawes Plan Commission, by law on August 30, 1924, the new currency was tied to gold. The basic unit became one Reichsmark subdivided into one hundred pfennigs. According to paragraph 22 of the same law, the Reichsbank was obligated to purchase one pound of gold for each 1,392 Reichsmarks; or, as per paragraph 31 at its option, to exchange its paper money for either gold coins, gold bars, checks drawn on a foreign central bank or foreign currency. The purpose was to prevent the government from continued printing of paper money as it had done in previous years, contributing to run-off inflation.

In practice under paragraph 52 of the same law, it was permissable to back the Reichsmark with foreign currency or checks drawn on a foreign central bank. Gold convertibility was as good as suspended.

The Reichsmark's stability did not have a long history. In 1926 there were heavy outflows of gold. The 40 percent gold cover for currency in issue was barely maintained. The outflow was reversed by classic central bank "open market" operations. The discount rate was raised with a consequential tightening of credit. The Owen Young Committee had expressed doubts whether the Reichsmark was really a safe currency. Dr. Schacht responded with a letter to Owen Young in which he assured him categorically of the currency's soundness. He reinforced this assurance by implementing paragraph 31 of the August 30, 1924, law enforcing a minimum 40 percent gold cover for all currrency in circulation.

In the early days of the Reichsmark in 1924 the discount rate rose to 60 percent. This still did not attract foreign money — it did the opposite. Father applauded Dr. Schacht for, instead, rationing credit to be available only for essential but not for speculative purposes. The rationing caused a bear squeeze among speculators who in 1926 had gone short of the mark, and were forced to cover, which in turn triggered the desired rally in the currency. When conditions were relatively calm and rates broadly in line with other major financial centers, discount rate changes worked, causing desired inflows or outflows of foreign exchange and gold. Father criticized German municipalities for incurring short-term debts abroad, especially in the United States, competing among each other with higher rates to get the money and using it to finance not-for-profit infrastructure projects. He thought this was a sure recipe for financial trouble, the more so as on account of rising rates foreign lenders became increasingly reluctant to make any new commitments.

Father did not sound like the run-of-the-mill banker. Making money was important but not if it damaged a country still politically and financially fragile. The central bank might be able to defend the currency, but what if the cost was strangling the economy? The need to earn foreign exchange beyond normal needs, to meet reparations payments, burdened the picture. He thought with some domestic belt tightening by the private

and public sector the reparations could be handled. He called for spending restraints by the central and local governments. Because of deficit
spending, domestic interest rates had risen to 11 percent, which he considered "unacceptable for a civilized western European society."

According to one way-out German economist, the reparations money
could be raised if Germany reduced its alcohol consumption by one-third
and cigarette smoking by half. Gustav Streseman suggested something
along the same lines. The newly created Bank for International Settle-
ments (BIS) in Basel, of which the Young Committee was a founder, took,
in Father's opinion, a more realistic approach. It oversaw the reparations
payments and had the authority to defer transfers in the event of a
German foreign exchange crisis.

In conclusion the Hamburg retailers were told that if Germany
"wanted to live up to its obligations and strengthen its economy, once
again to be master in its own house, it could not continue to live beyond
its means."

A few weeks after this dinner the Wall Street crash occurred. On November 29, 1929, Father's anxious father thanked him "with all my heart
for your very nice letter." He was "greatly comforted by its contents and
relieved to hear that [not withstanding the Wall Street crash] you continue to be in a position to help your brother and sister financially without undue burden to yourself." He went on to write about his securities
portfolio: "To sell securities now would hurt greatly. I would only do it if
you need the proceeds. To have *Sitzfleisch* — to sit it out — seems the
right principle even though it was our ruin these past two years. In other
words, all theories can fail. When you worked out the value of my portfolio, did you include the securities which are really yours? . . . I won't write
more today. If I live long enough for conditions to recover and hear from
you of successful deals, I will again be sending you cheerful letters. Meanwhile have Edith write me; she is so good at it; her letters give me great
pleasure — Lots of love and kisses, Father."

7

End of the Good Times: Depression and Hitler

The year 1930 was troublesome. Behrens lost a large part of its capital, not in the stock market, but due to severe credit losses. Not surprisingly for a Hamburg banking business, the credits were highly sensitive to commodity prices and foreign trade. Both were severely impacted by the onset of the Depression. A leading company in the wool trade, Nordwolle, which owed Behrens money, went bankrupt. Coffee prices collapsed. The family of my schoolfriend Jan Schlubach, long-established Hamburg coffee importers and Behrens clients, went broke. They had to sell their house on one of the Alster canals and move into a small apartment over their nearby garage. These were not isolated episodes. Father's participation in the losses more than wiped out his capital in the firm.

Despite business worries, family life continued. Eberstadts, Edingers, and other relations came together each spring around Easter in Jugenheim, a small resort in the Bergstrasse ridge of pretty hills south of Frankfurt. The gathering of the family was usually so large that most of the bedrooms in the only two inns, the Hotel Krone and the Pension Waldfrieden, were filled. The latter inn was more modern and had slightly better plumbing. It was the time of Albert Eberstadt's birthday and Mother and Brigitte had already joined the family in Jugenheim.[1] Nowadays there is an exit off the Autobahn marked Jugenheim. Another nearby exit is Eberstadt. It is not the Eberstadt our family came from before they went to Worms; that is another and still smaller Eberstadt in the same region but farther south.

In a letter of April 12, 1930, my father, who was still in Hamburg with me (I was nine), congratulated his father on his eighty-third birthday. He was writing late, but hoped a special delivery letter (*Eilboten*) might still make it. Father wondered in which hotel the birthday would be celebrated. "And with *Zimtkuchen* [cinnamon cake]?" Father would be in Jugenheim in a few days and would drive with Mother and the Flersheims to Zurich for a holiday. Even in Hamburg it was spring and that afternoon he had been with me on the Elbe. "We were able to have tea outside at Jacob." This was the name of a favorite *Konditorei* and restaurant overlooking the river. "Tell Edith we walked for two hours; that will put me in her good graces. On top of it I walked nearly the whole way to the office this morning. Walter was very sweet. I believe he greatly enjoys these rare occasions when he and I go off alone. Tomorrow he and I will again be off to do something. I lived virtually out of a briefcase in Berlin for two days to do with the sudden crisis at Gothaer Grundkredit." Here Father was referring to a mortgage bank on whose board he served. Fortunately, he wrote, it did not affect him personally as the losses had been incurred before he joined the board and was therefore not liable. "Everywhere they cook only with water, especially if some big shot is chairman and pays himself a small fortune. How is our adorable little one [Brigitte]? If she is only half a sweet as she was the day she left that is still plenty."

By 1930 there was not a problem-free bank in Germany. It was only

---

1. Near Jugenheim is Battenberg, the seat of the family that in England during the First World War anglicized its name to Mountbatten. The Battenbergs had little money, but had "looks" and brains. Through strategic marriages they were connected to many ruling families in Europe, including Czarist Russia. The best-connected present day Battenberg is Prince Philip, Duke of Edinburgh, husband of Queen Elizabeth of England.

a matter of degree. Deutsche Bank and Dresdner Bank were wounded, Dresdner worse than Deutsche, Darmstädter, and Nationalbank (Danat Bank) mortally so. Behrens suffered further significant losses after the Wall Street crash and the Flersheims advanced Mother the money to even out my father's capital account at Behrens. With little to fall back on, Father needed an income. It was an anxious year.

Under the circumstances Father was fortunate to find a position as joint head of Dresdner Bank in Hamburg. The conversations with Dresdner were off again, on again, with ominous interludes of silence. On August 13, 1930, sounding worried, he described the conversations to his father. Dr. Pilder of Dresdner Bank, Hamburg, was being promoted to a post in Berlin. On his initiative, without consulting the Berlin head office, he suggested Father become his successor. In the course of their conversations he inquired about Father's personal financial situation. Apparently he was taken aback to hear Father was in debit to Behrens. He had heard that Behrens had suffered stock market losses attributed to Father. Evidently Father's explanation about the true source of the Behrens losses satisfied him. Father wrote his father to say that since he had been given credit for his successes, it was inevitable he should now be blamed, no matter how unfair. He was annoyed at himself for having been so candid with Pilder. He wanted the job badly and wrote, longingly, how well it paid, with good additional potential from a participation in the earnings of the Hamburg branch — a base salary of RM 55,000, which might well be doubled by the override. Father next was to meet Geheimrat Frisch, the Berlin board member responsible for Hamburg, and confide to him about his personal finances. Any decision also had to await the return from vacation of Anton Hübbe, who would be Father's colleague managing the Hamburg business.

After worrisome delays Dresdner took him. In a handful of years my parents had become accepted in Hamburg, doubtless a consideration in the minds of those who offered him the post. On December 31, 1930, Behrens announced Georg Eberstadt's resignation and, on January 2, 1931, Dresdner Bank his appointment as director of the Hamburg branch. Previously, on November 12, 1930, Father had signed a contract, initially for two years. His base salary was RM 21,600 plus RM 32,400 for general expenses. For 1931 he was to receive 1 percent of the Hamburg profits, rising to 3 percent in 1933. In addition he received RM 5,400 annually "to live while at work and at home in the style befitting his position." In 1934, however, there was a general salary reduction. Under a law dated June 30, 1933, businesses that received government subsidies on account of their financial situation had to reduce executive pay.

Still, Father greatly enjoyed his new job. On January 10, 1931, he described some of the work to his father, saying that he had made the rounds of the branches, liked his colleagues and found them competent. He was glad business was quiet, which gave him a better chance to become familiar with the organization.

He continued to speak at various functions. On December 17, 1931, he lectured at the Gesellschaft für soziale Reform (Society for Social Reform) on "Monetary Problems and the German Economic Crisis." It was his most scholarly and, for me, most interesting paper. The year had seen the low point in the German depression, which had become a classic deflationary slump. Everyone was wondering how they got into it and how to get out of it. Theories abounded. "We have to be candid with ourselves. German bankers rarely have much command of even the most elementary economic theory. Intuition and instinct, they claim, are all that matters. But look where that got us lately." He quoted from the famous MacMillan Report — the British government-appointed Committee on Finance and Industry: "It is as foolish to disregard the analyses and generalizations of the scientific observer, as it would be to believe that the world of finance could be successfully conducted by university professors."

He went on to describe how booms and slumps come about. In equilibrium everything not consumed is saved. The savings are invested — in plant, equipment, home construction, stocks and bonds. Personal savings and business liquidity on deposit in the banks are reinvested through loans to borrowers or the purchase of securities. In a business expansion the banks "create" additional investment capital and consumer purchasing power by lending more than they have on deposit (which in turn creates more bank deposits, more consumption, and more investment).

Credit creation in excess of savings leads to an expanding economy that crests in an inflationary boom, and eventually ends in a bust. Bad loans are made, losses incurred, good loans called in to defend the banks. "If more is invested than saved there is a boom, if less it leads to a depression." There had been a boom in silver fox furs. The price of foxes rose. More foxes were bred. In the end there were too many foxes. Prices collapsed.

The American economic situation was analogous. Excessive investment financed with borrowed money led to "one of the worst economic depressions known in history." The Federal Reserve and private banks had committed huge errors. It reminded Father of the German economic and stock market boom and collapse in 1927, fueled by plentiful and cheap credit supplied by the banks which in turn had refinanced themselves abroad. Industry and speculators had overborrowed and invested beyond the level of actual savings. As the intermediary between lender and borrower the banks were vulnerable in such times. "The line is fine between a frozen and a lost credit. Withdrawal of deposits decreases liquidity. The banks are forced to call in loans. Confidence in the banks erodes. Next it spreads to the rest of the economy."

Germany's problems in his opinion were greatly aggravated by the reparations. Germany had overexpanded its manufacturing capacity to produce enough for reparations. Since domestic savings were insufficient, the banks borrowed from countries which themselves were in a credit-fueled boom. The Kreditanstalt collapse in Vienna shook confidence everywhere. Germany's ability to meet its obligations began to be questioned. "Of course everyone knew Germany, and in particular the banks, could never repay over a mere twelve months the five billion marks that had been borrowed abroad, but then nine out of ten people would have said, no one is going to ask us to do so." Father thought that France had set off the repayment crisis. The French withdrew some of the huge sums they had on deposit in London. They were afraid of the City of London's German commitments. The French withdrawals forced Britain to go off the gold standard. Going off gold cost the Banque de France 2.5 billion francs, caused the Netherlands Bank huge losses, and led to devaluations

by other, smaller countries. Gold was replaced by the gold exchange standard, which Father considered inherently more risky than the classic gold
standard. Meanwhile British officialdom and papers such as the *Times*
were doing their best to play down the German commercial risk for the
simple reason it was vital for the survival of the City of London to avoid a
German breakdown. Britain allied itself with Germany, calling for reduced reparations (which ranked ahead of German commercial debts).

Father thought the policymakers had not reckoned with a deflation.
The purchasing power of money had declined steadily all over the world
since the last century, the German inflation quite aside. Now suddenly
there was a worldwide deflation. The purchasing power of money surged.
Commodity prices had fallen on a scale inconceivable two years previous.
The Dawes Plan payment schedule projected steady improvement in the
German economy, not a depression.

It is fascinating today to read the theories on how to reverse the German deflation-depression. Some advocated inflation, others a currency
devaluation to make exports more competitive, still others a new dual
currency, one internal, the other external. Father did not think any of
these ideas could work. Great Britain's devaluation, for instance, had
stimulated neither exports nor the domestic economy. A German devaluation would aggravate the situation by causing a capital flight. Devaluation of the mark would cause limitless distrust; nobody could say what it
might lead to. It would severely increase the cost of foreign currency liabilities. It would further weaken bank balance sheets. He was against
import restrictions. Without imports you cannot export. An autarchic
economy would be a disaster with two-thirds of the German national
product industrialized. He thought there was plenty of purchasing power
and the economy would revive on its own once people started to spend
rather than hoard their money.

The government issued a series of emergency decrees to balance the
budget. Salaries and wages were cut. Sales tax was raised. The most con-
tentious decree was a top limit of 6 percent on interest rates. An 8 percent
coupon, for instance, was reduced to 6 percent, but if a 6 percent bond
stood at a discount from par the rate was not changed. Father deplored the

interference with the free functioning of capital markets. Prices and interest rates should be set by demand and supply, not official fiat. Bankers and economists alike were up in arms and foreshadowed the end of capitalism, but politically the measure was not unpopular.

"There have been times in history when interest was immoral. I only have to remind you of the Old Testament and canon law. There are present day prophets around who would break the power of the money lenders." Father distanced himself from the extremists who saw the end of capitalism: "Human memory is short. If a volcano destroys a town today, tomorrow the population begins to rebuild it. Is it socially just to cut wages and salaries but not to touch the bondholder?" However irrational on economic grounds, politically it was perhaps understandable. Whether the emergency measures were a step in the right direction depended in the final analysis not on Germany alone but on whether Germany's creditors would see the light of day and modify their claims. "The heroic efforts the German people are making will be condemned to failure if our creditors do not come to their senses. If they do, a people as hardworking as the Germans, bearing its burdens with heroic patience, will once again work its way back to better and happier days."

There were only two years between the time Father joined Dresdner Bank, had a good reliable income, made friends with the bank board in Berlin, and Hitler's takeover on January 30, 1933. Even though he kept his job until 1936, life was a holding action after 1933.

One week before Hitler came to power, Father was still campaigning for the Deutsche Volkspartei. At a meeting of the party's wholesale trade association he spoke on monetary and credit policy. He did not think government prime pumping had done much good. What had helped the German economy in 1932 was the "quite extraordinary" recovery of the stock and bond markets, admittedly from very depressed levels. He thought the market recovery was soundly based, in part because there had not been any new issues for several years. The public and institutions had become quite liquid and had begun to reinvest some of this liquidity. Capital which had taken flight outside Germany was being repatriated. Interest rates outside Germany, especially in the United States, had declined. He thought the improved capital markets were far more helpful to the creation of jobs than any artificial spending programs by the government.

As *Pfandbrief* prices — the German equivalent of mortgage bonds — recovered closer to par, he saw the beginnings of a housing boom, a better way of job creation than ill-conceived government spending. Scrap metal prices, one of the few indicators he followed, had recovered by 50 percent. Huge government expenditures in the United States — this was Republican Hoover's spending before Roosevelt's New Deal — had done little to decrease unemployment. German government deficits were no worse than elsewhere; in fact, rather better than a $3 billion budget deficit in the United States or 26 billion francs in France. Father thought that instead of reducing bond rates by fiat, German capital markets were ready for refunding at lower interest rates based on improved market conditions. The municipalities seemed to be over the worst of their financial crisis. Although still in arrears on interest, they were able to borrow new money for job-creating projects. The balance of payments had improved. Some foreign-held debt had been repurchased. He felt that the full resumption of external debt service eventually could be handled. For the time being funds belonging to external creditors should be set aside internally in Reichsmarks. The foundation for resuming external payments was being laid by a strong export surplus.

On the eve of Hitler, Father thought the German economy had begun to recover, a recovery for which Hitler later took credit. "For the business world political details are secondary; we need political peace and quiet. Once we know where we stand we can deal with almost anything. . . . Leave business to its own devices and you won't need fancy ideas and projects."

With the advent of Hitler in 1933 Jewish careers came to a standstill. In the banks and in industry, Jews were left in most cases in their posts until 1937–1938, but advancement became a rare event, especially at a senior level. The possibility of Father advancing to the Berlin Vorstand became out of the question.

In the early years of the Nazis, Jews who had seen frontline service in

World War I were left alone. This helped Father keep his position. His baptism did not "protect" him then, and would not have saved him from the Holocaust. In his business life, with colleagues in the bank or clients, he was never made to feel the official anti-Semitism. Hamburg was not an ardent Nazi town. The working class had been politically quite radical on the left. The middle class were conservative but no great Nazi sympathizers. The haute bourgeoisie, which consisted largely of the international merchants and shipowners, were liberals in their way of life, Anglophile, and anti-Prussian. Hitler avoided visits to Hamburg. On one occasion, in 1934, he came to the city and had a cool reception. My entire school, including the Jews, was turned out to line the streets. My teachers thought I would feel discriminated against if I were forced to stay behind. In a weird way it was a well-intentioned gesture. My parents should have made me stay away, but they deemed it impolitic, and by then Father wanted to avoid provocations that might affect his livelihood.

One or two non-Jewish social friends avoided our family after 1933, but on the whole our daily life did not change greatly. In April 1933, the Nazi regime had appealed to the public to boycott Jewish businesses and products. Later in April, Jews and "other undesirable elements" were dismissed from lifetime civil service status.

We happened to hear that Heckemüller, our former chauffeur, had become an even more ardent Nazi. None of our three maids displayed interest in politics or any desire to leave our employment. Martha Knüttel, who had raised my sister and me, stayed and came to England with us in 1936. My mother remained friends until her own death with the grandchildren of Hilde Brunschön, the housemaid. We continued summer vacations, mainly in Switzerland. Foreign exchange for travel, in particular for vacations, was rationed, but sufficient for the four of us to summer abroad for a month. Longingly Father looked at trains with Swiss destinations and mumbled enviously that they were full of "criminals" getting out of Germany and wished he could find a way to be one of them.

Father did not know how to use a razor. We could not take a summer holiday unless there was a barber in the village. In those days Baedecker listed barber and newspaper shops. Till the day he left Germany, his barber Strohdieck came to shave him every morning. Strohdieck was no Nazi but no hero, either. He preferred that his calls to a Jewish house be handled discreetly, but business was not what it used to be. Not many needed a daily barber. As a sideline Strohdieck had taken up chiropody, but that was fraught with problems. A high Nazi official died while having his corns removed. In a panic Strohdieck put the corpse on the pavement, hoping to disassociate himself from the incident. But he got into trouble with the police. (Which reminds me of a famous pre–World War I episode in Hamburg's St. Pauli red-light district. The then King of Denmark was amusing himself, incognito, but in the act died of a heart attack. The madam had no inkling of his identity. She simply did not want a corpse on her premises and put it outside on the pavement. Hue and cry the next morning: Where is the King? Meanwhile the unidentified corpse had been removed to the police morgue and it took days until two and two were put together.) Father finally learned to shave himself. He was taught by Henry Sonnenberg when the two wintered together at the Carlton Hotel in St. Moritz early in 1936.

How and when to emigrate increasingly occupied my parents. England was the only country they considered seriously, but the City was in a deep slump.

It was not advisable to travel abroad too often after 1933, but when in London, Father sought out his old connections in the hope he might be offered an opening. He knew best Lazards, Guinness Mahon, Erlangers, and Barings. None needed or wanted what he might have brought to them. On the contrary, they were struggling to survive their Continental involvements. (They would stay away from international business for over thirty years and miss out on the post-World War II recovery.) Around this time Bob Brand (later Lord Brand) of Lazard Bros., who themselves had been hobbled by the collapse of the Kreditanstalt of Vienna and other crises of the early 1930s, suggested Father as chair of an international creditor committee. Father was very interested in the proposal. It would have given him an exit from Germany and an entrée into the international arena. By this time, however, a German-Jewish banker was persona non grata in Schuschnigg's Austria, even if acting for the City of London.

Still, Father continued a rearguard action. In 1934 he resigned from the board of Maizena, the German subsidiary of Corn Products. He steered the directorship to his Dresdner Bank colleague Anton Hübbe. In a friendly letter between the two, Hübbe confirmed he would pass half the board fee to Father.

Father, much more than Mother, was the driving force to leave. In 1935 after the Nuremberg Nazi Party rally he made up his mind to go. Hitler's racial laws made him realize, danger aside, that self-respect demanded the break. It was only a question of time when he'd lose his job. As a result of the new laws (the Nuremberg Laws), female non-Jewish domestic staff below a certain age had to be discharged. Father was not willing to accept the status of second-class citizen for himself or his family. He was afraid anti-Semitism in school would make Brigitte and me feel inferior.

While preparations for leaving went on, the Hamburg chief of police, on April 11, 1935, in the name of the Führer and Reich Chancellor, awarded Dr. jur. Georg Eberstadt the Ehrenkreuz (Honor Cross) for front-line soldiers commemorating their service in the 1914–1918 war. The medal was created on the authority of Reichspresident Fieldmarschall von Hindenburg July 13, 1934.

Between 1933 and 1935 there were still glimmers of hope that the Nazi government was not there to stay, at least not in its extreme form. On Hitler's orders there was the arrest and instant execution of Röhm, the disreputable and dissolute head of Hitler's storm troopers, the brown-shirted S.A., which was considered more "common" than the "elite" black-shirted S.S. There were widely if clandestinely circulated anti-Nazi sermons by Catholics such as Cardinal Faulhaber of Munich or the Protestant Bishop Galen of Cologne. The *Frankfurter Zeitung* still published the occasional discreetly critical article and few newspapers were supportive of the regime. Furtwängler and Richard Strauss were rumored to be feuding with Göbbels and his propaganda ministry. They were said to threaten resignation if Jewish musicians were dismissed. Hans Albers, the popular film star, refused any part in a political propaganda movie and ostentatiously continued his friendship with erstwhile Jewish colleagues.

The black-red-gold colors of the Weimar Republic were of course prohibited, but if a building flew only the colors black-white-red, resurrected from the Kaiser's era, or the Hamburg flag, rather than the swastika, it signaled an element of nonconformity.

Giving in to the racial doctrines, however, came in many forms. The owner of the neighborhood shoe store used to dress up for us as Santa Claus on Saint Nicolas Day. The second year after Hitler, he said he could no longer come to a Jewish home. In the spring of 1935 Mother bought four dahlia bulbs from the Kurt Heimart Holscher store in Travemünde, the pretty seaside resort on the Baltic coast. The invoice amounted to RM 2.10, including one free bulb. This was hardly a political event but on the bill he typed a dedication, presumably his own work, to Erich Ludendorff, Hindenburg's chief of staff in the First World War and later a Hitler supporter:

> German, upright and fearless — confused by nothing —
> You unraveled the knots of Fate
> And show that from a dependent spirit
> The German can free himself if he so wills.
>
> Petty spirits of the indolent minds of the masses
> You will never grasp the splendor he gave us
> Rather you will trot along on the leash
> Of some supranational fate.
>
> With the others, though, their genes are aroused
> When they hear what House Ludendorff holds out for them
> Fear, astonishment, habit, and tyranny
> Lose their hold as the spirit soars free.

The invoice was not dated April 24, but "Ostermonds 24," the Nordic month of April.

In 1935 Father implemented plans for leaving Germany. Many Jewish families with money had always had some assets outside Germany or started to make secret illegal transfers abroad. Somehow in 1934 or 1935, Father had obtained three 1,000 pound notes, which he decided to get out of the country. He had a small, flat leather case for nail scissors and similar accessories given him by his mother shortly before she died and to which he was sentimentally attached. He had Mother open the seams and place the notes inside the lining. With it they drove by car to Switzerland. Between Frankfurt and the Swiss frontier he boarded a train for Basel with the little leather case in his baggage. Mother drove on alone to Basel. Both made it safely across the border. The money was deposited at Dreyfus for remittance to his London stockbroker cousin and friend Alfred Marx. Three years of living expenses were safely abroad. He used the scissors case for another thirty years.

Father was going to start a small banking business in London for Willy Dreyfus and the German Dreyfus bank. In the mid-1930s it was still possible to transfer some money abroad officially at a favorable exchange rate for business purposes. The new firm would "promote German economic interests." The capital came from Willy's wife, Martha Koch, rather than the bank, which was in low waters whereas the Kochs were relatively well-off.

Gradually, Father had also prepared for our emigration. We were given English lessons at home by a Miss Stange, who was half English, half German. The lessons were supplemented by an English au pair girl, Joan Parry. She was quite beautiful, the picture of an English rose with a peach complexion and long blond hair. She lived with us almost two years and remained a good friend once we lived in England. In Hamburg she caught the fancy of the young Eric Warburg. He frequently took her out, safe from the racial laws because she was English. After the war Eric Warburg never failed to inquire nostalgically after Joan Parry. She was a personal and a linguistic asset. At mealtimes only English was spoken. Father read mainly English books.

Meanwhile life on the surface in Hamburg continued almost as if normal. However, profound changes were taking place almost daily. The Flersheim family as well started to suffer under the impact of Hitler's policies and the increased anti-Jewish attitude in Germany. Ernst and Gertrud

Flersheim emigrated to Holland in 1936. Their daughter Margarete and son-in-law Rudolf Wertheim established a home in Brussels, after leaving Germany in 1937.

In his memoirs, dictated to Rudolf Wertheim on several of his visits in Brussels during 1939, Ernst Flersheim describes these years of the depression and the years when Hitler came to power.

In 1931 Germany introduced foreign exchange controls which robbed us of our business freedom and flexibility. Our entrepôt business on the one side, and imports into Germany on the other, had to be handled and booked quite separately. For the entrepôt trade — that is, business between two foreign parties without touching Germany — the authorities allocated us a certain amount of foreign exchange. We were able to trade as before, if on a reduced scale. For actual imports we required on a case-by-case basis a series of licenses that were tightly supervised by the government in Berlin. The foreign currency control looked at our books constantly.

Well into the Nazi period, in 1934, Herbert [Flersheim, Ernst Flersheim's nephew] was appointed by the Party as head of our business [Betriebsführer]. Our staff, which was almost totally non-Jewish, continued to stick to us loyally, though with a single exception. In the 1920s we had hired a young man for the mother-of-pearl department. He was able and hardworking and became head of the department. After Hitler came to power this man became the official Party representative (Betriebszellen Obmann) in our firm. In 1935 he took it upon himself to denounce us to the Party claiming we charged excessive import prices. There was no truth to this charge as Herbert and Rompel were able to demonstrate when they were hauled before a party tribunal. In fact, nothing seemed to happen to us and no more was heard of the matter.

Even so, this episode made Herbert decide in the autumn of 1935 to leave Germany. At the end of 1935 we applied for permission to take the entrepôt business with us, as my wife and I had also decided to leave the country. After prolonged negotiations we were granted permission in October 1936 to relocate the ivory business outside Germany on condition the rest of the business was formed into a limited liability company headed by Rompel. As soon as this was completed I terminated my sixty-year association with the firm and left Germany for good. In 1938 a law was passed to "Aryanize" all Jewish businesses. We were forced to sell the firm. It was bought by Rompel and two former employees for one-third of its net worth.

Hitler came to power in January 1933. I need not enlarge on what this meant for any Jew then living in Germany. In October of the same year we suffered the unspeakable tragedy of losing our son Hans from the consequences of food poisoning. He had been on a business trip in London and arrived already sick in Paris. We had been traveling in Italy and the news of his illness reached us only days later in Lugano. By the time we arrived in Paris he had died the previous night. Edith had managed to get there a few hours before he died and was able to be with him during his last moments. It will be understood that I do not wish to dwell on this tragedy. We had the closest of relationships. We worked together daily. He was going to be my successor. My hopes and expectations for the future centered on him. Until he died he lived at home and with his warm ways knew how to make our lives happier. He had survived the war and prison camps but died with us not even by his side. He had a close relationship with his mother and understood her well. She has not been able to overcome her grief and lives in memories of him.

He was a first-class horseman who won many prizes. He enjoyed the companionship of his fellow riders, civilians as well as army officers. He was on the board of the Riding Club of Hesse, and also on the board of the Old Boys association of the Goethe Gymnasium, his former school. Some months after his death he was memorialized at the mother-of-pearl auction in London. According to our English agent it was the only occasion to his knowledge when a non-Englishman was so honored.

My first reaction after his death was to liquidate our firm, but I was persuaded otherwise at a family meeting. In 1935 I lost my brother who had been unwell for some years. My sister Alice died in 1937, soon after she had emigrated from Germany to live in Lugano. This left no one with whom I could reminisce about childhood or parents.

The Eberstadts moved to England in 1936. Walter attends boarding school at Tonbridge and expects to go to Oxford. Brigitte attends a day school in London. The Wertheim family stayed in Frankfurt until 1938. My son-in-law Rudolf was able to continue practicing law, as he had been a frontline soldier in the war. Their son is in a children's home near Paris but will join his parents in Brussels as soon as they have found an apartment. In the spring of 1938 Rudolf became aware in the course of handling the sale of our Frankfurt home that the house, our money, and other assets had been confiscated by the Gestapo, and that we were in the process of having our German nationality taken away. The reason given was "disloyal acts" by my wife toward the Third Reich. There were charges made under oath of supposed "subversive" statements by her. Attempts to get to the bottom of the affair were rejected on the ground the proceedings were secret. We first became aware formally of our "*Ausbürgerung*" by reading our names in the official German legal gazette. We have no idea what really occurred or who had denounced her.

Since leaving Germany we have been to London several times to visit the Eberstadt family and at present are in Brussels with the Wertheims. As we sat together after dinner one evening they urged me to write my recollections. My life, they said, spanned the rise and fall of an era, and my childhood goes back to an age hard to imagine by the younger generation. Thus I came to dictate these notes to my son-in-law Rudolf in the course of several weeks.

Later chapters will describe the fate of my Flersheim relatives. For now, back to my father's world of banking. His good friend, Cornelius Freiherr von Berenberg-Gossler, a member of an old German aristocratic family, described something about the lives in those years of upper-crust Hamburg Jews, many baptized like Father, mainly bankers and lawyers, in a memoir published in *Hamburgische Geschichts- und Heimatblätter* (vol. 12, no.1, April 1988). He was a senior partner of Joh. Berenberg Gossler and Co., a private bank with roots from the middle of the sixteenth century and politically quite conservative. After the First World War he belonged to the Deutsche Volkspartei which lost its influence with the death of Gustav Stresemann in 1929. Gossler joined the Deutsch-Nationale Party. In March of 1933 he became a Nazi Party member for one reason alone — in the hope that if decent people joined the party they might be able to exercise a moderating influence. Jewish friends such as Max Warburg and Father's Dresdner Bank colleague Paul Salomon agreed with him. By August 1934 he concluded this was a vain hope and submitted his resignation to the Party boss in Niendorf outside Hamburg where the Gosslers lived. He gave five reasons for quitting: 1) anti-Semitism, which had always disgusted him, even in the Kaiser's days; 2) replacing existing bishops in the established church with Nazis; 3) suppression of all political opposition or independant opinions; 4) seeing nothing in National Socialism which held out a better future for Germany; 5) Hitler's policies would lead to war. Germans had a belligerent temperament to begin with which was being fanned by Hitler's demagoguery. Germany was inviting the hatred of the entire world.

Without compromise he opposed Hitler's regime. He was appalled by the Nazis' anti-Semitic and anticlerical measures. In a plebiscite he voted against combining chancellor and president into one post. He put a blank into the ballot box to vote against the reoccupation of the Rhineland in 1936 and the annexation of Austria in 1938.

In his diary Gossler described the gradual dispersal of his Jewish friends. The first was Father. At Dresdner Bank Father had supported the Gossler bank which "due to the world economic crisis in 1932 had encountered difficulties." Gossler's longtime neighbor and business friend

Kurt Bambus went to South Africa. (Bambus's brother Erich did not leave and died at Auschwitz.) When the Nuremberg racial laws were promulgated in 1935, Gossler called on Max Warburg at his bank to express his horror. When Warburg was forced to resign from his own bank, Gossler wrote expressing his deepest sympathy. Max Warburg's exile to the United States "greatly shook" Gossler. In April 1938, Richard Kauffmann, a friend of Gossler's and partner in Wm. F. Ree Jr., a well-regarded Hamburg banking firm, sought Gossler's help on how to save his firm. Since Schacht's resignation in the fall of 1937 as *Reichswirtschaftsminister* (Minister of Economics), restrictions on Jews in business had tightened further. A business was deemed Jewish if it had one Jewish partner. A bank was considered Jewish if a single board member was Jewish. Ownership of the Ree bank was vested in a previous senior manager, but Cornelius Gossler was given full voting power to protect Kauffmann's interest. Kauffmann sought refuge in England. Gossler accompanied him to London on a Danish airplane, helped him remove some of his assets outside Germany, and introduced him to his English business friends.

Day-to-day life became increasingly onerous. Gossler used to lunch most days with Percy Hamberg and George Behrens at the Harmonie, Hamburg's elite luncheon club. He resigned in 1935 because his Jewish friends were no longer welcome. Instead they met at the Cafe Vaterland. They were generally joined by two lawyers, partly Jewish, Kurt Dehn and Edgar Wiegers. Both were good friends of Father's. The Vaterland luncheons ended in 1938 when the restaurant posted a sign on the door that "non-Aryan" customers were undesirable. In 1934 a Führer edict prohibited all social contact between Jews and party members. Gossler noted, "Thank goodness I no longer belong to the Party."

The worst was yet to come, Kristallnacht, on November 9, 1938. Gossler wrote in his diary about the "appalling destruction in the streets." He registered the "disgust of the Hamburg haute bourgeoisie" with the way the "Nazi government mistreated innocent Jews," a disgust shared, according to Gossler by many in the working class — for instance, at the Jewish-owned Beiersdorf pharmaceutical company, which employed 4,000 workers. Among Gossler's friends, George Behrens and Kurt Rosenmeyer, also a banker, were arrested and sent to Oranienburg, a concentration camp near Berlin. They had to wear prisoner clothing and their heads were shaved. Under the supervison of "criminals and frequently bestial S.S. men" they dug canals. Inside the camp they were supervised by "Communists, most of them educated people who were very nice to them." They slept on straw mats, "too narrow to turn, 150 per hut." After his release Rosenmeyer described these conditions to Gossler. He said of 14,000 inmates at Oranienburg, 6,000 were Jews. George Behrens, kept till Christmas, told Gossler how he had been beaten up and Gossler relates how he had such frostbite that they were barely able to shake hands."

Only the back door to the bank was open when Gossler went to welcome him on his release. The front entrance was officially sealed. The Behrens firm, founded in 1780, in the same family for five generations, was for practical purposes closed. It made no difference that George Behrens' great-grandfather had been baptized, or that the family for generations had supported good causes, in particular the arts, in Hamburg. "His world has come to the end, he is very run-down and will be emigrating shortly." Percy Hamberg suffered a nervous breakdown. On Kristallnacht he was convalescing in a sanatorium. "Solely because he was Jewish and over the protests of his doctors, on November 16 he was taken to the penitentiary at Strelitz." On December 25 he died in an insane asylum. Five days later he was buried in Hamburg. "It was an incredibly sad funeral, formal words by a rabbi. Few people attended, among the few Hermann Willink" — Father's friend who after the war helped reestablish the Behrens firm.

Other Hamburg Jews who emigrated, many with Gossler's help, included Heinrich Embden, a prominent neurologist, Reinhard Friedländer of the Anglo-South American Bank, Kurt Rosenmeyer (whose mother later died in Theresienstadt). A Professor Poll went with Gossler's help to Sweden but died there of a heart attack shortly after his arrival; his widow took her life a few days later. The Gestapo caught up with George Behrens in Belgium where he had sought refuge. He was sent to a camp in the

South of France from which he fled to Cuba. He was the only one of
Gossler's friends to return after the war, which his half-Jewish mother had
survived in Hamburg.

Fritz Warburg, a partner in M. M. Warburg, had emigrated to Sweden
but came back to Hamburg in November 1938 to attend a board meeting
of the Jewish hospital. He was arrested after Kristallnacht and had his
passport confiscated. According to the Warburg bank's history it was only
thanks to the intervention of the Christian partner in one of Hamburg's
oldest banks that finally in May 1939 Fritz Warburg was permitted to
return to Sweden. Gossler was of course the Christian banker. He saw
Gruppenführer Wolff, Himmler's adjutant, at the Prinz Albrechtstrasse
Gestapo headquarters in Berlin. Ahead of the meetings Gossler had conversations with Kurt Sieveking, a postwar Hamburg mayor, with Max
Warburg, by then in London, and with Christian Niemeyer of M. M.
Warburg. They believed Fritz Warburg was being detained as a prominent
Jewish hostage in the event of some new international crisis. Wolff and
his boss Heydrich were amenable to Warburg's release but demanded a
price. On April 27, 1939, Gossler noted in his diary that on Warburg's
behalf he offered to finance the emigration of one hundred Jewish children and some impecunious adults from Germany. As the upshot of this
initiative the Hamburg Gestapo instructed the head of the Jewish school
to encourage the emigration of its students. The school worked in England
with the Movement for the Care of Children, headed by Lola Hahn-
Warburg, Max Warburg's oldest daughter. The connection with the
Swedish Jewish community was established by Fritz Warburg's Swedish
wife. War broke out before all the children could be brought to safety.

During the war Gossler had numerous meetings with Klaus Göttsche,
head of the Gestapo department in Hamburg responsible for Jewish
affairs, trying to intervene on behalf of his remaining Jewish friends, sometimes with success, mostly without. Göttsche seems to have played an
ameliorating role and, in particular, took no active measures against
Gossler, who never minced words with him. Once in the war a Gestapo
official, presumably Göttsche, objected to something Gossler wanted to
achieve. Gossler responded, "All right, arrest me, but then see what the

consequences will be." The matter was resolved satisfactorily. No one will ever know whether Göttsche disagreed with his superiors or simply wanted to protect his postwar survival.

The war came as no surprise to Gossler. When Germany broke the Locarno treaty in 1936 and occupied the demilitarized Rhineland, when Austria, the Sudetenland, Czechoslovakia, and the Memelland were annexed, the additions to German territory gave him no pleasure. It only made him fearful of a war which he thought Germany was bound to lose. After Kristallnacht he wrote in his diary: "What do all these conquests and successes of Hitler amount to compared with bestial atrocities which horrify civilized people all over the world? Better a small, decently governed state than the powerful nation Germany has become, governed without law or dignity by robbers and murderers. Appeasement will come to an end. It will lead to war and disaster." In that war Cornelius von Berenberg-Gossler's oldest son, an army surgeon, was killed on the Russian front. His youngest son — my friend Heinrich — was seriously wounded as an infantry officer. Soon after the outbreak of the war he noted in his diary: "If National Socialism conquers the world it means the end of civilized life, and yet I tremble for my Germany, betrayed by the Nazis."

After the war, Dr. Max Plaut, for many years counsel of the Jewish community in Hamburg and a Holocaust survivor, was asked if there had been Gentiles who stood up for the Jews, not only in isolated instances, but for the community as a whole. He named three — Dr. Rudolf Brinckmann of Brinckmann Wirtz, the M. M. Warburg successor firm; Cornelius von Berenberg-Gossler; and Theodor Boe of Boe and Ketelsen, coal merchants.

It was my privilege to know two personally and to have gone to school with a Ketelsen son.

My great-great grandparents: August Ludwig (Amschel Löb) Eberstadt
(1770–1839), and Esther Eberstadt (1775–1819).

My Edinger great grandparents: Heinrich Edinger (1822–1886) and
Florestine Seligmann Edinger (1830–1899).

My Eberstadt great grandparents: Abraham Eberstadt (1812–1892), and Betty
Seligmann Eberstadt (1819–1905) with their children Albert (my grandfather),
Louis, Emilie, and Louise. The photo was taken in Worms, circa 1886.

My Eberstadt grandparents: Albert Eberstadt (1847–1931) in a photo taken in
Worms, 1927, and Marie Edinger Eberstadt (1855–1918).

My von Mayer great grandfather: Freiherr (Baron) Adolph von Mayer
(1844–1925), father of Gertrud Flersheim, with his second wife Freifrau
(Baronin) Flora von Mayer, taking the cure in Karlsbad, 1911.

January 1992, on my first and only day in Coburg, birthplace of my
grandmother Flersheim. *(Above):* On von-Mayer Strasse. *(Right):* In front of the
Albert of Saxe Coburg Gotha Memorial. Albert was Queen Victoria's
Prince Consort, and his father, Duke Ernst, ennobled the Mayer family.

Albert Eberstadt's 1890's business and home on Schnurgasse, Frankfurt am Main.

#10 Schubertstrasse:
Albert Eberstadt's Frankfurt home from 1904 to 1932.

Hans Flersheim, in German dragoon uniform,
circa 1912,
during his compulsory military service.

Leutnant Georg Eberstadt, 118th Landwehr Regiment, World War I

Somewhere in France, 1917: Lt. General von Oppeln-Bronikowski
(*center right, bottom step*) with his general and divisional staff officers.
Father is standing second from right, one step up.

Visiting Worms "roots" in 1927. *Left to right:* Hans Schaefer, Georg Eberstadt,
Maria Schaefer, Albert Eberstadt, Ludwig Eberstadt, Lise Eberstadt.

Ernst and Gertrud Flersheim
with their daughters Edith and Margarete circa 1916.

Our Hamburg home, #7 Willistrasse, taken in 1997.

Gelehrtenschule des Johanneums, founded 1529:
My Hamburg high school from 1931 to 1937. Taken in 1997.

Grandfather, father, and grandson Eberstadt in Switzerland, summer of 1928.

Waiting Room, L. Behrens und Söhne, Herrmannstrasse, Hamburg, circa 1927.
Georg Eberstadt was a partner here from 1924 to 1931.

PART TWO

WHERE WE WENT:

ENGLAND

8

The Beginnings in England

From 1935 on we were preparing our emigration actively. I was to start school in England in the autumn while my parents and sister prepared to move the household the following summer. Father had a meeting with Puttfarken, the Nazi principal of my school, the Johanneum. He persuaded him to improve my leaving report card — given the times a decent and politically courageous gesture. A prep school was found for me by Joan Parry's family in Tunbridge Wells, Kent, where they lived. Father found a (public) school. His Guinness friends had gone to Shrewsbury. He liked it but settled on Tonbridge, just a few miles north of Tunbridge Wells, mainly because the headmaster's name family originally came from Hamburg. Shrewsbury would have been the better choice.

Before I could start at Tonbridge, however, I was to spend a one-term prelude in the autumn of 1935 at the prep school mentioned above, Reverend Wheatley's Eversley School, on the Front Road in Tunbridge Wells. I was sent there to prepare for the common entrance exam I needed to pass to get into Tonbridge. Wheatley was a defrocked clergyman. One of the two assistant masters was fond of boys, the other of the matron. The place was cold and damp, the food a horror. I had never come across corned bully beef before. It looked like cat food. I hated the mauve color, the fatty texture of the cold thick slabs, but there it was, in Mrs. Wheatley's eyes, a treat squandered on the little foreigner. I have no recollection of the classes but apparently learned enough to pass the exam.

My English was not bad thanks to Joan Parry, our former au pair in Hamburg. Joan's mother in Tunbridge Wells lived with her sister, Mrs. Bomert, in a large Victorian house surrounded by a gorgeous garden full of rhododendrons, exotic plants, and trees. The house was on Broadwater Down, a beautifully laid-out, spacious and peaceful street. Tunbridge Wells, originally a spa, had and still has charm. The Pantiles, the main shopping area where at one time the waters were taken, are an architectural gem. The sisters were nice to me and had me to Sunday lunch, but first I had to go to church with them. Mrs. Bomert was skinny, Mrs. Parry heavy. Both suffered from flatulence and as we walked along Broadwater Down from church to their house they made noises reminiscent of the final chords from the closing organ voluntary. Both were widowed and not particularly well-off.

Mrs. Bomert had spent her honeymoon pre-1914 cruising on the Rhine, drinking hock, the English generic term for Rhine wines. These memories made her pro-German and well disposed to me. Mr. Bomert, who had been something in the City, was of German origin. Mr. Parry had worked in the Colonies. Mrs. Parry took me a few times "up to town," the English way of saying, took me to London. The train went to Charing Cross station. There was a Lyons Corner House next to the station where she treated me, really very nice of her, to Lyons standard fare such as its delicious sandwiches, cream buns, and a "cupper" (cup of tea), all served by the long gone "nippies," pretty or not so pretty, young or not so young, Lyons waitresses in black dresses and white aprons. All was superior to Mrs. Wheatley's corned beef. The Lyons chain, epitome of middle-class English catering, was controlled by the Salmon and Gluckstein families, decidedly less Anglo-Saxon than their clientele. Both families, as it happened, had sons at Tonbridge. Even if I was a fish out of water at Eversley, it helped me get used to English boarding school life and eased the transition to Tonbridge, its four-hundred-year history, nineteenth-century Ruskin architecture, and beautiful grounds.

I began public school in January 1936. Tonbridge was founded by the Skinners Company, one of oldest guilds in London. The Skinners were, and still are, wealthy. They own to this day valuable London real estate, particularly in the City, and agricultural land, though I hope by now they have diversified their assets into stocks. The Skinner Hall was among the oldest and most beautiful guild halls. Luftwaffe fire raids gutted it in 1940. Originally, to belong to the Skinners, hides and skins was your trade, but in modern times the Skinners, like other guilds, were more of a fraternal association, a lunch and dining club for like-minded public-spirited business men. The guilds, unlike the Pall Mall and St. James' clubs, were more middle than upper class. The warden of the Skinners Company was invariably chairman of the Tonbridge school board. The income from the Skinners property contributed toward the operating costs of the school and financed scholarships. The faculty was relatively well paid, though many English public school teachers in those days had some private means. Tonbridge was, thanks to the Skinners, more generously endowed than the majority of English public i.e. private schools. Father chose Tonbridge for two reasons. He liked the headmaster, and the fees were below those of most of the other leading schools.

In my day there were 400 boys in the school: 300 boarders and 100 day boys. Many came from families that had gone to Tonbridge for generations. The background of the majority was far from blue-blooded. In the City their fathers were joint stock (commercial) rather than merchant bankers, managers rather than directors. They came from the professions, solicitors more than barristers, doctors, civil servants, clergy, and the armed forces. The fathers were officers in county regiments, not the Guards, artillery not cavalry. In the navy they served below deck rather than on the bridge. Many came from parents in the Colonies or India. The boys were sent home to get a public school education and also on account of the climate. They would not see their parents from one end of the year to the next. School holidays were spent with grandparents who had retired back home in England. The fathers might have been judges or district commissioners in India, senior police officers in the Colonies, or overseas businesspeople. Few were in the Indian civil service, the Oxford and Cambridge-educated elite who really governed the Indian Empire. They were the sons of yeoman farmers, not of grandee landowners. A titled parent was a rarity, if so a knighthood, not hereditary. The officers were majors or colonels, rarely generals.

One "old boy" had become a field marshal (Lord Ironside) in the early years of the Second World War. He had made his reputation after the First World War leading an Allied force against the Bolsheviks. He was not one of warfare's great, but he looked a field marshal, and what a fuss the school made over him. Many families came from Kent and elsewhere in southern England. The day boys' parents chose to live in Tonbridge. Their children were educated at a fraction of the boarders' fees. There were two day-boy houses, Welldon and Smythe. The Welldon parents' social profile was similar to the boarders', but a Smythe boy might have come from local tradesmen's families. They were looked down upon by boarders and Welldon boys.

Back in Hamburg, many, many issues needed to be resolved before my family could emigrate. Should Maria Schaefer come with us or stay in Frankfurt? Though she was Jewish, as the widow of a World War I soldier the Nuremberg Laws posed no immediate threat. Her children were only half Jewish and in 1936 were not directly affected. We had helped them financially over the years and left some money behind for them, but our own future was too uncertain to take them along even had they wanted it. Father's brother Ludwig was still a judge. As a war veteran and husband of a non-Jewish wife he was expecting to retire on a pension even if forced to resign. His two children did not want to emigrate.

The most important conversations were with my grandparents Flersheim. It was decided they should leave as soon as possible. The Flersheim family had had some money in the United States since before the First World War. It was not a large amount but enough to live on and, if need be, help their two daughters.

Their move, however, turned out to be more complicated than that of my parents, and in the event, my grandfather and grandmother left helter-skelter. Flersheim-Hess was in the process of being sold to key employees. Ernst Flersheim's nephew and partner Herbert Flersheim believed someone in the firm got wind of the foreign assets and was about to denounce them to the Gestapo. Herbert and his wife went to Holland literally overnight, which forced my grandfather, who had hoped for a more leisurely transition, to follow hurriedly. My grandmother, left behind, was charged with disassembling their house, which became physically and psychologically too much for her. Finally she left without completing the task, also in a hurry, because she quarreled with everybody, including the Gestapo who supervised her packing. My grandparents wanted to give some of their art collection to us to take to England. Father was fearful to accept anything — other than a small Monet — as this would have constituted an illegal transfer of assets. Mother came to resent his reluctance in later years, on sentimental as much as financial grounds. The Monet was sold in London for less than a thousand pounds. Art can be almost worthless when there are more sellers than buyers. The painting is now in the collection of Mrs. Frederic Stafford in New York.

Our Willistrasse house was sold to Dr. Eduard Cadmus, a lawyer acquaintance of Father's. We received the market price, but the market was depressed by numerous forced sales of Jewish owners leaving Germany. After the war the Cadmus family, to their chagrin, agreed to a further payment. Mother was in charge of packing, selling what we did not take with us to England, buying a few smaller antiques such as my writing desk, now at 1035 Fifth Avenue. The furniture was typically German, too large for a more modest home in England. Most refugees were bedeviled by the bulkiness of their belongings but they could not get themselves to part with their past. German furniture was as alien as its owners in the new country. Mother was attached to her belongings. Father did not want to give away his library. The movers were decent. One apologized for his country as he packed father's Iron Cross and other war medals.

It was early summer of 1936 when our family took leave of Germany for good. I had returned from Tonbridge. We spent the last couple of days after the house was emptied at the Hotel Vier Jahreszeiten, a farewell treat, a parting view of the Alster lake and good-bye to Hamburg, to Eberstadts and Flersheims in Germany. Our governess, Martha Knüttel, agreed to work for us during our first year in England. Another treat was first-class travel on the Hapag liner *Deutschland*. As the ship cast off we stood on deck, but no one was ashore to wave us farewell. The band struck up the traditional "*Muss ich denn, muss ich denn, zum Städelein hinaus. . . .*" Mother cried and cried. Martha tried to comfort her. I don't recall Brigitte's emotions. I was dry-eyed. After all, I had already completed two terms at a stiff-upper-lip English public school. Another family member aboard was Cliff, our Bedlington terrier. Little did he know six months of a quarantine kennel awaited him on the other side of the English Channel, but we visited him many weekends while he was locked away.

During the first weeks in London that summer we had a superficially elegant but slightly shabby service flat in Gloucester Place. One of its assets, especially in the eyes of newcomers such as ourselves, was its prestigious West One (W1) postal code, which it shared with (south of Oxford Street and much classier) Mayfair. Gloucester Place consisted of late-eighteenth, early-nineteenth-century, narrow, originally one-family homes with red-brick facades and three stories of sash windows. By the 1930s most had been converted into flats and offices. They looked unchanged when I happened to be driving by there in 1996.

A full English breakfast was served by a butler — eggs and bacon most mornings. Mother usually had kippers. In Germany we never had more than one egg, soft-boiled, once a week. It was not going to be all bad, living in England. We walked in nearby Regents Park, the beginnings of Mother's love affair with the London parks. Mother looked for a larger furnished flat and found one nearby in Chiltern Court, an imposing modern granite building at the northeast corner of Baker Street and the Marylebone Road, built over the underground station. We sublet for six months from people by the name of Gee who could no longer afford the rent. Father told me that happened if you did not work hard and drank too much. Their fate made a deep impression on me. Otherwise I remember chintz sofas, uniformed doormen, and thought Chiltern Court was quite grand even if it was north of the Marylebone Road and we were demoted from West One to North West One. At a restaurant next door the three-course lunch cost one shilling and six pence. I was allowed, occasionally, to take new friends from Tonbridge there.

For himself, my father sublet a small office from Viscount Suirdale, an Irish peer and an in-law of the W. R. Grace family whose interests he represented in England. It was in the old Schroeder building in Leadenhall Street. His first employee was Ernst Collin of the Berlin Dreyfus bank, a kinsman of Willy's. He became father's bookkeeper. Probably he was supposed to keep an eye on Willy's investment in the new firm. Soon after we came to England father hired a bilingual secretary, Dora Irwin, as his second employee. Miss Irwin, a lifelong spinster, tall, ungainly, worked for him from 1936 until he died in 1963, and continued part-time till her own death to help Mother. She typed poorly. She did not get on with Mother but was devoted to her "boss." She came from a German-Jewish middle-class background. Her parents had settled in England before the First World War. They anglicized their name from Ehrmann to Irwin. She considered herself superior to newly arrived refugees such as ourselves except when father, more than once, bailed her out on account of an unfortunate kleptomaniac habit.

German refugees arrived in England from 1933 on. In 1936 we came before most did. Some were relatives and acquaintances, but few were close friends. Father had kept himself apart from the Jewish business community in Hamburg, hence had few links with those who had already established themselves in England. Mother never shared this attitude. Many they socialized with were relatives and connections of hers. Geoffrey and Edie Howard received us warmly. She was an Edinger cousin, he a pharmaceutical manufacturer from an old West Country Quaker family. They called on George Edinger, Edie Howard's clever but oddball journalist brother. The reception from Katie Lewis, an Eberstadt relative, daughter of Sir George Lewis, was correct but chilly. The same could be said of Lady Seligman, widow of Sir Charles Seligman, a well-known banker and cousin of my grandmother Flersheim. Louis Kiek of Erlanger's, from whom father had hoped for business support, did nothing. Father did a little better with Bob Brand (later Lord Brand) at Lazard's. The

Guinnesses were genuinely friendly but there was little they could do for him in business. Alfred Marx was a mine of helpful English know-how, but the recipient rather than giver of business, which he needed badly. They saw ex–Dresdner Bank colleagues who were trying to make a new start in London, such as Herbert Guttmann, the bank's former chairman and member of the founding family. Father explored a business link with Kurt Calmon, another ex–Dresdner Bank executive. It came to nothing but Brigitte later had a brief flirtation with his son and I with his daughter. We called him the hairy ape, but she was good-looking.

Toward the end of 1936 we rented a flat at 30, Lansdowne Road, a pleasant tree-lined street off Holland Park Avenue at the corner of the tube station. Two adjoining houses had been converted into flats. We occupied the ground floor. The rent was reasonable — 300 pounds a year. It was beautiful, which eased settling in a new country. The back overlooked a typically well-maintained London square to which only adjoining residents had access. We were able to walk into the garden from the living room. The Hamburg furniture reappeared. Our dog Cliff completed his quarantine. Our Ford V8 from Hamburg had its own garage next door. The car was not ideal. It had left-hand steering, but there was no money for a new one.

I can't imagine how the firm of G. Eberstadt made a living. They weren't stockbrokers, who at least earned a commission; Father did not want to be one. Anyhow, the London Stock Exchange did not admit aliens as members. The firm was on a register entitling it to a return commission from brokers. That cannot have amounted to much, and in any event they did not have many, let alone substantial, clients. They earned some money handling the transfer of the small capital refugees were permitted to bring out of Germany. They tried larger deals involving the liquidation of foreign-owned assets blocked in Germany, but I do not recall significant successes. The Berlin Dreyfus bank was supposed to be the main source of business but apart from providing some initial capital hardly anything originated from them. In 1938 the firm was "Aryanized." It was sold to Merck Fink, which ended the relationship.

With the little money Father had personally and some of the firm's capital, he traded in the London market and on Wall Street. (Don't be a trader if you cannot afford losses!) At dinner he'd receive a call from Alfred Ehrlich, an Austrian refugee who eked out a living as Hayden Stone's London representative. The mealtime mood depended on Ehrlich's prices, especially Allis-Chalmers and Bethlehem Steel. It was a nightly irritant to Mother when he interrupted our dinner. A few years later I served under Ehrlich, then a sergeant in the Pioneer Corps. He was bizarrely ugly but had a good-looking Scottish wife whose charms supposedly earned him his sergeant's stripes. Still later, when I was living in the United States, he became the not very successful New York representative of Watt and Watt, a small Canadian house. I was able to give him some business, which resulted in frequent phone calls: "Vatt and Vatt, Errrlick speaking." Eventually Frank Lloyd of the Marlborough Gallery who had also served under Ehrlich in the Pioneer Corps made him his confidential bookkeeper. Keeping Lloyd's confidences cost him a nervous breakdown and his health.

It is not surprising that G. Eberstadt was not successful. The times were awful, the territory unfamiliar. Expenses, which included father's salary on which we lived, were slowly eroding the firm's modest capital. Appearances were kept up, but in reality we had no money to speak of. We lived frugally. Bridget and I (anglicizing her name was part of a conscious effort on both our parts) had minimal pocket money. A movie was an event. Sundays we often drove to Chalfont St. Giles in Buckinghamshire. Mother could not get out of bed in the morning, so we'd leave late. Father would drive too fast. She'd make him stop. She threatened to get out of the car and go home unless he slowed down. He'd apologize and promise never to do it again. In the car they'd squabble over anything and everything. These were unhappy anxious times, and Sundays were the worst.

At Chalfont, the handsome traditional country house had been converted into a hotel with an adjacent golf course. We lunched on the prix fixe menu and afterward our parents played golf. Mother was a tolerable player. Father tried but was hopeless. Bridget and I walked behind them, half the time dying a thousand deaths and hating every moment. They saved on the cost of a caddy. Each time a ball was lost they looked and looked until the "Fore!" from the pair behind became too insistent. If they let them play through, they'd get excited because it was getting late, or why hadn't we all paid better attention where father had sliced or hooked or topped his shot. One hushed the other in loud German or bad English. Their clothes were foreign. They were foreign. The dog barked in the locked car. During the week at least Father had the office. It was so unfair; he tried so hard. But the times were wrong. Father wanted dinner parties for potential clients. Mother preferred friends or relatives, generally impecunious and of little business interest. If they were better off it was an irritant. Nearly all were Jewish, which he considered reverting to what he and his father had wanted to get away from.

During term time, thank goodness, I was at boarding school. Bridget went to an excellent day school at nearby Camden Hill and made new friends. Their parents were the few social contacts we had with the English. On the whole people were cordial and understanding of our efforts to make a new life. Probably they could not conceive why we should be quite so unsure or defensive.

Gradually we settled down. Both parents liked England from the beginning and came to truly love it. The office moved from Lord Suirdale's in Leadenhall Street to 27, Old Broad Street, where they subleased from Robert Benson and Co. (later Robert Benson Lonsdale and Co., then Kleinwort Benson, which became Dresdner Bank Kleinwort Benson and is now Dresdner Kleinwort Wasserstein). A good address mattered in the City, and 27, Old Broad Street was that, a handsome building with a pleasing curved facade, five stories high. It survived the Blitz but eventually gave way to the National Provincial tower.

We had three years in England before the war. Hitler, Mussolini, Mrs. Simpson, and Edward VIII's Abdication dominated the news. Abyssinia, German rearmament, breaking with the League of Nations, the Austrian Anschluss, the Sudeten crisis, Munich, Kristallnacht, occupation of Czechoslovakia — one ominous event followed another. The relief to be in England outweighed financial worries. In 1937 my grandparents Flersheim found a new domicile in the Netherlands. They lived quite agreeably in

Amsterdam in the Doelen Hotel. They came on visits to London. Neither political nor personal trauma were sufficient to steer my grandmother's relations with her husband or my mother into more tranquil waters.

My mother's sister Margarete Wertheim, her husband, Rudolf, and their son Hans emigrated to Belgium in 1937. Margarete's multiple sclerosis was worsening. Her deteriorating health overshadowed political worries for them. Fritz Flersheim and his mother, Florence, lived at the Doelen Hotel until they went on to the United States in 1939. Herbert Flersheim, with the support of his old Amsterdam friend Hans Wetzlar, carried on in the ivory trade. He had a pretty house in Sandvoort outside Amsterdam. Unlike most refugees, the Flersheims had no acute financial worries.

Willy Dreyfus and his family went to Switzerland; they were also by the standards of those days relatively comfortably off. He remained in Switzerland; his wife and children later went to the United States. Mother's favorite cousin and friend Mariechen Koch-Floersheim settled quite agreeably in Switzerland with her husband and children. Father's sister Maria Schaefer and her children, as well as his brother Ludwig Eberstadt and his family remained in Germany.

However little social contact we had with the English, we were grateful England had taken us in. We learned about royalty, Parliament, government, Whitehall, the garden squares, the parks, the English themselves, their haughty calm, their fairness — and up to a point, their tolerance, English history, and traditions. Tackling the new sidetracked our homesickness and loss of the familiar. It helped that both parents had spent a happy time in England before 1914. They wanted to like the English and be accepted. They wanted to become part of their ways and be fluent in their language. Mother had a good accent but a limited vocabulary. Father's accent was bad but his English was fluent. It did not bother mother in the slightest to speak German anywhere, and at the top of her voice. Father whispered in his guttural but grammatically perfect English.

What did the English, an insular people who looked down on foreigners, mocked foreign ways, and felt especially ambivalent about Germans, make of the likes of us? The First World War had ended less than twenty years earlier. There was hardly a family that had not lost a relative in the war. The survivors were in their forties or fifties. If politically minded and "upper class," they might be in Parliament or, like Anthony Eden, in the government. They were fairly senior in the civil service, the armed forces, the Foreign Office. They were well up in the business world or the City. They were the dons at Oxford and Cambridge, bishops, county gentry. A few were intrigued with Hitler and feared Communism more than the Nazis. More than a few believed the Treaty of Versailles had been unfair to the Germans. Some were anti-Semitic but it was a different anti-Semitism from German, let alone the Nazi German. Many simply did not like aliens. Notwithstanding the ingrained prejudice, which is part and parcel of human nature, England was a tolerant nation. It prided itself on having taken in throughout its history the persecuted and on benefiting from their talents.

One summer, in 1937, we vacationed at Le Coq on the Belgian coast. Belgium was inexpensive, close by, and it was the Continent. I fell in love with Claude Ravier, who was French, and like myself, she was fifteen years old. In 1938 we went to Shanklin on the Isle of Wight. The international situation by then was too precarious to risk leaving England. It was anyhow time to try an English holiday. I met my first English girlfriend, not in the same league as Claude Ravier. I do not recall her name, though we saw each other a few times after the summer in London.

In the summer of 1939, with war almost a certainty, we spent a holiday motoring through England. Both parents entered wholeheartedly into the spirit of discovering the country that was becoming our new homeland. We went to Stratford-on-Avon, the East Anglican cathedrals, Durham, Liverpool, and the Lake District. In Ann Hathaway's cottage father hardly endeared himself to our guide, fellow tourists, and me in particular by casting doubts, in heavily accented English, on Shakespeare's existence.

An even stronger influence than family in these prewar years in England was becoming accustomed to English public school life at Tonbridge. I was in School House, the largest of the boardinghouses, presided

over by the head of house, the Reverend H. N. P. Sloman. Though ordained, Sloman rarely took a service. He had graduated with a first in classics from Balliol but was indolent. Mrs. Sloman had immense bosoms and
wobbled unsteadily on high heels. They had living with them Brenda, a
younger, quite attractive relative, whom we considered a bit tarty because
she appeared flirtatious.

To be a housemaster was lucrative. He was expected to run his house
at a profit — the issue was how much profit — to save up for retirement.
The cost of food was the major variable. Financially more aggressive
housemasters or their wives went easy on second helpings. School House
food was quite adequate. Sloman had a good salary and some money of his
own.

The day-to-day operations and discipline of School House were in the
hands of C. H. (John) Knott, a lifelong bachelor, no scholar, but one of
England's leading all-round athletes. He had been a racquets, squash,
Fives, and cricket "blue" at Oxford; later he played county cricket for
Kent. At Tonbridge he coached the First (cricket) Eleven, the First (rugby)
Fifteen, and the indoor court ball games. The Knotts were a Kentish family with many Tonbridge connections. He was always pleasant to me,
though I was no asset for him. I was no athlete, nor a shining light academically. To be foreign was no plus, but it was not a negative. He loved
his profession and I doubt he ever questioned any aspect of the public
school system. He believed in corporal punishment. The day of my confirmation, after lights-out in our dormitory, my cousin Paul Marx and I
were whispering a while in the dark. This was overheard by a prefect, reported to Knott, who caned us, three strokes each. Depending on the
offense, it was three or five strokes. He caned with a powerful accurate
backhand stroke, as befitted England's erstwhile ranking racquets champion. Paul Marx played fifth string on the Tonbridge First squash team and
helped School House win the interhouse squash cup. This put him in
Knott's good graces but not sufficiently so as to avoid a caning.

I stroked the School House rowing Four, my only athletic accom-
plishment remotely worth mentioning. Knott was glad for me to earn my
so-called house colors this way, something that mattered in schoolboy life.

One year we reached the finals, which we lost. Rowing on the river Medway was pretty, though in the spring term it could be bitterly cold and windy. The steep, tree-lined Medway banks wound through muddy meadows. The river was narrow and shallow in the summer. It could not handle anything larger than four-bladed boats. Ours had fixed, not sliding, seats, which is rough on the behind. Everybody had to take some exercise every afternoon. Without, to my sorrow, the slightest talent I played Fives and squash, and in the winter term twice a week rugby football, or rugger as it was called.

As with most things English I welcomed and accepted the schoolboy way of life without many questions and wanted to advance up the seniority ladder. Public school was four years, from the age of thirteen or fourteen to seventeen or eighteen. I came when I was fourteen and a half and left at eighteen. Dress code codified seniority. In your first year as a "novi" you had at all times to button up all three buttons on your school blazer; in the second year you were allowed to unbutton the lowest; in the third year you closed only the middle button; and in the fourth you could wear an open jacket. In your first year it was not allowed to have either hand in a trouser pocket; one hand was allowed in the second; and both hands in your third. There was also some rule about how to wear your summer-term straw boater. You had to be a prefect to wear it at an angle. If a second-year boy met a novi with hands in pocket or jacket unbuttoned, or just did not care for the way he looked, he could "tick him off" or report him to a prefect if he did not respond or showed any "lip."

The School House layout was a long corridor. The study cubicles for the novi were at one end, followed by a row of comfortable prefects' cubicles that led to a long corridor of sleeping cubicles for all who were not prefects but too senior to sleep in the dormitories. When a novi went from his study to a dormitory, he had to tiptoe silently through the prefects' domain and then run as fast as he could along the main cubicle corridor. If we considered he did not run fast enough we'd be standing in our cubicle doors yelling at him to run faster.

The praepostors — prefects or pre's for short — were the power elite.

House prefects were the bottom rung of the elite. Each house had half a dozen or so, and they served under a head of house. Then there were school prefects made up from the heads of houses and all were under the Head of School. A house pre wore a blue and white band around his boater. A school pre's band was blue-white-blue. The rank and file, that is, myself, wore boaters with our house colors in the summer, caps the rest of the year. School House colors were black-blue-black. The life of a straw hat was brief. They got bashed or became rain-sodden and shapeless. They were quite expensive, which was a concern to me.

The prefects were served by "fags" recruited from the novi. Each prefect had his personal fag who did errands such as carrying his books to class in the mornings, shining shoes, or toasting buttered crumpets before the open fire in the common room. If his own fag was not around and a prefect wanted anything he'd shout "Fag," the novi came running, and the one who got there last had to do the chore.

In the morning the rank and file dipped in bathtubs filled with cold water, while the prefects soaked in hot water. Most of the prefects handled themselves decently. They took themselves seriously, were probably a bit conceited, but in my experience there was little if any of the sadism attributed to the system in books about public school life. In my last year one of the School House prefects was expelled for sleeping with Brenda, an attractive dark-haired Welsh "skivvie," schoolboy slang for a housemaid. If he had had sex with a boy probably nothing would have happened to him. It must have broken Knott's heart to expel him. He was the best fast bowler in that year's first cricket Eleven.

To have been a prefect was viewed as a prerequisite for Sandhurst, other service academies, or even a business career at Unilever, Shell, and the likes. I only got as far as a house senior. If prefects were lieutenants, heads of houses were majors, the school head a general. A house senior was a noncommissioned officer. In my leaving report John Knott said I should have stayed another year to become a prefect, not just for the character-forming experience, but because it would have made all the difference for my future life. Oxford was important, but in his opinion it could wait. To have been a prefect mattered more — maybe because I wasn't English. He and Sloman wished me luck at the House, the name by which Oxonians know Christ Church.

As for academics at Tonbridge I received above all a good education in the humanities. I continued with my Johanneum Latin but dropped Greek after a year. English literature and history were well taught. One of the masters was D. C. Sommervell, a first-rate scholar with a sense of humor. He had made his reputation condensing Toynbee's *History of the World* to a mere thousand pages. He came from a well-to-do western England shoe manufacturing family. His brother was Prime Minister Stanley Baldwin's attorney general in the 1930s. With S. H. Vere Hodge, a civilized scholarly teacher, we read Shakespeare. We did *Richard II*, parts of which I can recite to this day. But I missed much English literature. An English schoolboy in those days had read the classics before he got to his public school. French was taught by a World War I veteran, Lieut. Col. W. W. Chard, M.C. He had been a liaison officer with the French army. Several masters were ordained Anglicans. The natural sciences were taught but played second fiddle to the humanities. An overdue science laboratory was built while I was at Tonbridge, paid for by the Skinners and opened with royal pomp by the handsome young Duke of Kent.

My academic record at Tonbridge could have been worse, but it was not distinguished. The report card comments were well meaning but rightly not enthusiastic. They got better in the sixth form, which was the most senior. In the Michaelmas Term 1938 report, according to N. R. Ridgeway, I "showed a very real interest in Economics and made unusual progress, but was, of course handicapped by my inability to express myself concisely and write legibly." In Political Science I was "very good indeed, read with discrimination and thought for myself." In History and English, according to D. C. Somervell, I did "most industrious and intelligent work" but my written English was still "rather faulty at times." French was "satisfactory" and I placed seventh out of twelve. In the Lent Term 1939, I placed second out of fourteen in current affairs, sixth out of fourteen in economics, a "very thorough and logical thinker." In English and History Somervell wrote I had done "excellent work" and was an "industrious and vigorous boy." In Latin, J. M. McNeill graded me "a good worker who has a very fair knowledge of the subject." It had been a mistake on my father's part to make me take Latin and Greek. He had excelled at classics and thought "one" should have a humanistic education. I had a hard time with both languages. Much later, when my sons George and Michael took Latin at St. Bernard's I never admitted to them I had not enjoyed it much in my own school days, though to my surprise I still remembered enough to help them with their homework.

John Knott summed me up as a "delightful boy to deal with in every way, whose athletic activities have been praiseworthy and have been very good for him." In my final (summer) term in 1939 I was second of ten in Economics, fourth of ten in Political Science, a "good and vigorous worker," fourth of nine, in English and History. McNeill wrote that I had "worked well at a difficult book" in Latin (if only I remembered the book) and "my knowledge of it should be a considerable help next year"; seemingly he was not aware I was leaving and there would be no next year. I weighed 11 stone 2 lbs., stood 5 ft. 8½ in., full chest 38 inches and empty 35 inches. John Knott summarized my Tonbridge years as "a most creditable career" and predicted that I would do myself "and the school credit at Oxford." Sloman sent me off with best wishes; he was sure I'd "do well at the House, had had an admirable career at Tonbridge, and a well-balanced mind" which would take me far.

Barring a chance visit on my way to the South Coast through Tonbridge town I have never again set foot on the school grounds, have never been to an old boys' reunion or had contact other than at Oxford, with my school contemporaries. Still, I belong to the Old Tonbridgian Society, read its literature with interest, and have an unused O.T. tie in my closet. It would be untrue to say I hated Tonbridge. I wanted very much to be accepted in the ways of an English public school. It was part of the process of becoming English. I looked up to the masters. They came from families often a cut above the boys' background. They were tweedy pipe smokers. I don't believe there was a Jewish master among them and that has not changed. Few of the boys were Jewish. The wealthy Jewish families often went to Harrow, though on the whole Jewish families did not like to send their children to boarding schools. If they lived in Manchester, they got a superb education at Manchester Grammar School. Elsewhere in the provinces they'd also go to the local grammar school rather than a boarding school. If they lived, like the preponderance of Jews, in London, they were day boys at Mill Hill or Highgate which are close to Hampstead, Golders Green, and St. John's Wood. Or they might have been day boys at St. Paul's, occasionally at Westminster School.

I had friends but not many. In my house there was Roderick Paterson but I never saw him again after we left. He went into the navy. I was good friends with Ben Yeats-Brown, a day boy at Welldon. His father was an impecunious retired Indian army colonel, brother of Francis Yeats-Brown, the author of a best-selling novel about the Bengal Lancers. They were an intellectual family involved in Eastern mysticism. The father, tiny in stature, was more ambitious for his children's athletic than scholastic attainments. Every afternoon he watched his older son David play racquets or cricket. David excelled at both and was a schoolboy's idol but did not get far in later life. Ben never went to university; instead he joined the 60th Rifles. For a while we were in the same brigade in Normandy, where he commanded an armored carrier platoon. I came upon him by chance and was given a welcome lift during an attack in the Bocage country. He became important in the City. He was a protégé of the fabled "Kit" Hoare, senior partner of Hoare and Co. (now Hoare Govett) and eventually succeeded him. I was friends with a Yeats-Brown sister, who later was at Oxford with me. The Yeats-Browns were friendly to me, even though the author uncle had a fascist reputation.

My Tonbridge recollections have little to do with games or classes but with atmosphere and specific events. Meals were served in a monastic refectory with long wooden tables and rickety benches. Grace was said before and after meals other than breakfast: Benedictus Benedicat before food, and Benedicto Benedicatur after. John Knott and the prefects had their separate high table. He had the same breakfast every morning, grapenuts with heavy cream. Our food was brought to our places by skivvies who were supervised by Tom, a wizened elderly manservant.

The Church, the classics, army, and sports were at the core of our education. The OTC, the Officers' Training Corps, played a major role in our lives. It was led by several of the numerous masters who had been officers in the First World War. In my time it was commanded by Major Hoole M. C. housemaster of Parkside. I forget the scholastic subjects Hoole taught, but he was an impressive figure in his breeches, highly polished cavalry boots, and bemedaled uniform jacket. I was a member of this paramilitary training corps, which proved helpful when later I applied for a commission in "my" war. We were equipped with First World War Lee-Enfield 303 rifles. I turned out to be quite a good shot. Among all the junk I should have long ago thrown away there is a target of mine with five bull's-eyes, and that was with a 22-bore rifle. We had a weekly drill parade, lots of marching, feet stamping, "General Salute, Present Arms!" not to mention all the spit and polish that went with a soldier's training. There were TEWTS (tactical exercises without troops) and an annual field day run jointly with the regular army. We had a band under a retired regular army bandmaster from the Irish Guards, Fitzsomething by name. He relished reunions with German veterans from the First World War and could not understand that I did not relish his relishing. It was open-minded of Hoole and his fellow officers to welcome me into their OTC. I herewith offer my thanks to the Almighty that I was prevented from joining that other paramilitary body, Germany's Hitler Youth. I probably would have, if I could have. . . .

Like the majority of English public schools Tonbridge raised young Christians. Chapel was the spiritual center of school life. The Church of England, the Established Church, was at the core of our daily routine. Jews and Catholics attended Anglican morning prayers in Chapel and evening prayers in their boardinghouses. Sundays the Catholics went to their own church in town. For the few Jewish boys there was weekly separate religious instruction. Chapel was taken quite seriously by most of us. I liked the aesthetics. I still find comfort in the serenity of the Nunc Dimittis: "Lord, now let Thy servant depart in peace, according to thy ways, for mine eyes have seen thy salvation." Organ voluntaries and hymns remain among my favorite music. The chapel was red brick Victorian Gothic. In the summer the west door stayed open, and warm fragrant breezes drifted in. You could see the Head, the grounds on which the school cricket matches were played, a lovely field bordered by tall trees. At even song in the summer the late afternoon sun set the chapel isle aglow. In winter it was poorly, if at all heated, and damned cold. I got little out of most sermons, and even less out of Holy Communion.

Before my confirmation on June 9, 1936, by the Lord Bishop of Rochester, the Right Reverend Chavasse, a heavily decorated World War I veteran with a couple of DSOs, we were cautioned not to expect too much from the actual confirmation. "It is the feeling of those who have drawn up this form of service that many people are disappointed in their Confirmation and in the subsequent life as communicants simply because they are not definite enough in their aims." And, "If your Confirmation seems to have passed without any great emotional uplift, that is no reason for surprise or disappointment. Your feelings are very rarely an index of your spiritual condition. The important thing is to cultivate the will to serve God and man." Weekday evenings in the School House dining hall there was a hymn and a prayer. On stormy winter nights Knott chose what became a favorite of mine: "Almighty Father, strong to save. And hear us while we pray to Thee, for those in danger on the sea." In bed I'd listen to the mainline London trains thunder in the distance and wish I were aboard.

We were allowed one Sunday a month to miss morning service or evensong, which gave enough time to visit my parents. Even better there was half-term when we were allowed a night away from school. The Southern Railway trains came up from the South Coast. After Tonbridge the express trains stopped only once, at Sevenoaks. They came into London at Charing Cross Station. There was a long tunnel under the Weald of Kent between Tonbridge and Sevenoaks. Coming back it foreshadowed the imminent arrival at Tonbridge. Sometimes I treated myself to a ride in the Pullman car, tea included, for six pence extra, though I felt guilty. For us every shilling mattered, but it seemed grown up and sophisticated to travel in those plush cars. I feel almost as guilty to this day if I fly business class, let alone first class, when economy does perfectly well.

The brief breaks in London meant a lot to my parents and I was spoiled with a good lunch. I preferred going to them, as their visits to Tonbridge made me uncomfortable. I was embarrassed by their non-English appearance, their foreign accents, and their not knowing the first thing about cricket or rugby.

During my three and a half years at Tonbridge the world did not stand still. There were almost nonstop international and domestic crises. Neville Chamberlain succeeded Stanley Baldwin as prime minister. Winston Churchill's warnings in Parliament began to be heeded. Anthony Eden and Duff Cooper resigned from the government, Sir Robert Vansittart from the Foreign Office.

The first month at Tonbridge — my parents were still in Hamburg — I got permission to go up to London for the funeral of King George V. Mother's cousin Herbert Flersheim happened to be in London for a tortoiseshell auction. He stayed at the Park Lane Hotel on Piccadilly and from his room we watched the funeral procession. Knott first made a fuss, but in the end let me go, deciding it would be good for me to witness an episode of English history. It was quite wonderful. It was bitterly cold but a weak sun had worked its way through the misty sky. All in the procession wore their splendid but weighty greatcoats. John Wheeler-Bennett described it in his biography of King George VI:

> On the gray and wintry day of January 28 [1936], King George V was borne through the streets of London and of Windsor to his grave in St. George's Chapel. Behind him walked his four sons, and five foreign rulers bore him company. The five were King Christian of Denmark, King Hakoon of Norway, King Carol of Romania, Tsar Boris of Bulgaria, King Leopold III of the Belgians, and the President of the French Republic, M. Albert Lebrun. There followed a great concourse of foreign statesmen and warriors, some of whom made strange companions: Marshall Petain, the hero of Verdun and the man of Vichy; Maxim Litvinov, then in fleeting popularity as the entrepreneur of a short-lived honeymoon of amity between Russia and the West, Marshal Tukachevsky, destined to be executed as a traitor a year later, and the Grandduke Dmitri,

a cousin of the murdered Tsar; Freiherr von Neurath, the German Foreign Minister who ten years later was to be condemned at Nuremberg as a major war criminal, Field-Marshal von Blomberg, a future victim of the Führer's caprice, and the aged and arthritic Duke of Saxe-Coburg-Gotha. From Austria came the dashing Prince von Starhemberg who endeavored unsuccessfully to enjoy the protection of both Hitler and Mussolini — and suffered accordingly; and from Finland the veteran Field-Marshal Baron von Mannerheim, that romantic figure who was to resist so gallantly the assault of the Red Army upon his country. All these followed King George V to Windsor, and with them went the mourners of England and the Empire, the greatest and the humblest in the land, to take their sorrowful leave of one whose passing marked the end of the Victorian era.

Two other royal events occurred during my school days. The first was the Abdication Crisis in December 1936. John Knott let me listen in his study to Edward's abdication broadcast. We were teary when Edward ended: "And now we all have a new King. God Save the King." To see the coronation on May 12, 1937, Knott gave me leave to go up to London. My parents had taken four seats at great expense in the windows of a shoe store on Regent Street. The store served a champagne lunch while we waited for the procession. We were in a good spot and got a good view into the carriages as they went by. The crowd reserved its loudest cheers for Stanley Baldwin, the prime minister. They considered him the king-maker who had forced the abdication and preserved the monarchy. He sat in his own state carriage with his wife, beaming and puffing on his pipe. Mother was the one who liked it the most. We had lived in England a year but that was long enough to start her love affair with the English royal family.

Notwithstanding what was going on in the world, much of it of monumental importance to the refugees, school life more than world affairs absorbed me. I did not cover myself in glory in school, but I managed. For most of my last year at school the prospect of Oxford, which I expected to be heaven on earth, kept me going.

Our arrival in England came at the tail end of Britain's greatness and power while on the surface all was still intact. Gandhi was already preaching and practicing passive resistance, but I doubt that at Tonbridge he was considered anything other than a mendacious menace, undermining the civilizing influence of the Empire. Schools such as mine were the training ground for future colonial administrators. They considered the white man's burden heavy, but for the good of governing and governed alike. Tonbridge was a product of the Empire. I got a whiff of what it meant to be the son of a soldier in the Indian army, a sailor still trained in Nelson's shadow, a tea planter in Ceylon, or a bishop in Mombasa. Today's parents lead by comparison a humdrum, if more comfortable life, but are bereft of the self-confidence, indeed the arrogance, of a governing class. For better or worse, my English public school had a lifelong impact on me, however much I wanted to shed its notions the day I left.

9

Wartime England

I had been accepted at Oxford. I was glad to have Tonbridge behind me. I left at the end of the 1939 summer term, barely three months before the outbreak of the Second World War. No more jingoish school song: "Here shall Tonbridge spirit, here shall manhood be, Serving God and Country, Ruling Land and Sea." It grated even when Britain still ruled land and sea. Many O.T.'s (Old Tonbridgians) went to Oxford or Cambridge, but few to Christ Church, which for some Tonbridgians was too exclusive and for others too intellectual. I was fortunate to get into the "House," as it was known. I was neither an English aristocrat nor had a first-class brain but I had an introduction to the "Prof," F. A. Lindemann, Professor of Experimental Philosophy at Oxford and a Student (teaching fellow) of Christ Church. He was extraordinarily kind to me. I spent the best part of an afternoon with him. He was aware of the military dangers of the Nazis. He was willing to help me on account of my origins and put in a good word with the admissions authorities. The Prof, independently wealthy, was close to Winston Churchill. I have read that from time to time he helped Churchill financially. In the war he was Churchill's chief scientific adviser and became Lord Cherwell, a title he took from the river which flows into the Isis, not far from his Meadows rooms in college. In *The Gathering Storm*, Churchill describes him as an old friend he had met "at the close of the previous war, in which he had distinguished himself by conducting in the air a number of experiments, hitherto reserved for daring pilots, to overcome the then easily mortal dangers of a spin." Lindemann was British-born, though the family was of German origin. He had studied in Göttingen under Prof. Walther Nernst, winner of the Nobel Prize for Chemistry in 1920. Nernst was the father-in-law of Heinz Cahn, a Berlin banker now in London who with his wife, Hilde, Nernst's daughter, had become my parents' closest friends in England. They generously had written to Lindemann about me.

In April 1939 I received a brief but welcome note from the Senior Censor, on behalf of the Dean. He was "glad to inform" me that I had been "successful in the recent Entrance Examination for admission in October next. Kindly send to The Senior Censor, Christ Church, as soon as possible, your Certificate exempting you from Responsions (for registration), together with a cheque for one pound made out to The Assistant Registrar, Oxford University." The Censor wrote he was not sure that he'd be able to find me rooms in college during my first year — in fact he did — and how much bed linen and crockery I'd have to bring up with me.

The more significant information was about money: "It is not possible to estimate exactly the cost of a year's residence at Oxford for an undergraduate at Christ Church, as this varies with style of living and to some extent with the subjects studied. The Board of Education estimate of 225 pounds per annum as a practical minimum, covering vacations and terms, is about correct. Considerable economy has to be used to keep expenses as low as this; but it can be done and is done by a number of undergraduates without undue stinting. Of course if an undergraduate travels or has to pay board and lodging during vacations, the amount would not be sufficient."

Furnished rooms, we were advised, "are assigned by the Senior Censor. The rent, including hire of furniture, the use of household requisites, carpet beating, chimney sweeping, etc., varies between six and seventeen pounds terminally. Scouts, waiters, messengers, and other college servants are paid by the Steward, but the House recognizes a terminal gratuity from each undergraduate of one pound to the scout and ten shillings to the scout's assistant. The House also recognizes a gratuity of one shilling to a college messenger when employed by an undergraduate to carry luggage to and from his rooms at the beginning and end of term."

The rest of the information was about the Junior Common Room, the Amalgamated College (Sports) Clubs, and no car during one's first year. Average total college bills incurred by undergraduates resident in Christ Church in 1938 amounted to 188 pounds, 11 shillings, and 11 pence. It all sounded good and wonderful. Father said he would allow me 300 pounds in my first year. The Senior Censor allotted me a pleasant inexpensive attic suite, bedroom and living room, on Killcannon, the staircase between Peckwater Quad and Tom Quad.

I could hardly wait for the beginning of term in October. We had our summer holiday driving through England. The "gathering storm" was on hold till Hitler's invasion of Poland. Not the ultimata from Great Britain and France, nor the last-minute attempts of Sir Nevile Henderson, Britain's ambassador in Berlin, to avoid war were of any avail. Hostilities broke out on September 3. Moments later the first air raid sirens wailed. I offered my services to dig trenches in Hyde Park. They were graciously accepted by His Majesty's Secretary of State for War, Leslie Hore-Belisha. Antiaircraft balloons floated over the park. Windows and car headlights were blacked out, gas masks issued, the Territorial Army called up.

Father's business in the City had come to almost a complete standstill. He had been working on a deal which would have made him enough money to keep us safe for years. He had a mandate from the Petschek family who had come to England from Czechoslovakia after the Sudeten crisis, to sell their stock in the Skoda Works, the Czech armaments maker. The Germans were the logical buyers. It was not a transaction that would endear him to the British. Its implications would have been misunderstood even if de facto the stock sale would make no difference. The Germans had already seized Skoda, but the transaction would legitimize the ownership.

To buy the stock they were willing to part with scarce foreign exchange. For the Petscheks it would have meant receiving money outside Germany. The outbreak of hostilities prevented the deal from closing, and just as well. Surely it would have caused Father trouble in the end. Speaking of trouble, he was on a bus with his Skoda files, but when he got off, he left his briefcase behind. Frantic, he took a taxi, caught the bus and retrieved his documents. At the lost property office if they had had their wits about them they would have called in MI-5 or Scotland Yard. The episode so scared father that he thought he'd better get rid of anything incriminating, such as his World War I sword which might have given the impression he was a Prussian militarist. Under cover of night we dug a hole in Lansdowne Square behind our flat and buried the sword. Decades later I was dining with the brother of my friend Ian Fraser, head of Lazard Brothers in London. He lived on the same square, was intrigued by my story and with a metal detector looked for Father's sword. He spent hours unsuccessfully searching for it. In the intervening fifty years it must have rusted away. In a similar vein, years earlier in Hamburg, Father and I had dumped his World War I revolver off the Krugkoppel Bridge into the Alster because he was afraid of the German police. This time it was the English police. It was tough to be a German Jew in the 1930s; baptism was no help.

Soon after war broke out Father's old business friend Heinrich Sonnenberg asked him to keep an eye on his British interests. Sonnenberg, self-made and very successful, manufactured and dealt in machine tools. In the 1920s he had become wealthy, in part by exporting machine tools to Russia. Fellow German refugees ran his British subsidiary, SOAG, but Sonnenberg wanted someone not involved in the day-to-day operations and squabbles to report to him independently. Sonnenberg was leaving the Netherlands where he ran substantial operations for the United States which made it all the more important to him to have Father, whom he trusted, become his "eyes and ears" in Britain.

He paid him a good salary. Father spent several hours most days at SOAG, somewhat to the annoyance of the full-time management. First and foremost he succeeded in keeping SOAG away from the enemy property custodian. Even though Sonnenberg was a Dutch subject, SOAG had become in danger of confiscation under the Trading with the Enemy Act and exclusion from defense contracts.

Father had become friends with Major General Sir Edward Spears, a prominent Conservative member of Parliament. Spears, the senior Anglo-French army liaison officer in the First World War, was close to Winston Churchill. His American wife, Mary Borden, a popular novelist, was a member of the Chicago Borden milk family. Father got Spears on the SOAG board. From that day SOAG was left alone by the authorities. Spears also saved Father from internment. In the spring of 1940 the British interned all male "enemy aliens." A policeman from our neighboring Notting Hill Gate station appeared one morning with a warrant to say he would be back the following day to take Father away. Spears managed to intervene in time and Father remained unmolested. Instead, they interned me, but thanks to Spears and Sonnenberg we were financially secure throughout the war.

The outbreak of war did not prevent me from going up to Oxford. I completed one academic year before I was interned in May of 1940. It was a wonderful year. I read Modern Greats, commonly known as PPE — Politics, Philosophy, and Economics. As luck would have it my Economics tutor, until he went full-time into the government, was Roy Harrod, Keynes's closest disciple. Harrod was a great teacher and a civilized, fascinating man. The Shakespearean actor Forbes-Robertson was his grandfather. His wife, Bella, was beautiful, brainy and, reputedly, flighty. For Harrod there was no question that the English way of life represented the best that Western civilization had produced and that it all came together, aesthetically and intellectually, unrivaled elsewhere in the world, at Oxford and Cambridge. For a man of his background and convictions, liberal and yet conservative, there was no doubt Hitler had to be fought. He had academic and personal ties with the United States and did not much care for the Continent, let alone Germany. He was sympathetic to the reasons that had brought us to Britain. He disliked some of the refugee scholars who were critical of his cherished English ways and found fault with its system. After the war he feuded increasingly bitterly with his fellow economist at

Balliol College, Tommy (later Lord) Balogh and, to not quite the same degree, Nicky (later Lord) Kaldor at Cambridge. Aside from disliking them personally he may have minded that his own academic maturing ended with Keynes. They were post-Keynesians who thought they improved on Keynes. He considered they diminished his legacy.

When I was Harrod's pupil he had recently completed a book on the workings of the Exchange Equalization Account, a fund managed by the Bank of England to stabilize the pound sterling–French franc exchange rate without increasing the money supply. He liked my interest in the subject and that I understood how, by sterilizing the newly created funds, it worked successfully. In prewar days I would have had him to myself at the weekly tutorial, but some dons had already gone off to the war and we had to double up. Generally I shared Harrod with Ivor Canning, a linear Canning descendant, in whom, alas, little of his forebear's mind had survived. However, it pleased me to share "tutes" with a Canning. He was killed in the war serving in the Guards. My other fellow pupil was Nigel Cayzer, from a titled family of more recent vintage. The Cayzers were leading Scottish shipowners. Nigel was not very bright academically but had a quick, almost sly, brain. He, too, was killed serving in the Scots Guards. He would have become an outstanding businessman. After the war I shared Harrod tutorials with Francis Dashwood, later Sir Francis, a descendant of the West Wycombe Hellfire Club family, no conventional academic brain, but brilliantly successful in life.

I remember less of my tutors in Politics or Philosophy. Patrick Gordon-Walker supervised the former. He was mostly away on government war work. My Philosophy tutor was the great Gilbert Ryle, one of Oxford's best minds. Ryle, a bachelor, was tall, athletic, and balding. He too joined the Guards. I had him again after the war. He was an incessant pipe smoker. With a flick of the wrist he cleared the spittle from his pipe into the fireplace where it sizzled a moment. He was a noted oarsman and coached the Christ Church boats from his bicycle on the towpath. I stroked the Second Eight. Both in Torpids, the winter race, and Eights Week in the summer, we did well.

After Harrod left Oxford to work full-time with Keynes at the

Treasury, I was again fortunate with my Economics tutor. Ian Bowen, an Australian by birth, a Fellow of All Souls and a senior member of the Oxford Institute of Statistics was helpful and friendly in every way. He was a good teacher. The Institute was of recent origin but highly regarded. A number of German émigrés were on the staff, including the economist Fritz Schumacher, who later became famous for his book, *Small is Beautiful*. Some of the Institute were soon to become fellow internees of mine. They made internment more interesting by their lectures behind barbed wire.

My rooms, in the attic of Killcannon staircase, were a long, well-proportioned living room and a small bedroom. There was, of course, no running water in those days. The nearest toilet and bathrooms were several staircases away in Peckwater Quad. My scout — Willis — woke me in the morning with a pitcher of hot water and a pot of tea. He lit the living room coal fire and emptied the chamber pot. Once the war got fully under way many of the scouts joined the armed forces and were replaced by women; some were the wives of scouts who had gone off to serve.

The prewar custom of entertaining at lunch or dinner in one's rooms was curtailed and later in the war stopped altogether. I had a few parties. One would consult with the chef, who suggested the menu and provided the staff for an elegant and excellent meal. How I loved it, so different from Tonbridge or the thickly accented refugees at my parents' home. I found friends among the numerous Etonians and Wykehamists at the House. Everyone seemed friendly but I can't believe I was accepted fully — and why on earth should I have been — by the *jeunesse dorée* whose families had been at the House for generations, or undergraduates who were intellectually my superiors. To be Jewish was no longer a major negative at Oxford in my time. Anyhow, I was an Anglican. The architecture, the music, the whole setting, made religion pleasurable. The times when Jews were to all intents and purposes excluded from the university, and especially the more exclusive colleges, were within living memory but so were the times when Catholics or the newly rich Victorians did not find a ready welcome.

My friends knew, of course, that we had come to England because we were Jewish. There were many Jewish undergraduates and faculty at

Oxford, but they were rarely devout. Jewish families to whom strict religious observances mattered tended to send their children to Manchester,
Glasgow, or London. Prewar Oxbridge was still largely about teaching the
humanities to upper-class Anglicans. Rutherford made science at Cambridge
famous. There were medical schools at both universities, but the majority
of doctors were trained at the teaching hospitals. Future solicitors more
often than not went straight from school to be articled to a law firm. The
merchant banking families and other City blue bloods gave their sons a
varsity education, but for commercial banking or general business there
was no need to have attended any university, let alone the senior ones.
Oxbridge was almost obligatory for the home and the Indian civil service,
to teach at the better public schools, for the bar, or politics. It greatly
helped preferment in the Church of England.

At the House there were some Jews. We had the Mond brothers,
grandsons of the Imperial Chemical Industries founder, and other members of establishment Jewish families, for instance the Marquess of
Reading's kin. In prewar England, not too different from Western Europe
or the United States, there still was a wide gulf between Jewish families
that had been settled for generations and the more recent immigrants
from Eastern Europe or Russia. Since the war these families have gained
the "upper hand" over the establishment Jews, who have gradually lost
their Jewish identification, married non-Jewish spouses, and often lost their
intellectual vitality and business drive.

At postwar Oxbridge, family background counted for little, scholastic
grades for almost everything. Government-financed rather than privately
paid tuition is at the core of university education. The grammar school
boy has a better chance to be admitted than his academic equal from
Eton.

I was fortunate to catch the end of an era. Prewar Christ Church was
the most sought-after Oxford college. It was beautiful. It was ancient. It
was Oxford's wealthiest college. The library had a world-famous collection of Old Master drawings and paintings. Cardinal Wolsey founded it as
Cardinal College in 1525. In 1532 it became King Henry VIII's College
and in 1546 Christ Church with its own Cathedral. Because of the links

with the Church it was known in Latin as *Aedes Christi*, the House of Christ, and the lay part plainly became the "House." Its dining hall is the grandest and most beautiful in Oxford. The portraits there attest to its history: Holbein's famous portrait of Henry VIII, portraits of Cardinal Wolsey, and of five prime ministers — Liverpool, Canning, Peel, Gladstone, and Salisbury. There are paintings of four viceroys of India — Wellesley, Minto, Elgin, and Dufferin — as well as of many other major figures from Britain's past. In my time portraits were added of Lord Halifax and Anthony Eden.

John Locke and John Ruskin had been at the House, as had William Penn, Arlington, Charles Wesley, Charles and Thomas Pinckney, who emigrated to South Carolina, Charles Pusey, and the Earl of Shaftesbury. The Earl of Rosebery vowed while at the House he would marry an heiress (a Rothschild, as it turned out), win the derby, and become prime minister before the age of fifty. He did all three.

For almost half of the nineteenth century H. G. Liddell (1855–1891) was Dean. He was the father of Alice, made famous in Wonderland by C. L. Dodgson, alias Lewis Carroll, a Student (fellow) of the House from 1852 to 1898. In my time, R. H. Dundas lived on Dodgson's staircase. He was moral tutor to more than one generation of House undergraduates. "D," a lifelong bachelor, was a Scot of impeccable antecedents. He went to Eton where Keynes was a contemporary and among his closest friends. In the First World War he saw service as an officer in the Black Watch and was deemed to look particularly handsome in his kilt. He was a first-class scholar, grounded in ancient history. His life revolved around the House, his Scottish family, and the cultivation of the well connected. He was widely traveled and spent his vacations with his sisters. He was known for nude bathing with undergraduates at Parson's Pleasure, a tributary of the Isis. He took it upon himself to enlighten successive generations of undergraduates about the facts of life, a session I contrived to avoid.

Given a modicum of intelligence, family connections helped a great deal with admission to this glorious past. There were few ordinary mortals such as myself, neither academically nor by lineage distinguished. I made friends. My cousin Denis Howard was there, reading chemistry with the family pharmaceutical business in mind. Karl Neumann, a fellow refugee whose family we knew, was reading law. I became good friends with Adam Stainton, a Wykehamist, and John Armistead. They shared a two-bedroom and living room suite, one floor up on Peckwater Quad. The Armisteads were solicitors in Yorkshire. Adam Stainton's father was First Treasury counsel responsible for drafting financial legislation. Adam's father, Sir John Stainton, had also gone to Winchester and Christ Church. Lady Stainton was a Dewar; her father had founded the Distillers Company. The Staintons were "establishment," civilized, well-educated, unostentatious, very well-to-do. Another friend was Hugh Arnott, an Etonian from Gloucestershire. The family had a lovely house where the Wye joins the Severn. Hugh's father ran a steel mill nearby, across the border in Wales.

As the months went by it became increasingly obvious that our near-peace existence could not last much longer. My English contemporaries were beginning to think about military service. I had no clear notion what would become of me. At Eastertime 1940, Adam Stainton and I volunteered to help the war effort working on a farm in the West of England. It belonged to Rolf Gardiner, member of an old landowning Wessex family. He had a beautiful estate at Fontnell Magma in Dorset. He turned out to be a wooly sympathizer of the Germans, full of loony Nordic fiddle-faddle. We had to dance around a maypole, he in lederhosen, and sing old Wessex wassails. One with a pretty melody went something like: "Back and side, go bare, go bare, but belly, God send thee good ale enough, whether it be new or old." I enjoyed the work at the farm. Soon after we left, Gardiner was arrested under the wartime emergency regulations. The police claimed he was clearing fields as landing strips for German gliders. He remained behind bars for some years but was released before 1945. After the war I read letters of his to the London *Times* on agricultural subjects. They sounded perfectly sensible.

Not only Gardiner's, but alas my own days at liberty were numbered. After the German landings at Narvik in Norway, but even more with the invasion on May 10 of the Low Countries, the "phony war" ended. Neville Chamberlain resigned as prime minister. Churchill, who was by then back in the Cabinet in his World War I post as First Lord of the Admiralty, succeeded him. In the last days of May and the first in June the British Expeditionary Force was evacuated from Continental Europe on the beaches of Dunkirk. The Battle of Britain was fought over the South Coast of England. Internment of enemy aliens gathered momentum. I was arrested in the first days of June. It came to me as a terrible shock. During the year at Oxford I had become Anglicized, and I could not believe what was being done. The police took me from Lansdowne Road one morning and in a police van sent me to Kempton Park racecourse, where those rounded up, who were mostly German refugees, became the prisoners of a Guards regiment which had just returned from Dunkirk. Their attitude left a good deal to be desired. To have us as prisoners was better than nobody. There was a "reception committee" organized by fellow internees, headed by the half-Jewish Austrian Baron Pirquet, whom the British deemed well qualified because he had been *chef de réception* at the Dorchester Hotel.

After a few days at Kempton Park we were loaded on a train to an unknown destination. The journey took us through London. The train happened to come to a halt near Olympia in Kensington, a few hundred yards from Lansdowne Road and my parents. It seemed to stop forever. I found myself crying with homesickness. They had no right to do this to me. I had committed no crime. I wanted to get out of that damned railway carriage, make a dash for it, and run home. But there were all these armed guards, and wouldn't they see me and shoot? Of course, I did not make that dash but cried more when the train resumed its journey.

The vast majority of the internees were German and Austrian Jewish refugees. A few were "real" Germans — for instance, Captain von Rintelen, a World War I naval veteran. Rintelen had an interesting history. Before the United States entered the First World War, he served as a German naval officer with his embassy in America. His assignment was to prevent the shipment of war supplies to the Allies. His superior was Franz von Papen, military attaché at the Washington embassy. On Papen's orders Rintelen sabotaged Allied shipping destined for Europe. He incapacitated freighters by attaching explosives to their steering mechanism, which went off on the high seas, and left them to be torpedoed by German

U-boats. This went on successfully for a while until Papen lost incriminating documents which gave away Rintelen and led to Papen's expulsion
from his post in Washington. Rintelen thought he had managed a successful getaway with a forged passport on a neutral vessel, but the British
naval blockade, on account of Papen's indiscretions were tipped off; they
searched the vessel and arrested Rintelen who was interned in Britain for
the rest of the war.

Between the wars Rintelen made a living lecturing on his exploits at
British schools, including Tonbridge. In his book *The Dark Invader,* he
blamed Papen for being found out, which Papen in his autobiography
contradicted. Rintelen was anything but a Nazi. In 1939 he had no desire
to return to Germany. When the refugees were released the British authorities did not give Rintelen the benefit of the doubt, even though a
number of influential people vouched for him. Thus he spent two wars
behind barbed wire at His Majesty's pleasure. We saw quite a bit of each
other in the Huyton camp. I liked and trusted him. Papen, who was considered a dilettante cavalry officer, eventually became Germany's last
chancellor before the Nazis. He served later as Hitler's vice chancellor. He
was charged with war crimes at the Nuremberg trial but came off lightly
with a prison sentence.

In many respects internment was an interesting time. There were lectures. Several internees were university professors. Some I had known at
the Oxford Institute of Statistics. Some had not yet managed to make a
connection with an English university or were caught while waiting for a
visa to the United States. There was a large group of Cambridge undergraduates. Charles and Peter Cahn were with me, sons of my parents'
friends Heinz and Hilde Cahn. I saw a lot of my mother's cousin Franz
Fuerth. He had a little money and generously shared with me some of the
extra comforts he procured from our guards. For a while I worked in the
orderly room of Major Brewer, our camp commandant. I was on the look-
out for potential clients for father. I found one, Mundi Goldberger, a well-
to-do timber merchant, originally from Poland. He had been interned but
not his father who came to G. Eberstadt for investment advice. Ronnie

Grierson, then still Griessmann, was a fellow internee. Our paths were to cross many more times.

Huyton was one of several internment camps in various parts of the country. It was a middle-class housing estate of semidetached villas, still under construction. The army had requisitioned it and surrounded it with a barbed wire fence, which was patrolled, though not very effectively, by our guards. Civilians from the neighborhood were able to get to the fence and stare at us. Since our mail was censored and slow we used the neighbors to smuggle out letters, which they willingly did for a small tip. We were allowed to listen to the radio. There was a limited supply of greatly sought-after newspapers. The conversation and thinking centered on how to obtain our release. For me internment was not as hard as it was for men with wives and children, especially if their families were in cities that suffered from German air raids. How were their families surviving financially? Where were they? Had they been evacuated? There was no possibility of telephoning.

Nearly everyone thought they knew someone who had influence to obtain their release, but in the first months hardly any internee was freed. There were a few releases on compassionate and medical grounds. The Battle of Britain was being fought. Cheers went up in our camp after every news bulletin reporting the number of enemy planes shot down over the Channel or the English South Coast. Rumors were rife. Some turned out to be correct, especially the stories that we were to be deported overseas. The Home Office wanted to get as many internees as possible out of Britain by shipping them to Australia and Canada. Some boats were torpedoed. The horror voyage of the *Andorra Star* to Australia has been the subject of books. Vera's uncle Stephan von Kuffner was on that voyage. He had been a lifelong ardent Anglophile, like his father well known in British alpine circles, but he never forgave the British for the way he was treated. He refused ever to speak about his experience. It had never occurred to him he might be interned like everyone else. He was sure his British friends would protect him.

Each time a convoy was put together a list appeared of who was to be shipped overseas. Some, perhaps the more farsighted, did not mind being sent from war-endangered Britain to Canada or Australia, but the married men did not want to be separated from their families. The Cambridge University contingent was deported en bloc. My Cahn friends were encouraged by their parents to leave — they have lived in Canada ever since. I was determined not to be sent away. I wanted to be released in England and join the army. My name was on the list of what proved to be the final shipment. Before the roll call, I slipped away and for twenty-four hours hid under a collapsed tent. When I emerged the others had gone. It could have meant trouble, but Major Brewer decided not to pursue the matter.

The English behaved atrociously — and stupidly — over internment, but fortunately not all of them. Articles started to be written in the press; influential voices spoke up on our behalf in Parliament. The *Times* almost daily had letters to the editor calling for our release. Ultimately our fate was reversed in the House of Commons. The cause was championed by several M. P.'s. None were more eloquent than Eleanor Rathbone and Colonel Josiah Wedgewood. Both were the British at their best. Rathbone came from a liberal, well-to-do background in Liverpool. On many issues she had introduced legislation that sided with the underdog. During the Depression, for instance, she prevented insurance companies from seizing the equity in policies if the unemployed were unable to keep up their premiums. I have come across Rathbones since the war and have difficulties holding back a tear when I tell them of my gratitude to their kinswoman. The Association of Jewish Refugees in England has named one of its old age homes after her. Josiah Wedgewood was a Quaker. Though in appearance the caricature of a British army colonel, there was nothing Blimpish about him. It did not prove difficult to convince Churchill of the idiocy of the internment policy. Two of his closest advisers, Professor Lindeman, who had been my sponsor at Oxford, and Brendan Bracken, Churchill's minister of information, were on "our" side.

Once the wheels to release us were set in motion, the process worked quickly. The spirit of the parliamentary debates and the tenor of the press did much to restore my faith in the fair-mindedness of the English. Nor had my English friends abandoned me. Still, since internment I have felt different about the English. No doubt it was my fault that I had foolishly fancied that a few years at public school and a year at Oxford had made me part of them. Though not yet nineteen years old, I had been ostracized twice. "Don't you know there is a war on" was the flippant or irritated response to complaints about wartime inconveniences, including internment. First things first. England's survival hung in the balance. The rights and wrongs of internment were hardly top priority. Dunkirk, the surrender of France, the air raids were enough to scare any nation. Yet after a while, time and psychic energy were found to reverse this xenophobic hysterical spy mania.

I badly wanted to join the fight against Germany. Even if the Pioneer Corps was not the Grenadier Guards I was relieved to put internment behind me. I was discharged from Huyton after three months and enlisted in Ilfracome, Devonshire, where I received the King's shilling. We were given rudimentary military drill instructions at the Pioneer Corps training depot. Mainly elderly ex-regular army British officers and NCOs brought out of retirement staffed it. We were in theory a combatant unit. We were equipped with World War I Lee-Enfield rifles but never had much rifle practice. We did, however, drill in earnest: Slope, Shoulder, and Present Arms; Attention and At Ease; Slow and Quick March; by the Right and by the Left; formed four deep and two deep. We learnt to salute, shine brass, to "blanco" belts, blacken boots, fold blankets, and get used to military life. Our official name was the AMPC — Auxiliary Military Pioneer Corps. Auxiliary we were, but I am not so sure about the Military. Later in the war the name got elevated to Pioneer Corps, and after the war became the Royal Pioneers.

The weeks in Ilfracombe were pleasant, especially after internment. The Devon coast in summer is lovely. Despite rationing, food was still plentiful. My parents came to visit. They quite liked the idea of a soldier son, especially one never likely to fire a shot in earnest. With food and lodgings provided by the army and my pay supplemented with a few shillings a week from home I lived quite comfortably.

After training I was sent to 220 Company, commanded by a Major

Holdsworth. I don't recall his pre–Pioneer Corps military past. He was elderly, sluggish, but not unpleasant. I am sure he did not know what to make of us, three hundred aliens, mainly German or Austrian Jewish refugees, plus a handful of French foreign legionnaires. The foreign legion had been part of the unsuccessful Allied expeditionary force at Narvik in Norway. They were evacuated to England with the other Allied troops. They were given the choice of joining the Pioneer Corps or repatriation to France, which by then had surrendered to the Germans. Some of the legionnaires who stayed with us had criminal records which even by French foreign legion standards were impressive. Back in France they would have been demobilized and exposed as civilians to criminal prosecution in the French courts. I was on guard duty with one, Christmas 1940. His name was Delrez. I don't recall his life story, but we ended up crying on each other's shoulders. Another I happened to meet on the Piccadilly tube after the war. He rolled up his shirtsleeve. There were wristwatches on his arm up to his elbow. He explained he cut them off people's wrists, and did I want to buy one. Yet another had been a lion tamer at the German Hagenbeck circus and claimed he got into political trouble with the Nazis and joined the foreign legion. Like it or not, he'd strip to the waist and show the scars where he had been mauled by lions over the years. At least two became prominent Communist politicians in postwar France.

Our company was stationed at Lydbrook, in Gloucestershire, on the Welsh border, in the Forest of Dean. Our job was to do the unskilled forestry and sawmill work for a company of New Zealand foresters attached to the Royal Engineers. In some respects the year at Lydbrook — and this memory is not glorified by the mist of time — was interesting and satisfying. I enjoyed working in the woods and at the mill. It was physically demanding, but at the end of the day you knew you had accomplished something measurable. We cut oaks planted one hundred and twenty-five years earlier to replace trees felled to build Nelson's fleet in the Napoleonic Wars. Our oaks fullfilled a less glorious function — they became railroad sleepers (railroad ties in American English). The New Zealanders felled the trees and we stripped the branches. In the mill we cut the logs with a cross saw. These were huge logs, especially at the lower end. Some took over a thousand strokes back and forth. Once halfway, the cuts needed wedging, or else the saw jammed, but otherwise we got through a log without pausing. It was a welcome moment for a breather when our cross saw needed sharpening.

The cut logs were levered on the sawmill bench with a cant-hook, a tool I had occasion to use a few years ago and still knew to handle. On the bench the New Zealanders took over. The huge, machine-driven blades screeched and sliced the logs like butter. Now and then we staged a little industrial sabotage. The sawdust went into a pit under the rotary blade. An elderly Pioneer, Dr. Rosenzweig, in better days a judge in his native Königsberg in East Prussia, shoveled the dust out of the pit. This was strenuous work. When he got tired he touched the rotor blade "accidentally" with his shovel and it took the toolsmith maybe half an hour to reset the teeth. The finished product — the sleepers — were trucked to the local railway station and sent on their way.

I teamed up generally with Kurt Jellinek, an Austrian who had been at Oxford. Before internment he was picked up by the Oxford police for driving a car, which enemy aliens were not allowed to do. Kurt considered his talents wasted in the Pioneer Corps. He bitterly resented the work that I really quite enjoyed. As it turned out he was not well, and he died of tuberculosis in 1943 or 1944. He and I rented a room from a Lydbrook villager in which we spent our evenings, he mainly reading, before we had to be back by ten P.M. in our Nissen hut for the night. After a while Kurt's younger brother Ernest joined 220 Company. He eventually became a tank corps officer and was severely wounded at the end of the Western European campaign. After the war he became a respected psychiatrist in Edinburgh and married a Scot. Their home is straight out of Biedermeier Vienna. Its lovely furniture was the only valuable asset his parents had brought out of Austria. The father had been a professor in Vienna who reached England moments before the war. He eked out his existence on the periphery of the Oxford academic world and lived in a tiny basement flat, a broken man. My mother knew the family and approved of my friendship with them. Like many upper-crust Viennese Jews, the Jellineks were baptized. Father and sons had gone to the Schotten Gymnasium, where the classics were taught to upper-class Vienna.

What a mixed bag we were! There was Sergeant Hertz from Berlin, who had started his English life at Kitchener Camp in southern England, where refugees who had nowhere else to live were housed. He had gone from there to enlist in the Pioneer Corps as soon as war broke out, and hence had avoided internment. Hertz had been an infantry officer in the German army in the first war. He entertained, but did not amuse, his British fellow sergeants with World War I stories, in particular one of a British officer he shot in the head after he had taken him prisoner.

There were the brothers Murai, Austro-Hungarian intellectuals who could not contain their rage at doing manual labor unbefitting who they were. Major Holdsworth in his earlier career had commanded a company of native troops in Africa. At a morning roll call one of the Murai brothers went berserk, broke ranks, pretended to take command and ordered, "Matabele, attention! Quick march!" etc., etc. There was a terrible fuss. Murai had become convinced Holdsworth considered us no different from the Matabeles of his colonial days.

Ronnie Grierson, then Griessmann and now Sir Ronald had a hard time adapting after Balliol College to the Forest of Dean. Later he became a paratrooper and rose to be a colonel. Captain Beaumont, a Conservative M.P., was the patron saint of the Griessmann family in those days, the way General Spears had been to ours.

Kurt Jellinek and I were good friends with Ulrich Holländer, who had arrived from Berlin penniless moments before the war, very bright and very neurotic, a nephew of the composer Felix Holländer. From the Pioneers he went to be commissioned in the Intelligence Corps as Michael Thomas. In the occupation army he became a confidant of Konrad Adenauer and other leading figures in postwar Germany. He was so afraid he'd return to England a nobody without prospects that he had himself demobilized in Germany where he made sufficient connections while in military government to build up a prosperous business career. His autobiography *Deutschland England über Alles* is a good read. It captures complicated confusing times.

The seeds for the Marlborough Gallery, one of the outstanding post-war success stories in the art world, were sown in the Forest of Dean. Two of my fellow Pioneers were Hansi Fischer and Frank Levai, subsequently Lloyd. The two had a common bond in that both had left non-Jewish wives and children behind in their native countries. Fischer, a cultured Austrian, had been an antiquarian in Vienna, Levai a successful trader in etheric oils in Hungary (or was it Romania?). Fischer looked and was lethargic, a scholar, but behind a scholarly facade, shrewder and tougher than Lloyd. The latter had bounce, joie de vivre, a sense of humor sufficient to forgive him — almost — for his alleged calumnies in the art world. Fischer had the knowledge, Lloyd the business acumen and a little capital. As soon as the war ended they planned on opening an art gallery. Fischer hated shoveling sawdust and got himself invalided out of the army. He spent the rest of the war as the *Financial Times* librarian. Lloyd stayed in the army; eventually he became a tank corps mechanic. In 220 Company he was the invaluable procurer of supplementary rations. Each morning he bought up the entire output of "Bath" penny buns from a nearby bakery. He sold them to us for twopence, a profit margin surely even the Marlborough would later find satisfactory. He never once touched a saw or shovel.

Few of us had much, if any, money aside from our army pay. For the younger and unmarried it sufficed quite nicely, but many were older with wives and children. For them it was financially hard. Many wives found work, often as domestics. For most of the older men a labor battalion was a comedown from a more glorious past. There were anxieties of every kind. In 1940 and 1941 it was not exactly obvious that Hitler would be beaten — and what of us, if the war were lost? Optimism is not a Jewish trait. There were the air raids, especially on London where many of us had families. Few had escaped from the Nazis with their entire families and all too appropriately fretted over their fate. Some had started businesses and were trying to run them from Lydbrook. We listened to the BBC nine P.M. news, which opened with Big Ben and closed with "God Save the King." Sunday nights it ended with the national anthems of all our Allies. We were avid newspaper readers and usually managed to have the *Times* delivered by lunchtime into the woods or the sawmill. Kurt Jellineck did the *Times* crossword over lunch. Our British officers and NCOs must have thought us very odd, but on the whole they tolerated our ways. I don't think we felt cutting trees was crucial to the war effort, but we were pretty good workers and did not cause much trouble to our superiors. Our cooks were excellent. They turned our rations into quite good continental cuisine. The officers had never eaten better, which doubtless helped to keep them agreeable. We took turns at kitchen fatigue. Peeling potatoes was less arduous than cutting trees, especially in bad weather.

The Forest of Dean was beautiful but daunting, remote from the world. Lydbrook was the opposite of beautiful. The village ran the length of a narrow, dark, and damp valley. One end was Chapel, the other Church. The two were fiercely hostile. Many worked in nearby collieries. Some were away in the armed forces. The women were plain, to put it charitably. There were few romantic involvements, even if we seemed intriguing because different. The company tailor, a skinny little Pole named Gleicher, claimed numerous conquests. "I not work in de woods, I work in de fuzz," he told us. I, for one, had far too little sex. On one occasion I invited a girlfriend from London for the weekend. She arrived with her mother, who made it clear my intentions had better be honorable.

The nearby Wye Valley was famous for its beauty and fishing. There were pretty restaurants with good food. Gloucester on the river Severn, an old cathedral town, was a little farther away but at weekends we were bused there in company transport. I came to know the cathedral well, if only for want of more exciting entertainment. There were Tudor-timbered restaurants and pubs, but too few of the opposite sex. Occasionally I hitchhiked to Chepstow, a little town where the Wye flows into the Severn. The parents of my Oxford friend Hugh Arnott lived there, as did Mrs. Arnott's younger sister. They had had hopes I might befriend her, but no luck. Just before the war she had been sent to India to find a suitable mate from among the British Raj. Notwithstanding the shortage of British women she returned, still single. Need more be said?

I quite often had leave over a weekend, and sometimes a whole week. By then my parents had moved to Cobham in Surrey, where they had a modest but pleasantly situated house. It was big enough for most of our Hamburg furniture, which made it home for me. It had a little land that my parents turned into a pretty flower and vegetable garden. Father took up gardening. He liked it, all part of becoming Anglicized; Mother had always enjoyed it. Their life was not bad. They had sufficient income and, anyhow, there was not much to spend it on in the war. Father had a pleasant ten-minute morning walk to the Cobham station. The trains went every half hour to Waterloo Station, which took 40 minutes, and from there the tube to the City was another 15 minutes. At least once a week Mother came up to London, lunched with friends, and met Father for an early dinner, a movie, or theatre.

Father's office was at Daniel Castello and Co., a small, wealthy London Stock Exchange firm. His cousin Alfred Marx was associated with Castello. Business was extremely quiet. They read the paper and discussed the war. The news was not good. Singapore surrendered. Major battleships were sunk. The Germans were winning the U-boat war. There were occasional commando forays on the French coast, more to boost morale on the home front than to gain anything of military significance. In the Middle East the Eighth Army moved back and forth; several commanders were relieved of their posts, including Wavell. Montgomery had not yet made his mark. The hopeful news was the German attack on Russia, even if initially there was one German victory after another.

No wonder the City was deadly quiet. There was little reason to trade. Internationally, London was cut off from the Continent by the war and from Wall Street by exchange controls. Father had a few friends such as David Sachs at Guinness Mahon and Eric Körner at New Trading (later S. G. Warburg), who were good at spotting where the distortions of wartime controls created the occasional market opportunity. His faithful little band of clients and friends such as Heinz Cahn and Bernd Heymann, the "Stationmaster," were usually game for a little flutter. His main activity was looking after Henry Sonnenberg's SOAG; years later Sonnenberg told me Father had rendered him great service in those days. Once America was in the war and an ultimate Allied victory became a realistic expectation, the market developed innumerable scenarios as to what peace might do for different stocks and sectors of the economy. By then Father had come to know a high official in the Belgian trade union movement who had brought the Belgian North Sea fishing fleet to England in 1940. He had the very substantial liquid assets of the unions and the fishing fleet to invest. By rights they should have stayed in bonds, but their timing to be in stocks was good. He was a fascinating man and became a major client. Father took me to lunch with him in 1944 after I was wounded.

When home on leave I greatly enjoyed hearing about my parents' doings. Mother provided good if tense meals. For her to cook and serve was an emotional strain on all. None of us were as helpful as we should have been, for which somewhat belated but sincere apologies. Sundays were hospitable. Relatives and friends who eked out an existence in modest lodgings, usually in North London, came to Cobham for lunch, a walk, or the afternoon on a deck chair in the garden. No guests were allowed when I was home; they wanted me all to themselves! Most times Bridget was away at school. Later, when she was in the WAAFs, we managed some leaves together. Mother's uppermost concern was for her parents in German-occupied Holland. She heard from them fairly regularly. They wrote to Willy Dreyfus in Switzerland who forwarded their letters. They were better than nothing but left much unsaid for fear of the German censor. She blamed herself — unfairly — that they had not left Holland. She had gone along with their reluctance to uproot themselves yet again, especially because life initially, even under the German occupation, was not too bad for them.

I remained a private, later a lance corporal, in Lydbrook until in the spring of 1942, when the War Office decided aliens could become officers. I applied and was accepted, for all the wrong reasons. It did not qualify me one bit to command polyglot middle-aged or elderly Pioneers, that I had had an English education, had attended the Officers' Training Corps as a schoolboy, and was fluent in the language. But it might make me a conventionally more agreeable member of an English officers' mess. For the typical German-Jewish refugee, who had seen better days and was now shoveling sawdust or working in a stone quarry, I can't have been an easy pill to swallow. Would the ex-lawyer have found it easier to take orders from a fellow ex-lawyer or banker? Probably not; they would have felt, why him, and not me?

The British were the most readily accepted, but a shortage of British officers, even for a corps as lowly as the Pioneers, was developing, and that was one of the reasons for accepting aliens for commissions. Obviously I was delighted to be promoted, notwithstanding my reservations. For three months I trained at an OCTU, an Officer Cadet Training Unit, in Lincolnshire. In the *Supplement* to the *London Gazette* dated July 14, 1942 (Exhibit 6 A), I was gazetted as of July 6, 1942, as Second Lt. Walter Albert Eberstadt (serial number 237409), behind Pesi Chichgar (237408), whoever he might have been, and ahead of Rudolf Julius Falck (237410). I knew the latter from Oxford. After he was commissioned he married a quite gorgeous English girl, Pauline. I was an usher at the wedding in a fashionable London church. He was killed a couple of years later as a paratroop officer at Arnhem. For a while I remained in touch with his widow.

Aside from Rudy Falck and myself there were at least half a dozen other aliens, some of whom I knew. We were the first to receive the King's Commission, a week before my twenty-first birthday. Officers had to buy their own dress uniform. I got mine at Bernard Weatherhill on Conduit Street, and it cost £8.10. The Sam Brown belt and shoes came from Peal's and cost extra. I celebrated my birthday with my parents in my brand-new uniform with dinner at the Savoy. Bridget was there. My birthday present was a silver cigarette case with my initials, very appropriate and very English for a twenty-first, even if I never was much of a cigarette smoker. I still have the case. Once in a while it gets polished. How easy it was to pick gifts when smoking was in vogue: Dunhill lighters, cigarette cases, elegant holders for ladies, for men a straight-grain Dunhill pipe. Nor are champagne swizzle sticks fashionable nowadays. What a good present they made.

My first posting as an officer was to 87th Company in the Pioneer Corps, commanded by Major Woodcock, ex-regular army, elderly, white-haired with a military moustache, good-looking and quite charming. He had been in the First World War. Between the wars he had served in India, retired, and was called back to command a Pioneer Corps company.

We were stationed outside Swansea in South Wales. The fires in the docks of Swansea and Cardiff started by German air raids lit the night skies. We worked in a stone quarry, inland near Lannelly. I worked at least as hard as the men, even if I did not have to. It was the best way to get them to work harder. Quarrying stone is not much fun, especially in bad weather. Each rock had to be pitched into a lorry. Accidents were frequent. Major Woodcock came out to inspect our work, in jodphurs and polished riding boots, leaning on an officer's ash walking cane, monocle in one eye. We drove in open lorries at least twenty-five miles to work. If it rained we huddled under our groundsheets. Thanks to my exalted status I was spared the open-air ride by sitting with the driver.

Woodcock presided genially at dinner in the officers' mess. I was the only alien officer. I tried my best to have a good rapport with the alien rank and file and not betray their confidences. They felt slighted at the least provocation. Yet, an order was an order, and I could not let them get away with not accepting from me what they accepted from the British officers. It did not work too badly. Every now and then it was possible to help with a few days of extra leave or some other minor favor. One of the men, a Viennese refugee, just before the war had started a chocolate factory with a government subsidy to alleviate unemployment in a so-called depressed area in a nearby South Wales industrial estate. I was able to get him time off occasionally to look after his business. Their specialty was Pischinger torte. Usually he came back with a few for my parents, a great treat and quite illegal, as chocolate was rationed. Another chocolatier was Ackermann, originally from Berlin. He had restarted his business in London, which made it more difficult for him to get away, but it worked sometimes. Ackermann chocolates exist to this day in England and remain a favorite in our family.

Major Woodcock's batman was Hubermann, a middle-aged former Berlin tailor. He often cried on my shoulder about how difficult the Major was. I did not always see it Hubermann's way, but on occasion he had my sympathy. One weekend Woodcock had gone on leave and left his Welsh corgi in Hubermann's care. The next morning Hubermann stormed into my hut and threatened to kill the dog, no matter the consequences.

"What on earth is the matter, Hubermann? Calm down, man." The Major had ordered to have the dog sleep in his hut. But he did not tell Hubermann that he had trained the corgi, perhaps in the ways of the Indian northwest frontier, to crawl under his blanket and work on his genitals. Something had to be done. Hubermann and corgi slept in separate quarters, and the Major never found out that his orders had been disobeyed.

I wish I remembered more about the people or our daily routine in 87th Company. I do remember going to a local pub with some of my fellow officers and getting so drunk that I passed out and was virtually unconscious for twenty-four hours. I also recall windy lovely walks on the South Wales beaches at low tide to collect cockles, smaller than clams, but tastier. The cockle women of South Wales were famous. There are songs about them. They collected bending forward and down. Supposedly local males would enter them from behind while they continued with their cockling.

At one time we were outside Shrewsbury across the way from the Mytton Arms, an agreeable country hotel named after John Mytton, a famous highwayman. I should not and do not complain about my time in the Pioneers. I got to know lovely parts of England. I gained experience in manual labor. I learnt something about handling complicated subordinates, though probably not enough because years later in the Model Roland firm in New York I never managed to get on good terms with my colleagues who were the Wall Street equivalent of the Pioneer Corps. Actually, I did not have a good relationship with them because, unlike my fellow Pioneers, I never liked them particularly.

I came to appreciate Jewishness. I enjoyed and respected what I learnt, not least the humor. I acquired a German-Jewish vocabulary, an eloquent shorthand unlike any other. Not for the last time I had some regrets that I had been raised outside the Jewish tradition. What had we gained living that way? What had we lost? It is comfortable to be part of what you were born into — race, religion, customs, or culture. Traditions are made over generations. You absorb "who is who" with your mother's milk. To be part of the "club" provides a protective shield, a support system even if it is fiendishly competitive and full of intrigue and jealousy.

In present-day America it is possible to be part of the mainstream without giving up on being Jewish. In Germany it was not.

Prejudice is a deplorable but very deep-seated human characteristic ("*Gleich und gleich gesellt sich gern*"). If you demand a level playing field you must be willing to play on that field by the rules and customs of the majority which was there first. In nineteenth-century Europe this included baptism which opened many a coveted door. It was a challenge to be accepted socially and to succeed at work in a non-Jewish world. You had to work harder, learn more, be self-reliant. If it required adopting other traditions, the success in any walk of life made the extra effort worthwhile. Life in the Gentile world was a two-way street. It broadened the Jewish horizon and opened Gentile minds to overcome prejudices, to accept Jews into their world. It led to many interfaith marriages. In the Pioneer Corps I thought a good deal about the "Jewish Question" and came to differ with my grandfather Albert Eberstadt, who thought it best to move away from our origins. Father used to quote an old Latin tag, "*Cuius regio, eius religio*" (In whose land you live, their religion practice).

On with the war! The last year before I transferred to the infantry was spent agreeably at Long Marston in Warwickshire, halfway between Stratford-on-Avon and the Cotswolds. Long Marston was a railroad depot. Loading a railway freight car is strenuous and needs careful planning. Perhaps that is where I learned to use each cubic inch when packing a suitcase or loading a station wagon. We sent military supplies to various seaports from where they were shipped to the Middle East theatre of war.

Off-duty I spent happy hours at Stratford and in the Cotswolds. There was little gasoline for recreational driving and I mostly biked. I saw Shakespearean plays and spent pleasant evenings on the banks of the Avon watching the swans and boats. Ernest Thalmann, who used to work at Dreyfus in Berlin, had rented a lovely house outside Chipping Campden, a typical Cotswold village. Thanks to a relative in Argentina he not only had an Argentine passport but, better still, he and his brother had inherited a good deal of money, which they had wisely kept outside Germany. Thalmann was one of the few émigrés who were comfortably off. He shared the house with his long-standing friend (and, ultimately, wife) Edith Mannheimer, her nice but impecunious husband Willy, and their son, Bobby, a good friend to this day. I had great affection for Edith, an elegant, beautiful woman. The Thalmann-Mannheimers were close friends of mine until they died.

Ernest Thalmann joined Siegmund Warburg during the war when the firm was still the New Trading Company and Siegmund was glad to employ people with some means of their own. Notwithstanding wartime rationing, food at the Thalmann home was excellent. Somehow Edith always managed to get me a boiled egg, a rationed delicacy in those days. The bike ride from Long Marston to Chipping Campden was uphill, the way home sheer bliss. To coast down from the Cotswold hills in the quiet of the night through zones of warm and cool air, differing fragrances from trees, hedges, and flowers, each sweeter than the one before, made me almost delirious. I have loved the Cotswolds ever since. One of the best springtime school vacations with Vera and our sons was spent at the Lygon Arms in Broadway. George, aged eleven or twelve, liked it so much that he decided he would honeymoon there.

There was an RAF base next to Long Marston commanded by Henry Dalrymple-White, an air force wing commander with whom I had become acquainted. Unlike the typical RAF officer he came from a Guards family. His father had commanded a battalion of the Grenadiers in the First World War. The family were friends with George Spencer-Churchill, who had been severely wounded serving in the same regiment and declared dead until Dalrymple-White Sr. noticed slight breathing. He eventually recovered his health but was left with lifelong severe headaches. He never married and lived at Northwick Park, a magnificent Cotswold house to which I was invited quite often for Sunday lunch. He had a superb collection of old masters, in particular Dutch flower paintings with dewdrops and bees on the leaves and petals. Ever since I have wanted to own one, but the good ones are too expensive for me.

One afternoon Dalrymple-White offered me my first airplane ride, in one of the famous laminated wood Mosquito fighter-bombers. "We will cruise around the Midlands and you'll be back on the ground in an hour." Instead, he practiced dive-bombing. When we finally landed I was so disoriented that it took two days in bed for me to regain my balance. Dalrymple-White was a highly decorated bomber-command pilot with a DSO and DFC. He led major bombing raids, including the firebomb attacks that destroyed Lübeck. He became an insomniac and eventually turned to drink. He emigrated to Kenya after the war, tried coffee planting, and was murdered in a Mau Mau raid.

10

My Real War

In the spring of 1943 the War Office permitted enemy aliens to serve in combatant army units. In a letter dated June 3, 1943, I applied for transfer to the Intelligence Corps, the Royal Armored Corps, or the motorized infantry (a rifle regiment). I was turned down for the Intelligence Corps. The War Office wrote that "officers of Lieut. Eberstadt's age and medical category are not normally accepted for the Intelligence Corps even if of British nationality." On October 8, 1943, I was gazetted to the Oxford-shire and Buckinghamshire Light Infantry, retaining my present seniority. Before reporting to my new unit I had a relaxing interlude in the officers' wing of the Queen Elizabeth Hospital in Birmingham for an appendectomy. I had a truly beautiful nurse and became greatly enamored of her. I went home on convalescent leave for almost two weeks, the longest period at home all the time I was in the army. For years Mother and I reminisced about a walk up Box Hill near Leatherhead with our brown poodle Ricky. We lunched at the same hotel where almost fifty years later I used to take her from her nearby old-age home at Furse Hill. I also went to see my sister Bridget who was a WAAF (Women's Auxiliary Air Force) stationed in Manchester. She introduced me to a dark-haired beautiful fellow WAAF who became quite a serious girlfriend. She died in a London nightclub destroyed in an air raid.

I was posted to the regiment's Fifth Battalion. The senior officers were regular army. Most of the officers were territorials or held wartime commissions. I quickly came to like the infantry. Some of the officers and other ranks had served in France in 1939–1940 and were evacuated at Dunkirk. We trained for an invasion of Western Europe, wherever and whenever it was to be. We kept fit with long route marches. We attended courses to improve our fighting skills, in particular so-called battle courses that were quite strenuous. I usually had to be helped over the more challenging obstacles. We were stationed on the South Coast near Dover where we spent off-duty evenings in the local pubs. Dover was shelled regularly by German guns from Calais. Whenever they fired, a siren went off and we had a few minutes to take shelter before the shells landed.

That winter I became quite ill with pneumonia. I was treated at a pleasant nursing home on the South Downs where I spent my time reading *War and Peace*. After I had recovered I was posted to the Second Buckinghamshire Battalion, probably because our commanding officer could not make head nor tails of my background. The Second Bucks was a territorial army battalion of the Oxfordshire and Buckinghamshire Light Infantry. Most officers and men came from Buckinghamshire. Peacetime battalion headquarters were in High Wycombe, a pleasant small town in Buckinghamshire. Disraeli had lived at Hughenden, outside High Wycombe, which he represented in Parliament.

With my "real war" fresh in my mind I wrote about it soon after I was wounded. The following pages were written in September of 1944. The only additions I have made are identifications of some of those mentioned or the explanation of unfamiliar acronyms and terms. Punctuation has been Americanized, as it is throughout this book, but spelling has been left in the English style of the Walter Eberstadt of 1944.

My memory is appalling. After a few unsuccessful schoolboy experiments I never again tried to keep a diary. It has occurred to me to record some recollections of my first expedition to France. As I am duty officer tonight, a Saturday night at that, it seems a good way to spend a few hours.

My battalion, the Second Buckinghamshires, were stationed in Winchelsea, Sussex, during the weeks preceding and immediately after D-Day. It came as no great surprise to us to hear on about June 10 that we would be disbanded and sent as reinforcements to 21 Army Group. It was a bitter disappointment to those who had been with the Regiment for many years and trained it into a first-class fighting unit. My company commander was Major John Duxbury, a schoolmaster and charming man who made life in the infantry as pleasant for me as it is ever likely to be for anyone. Lieut. Col. Richards, a severe but efficient Regular Army officer, commanded us. He always showed great kindness to me, possibly for the wrong reasons as he liked everyone who was a German and considered them all good soldiers. His nickname was "the Baron" because of German family links. In his eyes some of the German military brilliance reflected — dimly — on me, though for his liking I had lived in England too long. Little did he know. . . .

On D-Day (June 6) John Duxbury and I were having breakfast in our comfortable little chalet when we heard over the wireless that we had landed from the sea and air in and around the mouth of the Seine. We took no notice of this and considered that it was either a German stunt, or a raid in force. That morning I took the company out on the range, where we did little apart from getting in the way of another unit who were there with a Major who was to be my commanding officer two months later under very different conditions. I had a row with him, or, rather, he with me just as John Duxbury came running out with the news that the invasion had really, at long last, started.

I have often tried to analyze my feelings about that momentous news. We had been waiting and hoping for over two years now, yet it came as an anticlimax. The world seemed to be going on in the same way. Only the squadrons and squadrons of airplanes that had been roaring overhead for weeks before and shaken the windows of Rye and Winchelsea were gone. There was not a plane in the sky. Our only contact with the real war had disappeared. It made our existence all the more unreal. We worked on, listened to every news bulletin on the wireless, wondered who we might know out there and discussed the campaign in our armchairs. How easy it is to be a General without an Army, how easy to make bold plans if you don't have to carry them out. We felt miserable as officers and men drafted. We said, Oh you lucky men, and felt, Thank God it is not me, yet. We moaned, "If only we were going as a battalion, but not as reinforcements to strange units." In reality we meant we did not want to go at all. Yet we did want to go, to see if we had learnt our lessons and would pass the examination of battle.

During those days the weather was glorious for all purposes bar a seaborne invasion: blue skies but high winds. The wind apart, our sector of the South Coast was quiet, no sign or sound of battle. Yet only a few miles away our divisions were holding a slender ring while masses of men and equipment were being assembled and shipped across the Channel. My parents and I were cut off. Mail was bad, and telephoning impossible. I was living in a fool's paradise, thinking because I had not gone over with all the other subalterns I might not have to go at all. I was 2nd in Command of the company, being the only other officer left and tried to imagine how pleasant it would be to remain in that position.

I shall never forget a few days before it was my turn to go — we went to a civic ceremony and church service at Winchelsea. The little church is situated beautifully among chestnuts and apple trees. It was really the farewell ceremony of the Bucks battalion. We formed a guard of honor for all the grandees of the

Cinque Ports, some of which were the base for the greatest military operation in history. We prayed hard and laughed more than I ever have done at a service, prayed officially for the Allied cause, and privately for our survival. We laughed because we sat in the Squire's box. I was wondering what irreverent thoughts and deeds must have been perpetrated by generations of churchgoers in these exclusive boxes.

One night, around the 15th of June, the flying bombs started. I had just come back from a lovely day with my parents and sister at Tunbridge Wells, which we enjoyed all the more because we knew it would probably be the last family meeting for some time. All that night loud and low droning planes with a flame shooting out behind came roaring over Winchelsea. We engaged them with every weapon we had. Secretly I dreaded lest we'd really shoot one down as I had seen one or two explode in the distance on striking ground. In the early hours of the morning after a filthy night of rain and howling gales we were called out with reports that parachutists and gliders had landed near Ashforth and were attacking communications in that area. It seemed quite likely. I was in a blue funk as I saw myself in action any moment. The preparation for battle was a complete shambles. I could not find my revolver. My equipment was still wet. The faithful Armitt, my batman, had once again drowned it in Blanco whitening. Everything went wrong. My relief was considerable when it was called off as a false alarm. This was not the first or last time when I swore to make a new start and devote myself to efficiency and keenness and learning to handle my weapons effectively.

We spent the next few days on some mild training, took mild interest in the invasion, and immense interest in how to overcome the flying bombs. It was rather a good sight to see thousands of tracer bullets streaming up at night, or fighter planes chasing the bombs during the day. Many were brought down in our area even in those early flybomb days. In the evenings John and I went off in the company jeep to the pubs in the district, meeting others of the regiment and singing "I don't want to be a soldier, I don't want to go to war. . . ."

On Wednesday, June 25, I was told I would be going on a draft. I took it the way I have always taken startling news: with a void in the region of my stomach, a mental blackout for a few seconds, then panic, more panic, and then I got over it. In a way I was glad the decision had been made for me. There were about ten officers, the bulk of the remaining NCOs, and most of the remaining men to go. For the next few days I was under the almost constant influence of alcohol which depleted my at that time shaky finances even further, and impeded Armitt's efforts to mobilize my personal effects for war. This consisted of dispatching quantities of surplus kit home. The official limit was 60 lb of luggage, but I never managed to get my kit below 100 lb.

On Friday morning after a final drinking orgy with all the old men we set off for a reinforcement holding unit at Aldershot. A band met us at Aldershot. It played us up the hill to our camp.Without it we would never have made it up the hill.

Before we arrived at the RHU, the Reinforcement Holding Unit, I imagined we would have many days or even weeks waiting for our turn, but that notion was quickly dispelled. I realized I would be lucky to get a few hours at home. Being Bucks boys there were of course no final kit inspections needed. I concentrated on getting home and managed to slip away after lunch on Sunday. Half by taxi and half by other means I got home in record time. It was really just as I imagined the last visit home before going overseas: outwardly calm and quite cheerful, why had I not done this or that, why did we not know anyone at the War Office who could get me a sensible job. We made a futile attempt to work out a secret code. I wonder whether anyone goes overseas without his pet plan of how to evade censorship, or whether any of these plans work. It is much better if one's family is in the dark. It is much more difficult for them than for those going off. I had tried ever since D-Day to work myself into a frame of mind where I was quite prepared to accept the likelihood of not returning alive. Surely it should be possible for those remaining behind to accept the likelihood that they would not see their sons or husbands again, but evidently it is more difficult for them than for those in a battle. During moments of real danger we are usually too busy to worry about our own safety. During a night of mortaring or shelling it is quite possible for a few hours to pretend nothing really matters. Either I am safe in my slit trench, however close it all comes down, or I get a direct hit, and what happens after that does not concern me. It is selfish because you ignore worries and years of mourning of those left behind. It is a blessing that most soldiers are that selfish, else no battle would ever be fought.

I was afraid during most of my first battle how I'd react and imagined subsequent spells of intensive unpleasantness would pass more manageably. I was to discover later that I reacted differently. My first patrol went off quite smoothly and I took ludicrous risks. The first shelling seemed not too bad, though it was the heaviest I was to experience. Every time I survived some danger I thought thank goodness I have survived this one but wouldn't it be a great pity to get blown up next time.

It was a lovely afternoon at home, this last one. Everything was as it should be largely thanks to the kindness and understanding of Heinz Cahn who was with us for the day. We took photos in the garden, silly ones but they helped. When it was time to leave I was fortunately in a rush. A quick good-bye kiss, the bus to Weybridge, and a train back to Aldershot. I felt more cheerful than in weeks. The account was closed. I was ready and looking forward.

The last evening at Aldershot became very merry and drunk. Benjie Yeats Brown who I had not seen since school turned up and we spent my last English (or foreign, for that matter) money on a first rate bottle of vintage port and lots of beer. I was much amused by the nearest lavatory, a bucket inside the prison compound where the inmates were handcuffed waiting to be shipped overseas. They took an inordinate interest in the most private parts of my body. The CO was kind and tried his best to make our last days pleasant. The food was excellent and for a canvas camp everything was very comfortable. I spent the late evening talking to Benjie and writing home.

The next morning we left. The draft consisted half of Bucks boys and half from our 5th Battalion. The officers, apart from me, all came from the 5th. I knew quite a few from the time I served in the 5th, especially Major Barnes who took us over. The band marched to the station and played for us on the platform. There were moist eyes and a bashful "Good luck, boys" from civilians waiting for trains to take them to their peaceful daily pursuits. I think I can say quite honestly, at that moment I did not envy them.

The journey to Newhaven was windy and cold. By now getting troops embarked had probably become a boring routine, but in those early days it still seemed thrilling to all concerned. What a funny spectacle we must have made on the railway sidings and quaysides, packed like sardines and loaded like mules, each anxiously guarding his possessions. The officers had to cope with their clumsy valises on top of everything else.

Newhaven harbour was a wonderful sight. The quayside was crowded. The little harbour was swarming with small naval vessels, landing craft of all sizes, channel packets and small cargo boats upstream. Dozens of white ensigns and U.S. Stars and Stripes were flying in what had become a gale. The sea was roaring outside the breakwaters, yet how sheltered we were inside. The army part was run largely by gunners from our old division, the 61st. We said to them: Are you lucky to stay behind on a job like this, but thought: Chum, I would not change with you for anything. Ours was a U.S. craft with the British 3rd Division insignia painted on the control tower. They had taken 3 Div over on D-Day. What better proof of Allied cooperation could one ask for? They made us most welcome aboard, especially as we offered to clear away some of the almost inconceivable quantities of junk littering the deck but which did not seem to worry the U.S. navy in any way. All army portions of the ship were filthy but their own quarters were spotless. Since they had been in every landing since North Africa they probably knew their business. One can hardly blame them if they had given up trying to clear the garbage that follows in the wake of a body of troops.

We spent our last shillings on chocolate bars with which the Army Council sweetened our departure. Actually morale could not have been higher. The men were packed like sardines below deck.

There was a constant surge of humanity pushing up and down the hatches. Luckily there was an issue of Naafi (PX) writing paper and the men settled down to letter writing. The officers settled in comfortable quarters kindly made available by the U.S. officers who gave up some of their own cabins. We shared our meals with them, and they were meals worth sharing. The men were allowed to use the ship's galley to warm up their Compo rations, all of which made us think well of our Allies. As the gale did not abate we had to stay in port for two days. No one minded. Food was plentiful and there was lots to watch. As I knew I would become a liability once we put to sea I worked hard looking after the men. 59 Div, which was to be split up as reinforcements after a few months of fighting in France, were embarking at the same time with us. The storm had calmed down when we put out to sea but the water was still too rough for me. Our lethargic U.S. friends came to life once we had moved off. They thought there would be some mines about and it was lucky we were the last boat in the flotilla. On the other hand, the last boat tended to be picked off by U-boats of which there were bound to be some. I turned green soon and retired to my bunk where I fell into a sickly slumber. Below deck the men were making plentiful use of the vomit bags.

By the next morning the sea had calmed down. I was fortunate to be on deck when we came within sight of the coast of France. The sea of mastheads cannot have given comfort to the enemy. It was inspiring to see hundreds of big and little ships discharging their cargoes along the newly built piers or via little lighters and ducks. It all was proceeding in an orderly and calm manner, more materiel and men pouring ashore constantly. The German boasts they would cut us off in a few days were being ridiculed. Hundreds of ships were handled simultaneously. By now we have become familiar with the story of the Mulberry ports. The sea looked like a 19th-century painting of harbor roadsteads. Beyond the beach innumerable army vehicles were moving up and down the newly built coast roads. Nonstop, trucks were moving inland. There were a few damaged houses on the dunes, the kind of large seaside villas found everywhere along the European coast line. The Navy was housed there sending out a stream of Morse signals, telling one vessel to come alongside and another to move further down, or giving a skipper a rocket for not responding promptly.

We had to wait a long time for our turn to disembark. We spent it eating too much, chiefly to ease the load of our packs. An occasional friendly plane flew overhead. Ashore there were explosions, which to the uninitiated like myself sounded like shells. Actually they were mines being blown up. At last an infantry assault craft came alongside to take us ashore, inclusive of our bulky baggage made even bulkier by bags of 48-hour assault rations. And so we went to "assault" the Normandy coast thanking our stars we were not the first wave and that we faced nothing more frightening than military police that set us on the right route. We deposited our kit in a field where it would be picked up later by transport. Nevertheless I carried a heavier load than I ever had. I was wishing I had not cheated on exercises, stuffing my pack with a couple of pillows. I was in charge of about a hundred men who I was supposed to take to a collecting point five miles inland. There was no danger of missing the way. It was marked by endless signposts telling one where everything was, from field cashier to a corps rear headquarters. I recognized flashes and designations which I had seen for months past in England. I used to think them silly but now appreciated what help they provided to find one's whereabouts. As a double check, traffic control had a policeman at every road junction and enquiry bureaux with long location lists. For those with maps there were signposts at crossroads show-ing the exact map reference.

Along the road we soon passed our first farmhouses which generally were not too badly damaged. Civilians were following their daily work. They gave us a friendly, but not overly friendly wave as we passed. One noticed which farms had fallen without a fight and which had been shelled. The roads, in the first place little more than tracks, were in terrible shape. The hamlets with their post offices, telephone boxes, and bus stops reminded me of Swiss villages. I was beginning to feel at home. The high stone walls around the farms, green shutters outside the windows, no-tice boards in front of the *mairies*, little churches and crucifixes, insulators on telegraph poles, looked so pretty even though every inch of the scenery was dominated by the army. Many of the little chateaux on the way had been taken over by military units.

It began to drizzle as we were marching, of which we were to experience a great deal more later. The men were fairly tired. I had to run a lot up and down the column to keep them going as a respectable body. Once used to a certain standard one is not pre-pared to relax, even if there is no superior officer around. As most of them were old Bucks boys it came naturally to them and me. There were tricolors in the windows but the novelty of liberation seemed already to have worn off. The concentration area was a long way inland. Quite touchingly, there was a RAF officer on the road who offered us some cigarettes, saying we needed them more than he did. This was the first of many episodes where the other arms seemed to demonstrate respect and sympathy for the infantry. I recall another occasion. We were slogging up an unending poplar alley on the road to Caumont, with the sun beating down mercilessly. Some gunners, stripped to the waist, walked over from their guns to offer us tea of which no doubt they had none too much. The nearer you get to the line, the greater the comradeship.

We had the first of many experiences of moving on as soon as we had dug shallow slit trenches in the concentration area. After a few hours we were taken by lorries to an RHU outside Bayeux. It was fun to see the countryside in comparative comfort. Driving through Bayeux our convoy lost its way and split up. Bayeux made a peaceful impression apart from innumerable soldiers walking the streets aimlessly the way they did back in England. I noticed saluting officers had been abandoned, a state of affairs the High Command fought as hard as the enemy, with fewer visible results. It was pretty to see torrents of rainwater run down the cobbled streets. I appreciated the flags, shuttered windows, the cathedral, the market square, full shop windows, Camembert cheeses, children playing in the streets, all that goes with a busy French market town. I was glad we had missed our way. While we finally got an MP on the outskirts to put us back on the right road, a batch of soldiers slipped past the MPs. They were supposed to keep any troops out of town without proper papers, a task doomed from the beginning. The only bordello was guarded by red caps and had barbed wire around it. I heard this led the girls to protest their livelihood was ruined.

The HQ of the RHU was in a nice farm. The troops passing through dug themselves into the hedgerows surrounding the fields. It was almost dark when we arrived. We quartered under apple trees in an orchard. To stimulate our morale we were issued a generous amount of rum. The smell of rum, apples, wet grass, and rain blended well and lulled us quickly into deep sleep. The men who had slept out on innumerable exercises in England were better than I at making themselves comfortable and warm but it did not take me long to become their equal. The next morning we moved into another part of the camp where we rejoined the other Bucks officers. I was especially glad to see George Revnell. We had always understood each other.

The next day most of us moved to the CRC, the corps reception area, again by transport and again we lost our way. This time we moved forward into the gun area, which I found terrifying. I saw my first large formation of bombers flying over and dropping their load a few miles ahead. Several were shot down.

The CRC was in a damp valley. I found a comfortable warm straw hut, which kept most of the rain out. Pud Rice, Derek Steward, and Macmath were with me. At the farm we got milk and eggs, also firsthand information of conditions inside Caen from a civilian who had managed to get through our lines. From there we moved another stage forward to the second echelon of the First Battalion, the Worcestershire regiment to which I was posted. I liked them from the first moment. They were very kind to me. The 2nd echelon was commanded by George Taylor, our 2nd in Command. After one noisy night in a barn, rocked by a nonstop barrage from our guns (it was not smart to sleep in the barn which was within easy shelling range; the experienced Taylor had dug himself deep in) we made our way forward to the battalion. It was holding a sector of the line at Mouen, a little village just beyond Cheux, and to the right of the heavily contested Carpiquet airfield.

So at last I had got there, had got what I always wanted, yet been terribly afraid of: a platoon of infantry. My doubts vanished as soon as I shook hands with Lieut. Col. Harrison, our commanding officer. He was sitting in his command post, dug in an orchard behind a badly battered farm. The battalion, he told me, had had a very rough time since their landing eight days previously, and had been engaged almost nonstop since. They had already done awfully well and made an excellent name for themselves, as indeed had the whole division, the 43rd Wessex Territorial Division, commanded by Major General Thomas, commonly known as Butch. It consisted of the usual three infantry brigades — 128 bde, 129 bde, and my own, 214 bde. The brigades were composed of two battalions of the Hampshire regiment, two of the Somerset Light Infantry, one of the Duke of Cornwall's Light Infantry, one of the Dorset regiment, and ourselves. 214 Brigade consisted of the Fifth Battalion, Duke of Cornwall Light Infantry, Seventh Battalion, Somerset Light Infantry, and First Battalion, the Worcestershire Regiment. The Worcesters had until recently been part of a Guards brigade, which shows how highly thought of they were. The attack on Mouen had been their first proper battle for which they got high praise from corps HQ, especially as the 15 Scottish Div. had been trying unsuccessfully and with very heavy casualties to get into this area. For days and days we found dead Jocks [Scots] in the lanes, covered by trees and branches felled by artillery fire.

I was posted to B Company, commanded by Major Algie Grubb, one of the most inspiring officers I met in the Army. He looked like a clergyman and appeared a complete pansy. In fact, he was one of the toughest men one could imagine. Before the war he had read law. He made me feel at home right away and put me in the picture in his clear and precise manner for which we were to be grateful at many rushed "O" groups later on. Grubb later became battalion 2nd in Command. Capt. Ronald Newman had just been made company 2 i.c. The other platoon commanders were Freddy Henry, a young boy who had just left Radley, charming and conscientious, perhaps lacking a little maturity, but an excellent leader and adored by his men. He was lucky to have the ideal counterpart as platoon sergeant, an old regular named Stupple, a big thief and excellent cook. He ran around in looted clothes and spent his time cooking and supervising the feeding arrangements for his platoon after whose interests he looked like a tiger. Jack Booth, who was killed just before I was wounded, was a different type. He came from a simple background in Birmingham and had served most of the war in the ranks. He was efficient and tough, never ruffled. His men had complete confidence in him, as did Algie who often consulted him. One could not have wanted a better or less selfish fellow officer.

10 platoon was mine. It had always been regarded the crack platoon in the battalion. Until the attack on Mouen it had been commanded by a Canadian named Brigadier who had won a DCM, a Distinguished Conduct Medal, at Dieppe. He was wounded the day before I arrived. In fact, the platoon were very weak in numbers. They had lost 16 out of 35 men, chiefly from our own shell fire. In the attack on Mouen they pressed forward so fast that they ran into our own creeping barrage. My platoon sergeant was a cheerful mechanic from Birmingham named Burr. He had been promoted the day before I arrived. So neither of us was too sure of himself. My three section commanders were Corporals Smith, a useless funk and nitwit, Fowler, a brilliant but somewhat unreliable southern Irishman, not at all the type one would expect to find in that position — he spent a lot of time painting from a slit trench — and lastly, Nyland, a devout Catholic for whom I had the greatest regard and liking from the first day. He was immensely hardworking and conscientious. He mothered his section in the nicest way, yet did not give them an inch of rope. He spent his time writing love letters to his girl who worked in a Naafi center at Dover. I soon gave up censorship. The letters were too frequent and too long.

Of my men I want to mention a few: Lc/Cpl Johnston, my mortar NCO, always calm and willing to undertake any job; Shakespeare, a somewhat frightened young boy from Birmingham who was not happy unless he had someone in his slit trench with him. He drove me mad at times. When others kicked him out of their trenches he'd find some reason to spend hours with me; Barlow, the platoon barber and cook, very dirty and very likeable. Given half a chance he went on the scrounge and would return with a few boiling fowl which he knew how to prepare very well. When everyone else was tired he raised our morale by coming up with a good meal. He threatened at least twice daily that he was fed up with me and the platoon, that no one took notice of him, and that next time he was made to dig a hole in another spot as soon as he had finished one he would complain to the Colonel. Day and night he mumbled about munitions workers, how much money they made and how many pints of beer he could buy for that. Then there were two cockneys, Smith and Turnbull, who did everything together and were my best fighting men. They took pleasure to match their skill against any Boche, whom they hated and despised. They both had happy homes and hated the Army almost as much as the enemy but were, rightly, convinced they were the superior soldiers. I liked the two very much. Turnbull seemed to require more kit than the rest of the platoon together.

Number 2 section was commanded by an 18-year-old named Cotton. He took over from Fowler after he was taken ill. Cotton was strikingly good-looking. His ideas of discipline would hardly have been approved by any colonel, but he succeeded in keeping his section the most cheerful. They were steady in bad moments and had a knack of always making themselves comfortable. None were over 18. They stuck together. Their spare time they spent eating, letter writing, and looking after their weapons. They produced photos of attractive girls and nice-looking families. One of the most engaging traits in the British Tommy is his desire to show his officer photos of friends and family of which he carries a large number in his wallet. In Nyland's section the best was Davies, a young Welshman from Carmathen. He had three girlfriends to whom he wrote passionate and identical letters. Each he promised eternal bliss. He would have succeeded, too. Then there was Grundy, an excellent soldier who lived for his Bren gun, often covering it with his ground sheet, even if he got wet himself. Finally, there was Wilcocks, a Yorkshireman and the oldest in the platoon. He was an excellent signaler. As long as he was allowed to work a wireless set he was happy. My batman most of the time was Harry Cross. Rosser acted as a self-appointed bodyguard for me.

In peacetime he was a telephone engineer at West Drayton where he had a nice modern house, wore double-breasted waistcoats, and had an attractive wife. He was a good, reliable soldier who hated the Army, but I could count on him to carry out any job to the best of his abilities. Of Cross I could write a great deal. He had not been a batman before and was by no means an old soldier. He had been in the Army for a year and a half. He was an orphan, brought up by his grandfather who was now in an old age pensioners home. Cross sent him a lot of his pay. He was married at the age of 17, and had a child almost a year old. Before he joined the Army he had been a milkroundsman. After the war he planned to work for his in-laws who owned a prosperous small firm of meat porters. He and Cotton had gone to school together in Birmingham and were good friends.

During the four weeks Cross looked after me there was not a moment when he would not be wherever I might be. We shared a slit trench. He was not content until we had dug the deepest and most comfortable hole. He used to make sure that as soon as platoon business was finished I would do my share of the digging. He managed nearly always to get me a mess tin of hot water for shaving. There was not an hour of the day when he did not have some tea on the boil. Once the platoon had become used to me I was quite shamed by their insistence I should have the best of what food was available. If I was away on a job Cross would keep it warm no matter how long he had to wait. He acted as a private secretary preparing mail for censorship, getting maps ready for a move or telling Sergeant Burr what I wanted for the platoon by way of ammunition or kit. He saw to it that I had a change of underwear or socks, and managed to do my laundry in the most improbable places. I always had a small haversack with a few books and other personal belongings stowed away on the company jeep where he kept his extra belongings as well. Even during the heaviest shelling, when I at times got quite fed up, he managed to keep cheerful which helped my own morale greatly. He was a cautious soldier with a good sense of direction. He would come up to me and say: "Now, let's wait a minute. Something stinks," and he was invariably right. If I was not sure where we should be going he found the right direction. He used to worry if he did not hear from his wife. When she sent a parcel he shared everything with his friends.

Mouen was an ideal place to get used to frontline service. It was a quiet sector with the enemy two miles away. Most of the noise came from our own guns, which were just behind us. Apart from heavy machine-gun fire there was little activity from either side. The company was grouped around a few fields. In a sunken lane we made ourselves quite comfortable. There was a lot of loot, especially quantities of butter and cream, a few little pigs and many chickens. There was quite a lot of money, supposedly stolen from a former German headquarters. At least that is what I liked to think. The day after I got there George Revnell arrived. Though he was posted to another company I was delighted to see him. When we first met, I found him in his slit, bathing his feet in hot water, reading a book while his batman was preparing a meal for him.

A hundred and fifty yards to our front there was an old and pretty church, only slightly damaged. From it one got a perfect view as far as Caen, and an excellent close-up view of Carpiquet for which the Canadians were having such a struggle.

The only thing we were short of was tools. A pick or spade were worth their weight in gold. As to my own dress I conformed to what the men wore, as that was supposed to make one safer from snipers. Personally I don't believe it. When the danger from snipers is real, an officer or NCO give themselves away by waving their arms or shouting. As it was more comfortable I did not mind. In my equipment pouches I carried a mixture of grenades, pipes, and tobacco. Alas I broke my pipes the first time a shell landed near us and I took overly hasty cover. At that time, too, I scratched my knee rather badly and still have the scar. Like every-thing out there it went septic in no time. My chief companion in that period was our MO [Medical Officer] who had his Regi-mental Aid Post near us. He was an awfully nice man, always calm and very brave. He smoked Dunhill tobacco and had a great array of pipes. All I did at that time was to carry out some "scrounging" reconaissances and keep my platoon fit and busy with running and physical training (PT). I scrounged a whistle from a French house. It had a squeaky hooter at one end. During awkward moments I used to signal with that squeak, which was a good morale raiser. During this time Parks who at first was my batman had come with me from the Bucks. He was so frightened and had so little grip on himself that I found him useless. After one week he went back to England bomb happy (or shell-shocked).

From Mouen I carried out my first night patrol, with Nyland and one man. I was supposed to find out whether some high ground overlooking Carpiquet was held by the enemy, as it was a potential threat to our flank. Freddy Henry went into Versons that night. The route out was along the Caen railway for the first mile and a half. To speed up matters I went along very quickly. A German outpost could have surprised us easily. I did a good deal of roaming around but there was no trace of the enemy. In the dis-tance there were noises, which I in my ignorance took to be the doors of the Carpiquet hangers squeaking. In fact they were Ger-man Nebelwerfer, luckily firing away from us. Finally I thought I heard human voices. We went down on our stomachs. I crawled forward alone until I came within thirty yards or so of what turned out to be an enemy post. They clearly were low German voices, and some strange whistling I could not make out. Under a tree there was a tank. It was all rather terrifying and nothing could have induced me to get any closer. I picked up some papers lying around. They were German cigarette cartons, quite dry despite the light drizzle, which had fortunately set in and was covering up our slight noises.

The return journey filled us with elation. It was a grand feeling to be back within our own lines. The platoon sentries had prepared some tea, after which I slept happily until 11 A.M. the next morning. From Mouen church I observed 500 British heavies giving Carpiquet a tremendous bombing, an awe-inspiring sight. Only one bomber was lost, and the target area was left well "alight." Our martial exploits from Mouen were few. I participated in a long-range daylight reconnaissance for an operation which came to naught and, another night, B Company was detailed to act as protecting force for all the Brigade mortars, which went off to fire fifteen minutes intense fire from a flank at 2 A.M. one morning. We expected an awful pasting in return. As soon as the job was over, we literally doubled down the Verson-Caen road. We missed what was meant for us. That night I got a good view of a small night attack on our right with tracers flying back and forth nonstop for hours. You feel rather smug if the shit is not directed at your own area.

From Mouen we moved a few miles forward to the area of Chateau Fontaine. The date was around July 5th. The system on these battalion moves up was that we moved by companies at short intervals with all the "hard" transport and some soft vehicles following behind. In one static week we had become quite immobile, having become overburdened with too much kit. On a five-mile move over bad roads one notices every extra pound badly. Parks was still my batman but so weak I had to carry some of his kit for him. Our route was marked for us by the Bn IO, the Battalion Intelligence Officer, and his men. These moves are not a simple affair of just marching along until you get there, but the few lanes and tracks are so blocked up, especially soon after a battle, that there is a stoppage every few hundred yards. We were being shelled a little on the way. Whenever there was a stop one took the best cover available. We had to cross a small river (not the Odon). From there it was all uphill work. Fontaine was a mess. There were hardly any civilians left. As we passed through we suffered one or two casualties. They got treated quickly by the company stretcher-bearers and were evacuated by jeep or carrier. Beyond Fontaine everything was a big mess, trees across the road, dead lying about, vehicles burning. It was quite a job to keep the company column together. A mile to our front was Hill 112, which was to be our home for the next few weeks.

Our first night was spent dug in a cornfield in the A Company area. I spent an uncomfortable night in a hole I had taken over from a dead German. He was lying beside me doing his best to disturb my peace of mind, but his greatcoat came in handy to keep me warm. Just behind us were units of the 7th Armored Division, quite a comforting feeling except when they came straight for us at night. I spent an unpleasant hour keeping friend Shakespeare company. The first smokescreen I had ever experienced came down just then. To begin with I could not make out the constant whizzing followed by a thud. I thought we were being gassed and made the necessary preparations. The next day the fun started. We were in full view of the enemy in the entire area and he soon settled down to endless mortaring and shelling. B Coy's job was to man the area just this side of the road at night, and to leave one platoon group there during the day (i.e., one platoon, one section of carriers, anti-tank guns and mortars, a few snipers, and an 18-set walkie-talkie to keep in contact).

We dug ourselves in during a fairly quiet night, and I was detailed to keep watch the first day. The weather was grand. We made ourselves as comfortable as possible, sunning ourselves behind the cover of the corn. I quite enjoyed that type of work. I could observe a bit of enemy movement, bring some fire down on them, amuse the men, read a little, and sleep. The constant milling around behind the ridge of Tiger tanks was a bit disturbing, but as they did not seem to be after me I did not mind. Anyhow, we had plenty of PIATS (anti-tank rifles) and around Battalion HQ there was a powerful concentration of 17-pounder antitank guns. These very forward positions came to be more and more popular as we discovered that the closer we were to the enemy the less mortaring we experienced. That particular morning our only fright was when one of my NCOs came back with a bullet from a German sniper which had grazed his chest. It was Smith who panicked completely over it and threw away his rifle, running like a hare. Apart from such minor upsets it was all quite enjoyable.

Going back we took up our new night positions. I recall a frightful schemozzle. My position had been pinched by another company. In the middle of searching for cover, an awful shelling started. After much haggling we finally found our area as indicated on the map. It was fortunate for me that we did not go to our original area. A few hours later the platoon commander there got a direct hit on his slit trench and was killed. His name was Roy Spicer, quite a nice fellow. We soon began to understand when the Germans were likely to mortar us. Every time our tanks moved along the road on our left the Germans saw the clouds of dust these wretched vehicles threw up. Almost instantaneously we got a pasting lasting anything up to an hour. We all got very fed up with the tanks. They seemed to cause us nothing but bother. I used to think we should deny the Germans observation by returning their shell fire. Probably it would not have helped greatly, as it would have been hard to position an OP [Observation Post]. During these weeks I did not lose any men while we were actually in our slits, though the number of shells that landed in our platoon area was fantastic. Around my own slit, within a ten-yard radius 8 bombs dropped, which I found very disconcerting.

The Germans were sending over more than we sent them. Our situation was really unfortunate. They had a better hold on Hill 112 than we did, but it was considered vital (why, I cannot

imagine) that we should hold on to what we already had instead
of simply retiring behind the next ridge and establishing OPs
there to stop any German moves beyond the 112 area. The nights
forward were a nightmare. First there was the move forward,
which invariably took place during a shelling. There was no point
taking cover. We simply moved forward hoping for the best.
There was not a single move forward or back when I did not lose
a man or two. I always arrived at our location bathed in perspira-
tion. The nights were noisy, though little or no firing was directed
at us. We generally stood to the whole night, sometimes only 50
percent of the men but more often 100. There was constant
movement around us, either our own patrols going out or single
enemy prowling around. Whenever I tried to get a little sleep I
had one man standing in my slit trench to rouse me as soon as
anything suspicious appeared. This meant rarely more than ten
minutes of consecutive sleep. Bn HQ was being mortared heavily.
Nearly every night some of our vehicles were blown up and burnt
for hours, providing a perfect aiming mark for the Boche.

   Shellings during the day were hard to endure. I tried to write
letters or read a book by Jane Lane called *He Stooped to Conquer*,
about the massacre at Glencoe. One could hardly have found a
more bloodcurdling story. Sometimes I fell asleep but usually
wandered from slit to slit chatting to the men, who on the whole
were awfully good about it all. It was a frightful job to keep them
from getting out of their slits as soon as a "stonk" was over, as that
would have indicated to an observant enemy that he had not yet
succeeded in accomplishing what he had set out to do. Tea was
heaven-sent and we had some on the brew all the time. Sergeant
Burr was excellent at distributing rations. He always kept a small
reserve, for which we were grateful. A good platoon sergeant is a
godsend. I gladly forgave him for his hopelessness at paperwork,
not that there was much of it. He would forget to indent for
ammunition or put in a casualty report. This did not worry the
men who liked him more than I did. Parks and a good many others

became bomb happy during that period and had to be evacuated. It is pitiful to see a man go to pieces completely.

Algie spent his time wisely in a deep slit sleeping all day except during the short O groups, when orders were given out. They were always a cheerful affair and excellent tonic, even if one had to run to and fro while the dirt came down. A little overhead cover provided an increased feeling of security. We all developed an ostrich complex. Everyone seemed to pray during shellings and make vows, few of which, I fear, were kept. By now I have forgotten most of mine. The absence of mail was very upsetting for me. Little did I realize that my letters were not reaching home, either. Only once I got back to England did I realize how worried everyone had been about me.

On the 13th of July we moved back to Brigade Reserve. We may have moved out of range of small arms fire, but the shelling was almost as bad and the noise worse. Everything was so crowded that these so-called rest periods took place on top of our guns, which meant we caught a good deal of the German counter–battery fire. During service one day, while singing a hymn, three of our men were killed. Cross had become my batman, which made life much more comfortable. He started with an orgy of washing clothes. It culminated with pouring bucket after bucket of water over me while most my platoon stood around me talking quite cheerfully. We established a small officers' mess in a well-preserved cottage where we had our first beer and whisky issues. Both were welcome, especially as it was my birthday, which was celebrated very cheerfully. After reminding my platoon they came to congratulate me. I received my first letter, a bill from Dunhill's.

I took a party to a bath unit just outside Bayeux. It was a horrid journey, hardly worthwhile as the water was cold. In fact, we all felt quite unsettled. Further back everything seemed so hectic. The roads were crowded. There was dust everywhere, much more than further forward, but there were none of the ubiquitous dead cows with their foul all-pervading stink. We were meant to go to a cinema but it had disappeared two days earlier. All of this put us in a bad mood. I was in charge of a 12-lorry convoy and two hundred men. I was jolly glad to get back to our forward place. That night we got drunk on whisky produced by Freddy Henry and listened to excellent dance music on our invaluable wireless.

A word here about the wireless: to get English stations even in the most forward positions is a boon that cannot be over-estimated. The excellent BBC news services helped keep the bigger picture before us. The men were equally keen on the news broadcasts and there was complete quiet on our part to listen, even if the enemy was not always obliging. Newspapers came out quickly. There were three or four per platoon, including the *Daily Mirror*, which was the most popular. There was also the *Wyvern News*, the first-rate divisional news sheet. It gave us the bigger picture as well as providing a day-by-day account of happenings in the divisional sector. It exceeded the *Mirror* in popularity. One naturally likes to read of one's own exploits, especially if they are praised. Many of us collected the *Wyvern News*.

We had quite a bit of German bombing, which was most unwelcome. The Germans dropped powerful flares, which created near daylight conditions. They appeared to be after the main road to Caen along which there were bumper to bumper transport columns day and night. One or two planes were shot down.

On the 16th we moved forward again, in better spirits but not really terribly well rested. We stayed about another week in the Chateau Fontaine area doing much the same kind of work and getting very tired of it all. I remember one amusing incident after a shelling when I went to follow nature's call. I was sitting on the edge of the slit made for that purpose when the divisional padre, a charming man who had spent one evening with us during the rest period, drove by in his jeep and waved to me. Alas, I waved back and lost my balance. Padres were immensely popular with officers and men alike. They were hardworking and cheerful. They were more effective than doctors at curing almost bomb-happy cases either by kindness or severity. Ours always had some presents with him, cigarettes, chocolate, newspapers, writing paper, in fact, any little thing that made life a bit more bearable. Actually there was never a shortage of cigarettes. Rations included one bar of chocolate and seven cigarettes per man daily. A specimen menu might consist of breakfast: tea, biscuits, butter, bacon or sausage; midday: tea, biscuits, steak and kidney pudding (excellent), potatoes, tinned fruit; afternoon tea: more tea, biscuits, jam or cheese or sardines, margarine; supper: biscuits, tea, soup, or stew. All this was frequently supplemented by some form of local thievery. Freddy Henry and I concentrated at one time on local red currants and artichokes. The sergeant major will never forgive me for having offered him artichokes. He categorized them as foreign muck, which only a foreigner like me or a silly young man like Freddy would eat. The next day I caught him in search of an artichoke, which he hid from me and then tasted in the privacy of his slit trench. We had some link in that he had served under the father of my friend Anne Coventry in 1939.

I do not recall the bigger picture during those days. There were lots of small-scale pushes all along the front. It was rumored that we were beginning to draw more and more of the crack German armor against us while the Americans were idling. No one at that time realized this was the plan. To us it was odious to see attack after attack put in on a battalion or brigade level, which more often than not fell just short of their objectives, or the gain was evened out by an immediate German counterattack. Whenever our attacks were successful it seemed as if they were not exploited properly, a feeling shared by Christopher Buckley of the *Daily Telegraph*. Our brigades made several attacks against Esquay and Etterville, with heavy casualties. These two places changed hands a good many times.

On or about July 21 we were again reserve battalion for two days. We again had a pleasant cottage and good slits. Most of my platoon took shelter in magnificent German dugouts, which were comfortable. The men were left largely to their own devices. They were quite happy cleaning themselves and their kit, scrounging for food, getting some new kit, writing, and sleeping. Morale was high. The platoon was at its best, weak in numbers but high in spirit. When we went back into the line we moved forward of Baron to where one of the Hampshire battalions had suffered heavy casualties. My platoon took over the most exposed position. The slits were dug deep with mortar-proof tops, which were essential. There were high trees overhead, which had a nasty habit of transforming bombs into airbursts. I am afraid we were becoming too slit conscious and siting ourselves to make fighting back difficult. That tendency had cost the 5th Welsh (?), part of 53rd Div., a whole company when they were surprised by a German attack. All bar one man were killed or captured. The German habits in the area were particularly obnoxious. They started mortaring without any apparent reason. The only warning we received that anything was afoot was their habit of ranging their mortars with one airburst in the direction of their later efforts.

After one day up there I got a message to report to Brigade HQ as liaison officer. It was already fairly late and no transport was available. Nevertheless, Cross and I decided to clear out straightaway as it would save us one night's unpleasantness on the hill. We set out packed like mules with our belongings and a bit more along the track back to Brigade HQ. It was a frightful lane strewn with dead animals, down a steep gorge at the bottom of which was the river Odon, and up again on the other side, only a bit steeper. In peacetime one would have considered it a beauty spot. After much searching around we found Brigade HQ just as it was becoming dark. The HQ was housed in an almost untouched large farmhouse. All the command posts were well dug in. Everyone slept in slit trenches as there was a lot of counter–battery fire. When I reported, no one knew anything about us, and the whole thing was a mistake. However, having got as far back as Brigade HQ I was determined not to be pushed off without having seen the Brigadier (named Assam), which I made clear to the Brigade major. I noticed terror written on the faces of the three LOs, who were afraid I had come to relieve one of them. They seemed a pretty dim lot with the exception of one Richard Wollheim who was possessed of great charm coupled with quickness in the up-take of our race. I never found out whether his background was the same as mine but thought it had to be. He provided me with hot water, which was welcome. I was in a really filthy mess. In any event, they took pity upon us and put us up for the night. My attitude was whatever the outcome I would at least have a peace-ful night and might get something out of the Brigadier the next morning. In the event we had an awful night. The Germans bombed and shelled us incessantly.

The next morning we found some UXBs — unexploded bombs — which turned out to be 500 and 1,000 pounders. Break-fast in the mess was pleasant. The food was well prepared and comfortably served. Otherwise the Brigade led a Spartan exis-tence. I saw the Brigadier who decided to appoint me IO of the 7 Somersets. They had recently lost two IOs, 3 COs, one adjutant, one signals officer, and most of the intelligence section. In fact, they were in an awful mess. That morning Lieut. Col. Nicol of the Oxf. and Bucks. had taken over. He was almost as raw at his job as I was at mine. We took an instant dislike to one another, which neither of us managed to hide successfully. Bn HQ was a minute dugout. It was by no means watertight and made work quite im-possible. I put Cross in the I section. The poor fellow had to try his hand at work, which was not exactly his cup of tea. The new I sergeant's name was Mully, quite good but it was his first week in the line.

Inside the dugout we always had one or two signalers. They operated the large 22 set which provided the rear link to Brigade, the 18 set which is the control set for the whole battalion net-work, and one telephone with lines to all the companies and a line back to Brigade. We had endless trouble with the lines. They were being cut up continuously by our own tanks. Apart from our own sets there were radios for the various OPs, which meant we had a big cluster of radios all around us. Feeding arrangements were lamentable, as were organized rest periods. Not once did I manage to get sufficient sleep. At night the CO, adjutant, two signalers, and myself slept in the minute dugout. It was enough to drive anyone mad. Not one night could we stretch our legs. On top there was work to be done day and night, preparing routes and photographs for patrols, keeping an I OP, keeping the log book, taking bearings on any shelling and mortaring which came down in our area, and digesting reports on the same subject from the companies. All this had to be coded and sent back to Brigade. A lot of intelligence reports came in from other sectors around us. There was a constant stream of enquiries from the gunners and tank people who wanted to be kept in the picture. The most important job was to mark innumerable maps to keep them up to date, at which I had little experience. This was made doubly difficult by the lack of facilities for proper work, nor was labor available to build another dugout. To crown it all we got the most incredible rain showers. Being on hard and chalky soil the water collected in our slits and dugouts and would not run off. Bailing did little good. We were ankle deep, sometimes knee deep in water. We did have oil lamps but had to maintain the strictest blackout. There were six maps to be marked: the CO's battle map, the visitors' map, my own map, a small sketch map for the CO, and an A and Q map showing lines of communication, etc. Lastly there was a map giving the bigger picture along the whole Army front. Each time another suspected mortar position had been located it meant alterations. There was endless information to be marked up which came in from our flanks and had to be sent out to our flanks. I made it my habit to visit all of the companies twice a day to put them in the picture as the CO did not believe in O groups so far forward. I had to go to Brigade patrol groups, accompany the CO to Brigade O groups and attend flank O groups that affected us. That was the routine, but each day there were a few extra jobs. I was really quite busy but enjoyed the work immensely notwithstanding the unfavorable conditions. They had no sense of humor at Bn HQ. As a result I enjoyed making facetious remarks which pleased no one bar me.

I translated a lot of German bumph for the Brigadier. I also made one broadcast in German to the lines opposite us. The broadcast was an unfortunate affair from beginning to end. It was made the day after the breakout attempts by the Guards Armored Division and some Canadian troops had begun. The Brigadier was under the impression the attempt had been successful. In fact, it was a costly failure. He wanted me to tell the Germans opposite us that they were surrounded by "thousands of allied tanks threatening their rear and cutting them off." This, however, was not the real state of affairs. Needless to say nothing came of my broadcast efforts. The forward platoon of C Coy (Maj. Chalmers) had a miserable night while I rigged up my broadcast equipment and prepared to speak from the comfort of a slit trench two hundred yards back. They went forward to lay my line for me and placed the loudspeaker. They were lost for over an hour, which did not help matters. The next morning we got a shattering shelling on Bn HQ. For half an hour the stuff came down very fast and very close. Each time a shell dropped the dugout rocked and we were covered in dirt. That and a rude CO as companion was a bit much. Later, back in England when I met two SLI officers, Majors Whitehead and Bailey, I was not displeased to hear Nichol eventually got the sack. Apparently he lost a company when the brigade forced the crossing of the Seine. Actually I was also told that the sacking was unfair but cannot say this worried me unduly.

During my tour as IO I motorcycled a lot between Brigade and Bn HQs. Each ride was a hair-raising experience. The road was appalling. I had to ride through the river Odon as the bridge was destroyed. Horrid! I was scared stiff. The bike slipped on stones in the water and started skidding up the opposite bank. By jeep the trip was great fun but that beastly bike was too much. Once it stopped I had a hard time restarting it. On a rainy day there was too much slush. On a dry one the mud was just as bad.

My last day as IO was particularly busy. 1 Worc. R. were to attack the triangular wood in front of C Coy, SLI, and another wood in the Hill 112 area. I attended the Worc. attack O group. The plan was to attack silently, with a noisy fire diversion from the Somersets. They had to evacuate two of their forward company locations. The danger to them was too great should the Worcesters be forced to use fire. My own old Worcester company were to hold the whole of their Bn area for the night. My job was to join the Worcester attack in order to keep Lieut. Col. informed. I spent the afternoon finding alternative positions for our two coys. This was an unpleasant job. I had to roam around on my own for several hours looking for slit trenches not in use for the moment. There was quite a bit of mortaring. The Germans were after a strong tank concentration in harbor to our right. Every time things came down I took shelter under one of the Churchill tanks. In many respects the tank people lead a more comfortable existence than the infantry does. They dig a shallow hole under their tanks, sit there quite comfortably, safe and dry, reading, brewing tea, or sleeping.

While up there I was able to watch small-scale tank engagements between ourselves and enemy Tiger tanks. Whoever poked their nose over the ridge got a bloody nose. On balance the Germans seemed to fare better. Their 88-mm guns are a real menace. For the infantry they are particularly unpleasant. They give no warning whatever. The mortar at least lets off a short whine, just long enough to take quick cover. With an 88 it is just a whack, a bang, and then a cloud of smoke where the beastly shell exploded. The German tactics seem to consist of sending over oil firebombs followed by 88 rounds. Time and again they set some of our tanks on fire and afterwards we would find charred limbs of our crews lying around. The German technique was to dig in their Tigers, with only the upper part of the hull above ground. We did manage to destroy some Tigers. In more open battle our Shermans equipped with 17-pounders proved almost equal to the Germans.

For an IO, aerial photos were the best means of pinpointing targets. Once I had got the hang of reading them they proved excellent for briefing a patrol. Even the most stupid subaltern got a good idea where he was meant to go, and what landmarks to look for. They amplified our excellent 1:25,000 defense maps. They provided up-to-date details of enemy positions, defences, mortar OPs in our own sector, etc. It was almost impossible to identify the mortar positions. We came to the conclusion that the Germans were deploying a relatively small number of these vile contraptions, and that they were mobile. We decided they fired from lanes and roads running parallel to the front and moved to another location before we could bring counterfire down on them. They had probably ranged on all the attractive targets from their various positions so that they were able to engage us with relative impunity to themselves. This theory was borne out by the experience of our infantry mortar platoons. They tended to suffer lighter casualties, provided the mortar platoon commander used his initiative and his CO allowed him to shift his positions frequently.

Even though we undertook more air reconnaissance than the Germans it was our impression that German shelling inflicted the greater damage. Part of the reason may have been that our camouflage tended to be careless and the men showed themselves needlessly. The most important reason, though, was that the Germans had better knowledge of the territory. They were withdrawing. They would range their weapons on their own forward troops before retreating. As they withdrew they already had ranged their weapons on what became our forward positions and counterattacked us with immediate fire. No army can have had as much training in the tactics of retreat as the Germans. Since Stalingrad and El Alamein they have been falling back continuously on all fronts, even if still winning important battles on the way. It remains to be seen whether, once they came to realize they no longer could win the war they decided to retire a certain distance and then make a stand or whether since 1942 they had lost control and were pushed back everywhere against their will.

My stint as IO ended after a week or so. Lieut. Col. Harrison did not sanction my posting away from the battalion. Lieut. Col. Nichol was glad to be rid of me, a feeling I reciprocated heartily. My return to the Worcesters was made pleasant by the warmth of the reception. My platoon appeared genuinely delighted to see me back. The officers also seemed pleased. I returned the night of the attack on 112, which proved only a very qualified success. It showed we had been in the line too long and needed a rest. George Revnell did not return from that show. As he is still missing there is little chance he is alive. The whole of his Coy HQ were killed. Apparently he was with them at the time of their death. Since my return to England I have both seen his people and corresponded with them. One can imagine their state after so many months of uncertainty.

After two more days in the 112 area we went back into reserve. On the way back I again ran into Major Harry Parker who used to be in the Bucks with me and now had a company in the DCLI. From reserve we did not go back into the line. We received the good news that the whole division would be pulled out for a week for rest, refit, and entertainment. We were very tired and glad to say good-bye to Mouen and Hill 112. We hoped we would never see that lousy part of Normandy again. Just as we were beginning our move a French gendarme arrived on a bicycle. He said he was coming on behalf of the mayor and mayoress of Versons who would like to pay us a state visit the next day to reclaim their bikes, which were standing in our farmyard. Algie replied he would be delighted to receive them in state. The march back to the rest area outside Bayeux was long and tiring. We had not realized how soft our feet had become. Had we been marching in the opposite direction I suspect more than one man would have fallen out. The entire division was concentrated into the rest area. The Worcesters were allocated a pleasant large farm and various fields into which the companies were split up. My platoon had the far corner, near a little brook, all quite pleasant. The officers did not really like to be parted from their platoons. We had become so accustomed to doing everything with our men. We were really happier living with them.

Cross rigged a comfortable bivouac for the two of us. I spent the day making lists — who wanted to see George Crosby, a horror mercifully spared me, or be entertained by a lesser star, or see a film, or taste the Bayeux night life (alas with red caps and barbed wire around the most important house in town). There were lists for new battle dresses, mugs enamel, or underwear. Cross washed and mended mine with commendable thoroughness. For the first time I saw my valise. It contained small but important comforts such as a pair of shoes and a pair of cherry red pajamas. We went to third-rate shower baths and took short walks. Most time, though, was spent getting shipshape for the next lap. We established an extremely nice and gay officers' mess. There was plenty of alcohol and lots of Camembert cheese. Col. Harrison would have felt deprived without a ceremonial march past of sorts. An old colonel in the Worcesters who was doing some stooge job was dug out and we marched past the dear old man. It seemed somewhat exaggerated, for the sake of making one man happy, to mess 800 soldiers around for a good many hours. I am glad to say the march past was a complete shambles, but no doubt will go down into regimental history as a fine show, and all that.

Our week was cut short to 5 days. But for George Formby it would have been only four days. Fortunately I was duty officer on the Formby night. An unkind Regimental Sergeant Major could have made me look the biggest fool under the sun, but this one liked me. I had helped him earlier to remove a corn from his left toe. He whispered each command into my ear, which still did not prevent me from offending Worcestershire traditions.

The move back to the lines was lengthy. We were the cycle company, which made it a fun day. With unfortunate results we led, or, rather, misled the battalion column. Instead of ending up in the corps concentration area (we had been shifted to 30 Corps commanded by General Horrocks, which consisted of ourselves, 50 Div., 11th Armored Div., plus Foxhead armored brigade) somewhere beyond Tilly we lost our way completely. Suddenly we were being machine-gunned by the Germans. We beat a hasty retreat. Without further mishaps we reached our destination, a little beyond the St-Lo Tilly line. I believe there was only one division, the 15th Scottish or the 53rd Welsh, between ourselves and the Americans. Tilly had been captured within three days of D-Day. Not more than three miles of further ground had been gained since. The sector where we were now concentrating had been held by Americans. Other than litter the ground with empty Lucky Strike and Camel cigarette packages they did not seem to have accomplished much.

We had wonderful weather, though dusty and almost too hot during the day. The nights were quite cold. There were notices everywhere telling drivers to go slow to minimize the dust, but it did not do much good. My friend Benjie Yeats-Brown and the 12/60th Rifles were just behind us. They were the motor battalion of the Foxhead Brigade. I spent a pleasant evening with them. For the first time we had our own tanks distributed down to coy level. Our troop commander was a chap named Nick. Algie made him a good friend and ally. Nick ran around in a green shirt, an M.C. pinned to it, suede shoes, and hatless. During really sticky moments he got out of his tank and walked in front of it so that he could see more. Our troop belonged to the 4/7 Dragoon Guards who were a particularly nice lot.

After two days of waiting we received our orders and plan.

We were to make for the river Orne around Conde sur Noireau. All this was part of the Falaise Gap battle. We started on July 30–31. The Americans, if I recall rightly, had already done their stuff to the right of St-Lo and were swarming into Brittany. During the next week we were given continuously more optimistic and ambitious orders, anticipating tremendous advances which never materialized. I suppose one had to do that kind of thing. There'd be complete chaos otherwise, if one ever got on as well as aimed for. Previous battles in the area had always been most costly to the infantry. It was the bocage, incredibly close country in Normandy known for its high hedges. The Guards armored division was in fact battling for the small town of Benny Bocage, close by. The Germans left a few automatic and armored guns behind which played hell with the infantry advancing in open formation across orchards and hedge-enclosed fields. Algie thought this would not do at all. In the best battle school manner he trained us in tactics developed by him. We were to advance from hedgerow to hedgerow, platoon by platoon in single file, firing with every weapon into the bordering hedges. Our four tanks were detailed to move up the middle, one by one.

The march to Caumont was hot and tiring. It was accompanied by a ceaseless and tremendous barrage from the guns massed along the roads. Caumont was still burning fiercely. Armored bulldozers were busy clearing the roads. Here and there was the body of a dead soldier. The smell of dead cattle was back. Beyond Caumont the going became downhill and easy. We heard reports that the Hampshires had been battling hard for a small village on our road. Actually they cleared it just in time for us to push through them. As they moved back, decimated and looking very much the worse for wear, they told us horrid stories, worse than necessary, about the pleasures in store for us. At the village the name of which I forget the Worcesters came to lead the show. We were ordered to advance on the road and on either side of it and capture the vital junction of the main Caen Avranches road. Our coy and Nick were to take the right side and we started to get on with the job.

It was vile country, with sunken lanes, raised hedgerows, high grass — in a nutshell no visibility. It was beastly country for the tanks. In fact, within five minutes one of our tanks got bogged. We did not really like their presence. Alone we could have advanced unheard and, in the failing light, along the hedgerows almost unseen. We were terribly lucky. It seemed the Germans had pulled out minutes before us. Not a shot was fired by anyone or a word spoken as our long-drawn file moved along the hedgerows. I don't think I shall ever forget the sight of a dead Tommy and a dead German facing one another, maybe twenty yards apart. They had obviously met in a chance encounter at night and killed each other. The Tommy must have been part of a patrol. We were shelled a little on the final stretch to our road crossing. Otherwise we got there safely.

By now it was quite dark. We were to hold the right forward area of the crossroads. The other companies were responsible for the rest of the area. We were in an orchard. The little one could see of it made it appear frightening. I should mention at this point that while we had been in the concentration area we watched 500 Lancasters bombing the place where we now found ourselves. The result was one hell of a mess. I doubt, though, whether this kind of bombing caused much damage in bocage country aside from morale shaking. Watching the raid had been quite a sight. Squadron after squadron appeared out of the clouds, dropped their markers and flew down as low as two or three hundred feet, directed by a master bomber. I found it quite moving that these black colossi flew in to help us but that half an hour later, lucky people, they would land at some green airfield back in England.

We had one big fright in the orchard. Sergeant Burr, the blithering idiot, shot himself in the foot with a tracer bullet. For a few moments no one could explain the noise or red light. We thought we were perhaps surrounded by trip wires. Now he is back in England, a hero from the wars.

Everything looked safer and more cheerful in daylight the next morning. I had found a spot from which we got a grand view of the enemy country in front of us. We established one of the Bn OPs with wireless and field glasses. I felt important and safe, but in fact was unimportant and unsafe. Our retreat in a sunken hollow was suddenly mortared to bits and pieces. No damage was done, thank goodness. I had quite an amusing job later in the day. After a first-rate airburst shoot on German positions opposite us, a German deserter came in. He said he and 24 others wanted to come over to us. Col. Harrison sent me off with two tanks to get them in. Cross came along with me. The beasts never appeared. Riding on my tank on the way back we were fired on by MGs and I was nearly knocked off by a tree branch. The birds had flown but evidently towards their own lines. Actually, we took a lot of prisoners that day, including a good deal of enemy transport which proved a useful acquisition.

Once again we had to leave our well-dug holes (which got deeper and narrower as one grew wiser and more cautious). We were to move forward another leap, bypassing Benny Bocage. This time we were lifted on all manner of transport. It turned out to be a most unpleasant night. We were held up for hours on the road by a traffic jam and were mortared fairly badly. I found cover along a slight undulation, which to my way of thinking reduces one's chances of being hit by 50 percent. The whole place was lit up by exploding ammunition lorries, not a good thing to have in one's neighbourhood.

The next morning we did push on, with the DCLI in the lead. They came up against a ridge held by the enemy. They suffered frightful casualties without achieving their objective. The DCLI had attacked up bare slopes. It was our turn next. Harrison, at Algie's instigation, decided to infiltrate through the tremendously

thick woods along the right. B Coy was to get to a plateau about
two miles behind the enemy, establish themselves and by way of
an elaborate artillery fire plan we were to maintain ourselves until transport could be brought up. From that position we should
make the country for miles around untenable for the enemy.
Once we were there the rest of the battalion was to follow up. I
was to reconnoitre another plateau a mile and a half beyond, and
if I considered it feasible, to hold it with my platoon. Our start
was not very encouraging. We were delayed until it was almost
dark. Even as we were covering our first mile we received three
conflicting wireless messages. To crown it all the artillery OP
found he could not FINITO.

I don't know why I finished in the middle of a sentence. I am glad I did
write then about Normandy, while it was fresh in my mind. Today, fifty
years later, names are forgotten and details blurred. I wish I had completed
the diary. I must have run out of time or energy the night I was duty officer at the Colchester depot, and what I recall of the rest of my time with
the First Worcesters is inevitably less detailed.

Maybe a week after the Carpiquet night patrol Algie Grubb sent me
on another patrol, which ended in disaster. We were either in no-man's-
land or inadvertently behind enemy lines when we heard loud voices in
German. My corporal, who was in front, stopped and asked for permission
to open fire, which I probably should have given rather than abide by the
instructions that we were meant to reconnoiter the area in preparation for
an attack the next day. It needed a split-second decision. The element of
surprise was on our side. We did not fire, but literally bumped into the
German troops. The three or four men ahead of me were taken prisoner.
At the rear I was able to disappear unnoticed into a ditch and hid until
the air was clear. To this day the episode haunts me and I remain bothered
by my decision. It probably saved lives on both sides. It did not lose us the
war, but still!

When we finally attacked, a week or so later, in August, we were supposed to capture Mont Pincon, a battle that is more than a footnote in the

history of the Normandy campaign. I was still smarting under the loss of
my men in the night patrol and was doubly determined to have us reach
our objective, which we did. I led a rather foolish charge across an open
field to the edge of a wood held by German troops. I lost a good part of my
platoon to rifle and mortar fire, but I was lucky and made it, I thought un-
harmed. I had captured one of the German infantrymen who had fired on
us and brought him back to our lines. I was quite pleased with myself until I noticed my tunic was wet, soaked in blood and that I had suffered a
gunshot wound in my right chest. The first-aid medics took it more seriously than I, and evacuated me into a most agreeable field hospital to the
rear of our lines. From there I was evacuated back to England, to Blightly
as it was called in the army, on a Red Cross train and Channel ferry. Our
final destination was a military hospital in Liverpool where they kept me
a couple of weeks. I must confess I quite enjoyed the fuss made over me.
Honor had been served. I had done my stint as a fighting soldier. I was relieved to be safe and comfortable, not only for my own sake but also for
my parents who had had sleepness nights over my safety. By then they
knew that my grandparents had been arrested in Holland and sent to a
camp; Mother's sister had taken her life in Belgium in 1940, her husband
and only son were known to have been arrested in Vichy France; the fate
of Father's brother and sister who had stayed behind in Germany was unknown; and my parents' own life in England was a makeshift existence.
Short of losing their own lives they had run the gamut of Hitler's doings.
If anything had happened to me, they had no inner resources left to cope
with more tragedy.

I had been able to get a message to them that I was out of the fighting
and safely on my way home. A week later they had a telegram from the
War Office: "Report received that Lieut. W. A. Eberstadt, Oxf. and Bucks.
Lt. Infty, attached Worcestershire Regiment was wounded on 9th of
August 1944 and admitted hospital with gunshot wound right chest.
The Army Council express sympathy. Letter follows shortly." Signed,
Under Secretary of State for War. My parents heard all this vacationing in
Exmoor together with Heinz Cahn, who kept them company and helped
keep them calm while I was in Normandy. "Enemy" aliens required police

permits to travel away from home overnight. Under the circumstances it gave Mother considerable gratification to ask the Exmoor police for permission to visit me in Liverpool. Bridget got leave from her WAAF station in Manchester. My first visitor was Elizabeth Freudenberg, one of the Labowsky daughters from Hamburg who lived in Liverpool.

After my discharge from hospital and a pleasant convalescence leave at home in Cobham I was posted to the Oxf. and Bucks. regimental depot, which for the duration had been moved from Oxford to Colchester in Essex. I was put in charge of training raw recruits who stood in awe of a "battle-scarred" young officer. I put them through immensely strenuous, though in the gorgeous weather of that autumn quite lovely, route marches in the Essex marshes and, a little farther away, Constable's Suffolk country. My boon companion was another young officer, Tony Paget, who had also been wounded. The Pagets were an old Oxfordshire family; one Paget had been Bishop of Oxford. Tony's father, General Sir Bernard, had commanded our regiment in the First World War and in the Second rose to be commander in chief of the Home Forces. We wenched and wined together. In connection with their official duties the Pagets had an apartment at the Connaught Hotel which became our base for exploring the nightlife of wartime London. Tony did return to the regiment and was killed in the Reichswald. He got a posthumous DSO, a rare award for a platoon commander, virtually a Victoria Cross. He was mourned by a girl he had inherited from me, pretty, Jewish, the daughter of a minor Hatton Gardens diamond merchant. Their background, worlds apart, brought them together.

I could have, and maybe should have, rejoined an infantry battalion. However, instigated by Father, who was implored by Mother to prevent my return to the front, the War Office interviewed me for psychological warfare and, upon cessation of hostilities, media control in occupied Germany. It sounded fascinating and proved to be in many respects the most interesting twenty months of my life.

Harbor tour of Hamburg, 1933. Edith Eberstadt, Rudolf, and Margarete
Wertheim are on the upper deck;
on the lower one, the by-then already inevitable Nazi.

Georg and Edith Eberstadt with Cliff, their Bedlington terrier, looking into the garden of their Hamburg house, 1935, shortly before leaving Germany.

Private W. A. Eberstadt, 220 Company, Pioneer Corps, with Bridget and Cliff on porch of Cobham home, probably 1941.

2nd Lieut. W. A. Eberstadt, 88th Company, Pioneer Corps, Cobham, 1943.

Lieut. W. A. Eberstadt, Second Buckinghamshire Battalion, with his parents while on 24-hour embarkation leave in the first days of July 1944 before posting to the First Battalion, Worcester Regiment in Normandy.

Major W. A. Everitt, Oxfordshire and Buckinghamshire Light Infantry, as a military government control officer at Northwest Germany Radio, Hamburg, 1945–1946, with Peter von Zahn.

Georg Eberstadt on his seventy-fifth birthday in front of Oakwood Court, London, with his daughter and son-in-law Bridget and James Collier, CB, his granddaughters Caroline and Lucy, and his poodle, Quicksy.

Independence Day Parade, Edgartown, 1994,
commemorating the fiftieth anniversary of D-Day.

With Vera at Buckingham Palace in 1986,
after Order of British Empire (O.B.E.) investiture.

11

Radio Luxembourg

In October of 1944 I transferred to one of the Information Control Units established to take over press, publishing, and broadcasting activities in what would become the British zone of occupied Germany. I had changed my name from Eberstadt to Everitt. I did not have my heart in the name change, but with the stigma attached to anything German I quite liked it at a time when I still wanted to be very, very British. Father and I picked Everitt from the London telephone directory. The name was innocuous and phonetically leaned on Eberstadt. There were no Everitts in *Burke's Peerage* or in *Who's Who*.

We were a polyglot group. Some British had worked before or during the war at the BBC. Others had publishing or newspaper backgrounds. Many were picked because they spoke fluent German. Some I knew from the Pioneer Corps. Most were Army officers or NCOs. Some were civilians who had worked in wartime ministries and looked upon military government to provide them with a postwar livelihood. Some of the British higher-ups were concerned that many of us had come from Germany, and were Jewish at that. They were afraid we might either take it out on the poor Germans or go "native." Nor did they consider us qualified to convert Nazis to the British way of life. The Americans did not share these typically British concerns. Most of their information control officers were German or Austrian Jews, but they were American citizens. I was technically still German. The British had stopped naturalization soon after war broke out. One of the last to have obtained British nationality was a stockbroker friend of Father's, a name-bearing descendant of Felix Mendelssohn-Bartholdy's. The Home Office made an exception with the explanation that they did not want a great-grandson of the man to whose music most of them had been married with to spend the war as an enemy alien.

I was promoted from lieutenant to captain to stay level in pay and rank with my civilian counterparts. We were quartered in requisitioned buildings behind Sloane Square. I shared a room with Peter Schnabel, a likeable and indolent ex-Viennese schmoozer and ex-Pioneer. Schnabel was a great ladies' man, a *Schnorrer* who was usually short of money, as well as a good cook who endeared himself to Mother in Cobham, where one night he conjured up a *Kaiserschmarren* with ingredients procured no doubt illegally from our officers' mess. Schnabel was, of all things, a kilt-wearing captain in the Black Watch, one of the grandest Scottish Highland regiments. He had a mother and a sister to support on his army pay. He was no hero, and notwithstanding the Black Watch, had never seen a shot fired in earnest. One morning when I was still asleep, the house adjoining our Sloane Street billet was flattened by a V-2 bomb. An ashen Schnabel reappeared, undressed, sank back into bed, and claimed he needed twenty-four hours of complete rest to recover from such a *Krawall*. After the war he went home to Vienna and was listed in the telephone book as "Schnabel, Peter, Königlich Britischer Major der Reserve, a. D."

It was fun to be stationed in London. Victory by then was a certainty, even if the failure to cross the Rhine at Arnhem added a dreadful winter to the war. Had Europe been spared those final six months of hostilities, endless lives and entire cities such as Dresden might have been saved. The gas chambers were at their busiest in those final months. The map of postwar Europe might have looked different. The war could have ended before the Russian armies advanced across the eastern borders of Poland. The Iron Curtain might have fallen several hundred miles farther east. The British contended that Eisenhower, in order to ensure an American-dominated victory, diverted supplies to General Patton which, at Montgomery's disposal, might have enabled him to win at Arnhem, to cross the Rhine in October of 1944, advance into the Ruhr, and force a German surrender before winter set in.

My information control unit received its (very rudimentary) training for our future work in London. I spent a few weeks at the British Broad-casting Corporation and at a training center that happened to be in Cobham, a couple of miles from my parents' home. Around Christmas we were considered trained and ready to be sent on our way. As the youngest officer and the only one with military experience, I was given a motorbike and put in charge of our convoy, which wound its way through V-2 terri-tory in the London East End to Harwich on the Essex coast where we em-barked for our Channel crossing. I was overbearing, considered myself rather grand, and was beastly to my nervous, weak-bladdered, elderly charges. I was adamant about not stopping other than for the prescribed five minutes before each hour. When we finally reached our destination, an elegant château between Brussels and Waterloo, I had got so cold on my bike that I was afraid my private parts had suffered permanent damage from frostbite. I did not stay long at headquarters. I was posted to Radio Luxembourg, which was in the psychological warfare division of SHAEF (Supreme Headquarters Allied Expeditionary Forces).

Life in Luxembourg was thoroughly enjoyable. The work was inter-esting. Many of my colleagues were a privilege to be with. We lived on American army rations, which meant plenty of everything, including lots of Hershey bars. The officers' mess was at the Brasseur, then the best ho-tel in town. I was billeted in comfort in a private home. The radio station architecture was art deco, set in a large private park. It had been built in the 1930s, really quite lavishly with lots of white marble. Radio Luxem-bourg had been highly profitable as the first commercial radio in Europe. Its staple was light musical entertainment. Audiences all over Europe

loved it. At Tonbridge it was the program we most listened to as school-
boys. Advertisers loved it. The station operated under a franchise contract from the Luxembourg government to which it paid a royalty. In
September 1939 the government required the transmitter to go off the air
to avoid being charged by the Germans with breaches of neutrality. In
May 1944 the government in exile of the Grand Duchy delivered to
SHAEF in London a letter authorizing the Supreme Commander to take
over and use Radio Luxembourg as long as required by the military situation. The retreating Germans destroyed the main control room but left
the transmitter intact. Luxembourg was liberated by the U.S. Twelfth
Army in early September. There were a few tense moments and some
casualties when the radio facilities were retaken. Two prewar employees
who, incidentally, had never collaborated with the Germans, were immensely helpful. The station was placed under SHAEF control with
William H. Hale as chief of station. Hale became well known in postwar
radio in the United States. Many advanced their future peacetime careers
at SHAEF, including, for instance, William Paley of CBS.

On September 23 broadcasts had begun with relays from London and
New York. On September 26, 1944, local origination resumed under the
direction of Captain Hans Habe, head of radio program production, Psychological Warfare Division, Twelfth Army. Habe, well known in the
Weimar Republic, was quite left wing. From Luxembourg he went on to
the American zone in Germany, responsible for newspaper publications.
He was controversial but fascinating. At Radio Luxembourg he had four
programs:

Story of the Day, based on front line intelligence, exposing weakness in
   units of the German army facing Twelfth Army units.
Letter Bag, consisting of readings from letters captured in German mailbags,
   field post offices, or headquarters.
Frontpost, based on the small Allied-produced newspaper of that name
   distributed by air to the German troops.
Leaflet Show, based on appeals to specific German units to encourage
   surrender.

In early October Radio Luxembourg was placed under the direct control of PWD, the Psychological Warfare Division of SHAEF. Its signal spread over all three army groups and could be heard in the western half of Germany. By the time I arrived, the programs produced by SHAEF personnel, which included me, were primarily strategic in nature, addressed to the German population behind the combat zone and ultimately to German civilians in occupied areas. Our commanding officer was Lieut. Col. Samuel R. Rosenbaum, an American who spoke good German. He and I got on well. Years later I visited him in Philadelphia where he lived. His wife played the harp. The repertoire for harp music is limited and he commissioned pieces for her. After the war he had an interesting prestigious job as head of ASCAP, which collects music royalties all over the world.

In late October a group of British civilians from the BBC arrived at the station to assist in the preparation and production of SHAEF programs. I became part of that team, which was outstanding. The general editor was Patrick Gordon-Walker, who had taught me politics at Christ Church. Gordon-Walker went on to prominence as a cabinet minister in postwar Labor governments. The features editor was Ralph Poston, who later became my boss in Hamburg. He was wonderfully supportive of me. In return he had my affection and respect. Poston had been head of broadcasting in the Palestine Mandate. Unlike many of his fellow English, he was sympathetic to Zionism. The Postons were a civilized family, the English at their best. His sister Elizabeth was the leading authority on Elizabethan music. After his return to England from Hamburg, he entered holy orders.

In the fall, programs were added to support military operations. German prisoners of war were employed to broadcast military intelligence reports, which had more of an immediate frontline character than the material provided from London or New York. Patrick Gordon-Walker's brother Robin joined as general editor of broadcasts addressed to foreign workers in their own languages. A daily program of news and intelligence provided by SHAEF had as its signature tune an excerpt from the Nimrod movement of Elgar's *Enigma Variations*.

Luxembourg also provided news programs about the military situation for use by the BBC and radio stations in the United States. The atmosphere was tense during Rundstedt's Ardennes offensive. In January 1945, Luxembourg was under intermittent rocket fire. In March broadcasts commenced to cover Field Marshal Montgomery's 21st Army Group sector. This was part of my daily work. We were commanded by Lieut. Col. Keith Thomson, a prewar Radio Luxembourg advertising salesman turned Tank Corps officer. Thomson later became military commanding officer of Radio Hamburg, while Ralph Poston became program head.

Luxembourg was the major allied broadcasting operation in Europe during the final months of the war. According to the official station history, "The SHAEF broadcasting personnel in May 1945 consisted of 4 U.S. commissioned officers, 6 British, 3 French, 1 Belgian; 70 U.S. enlisted men, 3 British; 22 U.S. civilians, 10 British, and three other Allied civilians. In addition there were 75 Luxembourg civilians."

My name appears on the staff manifest as one of thirteen feature writers. The most intellectual was Gottfried (Golo) Mann, one of Thomas Mann's children, who went on to academic fame in postwar Germany. Another was Leonard Miall, very nice, English, who later made his way close to the top of the BBC. We still correspond from time to time. P. J. Brand, a German émigré, married Charlotte Michaux, a Luxembourg-born colleague of ours. He went on to the World Bank. For many years we'd see each other. Among the news writers was Bill Ackroyd, a British army major, Etonian, urbane scion of a well-to-do stockbroking family, veteran of the Eighth Army. I can't now place where a Colonel Ward fit into our organization. He had an immense bushy moustache and in civilian life owned a store, the establishment of its kind, on Piccadilly which sold expensive canes and umbrellas. More important, it was among the leading taxidermists in the British Empire. They stuffed and mounted shooting trophies, from elephants to lions and tigers. In later years I used to drop in on him from time to time on my way to work at the *Economist* in St. James.

I do not recall features written by me. I was sent on field trips which, however, did not always lend themselves to broadcasting. For instance, I went into Trier with the American battalion occupying that lovely old town. Trier was called Trevoranum in Roman times and is a bishop's see to this day. To my horror I came upon one unit looting the cellars, which were filled with huge wooden wine vats and thousands of wine bottles. The troops, a black battalion, had tapped the vats, let the wine pour over themselves, and it was now inches deep covering the cobbled stone floor. Bottles were clanging, and intoxicating narcotic vapors had begun to overwhelm the cellars. It was a satanic scene. It was not the moment to moralize, but to pull the men out of the cellar before the alcohol fumes killed them. I was not beyond a little "liberating" myself and was complimented for having covered the liberation of Trier productively when I returned to our officers' mess with some good Moselles.

In late April I was given leave to drive to Belsen. The war had not yet ended. We knew my grandparents had been taken there from Holland. We also knew that my grandfather was dead. We did not expect my grandmother to have survived, but had no definite knowledge of her fate. I reached Belsen about ten days after its liberation. My visit is described in the next section of this book.

While in northern Germany I went to Bremen, which had recently been taken by British troops. It was devastated by fire raids. As in Trier, soldiers had found cellars filled with wine, more to the liking of the Hanseatic climate and palate, red rather than white, and French rather than German.

Just prior to V-E Day I had a few days of leave in Paris. I had acquired a German army staff car, the predecessor of the Volkswagen, roofless and rickety. It gave me trouble most of the way. It passed out fifty miles from Paris. I abandoned it, took my bag, and hitchhiked the rest of the way. I had never been to Paris. My introduction was like a fairy tale. I had a date with an ATS (WACS) officer, also a psychological warrior. The weather was perfect, the chestnut trees in full blossom, food and drink in the officers' messes plentiful and good. We had a meal at Maxim's, which was trying to make up for its collaborator years with the Germans by being particularly solicitous of Allied guests. We stayed at the Hotel Astorg, small and charming, in the Rue d'Astorg. The hotel has become an office, but sometimes I still walk along the street.

On V-E Day I was in Luxembourg. There were special broadcasts non-stop. Sam Rosenbaum organized a victory celebration in the studios. I managed some time off and went for a lovely long walk along the Moselle with Golo Mann. We stopped at numerous taverns, sat in the sun — the weather was perfect — and drank a great deal of wine. What could be more appropriate than to spend the first day of European peace with Thomas Mann's son? He was not yet famous, rather an oddball like the other Mann children, but interesting company. I have read some of the books that later made his reputation, but our paths never crossed again. In the early 1950s, when I was vacationing with my parents at the Waldhaus in Sils Maria, our dining room table happened to be between Thomas Mann's and Ernst Jünger's. Not exactly frivolous dinner neighbors! From a conversation I gained the impression that Mann father and son were not close.

PART THREE

The Flersheims and Wertheims in Emigration

The Flersheim family and their business had survived difficult times prompted by the world economic crisis, by tightened foreign exchange regulations, and the onset of Nazi rule. By the mid-1930s anti-Semitism affected every aspect of daily life in Germany.

In April 1933, there was already a call to boycott Jewish businesses in Germany. Jewish students started to be expelled from schools and universities. Civil servants who were Jewish, or others seen as disloyal to the Nazi regime, were dismissed from lifetime-tenured jobs. By April 1934, hundreds of university professors, an estimated 4,000 lawyers, 3,000 medical doctors, and thousands of artists and musicians lost their positions. By late 1934, over 60,000 Jews had left Germany.

Ernst and Gertrud Flersheim were still committed to their life in Germany, dealing as well as they could with the changes inflicted upon them. Domestic and international business operations were impaired. In September 1935, the Nuremberg Laws were pronounced, relegating Jews to second-class citizens with restricted rights. Marriages or intimate relations between Jews and Germans were prohibited. The assimilation and integration of Jews into western European society over the past hundred years was undone.

By the end of 1935, the Flersheims had received permission to continue part of their business outside Germany. They planned to emigrate to Holland. Their daughter Margarete also lived in Frankfurt, married to Rudolf Wertheim, a lawyer who, on account of his World War I service, was still able to practice law in 1936. In 1937 Rudolf and Margarete Wertheim emigrated to Brussels with their then ten-year-old son, Hans, who was born in 1928.

The Flersheims chose the Netherlands because they knew the country from holidays and business. It was not too far from the Eberstadts in England and it was close to the Wertheims in Belgium, and they visited their children repeatedly before 1939. Their nephews Herbert and Fritz Flersheim had relocated to Amsterdam as early as 1935.

In the late 1930s war had become a near certainty, and with the benefit of hindsight the Netherlands and Belgium were endangered countries, yet neither the Flersheims nor the Wertheims seemed to fear they'd be overrun in the event of a war. Father tried to get them to move to England, but they had come to quite like where they lived and could not get themselves to face another move. In 1939, Ernst Flersheim was seventy-seven years old and Gertrud sixty-seven.

As long as the Netherlands and Belgium were neutral during the "phony war," it was possible to communicate from England. After the Low Countries were overrun in May 1940, they became enemy territory and communications between England and the German-occupied countries were cut off. However, the Flersheims and Wertheims were able to write to one another. The Flersheims and my parents also continued to correspond, now clandestinely via our Swiss cousin Willy Dreyfus, until the Flersheims were arrested in Holland in 1943. Much of their correspondence survived and found its way after 1945 to my parents.

12

Last Years of the Wertheim Family, 1940–1942

Margarete Wertheim suffered from multiple sclerosis and by 1940 was fairly immobile. She feared she would be a hindrance to her husband and son. Two days after the German troops marched into Belgium and Holland, she took her life, though at first we were led to believe she had suffered a heart attack.

On June 27, 1940, Willy Dreyfus cabled Father in England: "Gertrud writes Margarete died heart failure May 12th. Rudolf's whereabouts unknown since May 10th. Impossible communicate Belgium. Parents [Ernst and Gertrud Flersheim] unmolested. Most heartfully mourning with you both. Love Willy Dreyfus"

Gertrud Flersheim managed to establish contact with a family in Brussels named Rosenberg who had been friends of the Wertheims and were one of several families looking after the Wertheims' son Hans. Following is a letter written by Mrs. Rosenberg to Gertrud Flersheim, nearly five months after her daughter's death. It describes the last days of Margarete and mentions the Bergers, who had sons of about the same age as Hans. I do not know where the Berger family came from but seem to recollect that their name came up in pre-1939 correspondence and conversations between my mother and her sister. To the best of my knowledge Mrs. Berger had been the Wertheims' housekeeper. The letter mentions Mrs. Berger visiting the men (her husband and Rudolf Wertheim) after they were detained. On the day of the invasion, Belgian police had arrested any person considered a potential threat to the interests of Belgium, including German nationals and refugees from other countries.

KAETHE ROSENBERG TO GERTRUD FLERSHEIM, OCTOBER 3, 1940
110 Avenue des Nations, Brussels

Dear Mrs. Flersheim,

Thank you for your letter. I fully understand that you want to know more about your daughter. In the final months before the outbreak of the war I saw a good deal of her. I liked her greatly. She was courageous. Notwithstanding her illness she was always there for others, and gave of herself. With her bright mind she was determined to the end not to stagnate but to learn and absorb new knowledge and ideas. She had made plans to attend classes at the university, and to go to concerts, as well as lectures. The last time I saw her was on Saturday, May 11, when Mrs. Berger asked me to keep her company. She was very restless and nervous. She was greatly worried about her husband and afraid of the air raids. The idea of having to go into an air raid shelter in the event of an alarm troubled her greatly. Notwithstanding all this she wanted to write to you to put your mind at ease. I tried my best to encourage and divert her. After she had written to you she telephoned a few friends and shops. It was all a big strain on her. We lunched together, rice pudding with applesauce. She had her meal with evident pleasure and we were all cheered by the presence of the children. However, her main concern was about her husband and whether he would come home soon. She felt so lost without him. Mrs. Berger meanwhile had been to visit the men, brought them their laundry, some tobacco and chocolate. She sounded positive about their situation when she came back. On Saturday we had no idea that by Sunday they would be gone. Your daughter spoke a good deal about you. She was so afraid that her father might not be with you and that she would no longer be able to correspond with him. The poor woman could not move from her armchair. It bothered her so much that in the tense and exciting first days of the war she was unable to do anything helpful, yet she never complained with as much as a syllable. She was a sensitive, thoroughly good person. She tried her best to fulfill her role as wife, mother, and daughter. But don't begrudge her the peace she now has.

With my deepest sympathy, dear Mrs. and Mr. Flersheim, I extend my hand to you. A prolonged separation from her husband and the generally terrible times in which we live would have overwhelmed her. God meant well with her to release her from life.

Hans is a splendid dear boy. He looks so much like his mother. He does well in school. He takes a lively interest in political affairs. He is well looked after by particularly nice and decent people, and feels at home with them. Mrs. Berger feels as responsible for him as she does for her own children. In all likelihood he will be able to join his father shortly.

If there is anything else I can tell you, I am of course at your disposal. All we womenfolk now have grave worries about the fate of our husbands who continue to be interned in the south of France. Let's hope they will survive the coming winter in good shape.

With warm and friendly greetings to you and your husband. May you both prove to be as courageous as your dear daughter.

Yours, Kaethe Rosenberg

(Received October 9 and answered)

Considering that letters could fall into the hands of the occupying German authorities, it is possible they do not fully state the events. When Kaethe Rosenberg writes about the men: "On Saturday we had no idea that by Sunday they would be gone," we know that this refers to Rudolf Wertheim escaping to the South of France with Mr. Berger. The details of this escape are unknown. I believe that Rudolf Wertheim, when he went to the South of France, left money behind to take care of Mrs. Berger, her children, and his son Hans. It also seems this money had been given to another person, Mrs.Friedmann, to distribute. Isn't it interesting to see how quickly mail went between Amsterdam and Brussels notwithstanding the war? It also seems that Gertrud Flersheim was able to send some money to the Rethys, a family with whom Hans was living later on. Notwithstanding everything, in some respects life went on "normally."

R. RETHY TO GERTRUD FLERSHEIM, SEPTEMBER 23, 1940
Brussels

Dear Mrs. Flersheim,

  I received your lines this morning. I was on the verge yesterday of writing to you to advise you that since Saturday little Hans is living with us. Mrs. Wachsmann was no longer in a position to keep the child. In any event Hans is due within the next ten days to two weeks to leave together with the Berger children for the South of France. For the time being, he attends the nearby school and he enjoys being with us. It is a real delight to see him eating. Considering his age he has undergone a lot these past months. He appears to feel at home with us and has no desire to go back to the Wachmanns'. I hope there will be an opportunity to meet you personally so that we can exchange some of our thoughts.

         With kindest regards, Mrs. R. Rethy

(Received by Gertrud Flersheim on September 28, 1940)

As early as August 23, Hans was writing to his grandparents in Amsterdam that he had moved and was living now with the Rethys. He told them that he liked it better there than at the Wachsmanns'. He apparently spent four weeks with the Wachsmanns after living with the Berger family. Plans were under way for Hans and the Berger children to join their fathers in southern France, leaving in early October.

MRS. R. RETHY TO GERTRUD FLERSHEIM, OCTOBER 7, 1940
Brussels

Dear Mrs. Flersheim,

Thank you for your kind lines, which we have received with thanks. I hasten to let you know about your little Hans. He is always well behaved and does his school homework every day. He is allowed to stay up till 9 P.M. to listen to the radio, and Saturday night a bit later which makes him blissful. Everybody agrees that Hans looks really well by now. He is not gaining too much weight. Since the meals are plentiful, he does not want to eat excessively. There is fruit every day. (That is the region where I come from) and for today I have promised him potato soup. Klaus [Berger] suggested to him to trade places; Hans should go back for a fortnight and he would come to live with us. Hans answered promptly this was fine with him but on one condition, namely that Klaus should first spend four weeks en pension with the Wachsmanns'! Isn't that touching? My daughter Irene went yesterday to see Mrs. Friedmann and Mrs. Haas, where she also met Mrs. Lazarus. They went through everything and Wednesday afternoon Hans will go shopping with Irene and Mrs. Friedmann. They have made a list of what to buy.

I trust you and your dear husband, to whom please extend thanks for his kind lines, are keeping well.

With cordial greetings, respectfully Yours, R. Rethy

This note was added to a letter that Hans wrote:

R. Rethy to Gertrud Flersheim, October 14, 1940
Brussels

Dear Mrs. Flersheim,

I'd like to add a few lines of my own to Hans's letter. He seems in good shape and spirit at all times, and we have become very accustomed and attached to the child. He is, for his age, so sensible. One can have really good conversations with him. We have waited with this letter since we had been expecting to hear from you any day.

With friendly greetings,

Respectfully, R. Rethy

R. Rethy to Gertrud Flersheim, November 2, 1940
Brussels

Dear Mrs. Flersheim,

Many thanks for your kind lines of Oct. 25. We are utilizing the holidays to catch up with our correspondence. Hans, too, has just written to you. He is really all right with us and can enjoy his life, which is to the good because he has been much sinned against, even though sufficient financial means were left behind by Mr. Wertheim.

My daughter has posed the question to Mrs. Friedmann on several occasions — how many sons was Mr. Wertheim responsible for, three or one? This is in line with Mrs. Berger's instructions to spend at the most 15 francs a day on Hans's food. For that amount of money it is impossible under current conditions to take care of a growing child and feed him properly. To which she responded that, vis-à-vis Mrs. Berger, she could not justify more than 20 francs. It was left that she would pay 30 francs a day from October 15th onward, and between Sept. 21 and Oct. 15 pay an extra 10 francs a day, or 250 francs all told. The excursion to Tarmat cost 20 francs. Would you be kind enough to send me this sum?

My daughter has gone on numerous errands and missed out on several days of work. With Mrs. Berger she went several times to the *juge de paix* and elsewhere. With Mrs. Friedmann she went to the cemetery and did all the shopping with her because she does not speak much French. I leave it to you, dear Mrs. Flersheim, if you want to give her a present.

Here it is still possible to buy quite a few things such as underwear, materials, and tulles. People are buying up a lot, but so far it is still possible without coupon rationing.

We see the time approaching when Hans will be leaving us. We will be quite sorry because we have become used to him. He visits the Berger children only on Sundays, which he considers quite sufficient.

I am full of admiration for all your doings and efficiency, dear Mrs. Flersheim, and only hope you are not overtiring yourself. I do hope you and I will meet at some point in this life. A letter you wrote to Hans moved me to tears. I said to him I loved his grandmother without ever having met her.

Yesterday we had Indonesian rijstafel to eat. It's heavy, but Hans liked it a lot. In my youth, I lived nine years on Java, where my father was a colonel in the medical corps.

Enough for today.

With best regards, also to your husband, Yours, R. Rethy

(Received by Gertrud Flersheim, November 7, 1940)

R. Rethy to Gertrud Flersheim, November 18, 1940
Brussels

Dear Mrs. Flersheim,

My best thanks for your kind lines which I hasten to answer. First, to settle the business part, I would like to tell you that I am of course agreeable to your suggestions. I can well believe you that you have to count your pennies carefully; no one these days sleeps on a bed of roses; but isn't it paradoxical that meanwhile Mrs. Friedmann has *plein pouvoir* to spend money as she sees fit, and on the other hand, you, dear Mrs. Flersheim, have to deny yourself a dress you want to buy? Why should you send Frau Friedmann money when she has sufficient at her disposal? Frau Berger left 24,000 francs behind; I don't know whether you are aware of it. It is not to tell tales, but I feel it is my duty to make sure you know. Once the children leave, in any event all they will be allowed to take is 100 marks each. My daughter has had conversations with Frau Dr. Mayer about various matters, but it is very hard to talk to Frau Friedmann about some subjects because she has some fixed ideas; for instance, she is of the opinion that anything Hans gets, the Berger children should have the same. After we had bought various items for Hans, right away Klaus Berger also got a jacket, which cost 450 francs. I don't consider this right since it is all Dr. Wertheim's money, and there is more we don't even know about. None of this is our business, but it is difficult to keep quiet after all one has witnessed. Yesterday my daughter took Hans to the Avenue des Scarabes (where Frau Friedmann lives), as every week she goes to pick up fresh laundry for Hans, but Frau Friedmann was in town with the [Berger?] children to look at the St. Nicholas' Day festivities. They had to wait an hour. Frau Dr. Haas said she could not stand all the noise from the children any longer, and that she intended to put a stop to all the laundry plus laundress; she sends her and Peter's laundry out, and Frau

Friedmann should do the same. I never refused to wash Hans's handful of laundry at home, but Frau Friedmann would not let me keep anything at all of Hans's at our house. The other day, half an hour before he was due to go to school my daughter had to mend a pair of socks of his; we did not have a second pair.

Thank goodness Hans is well and happy with us; he is being spoilt by all. Every Sunday, he is given 5 francs to go to the movies by a lady we are friends with and who lives in our house. Last week he used the money to buy a book which he means to save to read when he leaves us [to join his father]. He is a good child, easy to raise; one need never tell him to do his homework; he has good manners; *jamais UN mot deplacé*. I rarely dare mention his dear mother. I have to be very careful because I notice how sad he becomes any time I speak of her. I cannot bear the helpless expression that overcomes him, and it also affects me.

As for further shopping, Frau Friedmann will presumably take care of it. She works as a domestic for Frau Dr. Haas, and gets only one afternoon a week off. She should have been candid about telling you of her situation, and a friend would have been glad to help her. Frau Dr. Lazarus is a charming woman, according to my daughter, as is Frau Dr. Mayer. These two ladies would doubtlessly have taken care of everything. But now I am going to stop. I have become quite dizzy from all this writing. My normal habit is to write short letters and I have still not written everything that is on my mind.

Next time more.

Yours, R. Rethy
(Received November 21, 1940)

R. RETHY TO GERTRUD FLERSHEIM, DECEMBER 8, 1940
Brussels

Dear Mrs. Flersheim

We are late in writing, my apologies. Last week there was a lot on, and Irene was out a lot with Hans shopping for all sorts of things before he leaves.

Now that the travel permit has been received, the children should be on their way soon.

We celebrated St. Nicholas pleasantly. Hans enjoyed his presents greatly. We, too, had a surprise. In the evening he would not allow us back in the kitchen, and the next morning he [St. Nicholas] had been there for us as well. We thought that was so sweet of the child. I asked him once whether he would give us a good-bye kiss before he left. He answered that aside from his parents and grandparents he had never kissed anyone, and did not think he'd like it. I think that is honestly spoken, and I like it that way. Tuesday Monsieur Jean and Irene are going to the opera — I ask you! They are going to see *Traviata* with Clara Clairbert. It was his idea. He has never before been to the opera.

The lady from upstairs has asked us to buy Hans a nice book. We found one for 26 francs. She has written something personal in it for him.

Otherwise there is nothing special to report. With very warm greetings from both of us, also for your husband,

Respectfully, R. Rethy
(Received December 16, 1940)

R. RETHY TO GERTRUD FLERSHEIM, JANUARY 4, 1941
Brussels

Dear Mrs. Flersheim,

For days I have been meaning to write and acknowledge receipt of your kind letter; I was very busy and when I did have time to write I was too tired. I was very pleased with your kind letter; unfortunately it arrived too late to give Hans his letter from you. He left on Dec. 15th. According to what I just heard, on the 23rd he was still in Paris. I hope by now they will have received their permits to move onward. We were sad when he left us. We had become very attached to him. The day before he left, Irene took him once more to the cemetery to take leave. He seemed deeply moved and had a hard time leaving the grave. Now he is gone, and let's wish for him that he will be soon reunited with his father in good health. Maybe while I am writing, he is already there.

The lady in the house who spoiled him so is at the moment quite sick: a nervous breakdown. She is waiting for a vacancy in a sanatorium; everything at the moment is overcrowded. If she can find a few months of complete quiet we hope she can be fully restored. It came so suddenly. We had still spent such a cozy Christmas together.

Before Hans left, her husband still gave him two beautiful books by Hector Malot [Sans Famille]. He was so pleased with them. If only we had news that he has arrived safely. I was not very pleased he went in a car, because traveling by car does not agree with him. We had lined up a very nice gentleman who has taken numerous people in his car to the South of France. He had plans just now to travel there by train; it would have cost half the price (instead of 6,000 francs, 3,000). But there was nothing we could do and Frau Friedmann thought it would be difficult to cancel the other person. Now it has happened and let us just hope he gets safely to his father.

No more for today but cordial greetings to you and Mr. Flersheim, also from my daughter.

Sincerely yours, R. Rethy

(Received January 16, 1941)

This concludes the Rethy correspondence. One wonders what Gertrud Flersheim wrote to her. Some of it one can guess from the contents of Mrs.

Rethy's letters: concern over Hans on every count; financial matters, including help, but concern that the Flersheims' means were restricted. My grandmother was a complicated lady and tended to write long letters.

Following are three pieces of correspondence from Ruth Friedmann to my grandparents. The first is a postcard addressed to them at 114 Michelangelo Straat in Amsterdam.

RUTH FRIEDMANN TO GERTRUD FLERSHEIM, DECEMBER 14, 1940

Respected Frau Flersheim, respected Herr Flersheim,

Today just briefly to advise you that at noontime today the three children left by car for the South of France, via Paris. They are being taken by a very reliable Belgian who works for the local Red Cross. I will write to you about business matters in the next days. Hans left radiantly happy. He was so very glad that he would be seeing his papa again. For the Rethys (as for me) the parting was very hard. He is an exceptionally nice boy.

With cordial greetings,

Sincerely, Ruth Friedmann

RUTH FRIEDMANN TO GERTRUD FLERSHEIM, DECEMBER 23, 1940
Brussels

Respected Mr. Flersheim,

I would like to acknowledge today receipt of three letters from you, one dated 12.8.40, one brought by a messenger on 12.14.40, and an express letter of 12.17.40 received today. Many thanks.

To this day Mrs. Weissmüller has not been in touch with me. I do not know whether she was in Brussels or whether perhaps she had heard that the children had left on the 14th and, therefore, there was no point in meeting to discuss her escorting the children. As I wrote to you in a card on the 14th in the evening, the children left at midday in excellent spirits, knowing that they were on their way to rejoin their families. Hans looked very nice in his new loden coat and new boots (notwithstanding his urging I would not let him wear his new suit for the trip). All sorts of people in the Rethy house gave him good-bye presents. The Rethys themselves were sad to see him go. In everybody's opinion Hans has developed well during the past few months, both in his appearance and mentality. I hope you can see this for yourselves, both from the photo I sent you recently and the one enclosed with this letter. Now, of course, I am awaiting eagerly news that they have arrived safely at Les Martys.

There is nothing new to report about the [Wertheim] apartment. De Preter has not written as promised, and Miss Rethy will go to see him once more after the holidays. Nor has Novgorodsky answered my letter, so that Miss Rethy will have to pay him another visit. Regarding the banking matters I have already written to you. Now that the children have gone, there seems little sense in going to the Commission for enemy property to have money released for the children's trip. The president of Lloyd's Bank promised me, after I had seen him three times, to arrange a meeting for me with the bank's commissioner who was, however, reluctant to receive me, and generally proved not amenable to any sort of cooperative attitude. He refused even to release the Belgian franc credit balance in the account. I had previously explained to the president of the bank that I was only asking for the unfreezing of money to pay for the living expenses of Dr. Wertheim's child, who was my ward. The president did tell this to the commissar, but so far to no avail. I further explained to the president of the bank that Dr. W. did not fall into the category of those who left Belgium voluntarily and had failed to return before the deadline when the money of those who had failed to come back was confiscated. Dr. Wertheim, I explained, had indeed been interned like all German nationals on May 10, but because he was Jewish was not allowed to return. The child, on the other hand, was here and had to be fed and clothed. One should at least give me the Belgian franc credit balance even if the English pound sterling balance remained blocked. The only response I got from the commissar was that he had no intention of doing anything for a Jew, and Dr. Wertheim was Jewish.

If I should obtain permission in the foreseeable future to en-ter the apartment and remove any of the contents, there would at the present be the possibility to have a shipment sent to the South of France. Hans and the Berger boys have taken their own clothing and each has a warm blanket (Hans has the beautiful sheepskin rug which used to be in the Longchamp apartment). Hans sat by the window in the car because he told me he got sick on long drives unless he got some fresh air. It was cold when they left but beautifully sunny.

For each of the boys I was able to get RM100, which equals 2,000 French francs, which means they will be getting to the South of France with almost 6,000 French francs. (I am saying "almost" because they may have to spend some of this money in Paris — depending on how long they will be there.) I was able to pay all the travel costs from here. It cost a considerable amount of money. I had to pay the driver 2,000 Belgian francs per child, though this is supposed to cover the cost of board and lodging while they are in Paris. It is quite possible that it will take several days to get the travel permit for going from Paris into unoccupied France. It would interest me to know how much Frau Weissmüller was going to charge for escorting the children to southern France.

I am enclosing a list of what I bought for Hans. There is no need for you to send me more money, . . . as I have enough to cover all expenses and a reserve for unanticipated further costs — provided they are not too high. At present I have about 3,000 Belgian francs left over.

Well, this is really all for today.

With best wishes for you and your wife, Ruth Friedmann

(Received January 4, 1941)

Enclosed in Ruth Friedmann's letter was a list of purchases for Hans:

Purchases for Hans

1 suit	400 Belgian francs
1 loden coat	320
1 pair of boots plus soles	233.25
1 suitcase	120
2 shirts	42
1 Basque cap	10.50
1 windbreaker	145
1 pair of gloves	17.50
1 pair of socks	28.50
1 pair of overalls	59.95
1 pair of scout pants	65
3 undershirts-underpants	66
1 long-sleeved polo sweater	50
4 pairs of socks	70
1 pair of shoes	204
1 gabardine raincoat	345
2 pairs pajamas	153
1 stamp album (present from grandparents)	22.50
1 pair of boots & grease	247
1 cap	11.50
1 briefcase (present from grandparents)	65
1 pair of socks	25
1 wool scarf	29
2 pairs of flannel pajamas	118
1 rucksack	37

1 pair of gloves	13.50
1 blanket cover	30
1 blanket belt	60
Total	3,030.70

Additional expenditures

Payment Rethy	260
Dentist	40
Tombstone Frau Wertheim	100
Grave preparation	80
Grave maintenance 1 year	40

Out-of-pocket expenses

Frl. Rethy, 5 francs per hour	170
Total	60

RUTH FRIEDMANN TO MR. AND MRS. FLERSHEIM, APRIL 17, 1941
Brussels

Dear Mrs. Flersheim, dear Mr. Flersheim,

Many thanks for your letters of March 4 and April 6. Unfortunately I have not been able to write to you sooner, but I had a bad abscess in my right hand and for two weeks was unable to write. It had to be operated on and only since a few days I can write again. Excuse my long silence, but you can see that I could not help it.

A few days ago I was again called to the district offices. Apparently van Kampt had raised objections to the removal of items from the apartment. I was told the inventory made at the time was no longer accurate, and I would have to see to it that the inventory list was adjusted accordingly. If this was not done I could find myself responsible for having to pay for missing items. I should get in touch right away with van Kampt, who is the building superintendent, or with Sohet, who is the lawyer. For me it is out of the question to negotiate with van Kampt, but I called Sohet, only to hear from his assistant that he was away. The assistant told me it was impossible to adjust an inventory listing ex-post. Still, I am going to try to see Sohet in the next few days. However, it seems to me most unlikely that I can regain access to the apartment. As I told you the only things I was allowed to remove were items of personal clothing. Apparently I failed to tell you previously that in the cellar I found neither a suitcase nor indeed anything. Now, however, I have a letter from your son-in-law and Berger that a suitcase with personal laundry was in the garage. I wish they had told me before. I could have removed it at the time, and might have found other items there. Maybe that is where your daughter's clothing items which are missing might be. If at all, I cannot apply for reentry into the apartment until I have spoken to Sohet. It is out of the question to get permission for the removal of any jewelry. Now that you see the problems I hope you will understand why I would not get anywhere with the jewelry or, for that matter, get permission to move anything from her writing desk.

I do not have a black woolen dress. There was one in the suitcase I sent to your son-in-law. I do have a muff and two pairs of woolen underwear. There is no suitcase to send these things to you. Should I buy a cardboard box and mail them to you?

I have sent the various items to your son-in-law, but I was not able to buy him any underwear. For that I would have needed ration coupons, which of course I could not obtain in his name.

According to your son-in-law's letter his plans to go to America are making headway. The affidavit is on its way. Meanwhile they are farming and have planted potatoes. Your son-in-law seems to enjoy his rural existence. No doubt you know that the two fathers are teaching Hans and Klaus. The Berger family is equally anxious to get to the U.S.A. as soon as possible. All this he writes in a letter dated March 27.

On May 12, I plan to go to the cemetery, after which I should be in a position to answer your questions. I wrote previously that the cemetery is in Uccle, Dieweg. The first time I went I also knew nothing beyond name, date of death, and address of your daughter. At the cemetery the caretaker told me where I would find the grave, but he gave me the wrong row number. It was difficult to locate it since there was no tombstone as yet. Now that a stone has been placed it is easy to find the right spot. In any event Frau Meyer also knows where it is and for the time being I will continue to be in Brussels and no doubt shall see you here before I can get away to America. In any event you may want to make a note: *Uccle Cemetery*, Dieweg; by streetcar take # 6 or # 10 and a light at the Dieweg halt.

One other matter regarding the upkeep of the grave (I just reread Frau Flersheim's letter): I have paid for one year's maintenance and when I go out there on May 12th I should be able to see whether they have done a good job.

Miss Rethy, Frau Dr. Wachsmann, and Frau Rosenberg all have been given something from the items we were allowed to remove from the apartment.

Well, this is all for today. Please let me know how I should dispatch the various items to you.

> With cordial greetings, Ruth Friedmann
> (Received April 25, 1940)

The letters that follow were written by Hans Wertheim, son of Rudolf and Margarete Wertheim. They start in 1940 in Brussels and end in the Pyrenees. They were written mainly in German, a few in French, to Gertrud and Ernst Flersheim, Hans's grandparents in Holland, and to his father, who had reached the Pyrenees ahead of him.

HANS WERTHEIM TO HIS FLERSHEIM GRANDPARENTS,
UNDATED (AUGUST 1940)

Dear Grandma and dear Grandpa,

Many thanks for the 25 F, the chocolate and the notebook.
All is very well with me. I go to school. I am done with my tests.
I believe I did well. I am now collecting picture cards made by
Blanche-Neige chocolate and am doing nothing about stamp collecting, because at the moment I don't seem to be able to get any
stamps. But card collecting is also very enjoyable. I would like as
a present a pocket flashlight that can be dimmed. It would be
most useful just now. They are continuing to fire at aircraft, which
are trying to bomb Everen.

Many greetings, Hans
(Received August 24, 1940)

HANS WERTHEIM TO HIS FLERSHEIM GRANDPARENTS,
AUGUST 23, 1940

Dear Grandpa and dear Grandma,

At the moment I am with the Rethys. It is very nice, much
nicer than at the Wachsmanns'. It is also very close to my school.
Thursdays, Saturdays, and Sundays I play with the Berger boys.
My stamp collection is not making much progress. I read a lot.
Once a week I go swimming at the pool with my school.

Many greetings, Hans
(Received August 28, 1940)

HANS WERTHEIM TO HIS FLERSHEIM GRANDPARENTS,
SEPTEMBER 4, 1940

Dear Grandpa and dear Grandma!

Many thanks for your letters. I am very well and how are you?
I have started again collecting stamps but don't as yet have an
album. The weather is very nice at the moment. I play a lot
outdoors. Soon school starts again. In the tests I ranked sixth out
of 25, and first in swimming.

Lots of greetings, Hans

P.S. I need a pair of gray trousers. Could you pay for them but
not buy them, as they need to match with a jacket.

(Received September 29, 1940)

HANS WERTHEIM TO HIS FLERSHEIM GRANDPARENTS,
OCTOBER 6, 1940
Brussels

Dear Grandma and dear Grandpa,

Many thanks for your letters. I am very well. I shall be leaving
in about one week. I am greatly looking forward to it. This week I
got very good grades — 21 out of 22. I have the same teacher as
last year (the awful one). We go swimming once a week. I can
now dive headfirst. I am in the sixth grade. Every Thursday I visit
with Ulrich, Klaus, Peter Schrag, and Wera. We go to collect
chestnuts. The weather is bad at the moment. This week I have a
math test. The food at the Rethys' is good. Today we had fritters
and tomorrow we are getting potato pancakes.

Many greetings, Hans

HANS WERTHEIM TO HIS FLERSHEIM GRANDPARENTS,
OCTOBER 13, 1940
Brussels

Dear Grandma and dear Grandpa!

The other day we went to buy everything I need: one suit, a cap, an overcoat, a pair of shoes, three shirts. We still have to get six pairs of socks, two sweaters, a pair of gloves, and a pair of trousers. The other day we had a math test. I scored 59.5 out of 60. I was ranked second in my class. Two weeks ago we went on a school outing. The weather has turned very nice. The day before yesterday we had potato pancakes, and yesterday we had mussels. Monday I went to the movies. I saw *Carnet de Bal.*

All good wishes, Hans

The following two letters to his grandparents were written in French by Hans, who signed his name "Jean."

HANS WERTHEIM TO HIS FLERSHEIM GRANDPARENTS,
NOVEMBER 2, 1940
Brussels

Dear Grandma and dear Grandpa!

Many thanks for your letter of Nov. 25 [he must mean Oct. 25]. The day before yesterday I went on a small excursion with Mlle Rethy. We went to Gernat. We took a train from the Gare de Schaerbeck at 18 minutes before three and returned at ten past eight to the Gare du Nord. We took our food with us. Yesterday I went to the cemetery. The grave is now very well taken care of. They have planted some ivy and some other plants. The stone is expected in a week's time. A few days ago we wrote an essay in French. I got 54.5 out of a possible 60 rating, which placed me third out of thirty in the class. The cemetery is well located. It is very large, very beautiful, and located on the outskirts of the town. When the stone has been placed I want to go there again. In the spring there will be beautiful flowers. I like Mme Meyer and Lazarus a lot. I have been invited several times by Mme Meyer. I have not seen Dr. Handel again nor the wife of the architect in our building as they have left for France. Copy if you can this letter for Grandma Else [Rudolf Wertheim's mother]. I don't want a stamp album because I do not have sufficient stamps. A little booklet would be enough for the time being and one of these days I shall buy one. The outing with my school was to the Roseraie where there is a big amusement park. The best grade in math is 60 out of 60 and in French 57.5 out of 60. We have a three-day holiday on account of All Saints' Day. This afternoon I will go to see a movie, but I don't know yet which film I am going to see. I am still with Mme Rethy and will stay there until we leave. I eat very well with them. Yesterday we had a magnificent soup, then mussels, followed by chicken and compote for dessert. At 4 o'clock we had crèpes and in the evening french fries. One can get all of this with food ration cards. I am paying attention that I won't get too fat.

Yours, Jean

(Received November 7, 1940)

HANS WERTHEIM TO HIS FLERSHEIM GRANDPARENTS,
NOVEMBER 17, 1940
Brussels

Dear Grandmother and dear Grandfather,

Many thanks for your letters. A few days ago we had a great storm around Brussels, A great number of large and small trees were uprooted in the woods and in the streets. One balcony was broken by a tree that fell on it. Plenty of windows were shattered.

But with us nothing happened. Now the weather is very nice. I go each week swimming. I can now dive from a 1 meter 80 board. I have not yet been able to buy the books I shall need in France because I don't know what grade I'll go into and the schools are very different. One of these days we will go again to buy the clothing I shall need such as pajamas, [. . .] a raincoat and various other items. This afternoon I shall go with Mlle Rethy to the movies. Probably we are going to see *Café du Port*. It is said to be very good. Thursday I am invited to Mme Meyer's for dinner. The day before yesterday we had jellied doughnuts. No one helped me with the letter I wrote you the other day in French, nor with today's. A lady gave me 5 francs for the movies.

Yours, Hans

P.S. I did not see *Café du Port* but *Grock*.

(Received November 21, 1940)

HANS WERTHEIM TO HIS FLERSHEIM GRANDPARENTS,
DECEMBER 7, 1940
Brussels

Dear Grandpa and dear Grandma!

Many thanks for your letter and the card. The other day I had a letter from Papa. I answered him right away. For St. Nicholas' Day I got a lot of candy. From the lady who has given me several times 5 francs I got a very nice book. It is written by Jules Verne and entitled *Cinq semaines en ballon*. We now have the permit to leave. We will travel in about one week. I am already very excited. This Thursday I have a math test. The other day I went once again shopping with Miss Rethy to get strong boots, heavy socks, a pair of warm pajamas, a cap, a scarf, a raincoat, and today we are still going to try and buy a pair of rubber galoshes. A loden coat* is not important. But I have a very sturdy windbreaker and pants, the kind worn by Boy Scouts. We got some grease for the boots. I am still going to get a rucksack and a thermos flask. I also thank you very much for the little stamp booklet. I picked a book- let. It has transparent sleeves where you slip the stamps in. I chose the booklet because it is much more practical than an album. I now have about 100 stamps. There are, however, some very nice ones among them. The other day I was at the dentist. He told me my teeth were all excellent only they stood a little crooked. He cleaned them for me. He knows Papa. At Frau Meyer's I ate very well. First soup which was wonderful. Then stuffed cabbage with potatoes and then a sweet dessert. I also got a little wine. Wolfgang is in America. I do not know Frl. Meyer. It is a pity that I can't see you before I leave. I went to a photographer. Soon, the pictures will be sent to you. I wore my new suit and overcoat in them.

Many greetings, Hans

Two handwritten comments were added by, it seems, Ruth Friedmann:

Just now it occurs to me that Hans, when he refers to wind- breaker, really means the denim jacket I bought him which is really very sturdy and waterproof.

*He means a windbreaker; he does have a loden coat! I don't know why he writes such nonsense.

(Received December 16, 1940)

The next letter, in French and signed "Jean" was written to his father in the Pyrenees while Hans was en route from Brussels. It was found in an envelope with all the other letters he sent to his grandparents Ernst and Gertrud Flersheim in Amsterdam. The envelope included the letters he wrote to them later in 1941 from Les Martys, after he had joined his fa- ther. At the end of the letter "Henri," one of the Berger boys, drew what he described as a "very big and very beautiful Christmas tree."

HANS WERTHEIM TO HIS FATHER, DECEMBER 25, 1940

Dear Papa,

We are now near Bordeaux. It is one and a half weeks since we left Brussels on December 14th. We got to Paris the same evening. We passed through Halle, Charleroi, Beaumont, St.-Quentin, and Ham. We stayed in Paris for just one week. Then we left for Bordeaux via Chartres, Fontaine, and Tours. Now we are on the Atlantic seacoast at the house of the gentleman with whom we have come from Brussels. We drink wine every day. The beach is not very big but we go there to play all the time. We also play a lot of croquet. The ocean is very calm. We are on a bay on the side of Cap Ferret. The weather is beautiful. The gentleman has four children, but they are a lot younger than we are, but we play with them.

Yours, Jean

As of February 1941 the letters sent by Hans to Ernst and Gertrud Flersheim were routed via Willy Dreyfus in Switzerland. Evidently it was not possible to write directly from unoccupied France to occupied Holland. The letters forwarded by Willy Dreyfus to Holland were all opened by the German censorship and the envelopes stamped: "Geöffnet Oberkommando der Wehrmacht" (Opened by Army Headquarters). The first of these letters from Hans to his grandparents was written in French and signed "Jean."

HANS WERTHEIM TO HIS FLERSHEIM GRANDPARENTS,
FEBRUARY 6, 1941

Dear Grandmother and dear Grandfather,

We have arrived safely in Martys after a 7-week trip. We have been here for five days. We have not written before because on our arrival there was a huge snowstorm during which there were no buses. Also the lights were out. Our toilet is in a little building in the open. . . . ? But now I want to describe our journey. We left Brussels on Dec. 14 with a gentleman and his car. On our way to Paris we went through Charleroi where we had lunch, and then via Beaumont, St.-Quentin, Ham. We arrived in Paris at 10.30 P.M. We stayed at a hotel called the Bradford, which is located near the *rond-point*. The hotel is in the rue St. Philippe du Rouleau. We were in Paris for one week and did a lot of sight-seeing. We went to the Trocadero, and to several movies. Then we left for Arcachon (Bassin d'Arcachon) which is south of Bordeaux on the Atlantic Ocean. That is where the gentleman (who drove us) has his house. On the way to Arcachon we went through Chartres, Vendome where we ate, then Tours, Poitiers, Bordeaux, and Arcachon. We stayed with him for six weeks. We played with his children on the beach and thoroughly enjoyed ourselves. But then we went by train to Bordeaux and from there to Toulouse where we spent the night. Then we took a train to Carcassonne where we met Mr. and Mrs. Berger, and Papa. We said good-bye to Monsieur and took a bus to Martys where our travels ended.

A thousand kisses, Jean

(Received February 25, 1941)

Sent with Hans's letter was this letter from Rudolf Wertheim to his in-laws:

RUDOLF WERTHEIM TO ERNST AND GERTRUD FLERSHEIM, FEBRUARY 6, 1941

Dear Parents,

Finally, finally after six weeks traveling the children have arrived here well and happy. It all turned out to be quite complicated and if Mr. Polgrims had not been such a competent person it would never have worked. The authorities in Paris did not accept the Brussels travel papers. The main thing is that they are here. Hans is in excellent shape. Mrs. Friedmann is right that he developed well these past months. He has grown a lot and is almost my height. He has lost some weight, which does no harm. Mentally he has matured, is lively and full of curiosity. Aside from an elementary school there is nothing within 20 kilometers from here. I have neither the money nor the desire to send him off to a boarding school and we have decided to teach the children ourselves. Mr. Berger will take physics, math, and the natural sciences. I will do English, French, German, and geography. We start Monday, in three days' time. I don't believe they will learn less than they would in a regular school. We are going to try to follow the French school system and are getting a curriculum from a correspondence course.

Our fellow inhabitants are away at the moment, which means the six of us have the house to ourselves at the moment. When they return, which is not for sure, we will have to break up. More than six do not fit into the house, even though we have learned that many things are possible which we would never have dreamed of doing. Hans and I sleep in a big room in one bed. He's cuddled up in a sleeping bag under two blankets and a coat. It has again turned cold and the snow was so deep that for three days we had no bus and no mail. We could barely get out of the house. We just huddled around our small fireplace to try to keep warm. The room itself could not be heated. Still, we felt cozy and comforted knowing the children had finally made it.

Regarding the United States I have heard nothing concrete. As soon as I know something I will write.

We have enough to eat. There is plenty of meat, vegetables, and fruit. There is enough bread and fats, but very few potatoes.

I hope you are keeping well and by now feel at home in your new apartment.

Best wishes, Rudolf

Accompanying the following letters from Hans and Rudolf Wertheim was a note from Willy Dreyfus dated "Ragaz, June 19." It read: "I send you greetings with Rudi's letter which I got two days ago. — Love, Willy."

HANS WERTHEIM TO HIS FLERSHEIM GRANDPARENTS,
JUNE 9, 1941

Dear Grandma and dear Grandpa!

Many thanks for your letters. We have almost finished seeding our field. We have put in beans, potatoes, carrots, peas, onions, spinach, radishes, and salad. Klaus and Ulrich [Berger] and I each have our own little garden and everything is growing well. A few weeks ago Papa and I visited the Reisses. They live about 50 km away from here. Papa bicycled to Carcassonne and I took the bus. From there it was another 20 km. We took turns biking and walking. It was very nice. We stayed a week. I played with their boys. They even have fig trees. Where they live the altitude is much lower than here. With us the weather is generally pretty bad. We are catching a lot of ladybugs, of which there are masses here. The other day Papa caught a most beautiful salamander. Yesterday there was a group of men in the village who put on a show. Nearly the entire village was there. It was very funny. I continue to collect stamps. There is a mailman in Les Martys who has a very good collection of over 10,000 stamps. A few weeks ago he came 'round to show it to us. Some are very valuable. We swapped some of ours with him. Papa and Mr. Berger continue to teach us school. We have learned a lot of English and we have covered the entire shorthand stenography system. We are learning modern history and the discoveries of Columbus and Ferdinand Cortez. In geography we have just finished with Africa. We have a cat, which we got as a little kitten. To begin she was quite ugly but she has come to look much better. The other day she caught a mouse. First she let it go and caught it back. Then she carried it into her basket and ate it, every last piece of it. I am being interrupted all the time while writing. We have just had a big thunderstorm which constantly makes the power go off. Apparently the long-distance overhead cables are in poor shape. We often go to look for mushrooms and have them for supper. They are tasty but not easy to find. I have hay fever. How are you?

Many greetings, Hans

(Received June 19, 1941, by Willy Dreyfus; received June 26, 1941, by the Flersheims.)

In June 1941 many U.S. consulates in Europe stopped functioning as they had previously or were closed altogether. From then on, all visa applications had to be made in Washington, D.C.. In addition, the number of visas issued was further restricted.

RUDOLF WERTHEIM TO ERNST AND GERTRUD FLERSHEIM, JULY 18, 1941

Dear Parents,

Many thanks for your dear letters of June 9th and 26th. The situation with regard to U.S.A. immigration has changed with us, too. Since July 1 the consulates can issue immigration visas only if they are instructed to do so by the State Department. Documents and applications have to be submitted to Washington by relatives or friends in the United States. Fritz [Flersheim] has cabled me that he will apply on our behalf. It's a pity because I had booked space for mid-August, and probably would by now have a visa. Now we have to wait again.

You ask for my view regarding Cuba. It is difficult always to have an opinion, especially after all the mistakes already made. However, if you push me I'd say you should risk the voyage, notwithstanding your age.

You, dear father, must have celebrated a birthday on the 13th or 14th of July. Belated, all good wishes. I hope you will celebrate your 80th [next year] with peace restored.

I can't say I am particularly depressed by the delays. By now one has got used to things like that. Still, I would have liked to go, but the summer here is so beautiful. For weeks the weather has been wonderful: sunshine day after day with just enough rain in between for the harvest.

We work a lot on our field and in addition help the local mayor and other farmers. The outlook for the potato harvest is good. We hope that from the 35 kg of seed potatoes we received we can harvest about 200 kg. In addition we expect to be able to buy potatoes to give us enough for the coming winter. For over six months we had none. As long as we have sufficient potatoes, our nutrition problems are solved. Already the situation is better than it was last winter, and it is my impression that as far as food is concerned, we are over the worst. In the past few weeks we collected huge quantities of wild strawberries. We received a special issue of sugar to make them into compote. We have bottled 10 kg of strawberries. The boys now have enough to eat. Even Hans the big eater rarely says: "I suffer from raging, biting hunger pangs." There is hardly any meat, but we all have come to notice how unimportant that is provided we have enough of everything else. We continue to make our own butter from cream and receive sufficient fats with our food ration cards.

My birthday was celebrated quietly but pleasantly. Hans made me a calendar and I collected two plates of strawberries all for myself alone to eat.

In the next letter Hans will give you another report. They seem to learn quite a lot in class. They are making almost surprisingly good headway with French, but they are also learning a lot in the natural sciences. They are not learning less than they would in a regular school. When I think back how little I knew aged 13 compared with what these boys seem to have learned by now! So don't underrate our "Odenwaldschule" [a respected progressive school in Germany].

Warm greetings, Rudolf

(Received in Switzerland July 24, 1941, in Amsterdam August 1, 1941.)

After this July 18 letter, there is a gap of ten months until the next letter that has come down to us from Rudolf to his father- and mother-in-law. Meanwhile, Hans wrote to his grandparents from a boarding school in Narbonne.

HANS WERTHEIM TO HIS FLERSHEIM GRANDPARENTS, OCTOBER 5, 1941

Dear Grandpa and dear Grandma!

I have passed my 8th-grade exam, and am now in the grade I should be in. I have caught up with everything. I had tests in English, French, math, physics, and chemistry. I am now going to take courses in English, French, Spanish (which will be new this year), math, physics, chemistry, natural history, geography, and history. Tomorrow the real school starts. I am now at a boarding school. The food is very good. In the morning we receive our daily bread ration of 350 grams. In addition we get a cup of coffee with milk and two lumps of sugar. At noon we get soup, meat, vegetables, or potatoes and for dessert cookies or fruit. For dinner we get more or less the same. The other kids and teachers are very nice. How are you?

Lots of greetings, Hans

(Received in Amsterdam October 23, 1941)

The above letter from Hans was accompanied by a note from Willy Dreyfus addressed to his Aunt Gertrud: "I have to thank you for your card of October 8. I am glad of the good news that uncle is better. I hope that now you can get some rest. . . ."

The letter of May 25, 1942, below makes clear that by this date the Wertheims had moved away from Les Martys. We know the following from Ernst Flersheim's letter to the Eberstadts in England, written May 15, 1942: "Rudi Wertheim writes that he has had to move to another, but nearby village, and has rented a small house together with the Bergers and a third family." Nearly one year later, a letter of June 23, 1942, mentions Rennes-les-Bains. The relocation meant much hardship, not in the least because new clearing of land for planting of food was required. What were the reasons they had to relocate? We do not know.

RUDOLF WERTHEIM TO ERNST AND GERTRUD FLERSHEIM,
MAY 25, 1942

Dear Parents,

Thank you, dear father for your dear letter of April 21. I am glad you have almost completely recovered from your bronchitis, and that the doctor is satisfied with your eye operation.

Today I received the sad news that my Aunt Berta, who for some time as you know had been living again with my mother, has died. It is a big blow for my mother, who had gained much support from the shared life with her sister. It is hard to be so far away from her and be totally unable to help her.

On May 12th it was two years since our dear Margarete left us. It still seems to me like yesterday that I said good-bye to her during those terrible days, expecting that I would be back a few hours later. Instead I was never to see her again. So much has happened since, new experiences, yes, a totally new world, hard times, yet also good things, though sometimes I feel as if in that hour something was torn in my life that cannot be mended. A void was created that cannot be filled. It is a different matter to live with other people, even if one gets on well and we are in harmony with each other, than to totally belong to one person.

We are more or less settled (in our new place). But so far it is still not the same atmosphere. There is something lacking which had made our old home so likeable. I can't really say — is it the scenery, the house, the people we meet here who don't feel to me so friendly, the poor nutrition (which should get better after the harvest is in), or the climate, which is much more tiring? But maybe it's just me and the mood I am in and tomorrow everything may be well with me again.

When all is said and done we have really settled in quite well. Together with the Simons we cultivate a large field, about 3,000 to 4,000 square meters. For decades, it had not been farmed and was covered with trees, grass, bushes, and brush. We have planted potatoes, peas, lima beans, string beans, carrots, beets, turnips, salad, cabbage, and lots more. Provided the harvest is reasonably good we won't go hungry. Above all, we should have a good supply of the most important, potatoes.

We have a lot of work. Just now, we tilled a vineyard and got all sorts of food supplies in return for it. After that, we'll do forestry work, for all sorts of food supplies. Come hell or high water, we'll manage somehow.

Fritz wrote a while ago that it was complicated but not impossible. The permits require the approval of several government departments for which Fritz and Georg T. have to be interviewed in person. As I happened to hear yesterday, some such permits have already arrived here, though not in large numbers.

Hans is home for the Whitsun holiday for one week. I am sitting next to him. He is still in bed studying his physics textbook and is offended that his breakfast (porridge) is not ready yet. He continues to develop well, is tall and strong, and totally absorbed by doings in school. He came home again with an excellent report card. Even in drawing he got a B, admittedly because his neighbor made the sketches for him. In return, Hans does his German homework. Everywhere we barter. Klaus Berger also came home with him. The boys work their own plot which they plant and tend busily.

All the best, Your Rudolf

(Received in Switzerland June 4, 1942, in Amsterdam June 13, 1942)

The remarks above about "Fritz" and the permits that were "complicated but not impossible" refer to Margarete's cousin Fritz Flersheim's attempts to arrange U.S. visas for Rudolf and Hans. United States visa regulations had been further tightened since the restrictions imposed the preceding summer, which had prevented the Wertheims' departure then. After the United States officially entered the war in December 1941, immigration visas became even more difficult to obtain. Apparently the process required personal interviews with references. Fritz Flersheim would have been one such reference and the other was "Georg T.," Georg Trefousse, a psychiatrist friend of Rudolf's then living on Staten Island.

In the letter that follows Rudolf Wertheim talks about several people who have not appeared so far in the correspondence. The letter itself was addressed to Valerie Uzielli, the wife of Mario Uzielli. The Uziellis, who were friends and kinsfolk of our families, lived near Basel, where they had moved from Frankfurt. Mario Uzielli had been a rare book dealer and antiquarian in Frankfurt.

I believe the "B" referred to below was Rudolf's Aunt Berta, mentioned in the previous letter, who had died. The Hedwig in this letter is Hedwig Blach, Rudolf Wertheim's sister, then living in England with Cornelia, her daughter, and Rolf, her son.

RUDOLF WERTHEIM TO VALERIE UZIELLI, JUNE 23, 1942
Rennes-les-Bains

Dear Valerie,

Forgive the hideous servant-quarter writing paper. There is nothing better left to buy in Rennes. I presume you received my letter written in late May in response to yours, telling me of B's death. Also I have to thank you for forwarding Hedwig's letter of May 9th. Further, I received yesterday the enclosed letter, which you had written to my mother but sent to me in error. Actually it interested me greatly, especially to read that Cornelia is too young for hospital work. If only a way could be found to let her stay in school when she seems so good at it.

I am enclosing an English language letter for Hedwig. It is a pity that a letter written in another language never comes across as intimately as in one's mother tongue. Anything one writes sounds so impersonal.

Hochberg has taken up my cause in a really particularly nice way. He has also spoken with another well-wisher of mine, Willy Dreyfus (I seem to have a number of well-wishers, including, for instance, the Uziellis!), and perhaps between them they will find a way out for me. If it does not work, I will have to see what else there is left to do.

I regret to say my spirits are still rather down, really for the first time in these past two years. But it really is incredibly miserable here, which I also say in my letter to Hedwig. Nor are our co-religionists here exactly a pleasure to be with. On top of it we are hungrier than at any other time, even though we spend on our food many times more than we did at Les Martys. All in all there is no drive in me since we came here. By now I'd positively like to get to the United States, if only because I am so damned hungry. Fritz Flersheim and my friend Georg Trefousse go before a commission in Washington this month to testify about me. By August we should know where I stand. I am not too hopeful, but it does not sound quite hopeless, either.

Our garden is in reasonable shape, but we are not doing too well with earning a bit of money from forestry. Berger is the only one strong enough to actually fell a tree. All I can do is chop firewood. For a week he has not been able to work. He has an infected finger, nor is he up to par in general. The same goes for me compared with St. [Les?] Martys.

Well, we shall have to see. In one form or another we'll find a way to get out of this pickle — almost a pity. In many ways it has been so stimulating to be rid of all this damned money. But what is not to be, is not to be. What matters now is not to let a depression get the better of one, to stay cheerful no matter how miserably down one feels in reality (and I'd so much rather be genuinely cheerful).

All the best to the three of you,

Rudolf

RUDOLF WERTHEIM TO VALERIE UZIELLI, AUGUST 17, 1942
Rennes-les-Bains

Dear Valerie,

Where should I start, with mind or body? Actually, why always the spirit, so I'll start off writing about all these delicious goodies. Believe it or not, in the last two weeks we have had not just one or two, no, four packages from Switzerland, one after the other. Two came from Willy Dreyfus, and two from you. I can only say they made some very special days for our entire crew which at the moment includes two more boys and [illegible]. The contents make one's mouth water. Not just nougat, but the very best! And date paste, to gobble down this instant, olives — which should keep, dried peas which should make many a plate of soup, almonds, and dried fruit to keep till winter. The packages from

Portugal are just not in the same league. I don't have it in me any longer to write don't do it, and instead say many thanks on behalf of us all. You gave us an enormous treat.

While on the subject of the body, I am glad to report that physically I seem all right again. The swellings in my leg and foot are gone, and, more important, so is the general weariness of all my limbs. I think I have regained my old energy and joie de vivre. Lack of food and general physical exhaustion rather than anything specific seem to have been at the bottom of my problems. We are now eating far better, though at considerably higher cost than previously. For the past six weeks I have worked less hard. I am indoors, in charge of cooking. The Berger lady, superwoman that she is, splits oak trees with a blunt ax.

Now that I don't have to drag my legs one by one up the stairs, thank God I don't any longer find life so tragic. Instead I ponder with considerable interest on the new blows which I see coming down on us almost certainly in the near future. Bravo, Hilde Lust! Something like that is a breath of fresh air blowing through all the mutterings about misfortune, self-pity, and rescue. Does it really matter so much whether we are sitting somewhere safe and pretty, or in danger? Does it really matter whether we are around for 50 or 90 years? In the final analysis the only thing that matters is to lead a fulfilled life, not to live it tied in knots, but in harmony with our personality and temperament. In this connection I had a letter a few days ago from a friend who spent a year in a camp (at Puis near Pau) but managed to get to Venezuela in July 1941. She writes: "On the face of it life is good, but inside me I feel a void and miserable. Basically, I am bored. . . . Like all the others in my situation I say one has to be happy and grateful to be here. But I ask myself, why do I have to be grateful for the privilege of being miserable, even if in comfort? Before I came here my life was exciting, even if often sad, but it was never without a purpose. Here I lead for the first time a life without any meaning." I don't normally quote anyone other than the poets. But she expresses it all so well. To me it seems it applies exactly to your sister, which is the reason why I wanted to share it with you.

Now for the rest of your letter. What Hedwig writes is really very good news. There must be quite something to her that she manages, without being pushy or calculating, to receive so much help from many different quarters. Her life has become better since she got rid of her miserable Paul. With him she was hemmed in from every side and had no chance to let her real nature come through. I shall write to her shortly.

As far as my mother is concerned, perhaps one should write to my friend Dr. Walter Lewald, brother of Prof. Lewald in Basel. His address is Bockenheimer Anlage 31a, Frankfurt. His wife is Jewish. Probably one would first have to ask him via someone like your brother-in-law whether it would be all right with him to receive letters. It is awkward to pose the question (in writing). Willy Dreyfus is also in contact with her. He has been passing on my news since May 1940. Another possible contact is Max L. Kahn, the Frankfurt lawyer, but I do not have his address. Finally there still is death as a way out for her.

I have been greatly interested in what you write concerning Theresienstadt. Notwithstanding everything, it seems a somewhat more humane form of deportation than the Polish ghettos. The parents of a family I am friendly with here — they used to live in Lintz on the Rhine — aged 88 and 78, were sent there. I am afraid that sooner or later all Jews living anywhere under German rule will be collected.

And as for Mario? Still an optimist? The plague on everything, but actually I think he may be right.

Once more, dear Valerie, thank you for everything.

Rudolf

As I read my letter it occurs to me that I did not write a word about my Hansel, maybe subconsciously in opposition to my sister who lives exclusively for her children and has given up on any life of her own. That, however, goes too far. He is a dear and decent boy. We talk a lot about school, which means everything to him, quite different from our attitude as children, or about politics where he is an optimist and is never in doubt about anything. At the moment he is into reading Karl May. Mariechen [Floersheim] sent him a four-volume edition of *The Land of the Silver Lion*. He is a good swimmer. The boys swim every day in the little stream behind our house. They also water the garden each day which is important as we have not had a drop of rain in months and our crop is in danger of being parched.

The prospects for getting to the U.S.A. do not seem good. The last attempt on our behalf was made by Fritz Flersheim and Dr. Trefousse on June 8th and I have not yet heard the outcome.

But now it's really enough. Thank you for the offer regarding reading matter. I am well provided for at present.

Rudolf

The exclamation above — "Bravo, Hilde Lust!" — presumably refers to the decision of this lady to end her life because she was going to be deported. I have been unable to identify her further.

"Finally there still is death as a way out for her." This part of Rudolf Wertheim's letter was hard to read in the original, and it is such a startling statement that I fear I may have misread it, yet it fits with the rest of the letter. Rudolf might have known at this point that his mother had been deported from her home in Frankfurt. His mention of parents of friends being deported to Theresienstadt seems to imply such knowledge. Gertrud Flersheim wrote to the Eberstadts in May 1942: "On top of all other things, Rudi must now cope with the fact that his mother is no longer at home."

The following letter was written by a certain Hugo to Willy Dreyfus in Switzerland.

HUGO [SURNAME ILLEGIBLE] TO WILLY DREYFUS,
SEPTEMBER 7, 1942
Hotel Beauport, Sanary-sur-Mer

Dear Mr. Dreyfus,

This minute I received a postcard from our dear Rudi Wertheim, dated August 28, to advise that he and his son are in the Camp de Rivesaltes, K Barracks #27. He expects to be transported away shortly. He asks that I pass this sad state of affairs on to you. He writes further, *"Je pris Willy Dreyfus de le faire savoir en Docteur Traugott, un cousin de mes amis Berger."* From the way he writes it is not clear whether the Bergers are also at Rivesaltes. He writes with extraordinary courage, *son bonne santé et bonne humour!*

I regret that such a sad reason should be the occasion for writing to you.

I correspond regularly with Mario Uzielli. When you are in Basel you no doubt see him. Give him my best.

With all good wishes, Hugo

Rudolf and Hans Wertheim were deported to Auschwitz in 1943, where they perished. The letter above is the last sign of life from them of which I am aware. It was written on stationery of Le Nautique, 6, Quay Victor Hugo, in Sanary-sur-Mer (Var). The letterhead carries one M. Schwob as proprietor. The restaurant has a *terrace sur la mer*, serves *bière*, and has a service *de brasserie à tout*. The telephone number is, or, rather was, 64; presumably it has since changed. Sanary is west of Toulon, on the Mediterranean coast.

Though Hugo was staying at the Hotel Beauport, he wrote from the restaurant Le Nautique. Considering the contents of his letter, perhaps he preferred not to write from the place he lived. I do not have the envelope of the letter. My friend Peter von Zahn has told me that the restaurant of the letterhead still exists and is near his house in the South of France. According to Peter, the restaurant was well known in World War II as a place where émigrés congregated.

Rivesaltes, located in the eastern Pyrenees near Perpignan, was one of the major camps in southern France. It had been built during World War I as temporary housing for colonial troops. Not far from the Mediterranean, it was subject to strong winds and extreme temperatures. In June of 1942 Himmler had set deportation quotas for France of 100,000. Foreign and stateless Jews were rounded up first. When the quotas were not met, the Vichy government, in early August 1942, canceled all exit visas. Regional prefects were secretly alerted to prepare for a major roundup, which took place August 26 to 28, 1942. Rudolf and Hans Wertheim must have been apprehended then.

The letters in this chapter were preserved thanks to Willy Dreyfus and Rudolf Wertheim's sister Hedwig Blach. In 1946, Willy Dreyfus sent Hedwig the correspondence between Rudolf and other family members that had passed through his hands during the war. When Hedwig Blach died, her daughter Cornelia Blaut copied some of these letters for me. They were hard to read, but I decided to transcribe some of them for the insight they provide, especially into Rudolf Wertheim's personality.

13

The Noose Tightens:
The Flersheim Letters,
1940–1943

From 1938 to 1943 Ernst and Gertrud Flersheim lived in Amsterdam. In the beginning they had comfortable lodgings in a pleasant part of the city, but after 1940 they were made to move several times, each time into poorer quarters. Before they were arrested and sent to the Westerbork camp they had an unbelievably primitive two-room apartment (I saw it for myself in 1996), up a steep flight of stone steps, without running water.

They managed to write regularly to Georg and Edith Eberstadt in England. Their letters were in German, sent for transmission to England to their nephew Willy Dreyfus, husband of their niece Martha Koch, daughter of Louis Koch, and Ernst Flersheim's sister Alice. Willy Dreyfus, a member of the Swiss-German Dreyfus banking family, had lived in Switzerland since 1938, when he left Berlin. He copied most of the letters and after the war gave the originals to my father, who kept them from my mother for obvious reasons. I found them after his death in his writing desk and have translated the following excerpts into English. The correspondence is a brave attempt to keep family links, at least by letter. No doubt for fear of censorship, little if anything is written about the war.

By the time the excerpted letter below was written, Gertrud and Ernst Flersheim had already received the letter from Kaethe Rosenberg in Brussels, a friend of the Wertheims, recounting Margarete's last days. Officials refused access to bank accounts and property left behind in Brussels ("Rudolf's affairs"). The letter also mentions their nephew Fritz Flersheim, who had emigrated to New York. He was safekeeping some Flersheim assets which they had long kept outside Germany.

ERNST FLERSHEIM TO THE EBERSTADTS, OCTOBER 31, 1940

. . . Since we last wrote each other, we have suffered the terrible loss of our beloved Margarete. It is impossible to express our grief in words. What terrible conditions our poor good child must have endured in the last days of her life. We imagine you know that Rudolf is in a small village in the Pyrenees (together with his friends, the Bergers). Hans and the Berger boys will soon be brought there. We tried, in vain, to see him and to look after Rudolf's affairs in Brussels, but did not get permission to travel.

We hear Walter is now in the country. What is his occupation? [Soldier!] We know Bridget goes to school in the country. George, do you still have your job with your friend S [Sonnenberg]? I hope you are making enough money, but should you be in need of anything, I am sure your cousin Fritz will support you.

Mother and I are in good health. We have our own small furnished flat and our landlord, not an agreeable person, provides our meals. Furniture and location are nice.

Your father, Ernst Flersheim

The omitted parts of the letters below inquire about the health of Father, who had just had a thyroid operation, about Bridget and Walter, and report that Hans Wertheim was shortly going to join his father, Rudolf.

ERNST AND GERTRUD FLERSHEIM TO THE EBERSTADTS,
NOVEMBER 14, 1940

Dear Children:

. . . We look forward to all your news. Let us have it as often
as possible. I greatly miss the company of my children.

Much love from your father, EF

To Bridget:

We have seen your handwriting only twice since Margarete's
death. . . . Talk to older friends about what you should do one day.
You are good at drawing, have good taste and clever fingers.
Think about fashion design. Study the history of fashion. Your
mother says you are thinking of secretarial work. Well, you will
see. Do you enjoy your garden and the out-of-doors? How about
swimming, rowing, skating? Does your father still spoil you? Is
your mother your best friend? [Indeed!]

We have not heard from Hans for quite a while. Do me the
favor and be nice to him. He is a good boy. Now, my beloved big
girl, do everything so that we can be proud of you, as your grandfather Albert used to say.

A big kiss from your best, old, friend, Gertrud

ERNST FLERSHEIM TO THE EBERSTADTS, APRIL 25, 1941

My dearest Children,

I wrote to you last month but found out my letter did not
reach you. We were so glad to get your good news at the end of
March from Willy. Our only wish is it will be the same in the future. We are anxious to hear as often as possible how you and
the children are. We understand you want us to get a visa [for
the United States]. Although the idea of another emigration is

troublesome for old people like ourselves, it would be reassuring to have a visa. Our only wish is to be for the rest of our lives with our children, and not to be alone. We know Rudolf has been to the U.S. consulate about his visa, but he writes he has not had an answer to date. Are you aware we have been registered at the U.S. consulate in Rotterdam since July 1940?

As for our life, we remain well. There is no important change in my eyesight. We have had to move several times, once quite suddenly because where we lived was requisitioned for other purposes. We are now lodged with a very refined family where we have three rooms of our own. There is only one other boarder.

Your father, Ernst

ERNST FLERSHEIM TO THE EBERSTADTS, MAY 29, 1941
Amsterdam

Dear Children,

We were happy to gather from your letter that you are well. We had not heard from you for a long while. If you don't have time to write, you can at least send us a telegram. I long for my little mouse [Bridget]. It is sad not to see her at this lovely stage in her life. Walter no doubt is busy.

As for us, we have had to move twice lately. At the present we live with very nice civilized people. We have two bedrooms and a living room. The food is good, and we will be sorry to leave them.

You are no doubt aware of the steps we have taken to go to America. It is hard to say how long it will be until we can go — quite likely several months until all the formalities have been completed. You will understand what a difficult decision it has been for us and we would not have done it but for the urgings from you, Rudi, and Fritz. I am afraid of the journey even though I really can't complain about my health.

A few days ago we had the first letter since Margarete's death from "Orchen," Ernst, and his wife. They live in a small spa not far from Rudi.

Rudi is expecting his visa at the end of the month, but I am not sure it will work. We have not heard a word from Herbert. Nor have any of his friends here. It seems the mail from Madeira does not function too well. We rarely hear from Florence, though we write her regularly.

I pray for your well-being and send you, Edith, a big kiss.

Your Father

The relatives referred to above as living "not far from Rudi" were Gertrud Flersheim's stepmother Flora ("Orchen") von Mayer, her half brother Ernst von Mayer, and his wife, Marcelle. The "Herbert" and "Florence" she talks about are Mother's first cousin Herbert Flersheim, who had apparently already left Amsterdam on his way to Argentina, and Florence Flersheim, Gertrud's sister-in-law, who was living in New York with her son Fritz.

GERTRUD FLERSHEIM TO THE EBERSTADTS, JUNE 1941

Your letter of May 18th gave us a welcome description of your life. We are so happy you are content. We read it again and again, as a makeshift substitute for being together. We are happy to read Walter and Bridget are happy to be with you, and like your house and the garden. Nature and good health are the best company. I am glad you are a good cook and housekeeper, but don't overdo it. Visitors make a lot of work. Tell your guests when you get tired. They will understand if they are sensible. Mariechen [Floersheim] overdoes it, as did my mother and Aunt Ernestine. The big flat [in London] was too much for you, especially the unending visitors.

I always thought well of Walter. His grandfather Albert thought we'd be proud of him one day. Hans [Flersheim] hoped he'd have him in the business.

If you have darning to do, first make sure before you start that it is worth it. I was once very disappointed when I was asked to darn a basketful of socks which were not worth mending. Do you know whether Eric Bruck's laundry business [in America] is his own? Before he worked in a clothing store. I am worried, I do not hear a word from my brother or most other family.

Rudi loves his work on the land. He writes rarely. After the day outdoors he does the domestic chores such as preparing the food, doing the laundry, etc.

We long for peace and the prospect of again seeing our children, grandchildren, and my brothers. Reading my favorite poet Fritz Reuter, "sitting by the side of a warming stove," lulls me to rest. I so much enjoy reading him, which reminds me of my childhood and where I was born.

What should I tell you? Stay healthy, be with friends. You, Bridget and Walter, learn whatever you can. You will benefit from it all your lives, even if you have to give up leisure time now.

I hug you with all my love, Gertrud

ERNST FLERSHEIM TO THE EBERSTADTS, JULY 14, 1941

Dear Children,

Thank you for your birthday telegram. You will have heard that our plan soon to visit Fritz is for the time being not possible. We had all the papers ready. We did not fail to do anything required of us, but it was too late. We have cabled Fritz to get us a visa to go to Cuba, but we would undertake this arduous journey only if we can be reasonably sure we won't have to stay there too long before we can go on to America. I must tell you quite honestly we dread the hot climate and all the stress of the long journey. Rudi has also not yet found a way to leave but is hopeful they can travel in July or August. Herbert wants to stay on in Madeira for the time being and writes he has no desire to go to the country where his mother was born [U.S.A.]. He writes, literally, that he never liked it. In any event please write whether you advise us to undertake the strenuous journey. We continue to be very satisfied with where we live, and also with our landlord.

Father Ernst

Ernst Flersheim's birthday was July 13. We have no way of knowing the background that would explain the mention about it being "too late," even though they had "all papers ready" to travel to join their nephew Fritz in New York.

GERTRUD FLERSHEIM TO THE EBERSTADTS, JULY 18, 1941

My Dear Ones,

It is now two years and nine months since we last saw each other in November 1938. Stay healthy, happy, content, and busy. Also, in wartimes you must continue to develop and learn to help your parents. Don't forget us and remember how much we need you. Your love and good fortune is our anchor. We are lucky to have many old friends and also some family here and I try to hide my grief from them. Our landlord and his wife are like friends. We have a nice view into the park and plenty of fresh air. Even in the heat wave we found a quiet bench by the water, surrounded by rose hedges. I am learning to darn and cook and try to help the sick and lonely.

Gertrud

TELEGRAM FROM MARIECHEN FLOERSHEIM TO THE EBERSTADTS, JULY 25, 1941

Maria and children very well. Edith's parents all right. Longing to see you all.

Mariechen Koch-Floersheim was Mother's favorite cousin, who had settled in Switzerland with her husband and children. The Maria she refers to was Georg Eberstadt's sister Maria Schaefer, who lived in Frankfurt. Her children are my cousins Jürg and Klaus Schaefer.

ERNST FLERSHEIM TO THE EBERSTADTS, AUGUST 11, 1941

When you cabled us not to leave at all cost, you no doubt had not yet received my letter of July 16, asking your advice. Meanwhile Fritz Flersheim has applied for a visa for us to go to Cuba and we expect to get it shortly. I have asked Fritz to apply through the State Department for our American visa. If it is turned down, it is useless to apply at the American consulate here. They can only issue a visa if instructed from Washington. The same would apply if we go to Cuba. We are most reluctant to go to Cuba without an American visa. We would also like to wait and see whether Rudi gets permission to go to America. If he does, the decision will be much easier for us. The uncertainty of not knowing what is right for us is disturbing, but it makes us feel better that you share our opinion not to rush into anything.

Father

P.S. This moment I heard from the Cuban consulate, which is in Rotterdam, that they have been instructed to issue us a tourist visa valid for six months once we are there.

Over the years Mother became increasingly troubled that she had not urged her parents to leave Holland *à tout prix*. But they were old and seemed reasonably comfortable and content.

ERNST FLERSHEIM TO THE EBERSTADTS, SEPTEMBER 28, 1941

Dear Children,

Our Cuba visa is valid until December. Even though we still have not decided if we should go, we have asked Fritz Flersheim to get an extension. Both he and Willy write you would like us to go to him soon, but we are so afraid of the heat in Cuba, and there is no guarantee we will be able to go on to the United States. Fritz writes that others our age have managed it perfectly well. After all the moving around, we are really comfortable where we are and like our host very much.

Father Ernst

WILLY DREYFUS TO THE EBERSTADTS, OCTOBER 10, 1941,
Zurich

Thank you for all the letters which have been forwarded. Walter's letter of September 9 will especially please them. I have written Ernst that you are now of the opinion they should go to Cuba soonest. Rudi is still waiting for his U.S. visa. Meanwhile his boy has been sent to a boarding school at Narbonne.

ERNST FLERSHEIM TO THE EBERSTADTS, UNDATED (EARLY 1942)

My dear Ones,

I last wrote you on January 4. My eyes are all right. I admire Rudi for managing all this heavy manual labor. We have not heard a word from Martin and Nini since their first Red Cross message. Fritz will continue to help us as much as he can. Herbert writes contentedly from Madeira and will also continue to be helpful. He wanted to send us a food package at Christmas but export from Madeira is not permitted.

Nothing gives us more pleasure than good news from you, also that you, dear Edith, quite enjoy your housework and are managing all right.

Last Sunday, I went with Albert to a concert by a newly formed orchestra. It was an all-Mendelssohn program. We went even though there was a heavy snowfall and the tramway was overcrowded.

I think a great deal of happy times we have spent in the past and in my mind give you, Edith, a big kiss.

Ernst

In writing about his eyes in the preceding letter Ernst Flersheim is referring to a cataract operation. The Martin and Nini he refers to are Martin and Nini von Mayer, Gertrud Flersheim's brother and his wife, who were sent from Germany to Litzmanstadt in Poland, where they died. Fritz and Herbert were of course their nephews Fritz and Herbert Flersheim, who tried to help them emigrate to the United States. Albert was the Flersheims' friend Professor Ettlinger, whose daughter Grete Salinger had gone to school with my mother in Frankfurt and now lived in London. It is slightly surprising that an all-Mendelssohn program was permitted in German-occupied Holland.

ERNST FLERSHEIM TO THE EBERSTADTS, MAY 15, 1942

We last wrote you in mid-April and have had your news meanwhile via Mariechen. Our greatest pleasure is whenever we hear you are well. It is good to hear George enjoys gardening and that Walter writes he likes to help when he is home, and that you, Edith, are such a good cook.

Rudi Wertheim writes that he has had to move to another, though nearby village, and has rented a small house together with the Bergers and a third family. They will again work a field and do some woodcutting. We have finally "heard" from Nini; she signed a receipt acknowledging money we had sent her. Various people we know have died recently, but there is really nothing much to tell you.

Ernst

Ernst Flersheim writes that "people we know have died recently" and that there is nothing much to tell. Nothing was safe anymore, including writing letters. Memories of better times and contact with family become more and more important, as in the letter below. Grandmother Betty (von Mayer, née Tuchmann) was known for her traditional *Stollen* — a rich white bread with candied fruit and nuts. The loss of her recipe leads to the suggestion the Eberstadts try to get it from cousin Lina in London.

GERTRUD FLERSHEIM TO THE EBERSTADTS, MAY 14, 1942

I'd like to write more often, but it is not easy. Your letters are our greatest joy. My one wish is to see you all, but time is not on our side. We are almost 70 and 80 years old. I am so pleased to hear you are a good cook. Your grandmother Betty was an excellent cook. At Christmas she baked 25 to 30 large *Stollen*. Maybe Lena Simon has her recipes. All mine disappeared when we left Frankfurt.

Does Bridget ever go dancing with Walter?

I miss my brother and his family; also my old mother. . . .

Gertrud

The letter continues with a long list of greetings to friends and relatives in London. The brother mentioned is Ernst, her half brother, and the "old mother" is her stepmother "Orchen." Both were in France.

The following letter was copied on a typewriter and forwarded from Switzerland by Mariechen Floersheim after a long delay. It mentions Rudi Wertheim and the fact that his mother, Else Wertheim, was deported from Frankfurt in 1942. Memories are mentioned of Domburg, a resort on the island of Walcheren in Holland where the Flersheims vacationed frequently prior to 1914. The painter friend is Charlie Toorop, daughter of an Toorop (1858–1928), a prominent Dutch artist whose work the Flersheims collected before 1914.

ERNST FLERSHEIM TO MARIECHEN FLOERSHEIM AND THE EBERSTADTS, MAY 1942

I last wrote to you in September [1941], the same day you happened to write to us. We are so glad you are happy and have good reason to be so. Like you, we think daily of Rudi and little Hans. We have not heard from them lately.

On top of all other things, Rudi must now cope with the fact that his mother is no longer at home. Rudi has had bad times, and who knows how [he] is now.

I, too, think often of the happy childhood days about which you reminisce in your letter. We speak often of Domburg. Just last week we had a visit from our painter friend and we talked with her about the happy times spent with her father.

We celebrated our 50th engagement anniversary having a glass of wine with our particularly nice, civilized landlord and his wife.

We greatly miss our good friend, Grete's father. He was so very nice to us on my 80th birthday. My health is all right, though I have lost over twenty pounds. I walk every day but it is a long way on foot into the center of town. I am sending you two old photos of ourselves. We much enjoyed Bridget's picture as a seventeen-year-old.

Ernst

Gertrud Flersheim included this P.S. to the Eberstadts:

Does Lena know the whereabouts of her sister-in-law Dora? It must help Grete [Salinger] that she can talk to you about her grief. She and Hedwig suffer from a similar fate: loss of Grete's parents, siblings, nieces and nephews, Hedwig's brother, mother, and nephew.

You'd find us much changed. Three days ago, I had three teeth pulled and I am losing my hair. Be glad you can't look at me. My love for the four of you is undying.

Gertrud

The good friend, Grete's father, was Professor Ettlinger. The Ettlingers together with their daughter and son-in-law were deported in 1942. On account of their age, they could have stayed behind, but insisted on not being separated from their family (the source for this information is Edith Eberstadt). Lena Simon lived in London and was a cousin of Gertrud Flersheim.

The following letter came with a covering note from Willy Dreyfus, dated June 24, 1942. "Billy" (von Mayer) was a nickname for Gertrud's brother Martin.

ERNST FLERSHEIM TO THE EBERSTADTS, MAY OR JUNE 1942

I last wrote you on May 14 and have meanwhile received your letter of May 10. It is a happy day when we hear all is well with you. I hope you, Edith, will soon get household help. I said how much work it is for Mother when we have nothing more elaborate than a few friends for tea in the evening.

At the end of May my friend Albert (Ettlinger) celebrated his 80th birthday. He is amazingly fit and looks younger than I, though the other day an official I had to see thought I was between 60 and 65. I don't want to celebrate my forthcoming 80th birthday [July 13]. I'd only be thinking of happy past celebrations with all of you. No news of Billy von Mayer. Herbert Flersheim has arrived safely in Argentina. I am happy Walter has developed well. He will always give you pleasure, I am sure (his 21st birthday is in July).

Ernst

GERTRUD FLERSHEIM TO THE EBERSTADTS, UNDATED (1943)

Nothing makes us happier than to have your news. It is a pity I can't write in more detail, but our letters are supposed to be kept brief. Edith, make sure you have sufficient household help so that you yourself don't have to clean the stairs. A household is more work in the winter, with heating, more cooking, and more laundry. I am happy you are able to see the children. Bridget is almost a grown-up and I am glad Walter is in a position to be helpful. We often speak of Albert [Eberstadt], what a good loyal wise man he was. I am so worried about both my brothers.

Albert Ettlinger is still full of energy, busy all day, helpful to many elderly and sick. He attends lectures at lunchtime. We are grateful for his friendship, and hers. She does beautiful needlework.

Ernst races around like a young man. I try to be helpful in the house, do some laundry and mending, but that leaves little time to learn anything new. Rudi and Hans miss mother and wife. Mail from them takes forever. Be sure one day you look after the two of them. It has been bitterly cold which used to be my favorite time of the year for skating. My feet would no longer be up to it.

Gertrud

(German censorship stamp, dated January 29, 1943)

There are more letters, but they don't add much to an understanding of the conditions under which the Flersheims lived in wartime Nazi-occupied Holland.

While the letters between the Eberstadts in London and the Flersheims in Amsterdam, dwelling as they do on greetings, love, and reminiscences are perhaps inevitably bland, Ernst Flersheim's correspondence with his nephew Willy Dreyfus is haunting. Fear and dashed hopes, failed attempts to leave for Switzerland or the United States, and pleas for help are the main subject of nearly every letter. In 1998 I obtained from the Dutch government archives financial and other records of their wartime life in Holland which, I can only say, would make anyone shudder.

It appears that the Dutch authorities were pressing the Flersheims for "ransom" money from Switzerland and that Dreyfus was trying to enlist the financial help of Ernst Flersheim's nephew and former partner, Herbert Flersheim. He had left Holland to go first to Madeira and then to Argentina.

As Jews tried everything to avoid roundups and arrests in Holland, several lists began to circulate that promised exemption from transport to camps. Emigration would be granted in exchange for substantial payments in foreign currency. Foreign currency was to be paid into bank accounts in Switzerland and the money would be transferred to the German treasury as soon as the emigrant reached his or her destination.

I have no record of any of the February 1943 correspondence that Willy Dreyfus refers to in the following letter.

WILLY DREYFUS TO THE FLERSHEIMS, MARCH 6, 1943

Since writing to you on 18th and 19th February, I have had your letters of the 19th, 20th, and 26th February. I have heard nothing further from Herbert. You are correctly informed that correspondence with Argentina has become very slow and erratic, but letters do get there eventually, provided they are not intercepted by enemy censorship. I continue to do everything possible to arrange the credit matter in the way you ask, so that it meets the requirements of your authorities. I have heard nothing from Fritz or Florence, nor anyone else over there since the fall.

ERNST FLERSHEIM TO WILLY DREYFUS, MARCH 10, 1943
Amsterdam

I last wrote you on March 4th and said I would let you have more details after I had spoken to the gentleman in question. However, so far it has not been possible to see him, and I did not want to delay longer writing to you that it is of the utmost importance for Herbert's credit to be placed at our disposal as soon as possible. I am hoping to see the gentleman in question in the very next days, after which I will write again.

Our health continues to be all right, but we think constantly about our mutual friend Albert. I hope we will soon have news from Edith.

By "our mutual friend Albert" Ernst doubtless means Albert Ettlinger, who had been arrested. The Flersheims were afraid the same would happen at any time to them.

ERNST FLERSHEIM TO WILLY DREYFUS, MARCH 12, 1943
Amsterdam

. . . Further to my letter of March 10 I have meanwhile seen the gentleman who is dealing with the officials in question. His delegate will probably come shortly to see you.

Please be sure that the sum mentioned in your letter of February 18 will be put at his disposal. This is of the utmost importance for us. Your letter of February 18 has already proven very valuable.

I don't have to repeat how grateful we are for all your help. Should you not be in Basel when the gentleman comes, perhaps you can arrange for someone else to see him. . . .

ERNST FLERSHEIM TO WILLY DREYFUS, MARCH 16, 1943
Rubensstraat 63, Amsterdam

. . . I wrote you on March 12 and have received yours of March 6. However, yours of Feb 19 has not reached me. If need be, send me a copy.

Words fail to express my gratitude to you adequately for all you are doing for us. We will never forget your help and goodness toward us. In response to your letter of March 6, I cannot fail to stress again how absolutely imperative it has become that the sum mentioned in the last paragraph in your letter is ready and available when the gentleman in question comes to see you. We hope that by the time of his visit everything will be in good order, because it essential that what we said will soon be implemented. In view of the unreliable mails to Argentina you may have to cable Herbert. . . .

ERNST FLERSHEIM TO WILLY DREYFUS, MARCH 25, 1943
Rubensstraat 63, Amsterdam

I wrote you on the 12th and the 16th but have not heard back from you. The foreshadowed visit to you by the gentleman in question has been delayed, and I don't know now when he will come.

Under the circumstances it would be of the utmost importance for us to have some written confirmation of the amount in question, which I could show to the authorities. I hope that in the meantime you have been able to complete everything, especially that you can send me a written confirmation. . . .

WILLY DREYFUS TO ERNST FLERSHEIM, MARCH 25, 1943
Basel

. . . I herewith acknowledge receipt of your letters dated March 10, 12, and 16. Their content has my full attention. I continue with all means at my disposal to arrange the credit along the lines requested by you and hope it will be done in due course. I don't have to tell you the obstacles in every direction that have to be overcome. I know full well what is at stake for you. Please be convinced that I am leaving nothing undone to get the matter done. . . .

Willy Dreyfus concluded this letter with good news from Edith Eberstadt, a letter from Herbert Flersheim that took six months from Argentina to Switzerland, and a photo of Bridget.

WILLY DREYFUS TO ERNST FLERSHEIM, APRIL 1943
c/o Dreyfus Söhne, Basel

Dear Uncle Ernst,

Our letters of March 25 crossed. I received yours today. I hasten to respond by writing that you can count on the money being available for you to pay to the authorities when needed. I herewith authorize you to show this letter to the authorities. I will be much interested to receive any further news from you.

Your loyal nephew, Willy

ERNST FLERSHEIM TO WILLY DREYFUS, APRIL 9, 1943
Amsterdam

Dear Willy,

I am in receipt of your letter dated March 25. I am unable to find the right words with which to thank you for what you are doing for us. They are in my heart but words fail me. I am convinced that you understand the necessity to conclude the credit arrangements as soon as possible.

I can only say that after what we personally experienced in the last few days, there can be no doubt left about our situation. They were extremely harassing and strenuous days! You inquire about our mutual friend Albert. We have not heard another word from him and therefore have no desire under these circumstances to come together with him. Even if I know that you are doing everything possible, please be sure to give me proof the money is there for me.

I hope to see the gentleman who is in touch with the authorities in the next days and to hear when his delegate is in a position to visit you.

In the hope of hearing from you without further delay, with heartfelt thanks,

Uncle Ernst

WILLY DREYFUS TO ERNST FLERSHEIM, APRIL 21, 1943
c/o Dreyfus Söhne, Basel

Dear Uncle Ernst,

I herewith acknowledge receipt of your letter in which you acknowledge receipt of mine dated March 25. I hope you have meanwhile received mine of April 1.

I herewith reaffirm once more that you can count on me as soon as the required sum has to be paid over. I look forward to hearing further from you. Please keep me posted how your negotiations are progressing. I have no doubt that they will recognize the exceptional position you are in, because it is exceptional under the circumstances to be able to make this kind of payment.

I hope that, notwithstanding what you write in your letter, your health is more or less all right. Greetings from your loyal nephew,

Willy

ERNST FLERSHEIM TO WILLY DREYFUS, APRIL 17, 1943
Amsterdam

Dear Willy,

I last wrote you on April 9 and acknowledge with thanks yours of April 1. I have meanwhile spoken to Herr Puttkammer of the Rotterdamsche Bank, the gentleman who made the application to the authorities on my behalf. The person who was supposed to travel to see you cannot come at the moment and I don't know when it will be.

I am relieved that the sum mentioned in your letter of February 26 is available when he comes. My informant [Puttkammer] says the sum is rather small as a first payment, but let us hope it suffices. He says it will be credited toward the sum needed to allow us to stay. For an exit permit the minimum needed is Swiss Francs 100,000.

In the past months we were four times in acute danger of being taken away and you will understand that this is the reason for
trying everything possible to obtain a larger credit.

I can't judge from here whether through Herbert or some
other way the money can be found. Please cable Herbert how serious our situation is. I hope someone in our family will be able to
help. I realize I am placing a great burden on you, but you are the
only one to whom I can turn, and so far you have stood like a son
at our side.

I must come to you with another request. I understand that in
order to get an exit permit from here we first need an entry permit
from the Swiss, and for this we need a residence permit from a
canton. We understand old people like ourselves are given a permit provided someone guarantees we won't be a financial burden
to the state. I hope such a guarantor can be found and perhaps
Georg [Eberstadt] in turn will guarantee to keep him harmless. It
would be good to undertake these steps now so that everything is
in order once we have the Swiss immigration papers. Please keep
a record of all your expenses so that Fritz can reimburse you in due
course.

Tante and I continue to be endlessly grateful for your support.
For the immigration authorities, I was born on July 13, 1862, in
Frankfurt, Gertrud on August 2, 1872, in Coburg. . . .

WILLY DREYFUS TO ERNST FLERSHEIM, MAY 4, 1943
c/o Dreyfus Söhne, Basel

Dear Uncle,

I herewith acknowledge receipt of your letters dated April 17
and 21. I have forwarded the enclosure [for Herbert Flersheim] to
Buenos Aires but considering the uncertainty of the post, I don't
know if or when it will get there. However, I have also telegraphed him. I would be so happy if I got permission soon, which

would enable me to make the financial arrangements that would satisfy your authorities. You can be totally assured that I am trying everything in my power. Without having to spell it out I can put myself in your situation. I fully realize how much depends on you making the demanded payment.

Realizing your situation I am now taking all steps possible to see whether I can get a permit for you to come to Switzerland. A number of formalities have to be cleared and I will let you know as soon as I have a positive decision.

I expect you have had my letter telling you of my son Richard's marriage [in New York]. I hear nothing but the best about my daughter-in-law. My wife is delighted with her.

Your faithful nephew, Willy

ERNST FLERSHEIM TO WILLY DREYFUS, MAY 8, 1943
Rubensstraat 63, Amsterdam

Dear Willy,

I wrote to you on April 9 and 17 but am sorry I have not heard from you since. I can tell you today that we have found someone who is going to Switzerland on May 19 and will come to see you. He will be there for a couple of weeks. I will be speaking to him before he leaves and ask him to find out from the Dreyfus office where you and he can meet. Please meanwhile arrange for the money to be available when he comes.

Here nothing has changed. Have you heard anything from Edith? Give her our best from both of us. Have you been able to give our news to Herbert?

I am awaiting with great interest your answer to my letter of April 17. I am assuming it has been delayed in the mail.

All the best, Uncle Ernst

In Holland, several major roundups of Jews took place in May, June, and September of 1943. Exemption lists, such as those kept by E. A. P. Puttkammer, apparently did provide temporary "protection" from these police arrests, adding to their credibility. However, between March and November, 43,000 Jews were deported.

ERNST FLERSHEIM TO WILLY DREYFUS, MAY 24, 1943
Rubensstraat 63, Amsterdam

Dear Willy,

We have now had your letters of April 22 and May 5. I wrote you last on May 4. I hope you have meanwhile seen the gentleman who is supposed to come to you and that the transfer of the money has taken place. It is of the greatest urgency because our situation here has worsened. We have been told we will shortly be taken to a nearby camp where we will be allowed to stay for the time being until the money has arrived.

Since it will be impossible to correspond with you from there, please write meanwhile to Herbert's friend Hans [Wetzlar] regarding the additional funds needed for an exit permit, also how you are getting on with our Swiss visa. I am enclosing six passport photos of Tante and myself in case you need them.

I am sure you understand that everything is now extremely urgent and the arrangements can still be made in time.

I won't waste words describing our situation. Please tell all our loved ones we are united with them in our thoughts, especially Edith, and also Mariechen.

Our best wishes are also meant for you and your family. Once more, thank you, thank you, for all your love and help.

Tante and your old Uncle Ernst

WILLY DREYFUS TO ERNST FLERSHEIM, JUNE 3, 1943
c/o Dreyfus Söhne, Basel

Dear Uncle Ernst,

I herewith acknowledge receipt of your letter dated May 24. I am glad to hear you and Tante are all right.

I have just this moment sent the following telegram: "Puttkammer, 187 van Eeghenstraat, Amsterdam. Concerning Ernst and Gertrud Flersheim am holding at your disposal SF 30,000 to be credited to correspondents of Handelstrust, West Amsterdam. Am attempting to get amount increased."

I hope my telegram arrived in time to prevent you from being sent to the camp. I don't have to tell you how deeply all you write affects me and I repeat I am doing everything within my power to help you. Thank you for the passport photos, which will be helpful in getting your visa, on which I am working.

Your loyal nephew, Willy

ERNST FLERSHEIM TO WILLY DREYFUS, JULY 5, 1943
Rubensstraat 63, Amsterdam

We are home after having been away 34 days, and this first message is for you and our children. Tell them we will think of them on their forthcoming birthdays and engagement anniversary.

I will write to you as soon as I have seen Herr Puttkammer. Our health is more or less all right. This is just a brief note to give you our news and thanks for your help.

The next letter reflects the extreme precariousness of the situation. Honduras is a new idea, and the fact that Ernst Flersheim has to refer to himself and his wife as "Walter's grandparents'" shows their fear.

ERNST FLERSHEIM TO WILLY DREYFUS, JULY 8, 1943
Rubensstraat 63, Amsterdam

Dear Willy,

I have not so far been able to see Herr Puttkammer or the
gentleman who came to visit you. I am writing mainly to give you
our news after the hard times we have just had. Now I must ask
you to get the Honduras papers for Walter's grandparents as soon
as possible. Is there any news about Switzerland for us? . . .

This telegram was part of the Puttkammer negotiations:

TELEGRAM FROM HANDELSTRUST, AMSTERDAM TO DREYFUS
SÖHNE, JUNE 23, 1943

Understand that in matter Flersheim you are holding SF
30,000 at our disposal. Our party asking when transfer will take
place and what if any obstacles there are. Please cable Handelstrust.

ERNST FLERSHEIM TO WILLY DREYFUS, AUGUST 3, 1943
Rubensstraat 63, Amsterdam

Dear Willy,

I wrote you on July 26 but don't want to mail Tante's long letter without adding a note, and to thank you for your letter of July
16. I was glad to have Edith's good news, and Herbert's. You say he
can no longer write from Buenos Aires, but I hope he is none-
theless in a position to send some more money to Switzerland.
Even if he can't do it, I hope you will find it somewhere. I know
Herr Puttkammer has also written to you.

We are very worried, as Tante has written, about having to move to another apartment. I hope you have positive news for us so that I won't be causing you more work and worry.

I am trying my best to keep going. Even if my age does not seem to show, my nerves have suffered greatly. Give our greetings to Edith and her family, also to Herbert and Fritz, and to your own family.

You have said nothing about whether you have succeeded in getting papers for Walter's grandparents.

Like an earlier letter, this next one ends with greetings to innumerable relatives, friends, and acquaintances, demonstrating how my grandmother was clinging to the life that once was.

GERTRUD FLERSHEIM TO WILLY DREYFUS, AUGUST 3, 1943

My dear good Willy,

You cannot imagine the pleasure your detailed letter of July 6, which arrived on my birthday [August 2], gave me. There is nothing more one wants at my age than good news from one's family, and rest and quiet for oneself. I don't seem to be able to get rid of my sinus infection, which I have now had for 15 weeks. On the 8th we have to move to Amsterdam East. It is hard to find lodging because we have no household goods or furniture of our own and people don't want to take lodgers because of the food shortages. Meanwhile we may have to find temporary lodgings. Mail sent here will be forwarded. We go apartment hunting every day which is hard at our age and I have to try to get well again. Don't tell any of this to your cousin [that is, Edith Eberstadt]. Why worry her. . . .

ERNST FLERSHEIM TO WILLY DREYFUS, AUGUST 9, 1943,
Amsterdam

Dear Willy,

I wrote to you on August 3, but meanwhile have not heard
from you. We are moving out of what had become a greatly liked
home for us these last 2½ years. Please advise Edith. We expect to
move latest in a fortnight into two rooms for which we are in negotiations. Meanwhile we have to stay in a large home with many
other inhabitants. I will let you know our new address as soon as
I have it.

I hope to have your early news that the money has been remitted to Puttkammer as per his instructions and that you have
undertaken steps to obtain additional funds. There is no other
news except to ask you NOT to undertake any further steps to
obtain papers for Walter's grandparents. [Why, why, why?]

Our health remains all right but looking for a new home has
been tiring. The strain has given me sciatica.

Uncle Ernst

[P.S.] As I sign this letter we received Mariechen's with welcome news and greetings from Edith. She should not do so much
now that she is without a maid.

ERNST FLERSHEIM TO WILLY DREYFUS, AUGUST 28, 1943
Amsterdam Oost, Krugerstraat 4, Third Floor

Dear Willy,

I wrote you on July 26, August 3 and 8, but got yours of July
26 only a few days ago. As I wrote you on August 8, there is no
longer any need for you to get papers for Walter's grandparents.
[Why so?]

I hope that meanwhile the money has been sent in accordance with the regulations to the Reichshauptbank, Berlin, and

that you are working actively to obtain additional funds. I look forward to hearing from you.

We have a tiny living room and a still smaller bedroom. There is neither hot water nor a bathroom but the rooms are nicely furnished. Our landlady, who cooks for us, is civilized but very high-strung. It is just very difficult to find any lodging. The two weeks before we came here we spent in a large home.

Last year when I was 80 I did not feel my age, but now it is a different story. Our best to Martha [Willy Dreyfus's wife]. Where is your sister, and how is she?

P.S. from Gertrud Flersheim

Dear Willy,

Please send an express letter to Edith wishing her a happy birthday. The old age home where we have just been was appropriate for my years, but sixteen people in the dining room made a lot of noise!

Tante Gertrud

"Foodschen Invaliden," mentioned below, was a charitable old age home in Amsterdam.

Ernst Flersheim to Herbert Flersheim and Willy Dreyfus, August 30, 1943
Amsterdam

Dear Herbert and Willy,

At the beginning of August we received your welcome letter [from Argentina] dated March 19. We were very pleased to have your firsthand news and to see you are content, and happy with your [young and new] wife. I think I can more or less visualize that life on an *estancia* is agreeable, the more so as it is not too far from Buenos Aires.

We have gone through a lot lately. We were interned for several weeks but were released thanks to your and Willy's help. Once we were out, we had to move to Amsterdam Oost. Before we finally found two small rooms we had to stay at the Foodschen Invaliden. In our new rooms the landlady cooks for us but there are no amenities — no hot water, no bathroom. You can see our old age is not lacking in variety, but one gets used to all sorts of things!! Rudi once wrote from his village in the Pyrenees that you find you really don't need more than one bed, one chair, and one table. Where could the poor man and his child be? We have been without any news from them for some time. Nor do we hear anything from Martin and Nini or Ernst and his family.

Most of our friends are no longer here [that is, they have been arrested]. I have passed your greetings on to your friend Hans [Wetzlar]. He is really the only one here who helps us, for which I am very grateful. You should write him a line. I am glad your mother and Fritz are well.

If I only thank you at the end of this letter for the help you have given us through Willy, that makes it no less heartfelt. You must know by now how much we owe to you for your help. As long as we live we shall be grateful to you, and one day it will be Edith or George or Rudi. Please, together with Willy, continue with your efforts to help us. You and Willy no doubt are thinking together what you can do for us. I know you will not let your old uncle and aunt down. It is not easy for us to come to you all the time for more help. Our health, all things considered, is not bad, but our nerves have suffered from so much excitement. . . .

Rudolf and Hans Wertheim had been deported from France and sent to Auschwitz in August 1942, and this was 1943. Martin and Nini von

Mayer, Gertrud Flersheim's brother and his wife, lost their lives in Poland. Ernst von Mayer, Gertrud Flersheim's much younger half brother, was married to a non-Jewish woman named Marcelle Mühlen, of French and German origin; he and his family survived the war in France.

ERNST FLERSHEIM TO WILLY DREYFUS, SEPTEMBER 9, 1943
Amsterdam, Krugerstraat 4, Third Floor

Thank you for your letters of August 7 and 19. I wrote you on Aug 22 and 23. You write that the payment will be made as soon as you have an answer from Puttkammer as to where he wants it. I saw him today, but he said he had not heard from you. He will write to you directly. Even though I know you are doing everything possible to speed up matters, I cannot stress to you sufficiently how urgent and critical the situation is. Please be sure the transfer is made in accordance with Puttkammer's instructions.

We live in two minute rooms as subtenants, which does not matter as long as we are left alone. I hope you have had news from Herbert regarding additional funds, though I am aware transfers from Buenos Aires must be difficult.

The following is the last letter Ernst Flersheim wrote before he and Gertrud Flersheim were interned in Westerbork, from which camp they were deported to Bergen-Belsen.

ERNST FLERSHEIM TO WILLY DREYFUS, OCTOBER 5, 1943
Amsterdam

Dear Willy,

We received your letters of September 5 and 16 a few days ago. Many thanks. We were happy to have good news from

George and his family and are glad that your wife and children [in New York] are well.

I don't know whether I will be able to write to you for the foreseeable future. In any event, please give Edith all our love and that we wish all the best for her. Our dearest wish is that they may live a healthy and contented life.

Also for you, dear Willy, our wishes are for the best. We are forever grateful for your love and assistance.

Please write for the time being to Herbert's friend Hans [Wetzlar]. Best regards from Tante. She has had to do all the housework and cooking lately. I try to be helpful, to the extent a man can be. Our nerves are in bad shape, but we try to pull ourselves together.

Your food parcel has not arrived as yet. I hope it will still reach us. . . .

The following correspondence is between Herr E. A. P. Puttkammer and Willy Dreyfus concerning possible payments from Switzerland on behalf of the Flersheims.

Please note at the end of this chapter Willy Dreyfus's postwar letter to Georg Eberstadt written in 1946 and sent along with the wartime correspondence reproduced here.

TELEGRAM FROM WILLY DREYFUS TO PUTTKAMMER, UNDATED

E. A. P. Puttkammer, Manager, Rotterdamsche Bankvereeniging, 187 van Eeghenstraat, Rotterdam

Concerning Ernst Flersheim and his wife am holding at your disposal SF 30,000 for payment to Handelstrust West Amsterdam. Am attempting to obtain additional funds. Willy Dreyfus.

WILLY DREYFUS TO PUTTKAMMER, JUNE 26, 1943
Basel

Respected Mr. Puttkammer,

Messrs Dreyfus Söhne, Basel, advise me they have received the following telegram: "Understand that in the matter Flersheim you are supposed to put SF 30,000 at our disposal. Our party is asking when the transfer will take place and what if any obstacles exist. Please cable. Handelstrust."

For good order's sake I would first like to explain that the Dreyfus Bank itself is not involved. This is a purely personal matter of mine as the Flersheims are close relatives of my wife's. Please advise Handelstrust accordingly and ask them to deal with me personally. I am not a member of the bank. I just get my mail there.

As far as the matter itself is concerned, please let me know to whom in Switzerland payment should be made.

I am most grateful for all your efforts.

Respectfully, Willy Dreyfus

PUTTKAMMER TO WILLY DREYFUS, JULY 20, 1943
Amsterdam-Z, 187 van Eeghenstraat

To the esteemed Willy Dreyfus, c/o Dreyfus Söhne, Basel,

I refer to your telegram of early June regarding Ernst Flersheim and his wife. As you are probably aware I was able to arrange for their [arrest] to be put on hold provided the offered sum of SF 30,000 is credited immediately to the Reichsbank in Berlin.

I must therefore ask you to undertake the necessary steps as soon as possible to effect the transfer. You should ask the Reichshauptbank to telegraph both me and the Herr Befehlshaber of the Security Police and the SD, Department IV B 4, The Hague, when the funds have been received.

In the interest of Mr. and Mrs. Flersheim I would ask you please to treat this as being of the utmost urgency.

Repectfully, E. A. P. Puttkammer

WILLY DREYFUS TO ROTTERDAMSCHE BANKVEREENIGING,
AUGUST 7, 1943,
Basel

The Management
Rotterdamsche Bankvereeniging, Amsterdam
I have been advised by Mr. Ernst Flersheim of the efforts you are undertaking on his behalf. I would like to express my great appreciation to you, and in particular to your Mr. E. A. P. Puttkammer. From my side I shall undertake everything to have the sum of SF 30,000 placed at your disposal.

Respectfully, Willy Dreyfus

PUTTKAMMER TO WILLY DREYFUS, SEPTEMBER 13, 1943
187 van Eeghenstraat, Amsterdam

Respected Herr Dreyfus,
On July 20, I asked you regarding Ernst Flersheim to transfer as soon as possible the sum you offered, SF 30,000, to the Reichshauptbank in Berlin. Since I have not heard any more from you I would like to stress that the matter has become extremely urgent and to make the required arrangements as soon as possible.

Respectfully, E. A. P. Puttkammer

WILLY DREYFUS TO PUTTKAMMER, SEPTEMBER 29, 1943
Basel

Respected Herr Puttkammer,

I acknowledge herewith receipt of your letter dated Sept. 13. Its content has my full attention. I should be grateful to hear from you at which address here in Switzerland the Reichshauptbank would like the SF 30,000 credited for the benefit of Mr. and Mrs. Flersheim. As soon as you give me the address, the funds will be remitted.

For your friendly endeavors, the significance of which I fully understand, please accept my grateful thanks.

With best regards, Willy Dreyfus

PUTTKAMMER TO WILLY DREYFUS, OCTOBER 12, 1943
Amsterdam

Respected Herr Dreyfus,

I am in receipt of your kind letter dated Sept. 29. To answer your question, the funds can be credited to any of the major Swiss banks in favor of the Reichshauptbank, Berlin.

I await your further news and remain respectfully,

E. A. P. Puttkammer

PUTTKAMMER TO WILLY DREYFUS, OCTOBER 19, 1943
Amsterdam

Respected Herr Dreyfus,

For good order's sake I must advise you that in recent days Ernst Flersheim and his wife were arrested and sent to the Westerbork camp. Their present address is Lager Westerbork, Post Hooghalen Oost, Barrakke #6.

Respectfully, Puttkammer

HANS A. WETZLAR TO WILLY DREYFUS, NOVEMBER 10, 1943
205 Prinsengracht, Amsterdam

Respected Herr Dreyfus,

I am in receipt of your letter dated October 21. Your uncle and aunt are not well. At the moment they are in the Westerbork hospital barracks. I do not know what exactly is the matter with them, but it is not surprising they are ailing. You can write to them: Herr Ernst Flersheim, Krankenbarakke #6, Frau Gertrud Flersheim von Mayer, Krankenbarakke #82, Westerbork, Hooghalen, Drente, Holland.

Should you be writing to Herbert Flersheim, please give him my best regards and tell him, considering the times, my family and I are well.

HANS A. WETZLAR TO WILLY DREYFUS, FEBRUARY 16, 1944
Amsterdam

Respected Herr Dreyfus,

I regret I have to inform you that your uncle and his wife have been moved to Celle in Germany. I do not have a more detailed address as yet.

With best regards, Hans Wetzlar

Celle is the city closest to Bergen and Belsen, the location of the Bergen-Belsen camp.

HANS A. WETZLAR TO WILLY DREYFUS, MARCH 23, 1944
Amsterdam

Respected Herr Dreyfus,

Many thanks for your letter. I regret to say I have not had any news from your uncle and aunt, and do not believe we can any longer expect to hear from them. Should I have any news whatever I will of course let you know right away.

Respectfully, HW

I found the above letters, and Willy Dreyfus's letter below, written in 1946, in my father's writing desk after his death in 1963. He kept them from my mother, and so did I.

WILLY DREYFUS TO GEORG EBERSTADT, UNDATED (1946)

Dear Georg,

I am enclosing a number of letters which I had indicated recently I would send to you. They show you the role played by Puttkammer. It is evident that he tried his best and succeeded for several months to delay the deportation of your parents-in-law.

It had to be clear to Puttkammer that my assurances to remit the money in question were not realistic. The Dutch were fully aware that nobody in Switzerland would dare contravene the Allied request not to make any payments to enemy or enemy-occupied countries.

We hoped that by going through the motions we could gain sufficient time to save your parents from the worst. Alas the Liberation came too late. Please give the enclosed letters to Hedwig Blach.

Cordially, Willy

Willy Dreyfus added a note to the above lettter, saying that a Puttkammer representative had dropped by to see him while he was away, but that Paul Dreyfus saw him instead and left the following memorandum of their conversation:

Regarding the Ernst Flersheim matter, WD should write to Puttkammer that the money is available, even if in reality this is not the case. He should write that it will take at least four weeks to make the arrangements, and then write again that more formalities still need to be cleared, but in a crisis SF 30,000 can somehow be made available. In his letters he should stress the complications. As for the Flersheims personally, they are so far all right.

The role played by Puttkammer is far from clear. Most of what I have read about him suggests he was nothing but a functionary working on behalf of the Germans.

The letters to be given to Hedwig Blach, referred to in Willy's letter above, are the correspondence concerning the family of her brother, Rudolf Wertheim. They make up many of the letters printed in the preceding chapter.

14

Bergen-Belsen

In February of 1944 Ernst and Gertrud Flersheim, aged eighty-two and seventy-two years, were deported from Westerbork to Bergen-Belsen. In February, Hans Wetzlar wrote to Willy Dreyfus in a guarded, brief letter that they had departed for a destination in Germany near Celle (the nearest town to Bergen-Belsen). Belsen was not an "extermination" camp but rather meant as a transit camp from which inmates were shipped to the eastern extermination camps. Deaths were from disease and starvation. Ernst Flersheim died a few weeks after his arrival, and Gertrud Flersheim some time later.

In England we knew they had been sent to Belsen. We first heard of my grandfather's death in a letter from a Frankfurt banker and friend, I. Bergenthal. Bergenthal had been in Holland, interned in Westerbork, and sent with his wife to Belsen. However, he had managed to get to Palestine, from which he wrote to my parents with news about my grandparents.

I. Bergenthal to Georg Eberstadt, September 9, 1944
Ben Maimon Ave. 27, Jerusalem

Dear Dr. Eberstadt,

. . . For weeks we have been trying to get your address to let you know about your parents-in-law. Unfortunately we have no good news. Your in-laws and we were interned at Westerbork at the same time and at the beginning of this year we were transferred to Bergen-Belsen. Your father-in-law died a few weeks later while your mother-in-law was placed in the so-called old age home. When we left on June 30 her mental condition was quite bad. She was told of her husband's death but according to what I heard she could not fully grasp the extent of this news.

As you probably know the two of them lived quite agreeably with a very nice family in a house in the Rubensstraat. They came quite often to visit us, which we always enjoyed, especially your father-in-law, who still showed such vigorous ability to look after his interests, even though his eyes gave him so much trouble. Later, like us, they had to move to Amsterdam Oost, where they found a very primitive apartment very near us. It was impressive to see how they managed to cope with these completely changed conditions. We saw a lot of each other. In the big raid of Sept. 29, 1943, they were arrested and sent to Westerbork, where conditions were not so bad for them. From there we were all sent to Bergen-Belsen, which was most unpleasant for all of us. What has since happened to your mother-in-law is beyond our means of knowing. We are unable to get any news whatsoever and do not know either what has happened to our [daughter] Hilde, her husband, or their child.

We can imagine the dreadful impact this news must have on you and especially on your wife. Please accept our heartfelt sympathy. We had become very fond of the wonderful old gentleman.

I will write about us another time. You may need a sworn affi-

davit regarding your father-in-law's death, which I can supply
with supporting evidence from others here.

Warmly,

Bergenthals

The following appeared on page 3 of the Palestinian newspaper *Aliya
Hadassah*, dated July 14, 1944.

Monday evening 282 Jews arrived at Athlit, directly from Hitler-
land. Such a group of miserable, emaciated figures, a kind of
arrival the likes of which Palestine had never before experienced.

Most of the immigrants came from the camp at Bergen-
Belsen near Celle, a few from Vittel in France. They fall under the
category "Exchange of civilian prisoners," that is, as Palestinian
citizens to be exchanged for German nationals. Only a few of
them really are true Palestinian nationals, while the rest are pre-
sumptive Palestinians, that is, holders of Palestinian immigration
permits. Of the 282, there are 45 children and 140 women; no
men of working age are in the group, though it does include a
group of "Chaluzoth" girls from Holland. About 50 people are
from Vittel in France.

The descriptions of conditions in the Nazi hellholes are grue-
some. The camp was built new in 1943 for people who already had
valid emigration permits for other countries (Palestine, America,
South America). At present there are about three thousand inhabitants, mainly German and Dutch Jews.

Life in the camp goes something like this: food consists solely
of turnips and tea, the workday is 12 to 14 hours. Everyone has to
work, from 6-year-old children to 80-year-old men. The work is
mainly cultivating silkworms and repairing military boots. Wake-
up is at 4 A.M. and roll call at 5 A.M. At roll call everyone must be

present, living and dead (that is, those that have died in the meantime). When someone is missing, everyone has to stand until everyone is accounted for. There were days when they had to stand for 9 hours, during which children who could not move collapsed and died.

Among the transport were eight people from Berlin who left there in March 1944. They spoke of the tremendous [air raid] destruction there. There is still a Jewish community in Berlin, but consisting only of Jews married to non-Jews. The congregation is located in the Jewish hospital in the Iranische Strasse (Exerzierstrasse). In addition a few thousand Jews have survived by going underground, helped by supportive non-Jews. In the group is James Ellenbogen, a former official in the Berlin Jewish community, and Frau van Tyn, the well-known Dutch Zionist and social worker. The leader of the transport was Dr. Israel Taubes, etc.

Some names from the list of the 282 exchanged persons:

Inge Aronstein, Dortmund
Johann Ascher-Morell, London
Ludwig J. Baruch, Hamburg
James Ellenbogen, Berlin
Mindel Färber, Düsseldorf
Jeanette Feuchtwang-Dunner, Cologne
Marion Bergenthal, Frankfurt
Gesina van Blitz, Amsterdam
Ursula Borchard, Munich
Pauline Cohn-Ettlinger, Mannheim
Otto Gassmann, Gleiwitz
Siegfied Glaser, Berlin
Elsa Hannach, née Broader, Berlin
Ruth Jacobsohn, Berlin
Paula Kaufmann-Adler, Frankfurt
Margaret Levy, née Hahn, Berlin
Walter Levy, Berlin

Ernst Flersheim and his daughters Edith and Margarete.

Ernst and Gertrud Flersheim, Hans Flersheim, myself and my sister,
Hamburg 1930.

The wedding of Rudolf Wertheim and Margarete Flersheim in the
Flersheim home, 32 Myliusstrasse, Frankfurt, 1927.
Train bearers are Jürg and Klaus Schaefer.

Rudolf Wertheim,
London, 1938.

Hans Wertheim,
aged 12,
Brussels, 1940.

Postcard from Rudolf Wertheim to Willy Dreyfus in Switzerland
to advise that he and his son Hans were in
a French internment camp, and expecting to be sent East shortly.

Steps leading to the Flersheim's two-room apartment at 4 Krugerstraat, Amsterdam Oost, where they spent the last months before being arrested. It had no hot water and extremely burdensome stairs.

Westerbork camp in Holland: railway spur to
Auschwitz, Theresienstadt, and Bergen-Belsen.

The two Germanys: Bergen-Belsen (*above*); and (*opposite*) a memorial for Generals Beck and Olbricht, Colonels Claus von Stauffenberg and Albrecht von Quirnheim, and Lieut. Werner von Haeften, five of hundreds who lost their lives opposing Hitler. "They died for Germany on this spot, July 20, 1944." They were executed in the courtyard of Gestapo headquarters in Prinz-Albrechtstrasse, now a Nazi Opposition memorial museum, after Stauffenberg's failed attempt to assassinate Hitler.

The Clara Schumann House, 32 Myliusstrasse, Frankfurt on Main, from1878 to1896 home of the pianist and composer, wife of Robert Schumann, and friend of Johannes Brahms. Flersheim home from 1897 to 1937. Now home of Klaus Peter Fischer and his wife Christiane Lampe, who affixed the plaque commemorating the Flersheim lives.

Unveiling of Flersheim plaque. *From left to right:* My Lazard partner Frank Pizzatola; Ursula Lichtenberg, wife of the late Paul Lichtenberg, chairman of Commerzbank; Anette Lichtenberg, Ursula's daughter-in-law; my cousin Klaus Schaefer; Sybille Reimnitz, wife of Jürgen Reimnitz of Commerzbank; Renate Schaefer; Klaus Peter Fischer, owner of the Clara Schumann house; me; and my cousin Gerhard Eberstadt of Dresdner Bank.

Gertrud Lewin-Hayn, Berlin

Klara Luise Wolfstein, Berlin

Hedwig H. Mittwoch, Berlin

Selka Ochsmann Bamberger, Frankfurt

Karl Ochsmann, Poppenlauer

Ilse Selka Jakobi, Berlin

Peggy Wallner, Hamburg

Ruth Zucker, Berlin

Ursula Flaum, Berlin

Vera Fränkel, Breslau

Julius Gans, Frankfurt

Johanna Gans-Meyer, Frankfurt

Hedwig Gassmann-Ginsberg, Breslau

Eva Goldschmidt-Schwarzschild, Cologne

Ellen Herz, Amsterdam

Jolante Katz-Ginsberg, Frankfurt

Grete Lehmann, Hannover

Siegfried Levy, Hamburg

Katarina Levy-Levinsky, Berlin

Jeanette Mayer-Rappaport, Vienna

Frieda Mittwoch Abraczk, Berlin

Bertha Mühlbaum, Berlin

Nora B. Rothschild, Frankfurt

Ruth Wolf-Adler, Dresden

Belsen was liberated by the British army in the spring of 1945, a half-year after we received the letter from the Bergenthals. At the time I was stationed in Luxembourg working at Radio Luxembourg, the PWD (Psychological Warfare Department) station of SHAEF. As soon as I heard of the liberation, I obtained leave and permission to go there. We knew my grandfather was dead, and expected my grandmother no longer to be living, but we had no definite information. The following diary entry was written immediately after my visit to the camp; I have retained my then British usage and spelling.

My Visit to Belsen, April 1945

I arrived at Belsen Concentration Camp on April 23, 1945, about ten days after the camp had been liberated by British troops. Halfway between Celle and Belsen large signposts with typhus warnings had been put up. Every few hundred yards a signpost said: To Belsen Concentration Camp. I was given a permit to enter the camp without any difficulty and, having been dusted with anti-typhus powder, was allowed to enter. There was a sweetly heavy odor of death as soon as one got near the camp. The layout of the camp is roughly as follows: A broad cinder track down the centre with huts going off to both sides, the cookhouses being at this end (near the entrance) and the "living" huts at the far end. When the British took over, there were about 35,000 of the 50,000 inmates who had been there a few weeks earlier left.

At the first moment looking down the central cinder track all I saw was a large number of reasonably healthy-looking people walking aimlessly — as people in camps are wont to do — up and down, but it did not take me many seconds to realize that they were the few lucky ones who were still fit, having arrived at the camp only a few days before it was liberated. I had only to look a little more closely to notice deathly-looking men and women, all pallid, skinny, haunted, unshaven, wearing rags or nothing on their feet, wearing the "white" and blue overalls that were the official concentration camp dress. As I walked down the centre lane, I saw the first dead: naked bodies of men and women, not an ounce of flesh left on them, hollow behinds, their stomachs caved in. No one had shut their eyes, and there they lay, in the same position, nearly all of them: their arms stretched up, their bodies slightly curled up; some lying on their backs, some on their chests. Those who were still living had taken their clothes off, either to sleep on them, or to use them to make little fires for baking potatoes.

I walked into the first hut compounds: imagine some long huts, all wooden, with open spaces in between. In the open spaces those men and women were hovering, dragging one another along, those lucky ones who had still strength enough to drag themselves outside their huts. The stench in the area between the huts was almost unbearable. It was a sea of mud and excretia: the camp authorities had tried digging latrines, but no one would use them: the women were sitting there doing their business, sitting there by the dozen, just outside their huts. It was just a sea of diarrhea. The women were too weak even to lift their skirts, and they did not seem to mind finding some support for themselves on a dead body. Some of them were lying there in the sunshine: I really don't know whether they were living or dead. In between all this they were squatting around little fires baking their potatoes. On the steps of one hut were sitting a young boy and a girl kissing one another.

I went into the first hut of the many I was going to visit. It was dark and the floors covered with the clothes of the dead. I don't know how many hundred women were in that hut, lying body to body. The dreadful stench was utterly overpowering. They were of all nationalities, but being mainly Jewesses, they understood my German. Immediately some of the stronger ones dragged themselves up and surrounded me. Nearly all of them had typhus. The hut was filled with the noise of their questions, and the groaning of the sick and dying. *Wann kommen wir raus? Wir wollen nicht sterben. Ich bin so krank, ach ich bin so krank. Sehen Sie mich an, Herr Doktor, ich habe solchen Durchfall. Ich habe solchen Durst.* — "When will we get out? We don't want to die. I am so sick, achh . . . I am so sick. Look at me, Herr Doktor, I have such diarrhea. I am so thirsty." Some started crying, whimpering, some started screaming. *Helfen Sie uns doch, wir können nicht mehr. Da ist schon wieder eine gestorben, schon die siebte heute.* — And so on, and so forth. *Ich kann nicht mehr, ich will sterben.* — "I cannot carry on; I want to die." Then a woman — she looked sixty, a sallow face, her black hair hanging down — came to me: *Kann ich nicht ins Hospital? Sehen Sie sich meinen Fuss an.* — "Can't I go to the hospital? Look at my foot." *Nehmen Sie doch meinen Fuss ab, Herr Doktor, sonst sterbe ich doch.* — "Please, doctor, amputate my foot, or I will die." She showed me a gangrenous foot, with the pus oozing out. I could not persuade them I was not a doctor.

Then I noticed a woman crying and screaming in a corner: *Mein Kind stirbt, helfen Sie mir doch.* — "My child is dying, help me." She herself was half demented. She implored me to come to her corner. I climbed over bodies and legs and she showed me her daughter: her right leg was festering, the girl had typhus and a high temperature. She had a bullet in her leg: a fortnight earlier she had been shot at by an SS guard who had caught her stealing a carrot after they had been kept without food for a whole week. I simply could not bear it and went away to get a little pushcart. We put the girl on the cart and pushed her to the hospital. The British medical authorities had been so overwhelmed that they had not yet been able to deal with that particular case. I immediately caused an uproar: *Nehmen Sie mich doch auch mit. Helfen Sie mir. Wir sind doch so krank.* — "Take me, too. Help me. We are so sick." I allowed the mother to come with me to the hospital: outside she became hysterical when I told her she had to go back.

The food situation in the camp was an unfortunate one: thousands of tins of bully beef were poured into the camp, as well as potatoes, vast quantities of black German army bread, and ordinary tinned milk. The recent and fairly fit arrivals thrived on this food, at least those who had come from the better *Arbeitslager* (work camps), but the starved and typhus-infected majority was in no position to get any benefit whatever from this rich and fatty food: many must have been killed by it, especially the little babies for whom tinned milk is neat poison. Raw potatoes were the only food they had been able to cope with.

In another hut I made the dreadful mistake of starting to distribute some ordinary ration biscuits. Before I knew what had happened I had literally dozens of women fighting for those few biscuits, fighting me, fighting with one another. I went back to them later on and they told me those biscuits had been the first food they had been able to digest.

I can't remember how many people I talked to: more clearly than most I remember a family of Polish Jews. They were happy because they were still together. They had been driven from camp to camp year after year: *Ist es wirklich wahr dass jüdische Kinder in England nicht in Lagern arbeiten müssen?* — "Is it really true that Jewish children in England do not have to work in camps?" She was such a pretty girl, fragile, large black eyes and the loveliest hair I have ever seen.

No one should imagine that all the inmates at Belsen were innocent of anything we would call crime: there were innumerable of the shadiest characters there who would have been locked up by any government, though needless to say not under such conditions. The vilest and pettiest political vendettas went on among the inmates: the Czechs and Poles carrying on unending feuds, each accusing the other of stealing their food and intriguing against them with the British camp authorities. A lot of the Russians went around terrorizing the remainder with arms they had hidden somewhere. Cannibalism was widespread — real cannibalism! A great deal of the Nazis' dirty work was done for them by the inmates, especially the Poles.

There had not been much cruelty by the Nazis at Belsen such as torture, no burning and no gassing, but everyone I spoke to on the subject was of the opinion that Belsen was worse even than the extermination camp at Auschwitz, or than Buchenwald or Dachau. At all those places living conditions — if one was lucky enough to be allowed to live — were infinitely superior to those at Belsen, especially as regards food and huts. Starvation was the deliberate means of keeping down the numbers at Belsen: there cannot be any doubt about that at all.

When the British arrived at the camp they found about forty SS guards and about twenty SS women. The SS men were being used to bury the dead from morning till night. They were under the constant supervision of a party of British soldiers. They were made to work until they collapsed, and then those ordinary British Tommies — and you could not imagine more ordinary types — hit the SS with rifle butts and kicked them till they got up again and went on working. I watched them loading the morning's dead from one compound and they started throwing the bodies up. *Wenn Sie diese armen Menschen, die Sie ermordet haben nicht jetzt wenigstens anständig behandeln, dann schiesse ich Sie über den Haufen.* — "If you don't treat these poor people you murdered decently, I'll gun you down right now," shouted the German-Jewish American corporal I had with me at the SS. It was a pleasure to see how they shook with fear and dragged themselves along to lift the bodies up more carefully.

I talked to the SS men. They knew they were going to die. We had shot two of them already while they were trying to escape. One committed suicide and one was buried alive when he collapsed into one of the mass graves. At the end of their day's work the SS men were drilled on the double until they literally collapsed. From what they said I realized what brutes and animals they were, that they still did not realize the enormity of their crimes, that they were completely accustomed to what they saw around them. One or two said: *In unseren alten Lagern war es längst nicht so schlimm* — "In the old camps things were nothing like as bad as they are here." The SS women were even worse. "We are not hitting them or anything like that. We are just making them work till they collapse," said the British soldiers. Some of the SS women had been to other camps before, and said conditions there had not been as bad: *Wenn einer gestorben ist, haben wir ihn immer gleich begraben und nie rum liegen lassen* — "When someone died we always buried them right away and never let the corpses lie around," one said to me. A German witness who had been forced to look at it all said: *Wer immer dafür verantwortlich ist, muss bestraft werden.* — "Whoever is responsible for all this must be punished."

When I told her she would be *bestraft* (punished), she was highly indignant. Other women told me — and I was prepared to believe it — that they did not actually volunteer for this type of work. They had been enrolled for some kind of *Hilfsdienst*, support services, and could not do anything about getting out of it. *Als Deutsche Frau schäme ich mich, und werde den Rest meines Lebens zubringen, dies alles wieder gut zu machen.* — "As a German woman I am ashamed and will spend the remainder of my life to make amends." Don't imagine that the British soldiers delighted in the rough methods they were using on the SS; but they looked upon it as their duty towards the inmates who had suffered so much all those years that their torturers should now get a dose of the same medicine.

The British soldier was an inarticulate and moderate man not given to emotions, but to see the flaming hatred that was driving these men on in their work was inspiring in itself. None of the soldiers who saw all this would ever want to fraternize. Many of the inmates told me time and time again how wonderful our men were; always kind and cheerful without speaking a word of German, too. They found all the British soldiers wonderful, the way they carried on their labours of mercy with a smile in all the horror.

When I was at Belsen the large-scale rescue operations had not started yet and all that was being done was spontaneous and improvised with local materials. Every conceivable unit in the district had lent ambulances, trucks, and water lorries. The plan was being prepared while I was there to shift up to 1,000 people a day to a new camp and/or hospital in a nearby barracks. In view of the fact that nearly all were too weak to walk even to the nearest lavatory, they had to be driven to their new camp, and most of them would have to be washed and deloused by nurses, as they were no longer capable of washing themselves.

Evacuation of a thousand a day was of course nothing like enough, as they were dying at a rate of 500 a day while I was there and were expected to continue to die at the rate of 300 a day. I could not understand how anyone who knew all this could continue to lead a normal existence; to know that here were thousands of innocent people we had liberated, and yet over a third of them would have to die for certain before we rescued the remainder, was a thought that haunted us day and night. And yet the people concerned with the clearing up of the camp remained incredibly calm — some of the most senior ones too calm, I feared. For example, we discovered a man by the name of de Vries, who used to be the chief editor of the Antwerp socialist paper *Volksgewart* and an underground leader. He was one of the closest friends of van Acker; yet this man had not been evacuated ten days after he had been found: he was free from typhus, and suffering merely from a most acute form of exhaustion. After I had been to see the colonel in charge, he finally promised to save de Vries. I do not know what happened, but anyway we sent a telegram to van Acker. The attitude that one life was as good as another was so wickedly wrong in view of the known facts; among other people I discovered, for example, three French women who had been sent to Belsen for helping British airmen get back to England. How could we allow people like that to die and ever hold our heads up again?

The highest praise of all the people who were doing so much with so little went to the Jewish Army Rabbi who had been at Belsen since the beginning. It was impossible to give justice to what he had done and how he did it. English officers who were at the first service held after the liberation told me they were moved to tears.

There was a continuous stream of visitors to the camp. Amongst others I met three young RAF pilots on their first 48-hour leave for many months; they had traveled right across Germany to come to Belsen; they thought it was the best way of spending their leave; that it would help them more during the last weeks of the war than going to Brussels. They stayed to help, too.

One, a mere boy with the DFC, collapsed when he saw the mass graves.

The first time I saw the mass graves was when the Mayor of Celle and four other mayors from the district were taken on a forced tour of the camp. I rejoiced in the horror on their faces as they saw what had been perpetrated because they did not want to find out what really happened inside a concentration camp; I believed them all when they said again and again: *Dass so etwas menschenmöglich ist, haben wir aber wirklich nicht gewusst. Wir wussten ja, dass es KZ's gab, aber wir haben ja nie geahnt, dass so etwas dort vorgeht.* — "That something like this is humanly possible we really did not know. Of course we knew there were concentration camps, but it never occurred to us that this sort of thing went on there."

Whenever we got near a particularly horrible sight, some would try to turn their heads; quickly a British soldier would appear who forced them to look at what they were meant to see. Constantly they mumbled: *Selbstverständlich werden wir unseren Mitbürgern berichten, was wir hier gesehen haben.* — "Of course we will tell our fellow citizens what we have seen here." But no offer of help, no offer that they somehow wanted to make up for all this. I was certain they had not known what was going on because they did not want to know.

When we got to the mass graves, the SS had just arrived there with their huge death carts and trailers; they were carrying the dead to their graves on the double, forward and backward, body after body, all the same dead faces, the sunken-in eyes, the shaved heads, the bony fleshless bodies. The most dreadful of all was that there was desperately little difference between the looks of the dead and the living. It was absolutely true to say that the living were just living dead. The slightest shock would take the last spark of life from them. And there, standing by the grave were crowds of inmates screaming at the SS: *Ihr Hunde, Ihr Schweine, was habt Ihr alles uns Juden angetan. Weshalb lebt Ihr denn noch?*

Meinen Vater habt Ihr getötet, meine Mutter, mein Kind, meine Frau, und so weiter. — "You dogs, you pigs, what have you done to us Jews? You have killed my father, killed my mother, killed my child, killed my wife, and so forth." In the end the crowd had to be driven away by the guards. I noticed two women watching the whole scene, apparently quite unmoved, while one was delousing the hair of the other.

The most dreadful hours I spent in the huts of the remaining German Jews: that was where I finally found out about Grandmother's fate. That she had died had become a certainty for me as soon as I got to Belsen; yet to hear the news and how I heard it was a fearful experience. [Today I have no recollection of how I heard about her death, nor have I found the letter in which I had apparently written about it.] Theirs was a fairly clean hut. They had homemade beds and by iron self-discipline they had managed to keep themselves clean and only half the hut had typhus. I was taken to the hut by one of the girls who was one of the official interpreters in the camp. She introduced me to her friends and we sat down. One, a very pretty woman, was fondling a kitten she had been given by one of the British officers: *Also Sie sind ein Englischer Offizier und kommen aus Deutschland: Sie Glücklicher. Ich war oft mit Ihren Grosseltern in Holland; sie haben so oft von Ihnen erzählt. Aber hier habe ich sie nie gesehen.* — "So you are a British officer and come from Germany. You are fortunate. I was often with your grandparents in Holland and they always spoke of you. But here in this camp I never saw them."

And we went on talking. They started to tell me of their experience during the last years: *Seit 12 Jahren sind wir von den Nazis verfolgt worden, und jetzt hat man unsn zu fühlen gegeben, dass wir noch immer Deutsch sind.* — "For twelve years we have been hounded by the Nazis and now we are still being made to feel [by the British] that all we are is Germans." One told me of her experiences at the *Verbrennungslager*, the extermination camp at Auschwitz: *Jeden Abend wenn die Sonne rot ist, erinnert es uns an die ewig glühenden Öfen von Auschwitz, gefüllt mit Menschen — mit Juden, mit unserer eigenen Familie.* — "Each evening when the sun is red I am reminded of the permanently glowing ovens of Auschwitz, filled with human beings, with Jews, with one's own family." She was saved because the day before she was taken away on account of the advancing Russians, they were burning even numbers, and hers was an odd number (they all had their prison numbers tattooed on them). Her son, aged 14, had been burned at Auschwitz. Then she started crying on my shoulder. *Ich bin doch so glücklich, dass ich wieder mit einem freien Menschen sprechen kann, der meine eigene Sprache spricht. Wir wollen doch nur eines. Dass sich wieder einmal jemand um mich kümmert, dass mich wieder jemand lieb hat. Wir sind doch so abgearbeitet, wir können nicht mehr. Aber wir müssen doch bald weiter kämpfen, wir müssen doch wieder irgendwo unterkommen. Wir sind die letzten paar Überlebenden von Tausenden von Deutschen Juden, die einmal hier waren.* — "I am so happy that I can again speak with a free human being, someone who speaks my own language. There is one thing we want, to find someone who will take care of me, who will love me. We are so run-down, we just can't carry on. But soon we must go on fighting for our survival. We have got to find somewhere to settle. We are the last small handful of survivors from what was once thousands of German Jews who were here."

Another girl had spent the last three years at a working camp in Hamburg. During air raids they were not allowed to go into shelters! The Hamburg women had been saved by Belgian officers from a prisoner-of-war camp who had secretly smuggled food parcels to them. Some had met their Belgians secretly and were hoping to marry them one day. Another girl had been writing under a code name to her "lover" for three years. She did not know his name either, but those letters kept her going and kept up her will to live.

Next to our group was the bed of what seemed a very old woman. She was 42. They all called her "Mutter." She wanted to get up all the time. She was very ill and they could hardly keep her in bed. *Ich will doch auch hören, was der Offizier zu sagen hat.* — "I, too, want to hear what the officer has to say." And all the time my women were quietly crying and talking to me, crying with joy because they could talk to me, merely to me of all people, because I took down the names and addresses of some of their friends and relatives whom they wanted to know that they had survived.

PART FOUR

VICTORY

15

Postwar Germany

A week or so after V-E Day I was posted to # 4 Information Control Unit in Hamburg, which was responsible for operating the radio station. My family had left Hamburg barely ten years previous. The last time there I was Walter Eberstadt, Jewish by race, Protestant by religion, fourteen years old, a mediocre student at the Gelehrtenschule des Johanneum, son of Dr. jur. Georg Eberstadt, managing director of Dresdner Bank's Hamburg branch and his wife, Edith, née Flersheim, whose parents were to die at Bergen-Belsen. I returned, not quite twenty-four years old, Captain Walter Albert Everitt, Oxfordshire and Buckinghamshire Light Infantry, stern, stiff-upper-lip English, a British officer still of German nationality in the Army of the Rhine, which after almost six years of fighting had defeated the Huns, Nazis, Germans — depending on one's mood on any given day. The Allies had secured Germany's unconditional surrender. We had taught the Huns a lesson in war and now would continue the process in peace. We were under strict orders not to "fraternize" with any German. Many villas on the Alster lake and elsewhere in Harveste-

hude, Hamburg's prime residential district, were requisitioned from owners who considered themselves more English than German, but still were
evicted from their houses. If lucky, they were allowed to lodge in the basement of their former homes.

Hamburg had been bombed heavily in 1943. The main destruction
was caused by firebombs which had done relatively little damage in the
town center but had flattened the working-class districts and the harbor.
Over forty thousand inhabitants lost their lives in the raids. Hamburg occupied a somewhat special place in the minds of Germans and British
alike. It had cosmopolitan, liberal traditions. It was Germany's most important port, home of some of the world's major shipping lines. It traded
with the world. Its leading families had worldwide business and family
ties. Its upper crust had modeled itself on its British counterparts and the
English way of life. Even the weather was English. It was Hitler's least
favorite German city. Of course, there were lots of Nazis in Hamburg, but
also lots of skeptics and opponents. Like every German state, it had its
Gauleiter who governed his region, directly responsible to Hitler. Hamburg's
Gauleiter — named Kauffmann — had by Nazi standards the reputation
of a moderate. Its mayor, Krogmann, came from an old shipping family
and should have known better. Still, he too had a relatively decent
reputation. To their credit, Kauffmann and Krogmann saved Allied and
German lives, and avoided further physical destruction by ordering surrender without resistance to the British. This required courage on their
part, as it flew in the face of Hitler's scorched-earth orders to continue
opposition, no matter the cost.

Anglophile upper-class Hamburg suffered a rude awakening from its
illusion that the British would right away resume prewar links. Many
greeted the British almost with open arms, more as liberators than
conquerors and thought all would be forgotten and forgiven. And they, in
return, would forgive the British for the air raids. Instead, their houses
were requisitioned, and any contact, other than in the course of duty, was
declared illegal. They painfully realized that the ordinary British officer or
soldier in those first weeks and months had no intention of forgetting
or forgiving. Toward the end of the war, as the Allied armies came upon

the concentration camps, the respect, soldier to soldier, in which our troops held the enemy forces, gave way to unbridled loathing and disgust. The concentration camps became the trigger for quite brutal behavior, the stuff dormant in most of us. Military government was at least as much concerned with ferreting out war criminals as administering the British Zone of Occupation.

What did I make of all this? Does it sound plausible that I arrived in Hamburg, consumed with hatred of everything German, determined to avenge family and everyone else persecuted by Hitler, to teach those bastards a lesson once and for all? Or that I would let on to no one who I really was, that this was the town in which I had spent my adolescence, gone to school, where many still lived who had known our family well? Or that I was Captain W. A. Everitt, just another British officer in the occupation army, *basta*? Or had this Captain Everitt arrived in Hamburg, teary-eyed, home after ten years in exile, the first night back in Hamburg walking familiar streets, standing before his parents' house, more tears, resolving to crusade for a new and better Germany, a new and better world? Or that this Captain Everitt had arrived in Hamburg not giving a damn, knowing he'd be demobilized soon, to spend his days and nights carousing, having a good time, enjoying the fruits of victory, maybe enriching himself in the black market?

Will the real Captain Everitt of May 1945 please step forward? Willingly he would, if only he knew today who he was then. It is over fifty-five years ago, and is one really expected to remember at eighty who one was at age twenty-four? I know what I did, but my memory of feelings and emotions is nebulous. I of course wandered around the streets, looked at our old house, but Hamburg was no longer all that familiar. I had spent ten years forgetting, suppressing my childhood, and quite successfully becoming English. I had spent almost half of my life in England.

In the event, there was not much time to sit back and reflect. From the first day the work at British Occupation Radio was demanding. Our billet and officers' mess were in a large villa in a cul-de-sac at the Alster end of Heilwigstrasse. The radio station was within easy walking distance on Rothebaum Chausse. Keith Thomson was our commanding officer and

Ralph Poston program head. I was put in charge of "talks and features." There were fewer than a dozen of us. We were "Radio Hamburg, ein Sender der Militärregierung," the military government station. We were on the air a few hours each day. Our main job was to relay military government announcements, regulations, and some news. The British personnel did the writing and broadcasting. In the first weeks there was no German program staff. Rumors were rife, German-language newspapers nonexistent. We advised our listeners about food rationing, monetary regulations, curfew hours, anything to do with daily living under British military rule. We were the main information link between the British military, German civilians, the disintegrating German army, released prisoners of war, and displaced persons from what had been German-occupied Europe. We took our first tentative steps to reeducate the Germans with programs about their Nazi past. To attract an audience we broadcast lists of missing persons, which reunited many families.

My relations with our German staff to begin with were formal and cold. I discouraged personal questions. I used the German language as little as possible. Off-duty was spent in our officers' mess or at the Hotel Atlantic, which had become a lavish officers' club for the occupation forces. Field Marshal Montgomery's anti-fraternization orders were not enforceable for long and were abandoned by midsummer. In June I spent a short leave in Denmark. I drove north through rural Schleswig-Holstein, fruit orchards in blossom, unravaged by fighting, but packed with British troops and German prisoners of war. Once I was on the Danish ferry, Europe really seemed at peace. The ship was clean, the crew friendly, the food delicious — a spinach soup with a white island of foamy cream in the middle. Copenhagen was a dream, untouched by the war, the population hospitable to anyone in British uniform. I was received warmly by a pretty blonde, a sales assistant in a millinery store. The Danes were, rightly, proud that they had been the only occupied country that one night had successfully spirited away its Jewish population and saved their lives.

As summer progressed work became much more creative. We started to originate programs and looked for qualified German staff. Once word was out we were recruiting, applications poured in. We wanted, ideally,

people who had been opponents of the regime, but they were in short supply. In most cases we settled for men and women who convinced us they
were well intentioned, had not been Nazi Party members, had not belonged to Nazi organizations that disqualified them from military government employment — Germans who, given the circumstances, had not
compromised themselves by being associated with anything particularly
troublesome after 1933.

The interrogations were searching and disagreeable for all concerned.
When I interviewed Jürgen Schüddekopf, who became one of the most
brilliant and well-liked commentators, I supposedly gave him such a hard
time that half in jest and half in anger he said, "Herr Major, I think I could
only satisfy you about my past if I stood before you, my head cut off." They
filled out the famous "Fragebogen," the questionnaires that probed all aspects of the applicant's life, from the obvious as to whether they had ever,
or since when, been members of a Nazi organization, to trick questions to
trip up the liar. Falsehoods were punishable with prison sentences.

We had the help of a military intelligence officer on our staff, a Captain Henry, who looked rather like Himmler but was really quite harmless.
I participated actively in the recruiting process and like to think my
method was more revealing than the standard Fragebogen questions. I engaged the people who interested me in discussions and debates, sometimes
well into the night. I'd give them a meal, whisky, cigarettes or pipe tobacco, and have them talk, talk, talk. If I concluded they were fundamen-
tally decent I was not put off by some affiliation with the late system. My
parents steered me to people they considered decent. Nearly everyone was
short of food and money and I was in a position to find employment for
people who deserved help. We wanted a "radio doctor" and gave the job
to Dr. Guido Möring, a friend of my parents, a society doctor, witty,
charming, a good-looking ladies' man, member of a socially prominent
family that had kept its nose clean in the Nazi years. He became a great
success as a broadcaster. We also hired his brother-in-law Dr. Kurt
Emmerich, a German army medical officer in two world wars. His real love
was writing, successfully, under the pen name of Peter Bamm. He was old-
fashioned, apolitical, reactionary yet liberal on issues that mattered, a

German patriot to whom the Nazis had been anathema. He was very, very funny and made us laugh at any hour of the day or night. He was responsible for the feuilleton broadcasts, which under his direction became hugely successful.

Bamm, especially in the early days, did not feel altogether comfortable working for British military government. He was not the only one who felt that way. Their exaggerated respect for rank and uniform bothered me. I did not like to be Herr Hauptmann, or later Herr Major. The war was over. I wanted to get out of uniform. I was a civilian. I wanted our German colleagues to rid themselves of their undue respect for the military — any military. We had to convince those who felt they were "collaborateurs" that they were working not for us, the British, but were in on the beginnings of rebuilding a democratic German society, working for themselves, not for the victorious occupying force.

The two key people on the staff were Peter von Zahn and Axel Eggebrecht. Zahn and I hit it off almost the moment we met and he is to this day one of my closest friends. I admire him as a human being and as an outstanding reporter. Before the war he was a young historian at the University of Freiburg. He had an English wife, Christa, who also became a dear friend. One of their five red-haired daughters is my godchild.

He served in the German army as a war correspondent on the eastern front. His unit retreated, eventually to Schleswig-Holstein, the final leg by sea across the Baltic. They were among the last German troops who made it to the West. They wanted to surrender to the British rather than the Russians. Though the war had ended they were still in camps to be interrogated for possible war crimes and to control an orderly demobilization. Zahn had been granted leave from his camp to offer his services to Radio Hamburg to broadcast the whereabouts of those still interned. We suggested a position with wider scope, which he was glad to accept. His background suited us — an English, or, rather, Scottish wife, politically not compromised, a historian who had worked as a journalist, an Anglophile who had lived in England for a period of time, spent his wedding night at the Cadogan Hotel on Sloane Street where Oscar Wilde was arrested. His family came from Dresden. They had been civil servants and soldiers of sufficient standing for his grandfather to be awarded a "von" by his Saxon king.

Before starting at Radio Hamburg, Zahn asked for help to visit his wife. She had survived scrapes with the Gestapo because she was English, staying with cousins of Col. Claus von Stauffenberg who had planted the bomb on July 20, 1944, that failed to kill Hitler and was arrested, sentenced to death by Freisler's "People's Court" and hanged. Stauffenberg kin had become suspect, even if not involved in the generals' plot. Christa von Zahn's Stauffenbergs had a castle at Wilflingen in the French zone. In the first weeks after the war it would have been difficult if not impossible for Peter to travel across a zonal border, let alone bring his wife to Hamburg, all of which we arranged for him.

The second German who wrote many of the programs we broadcast under the heading of "Talks and Features" was Axel Eggebrecht, a left-wing radical in the Weimar Republic who had wangled his way through the Nazi years with nonpolitical articles and film manuscripts. Eggebrecht was more polemic than Zahn, combative, more outspoken about his hatred of the Nazi period. He had bottled up twelve years of thoughts he had been unable to bring to paper. "Give me a typewriter, paper, a desk, some pipe tobacco, I will show you what I can do." Eggebrecht became a pathfinder for Germans who wanted to discover the truth about the Hitler years and wanted to find their way in the earliest days of democracy, albeit a democracy "imposed" by outsiders.

For me, at age twenty-four, to be in on creating the most influential radio programs in any of the occupation zones was unbelievably interesting and rewarding. I was part of the team laying the foundations for what would become the German equivalent of the BBC. The sensitivities were a constant challenge. It was our mission to "reeducate" the German population. It was our mission to explain and justify the measures of the occupation army and military government, to undertake the first steps of selling the population on democracy. If our programs were considered offensive, justifiably or not, nothing was simpler for listeners than to switch off the radio. It is one thing to say: you are guilty, you committed war crimes, you started the war, murdered Jews, deserve the conditions under which you now live — and another to be heard. It was more effective to use German commentators rather than relay broadcasts from the BBC in London, provided the broadcasters had credibility with the audience and were not considered mere collaborating mouthpieces of the victors. It was hard for Germans who had lived twelve years under dictatorship to believe that the Eggebrechts and Zahns were broadcasting of their own free will. If only to establish their credibility, we allowed them considerable latitude to question Allied measures.

Our most effective broadcasts were roundtable discussions guided by Eggebrecht, and talks by Zahn and outsiders under the caption: "Are we going in the right direction?" These talks were reproduced in one of the first publications licensed by the British and given to Axel Springer's tiny Hammerich und Lesser publishing house — the beginnings of Springer Verlag. His biggest moneymaker for years was the weekly radio program magazine, which evolved out of the printing of the radio talks. I became friends with Springer. He had immense charm and drive. His publishing house grew in size and influence partly by pursuing a more nationalist editorial policy than I cared for, but he never failed to support Israel or condemn racism of any kind.

Eggebrecht covered the trial before a British military government court of the commandant and guards of the Bergen-Belsen concentration camp. Night after night he was on the air, earning more opprobrium than approval from the listeners. It was a thankless task. He received hate mail rather than fan mail. In 1996 it is hard to realize it required personal courage in 1945 to be a reporter covering the Belsen trial.

We had started out as a station of the military government, and to make matters quite clear, we used as our continuity signal linking programs the opening bars of "Rule Britannia," while the signature tune beginning and ending the day was "Land of Hope and Glory." Few programs had originated from Hamburg. We had transmitted mostly from Radio Luxembourg or the German Service of the BBC in London. By July, however, we became state-owned as NWDR, short for Nordwestdeutscher Rundfunk. There was a satellite station in Cologne which eventually became the Westdeutscher Rundfunk, and a satellite in the British sector of

Berlin. No more English was spoken in the announcements. The inter-mission signal was changed to a few bars from *The Magic Flute*, the signa-ture tune from Brahms' *Academic* Overture: "Ich hab mich ergeben, mit Herz und mit Hand, Dir Land voll Lieb und Leben, mein Deutsches Vaterland." Since it was possible to miscontrue the first four words stand-ing on their own to mean "I have surrendered," we were accused by some of duplicity — as if using the stanza were an example of perfidious Albion's daily humiliation of the Germans. The music had in fact been chosen by the German staff, and what it really said was: "With all my heart and hands, I have given myself to thee, my beloved German Father-land." For my taste it was too nationalistic.

With these changes, our work became rewarding. Programs were added. Interesting people joined the staff, full-time and part-time. Reedu-cation was intermingled with literature, plays, classical and light music. Pre-1933 plays were put on, books long banned were read. Political parties reappeared on the air. Kurt Schumacher, head of the Social Democrats (SPD), was painfully long-winded in front of the microphone. One com-mentator particularly critical of the Nazi years received so much threat-ening listener mail he dropped politics and switched to literature. Another, a former foreign correspondent, had been recommended as politically clean. He made a good impression, reminisced in glowing terms about the League of Nations, but when we were shown some of his post-1933 articles, we saw a different side to his story. In July 1944, after the attempt on Hitler's life, he renewed his pledge to National Socialism. After my time, Hugh Carleton Greene, who did such a wonderful job heading the NWDR, had to fire over twenty staff members who had hidden a Nazi past.

Early in 1946 we hired as a political commentator Karl-Eduard von Schnitzler, a prisoner of war of the British. He came with seemingly ex-cellent credentials. The Schnitzlers, prominent bankers and industrialists in Cologne, had been early Nazis. The NWDR Schnitzler was considered an idealistic anti-Nazi, a man who had broken with his family over poli-tics. We failed to see that he did not object to dictatorship per se, that he was a rabid Communist who despised the West. Peter von Zahn never liked him and did not trust him. From Hamburg he was sent to Cologne. His political line there became increasingly unacceptable to British and Germans alike. He was unwilling to modify his position and defected to the Russian zone. From Berlin he broadcast on behalf of the Russian occupation forces. Later, in the DDR, he became one of the main German Communist government propagandists. He returned, a discredited old man, after unification, to an obscure existence in the West, but never forsook his belief in Communism.

We were the "only game in town." Licenses to publish newspapers were granted slowly, in part because of the newsprint shortage. Word got around that if you worked for the NWDR you could earn a little money, the place was heated, and it had a canteen. Some wonderful talent came together. We gave the postwar start to many people who would later become famous. To name some: Gustav Knuth, Werner Hinze, Hilde Krahl, Maria Wimmer, Rolf von Beneckendorf, Ida Ehre, and Helmut Käutner. The full-time editors included Bruno E. Werner, Jürgen Schüddekopf, and Gregor von Rezzori, the last then quite young and unknown, but later to attain international renown with his books. Bruno E. Werner belonged to a generation that had cut its literary teeth in Weimar Berlin. He made a promising start with Ullstein, was a liberal conservative, good-looking, a bit of a snob, talented though no giant, likeable. He had never been a Nazi party member, but I'd be surprised if there had not been times in his life under Hitler when he wished words spoken had never been said, episodes he was not exactly proud of — decrying the Weimar he once relished, dropping Jewish friends, acting as if there had never been a Heine, Mann, Kafka. A regular contributor to our programs, Walther von Hollander, was a friend of Werner's, intellectually his superior, internationally known, head of the German Pen Club, and politically of Werner's ilk. For a while two former general staff officers, Klaus von Bismarck and a brother of his, worked for us. I declined with great regret their present of an ex-Wehrmacht staff car, quite the most beautiful two-seater supercharged Mercedes. Both Bismarcks went on to distinguished careers in the Federal Republic.

A particularly effective job was done by the British control officers responsible for music. One was Jack Bornoff, artillery major with a love of music, another Howard Hartog, member of one of the founding families of the Unilever group. Under their leadership the symphony orchestra was reconstituted. They located musicians who had scattered to all four winds and brought them back to Hamburg — no easy task because the military were reluctant to give residency permits for people to live in the badly damaged city. Hans Schmidt-Isserstädt surfaced somewhere and was engaged as conductor. He once confided to me he felt awkward opening his concerts with "God Save the King" but came to terms with his discomfort over this order of military government by telling his orchestra to mumble to themselves the words of the old imperial national anthem "Heil Dir im Siegerkranz, Herrscher des Vaterland's, Heil Kaiser Dir" — set, of course, to the same melody. Later, with the NWDR symphony orchestra as his base, he attained worldwide stature. His life story was easy to censure in retrospect, yet unfair to condemn, given the circumstances. His first wife was Jewish. Under Hitler they divorced. This enabled him to continue conducting under the Nazis and to make a living. She emigrated with their child into economic hardship, but to safety. He remarried eventually, but he and his first wife remained friends and saw each other after the war.

In life one is blessed at the most with a handful of long remembered emotional high points. For me one of those rare moments was a performance in July of that first peacetime summer of the Mendelssohn Violin Concerto with Yehudi Menuhin and the NWDR orchestra under Schmidt-Isserstädt. It was Menuhin's first German visit since a trip he had made there as a child prodigy. He was touring displaced person camps and was persuaded to play for a German audience in the cause of reeducation. It may have been the first public performance of Mendelssohn since the composer had been banned by the Nazis, and at that by a Jewish soloist of world renown. The concert seemed a symbolic watershed, a moment of atonement for the past and of hope for the future. There was not a dry eye among the orchestra or the few of us in the studio watching the performance. Tears ran down Menuhin's face as the orchestra gave him a standing ovation at the end, shaking his hand, applauding over and over.

What to make of Germans in 1945? How to "treat" them, especially the ones with whom we worked at the radio station? This was a constant question then, and it remains a subject I turn over in my mind to this day. It was easy when they had been outright Nazis, and it was tempting, in the first flush of victory, to read the riot act to one and all. But who was I to sit in judgment over every nuance of everyone's conduct after 1933? I have never claimed moral credit for not having been a Nazi. There had never been a dilemma for me, mercifully removed by my parents to England. I was by default on the side of the good guys. It troubled me then, as it troubles me now, that many Jews, particularly American Jews who were an ocean away from where it all happened, claim too stridently the moral high ground for themselves.

I tried not to abuse my power. We had innumerable discussions, often late into the night, about the past and the future. I tried not to impose my opinions, let alone bully, because of the authority vested in me by a British officer's uniform, because Britain had won the war, because my parents had been kicked out of Germany, my grandparents had died at Belsen, because Germany had been responsible for two world wars, for killing six million Jews. By setting myself strict standards, I hoped it would become self-evident to those with whom I was in contact that Jews were not what they had been made out to be by Hitler. I wanted to earn respect by what I did, not because I wore a uniform and we had won and they had lost. Personal example provides the only effective form of leadership.

It is easy to fritter away the moral capital earned in the victory over evil and to wind up on the moral defensive. It is easier for the vanquished to conduct themselves with dignity, to earn respect and even sympathy, than for the victor. Victory goes to the head, defeat to the heart. One goes hungry, the other is well fed. One requisitions the best accommodation, the other is evicted from it. One submits applications, the other grants or rejects them. The one considers their complaint justified, the other barks "Come back tomorrow." One stands before, the other sits behind the desk. Dignity comes more readily to the defeated than to the victorious. Discipline is hard to maintain at the end of a long war. German troops, spic and span in their field-gray tunics, behaved with almost exemplary correctness in Paris in 1940. On the face of it they were disciplined, yet in reality party to heinous crimes. The Allied forces in 1945 were no longer all that well behaved. There was cause for petty and sometimes not so petty complaints, but even if they were a bit noisy or threw their weight about, their excesses were harmless. They killed no one.

Maybe I should become the Emily Post of "Etiquette for Victor and Vanquished"?

My British military and civilian colleagues were on the whole congenial. Only two of them mattered as far as I was concerned. Keith Thompson was our commanding officer, a dapper wartime cavalry colonel with an elegant little moustache, quite charming, with no knowledge of the language or interest in German affairs. He presided over us with a light touch. He had fallen in love with a perfectly beautiful German blonde, Maria B., even before fraternization was permitted, which rather sidetracked him from his military duties. He had also commandeered a twelve-cylinder, two-seater Maybach convertible, a stunningly beautiful car.

The other colleague was Ralph Poston, of whom I have written above. He was a great human being who took his job immensely seriously. He worked so hard and for such long hours it damn near killed him. He gave me all the latitude and support I could have asked for. He stood up for his views and principles. He had an uneasy relationship with higher authority when they seemed to interfere with the way he thought we should set about our work. He wanted our German program staff to be granted more freedom than our superiors were ready for.

We had a genial and competent peacetime BBC engineer, Paul Findlay, who had joined the Army Signal Corps. He was an invaluable asset and pleasant to work with. He, too, fell for a "Fräulein," whom he eventually married. Paul Findlay was the first to find in a basement studio two Magnetofons, a revolutionary German wartime invention that replaced the traditional phonograph disk. It recorded on magnetized tape. It improved the quality of the sound and, unlike a disk, played without interruption literally for hours. In the war the Germans were able to continue broadcasting with the Magnetofon machines during the worst air raids. Findlay dismantled one and had it flown back to the BBC in London for closer examination. These big machines were the forerunners of every tape recorder since made.

I was too busy with my work to spend much time in the officers' mess. Needless to say I, too, had fallen for a German girl. For many months we were truly devoted to each other. In addition I socialized with our German colleagues, in particular with Peter von Zahn and his wife, Christa. I saw banker friends of Father's, people he encouraged me to see, who had kept their noses clean and were relieved the Hitler years and the war were over, even if the defeat of Germany meant they were now in straitened circum-stances. In a small way here and there I was able to help them. I became friends with Heinrich von Berenberg-Gossler, son of father's friend Cornelius von Berenberg-Gossler, the man whose courageous efforts during the war to save the lives of those who had not emigrated and were about to be deported I describe in Part I of this book. In British eyes a banker-baron was suspect, even if his English was fluent and he had spent years at Barings in the City. The Gossler family, it turned out, had received help from my father — something I heard from them and not from him. In the 1930s their 400-year-old bank found itself in difficulties. Father was by then at Dresdner Bank, with whom they had a loan that was no longer fully secured and should have been called. Father looked the other way until eventually it righted itself. He had acted as a sound banker and friend.

Heinrich von Gossler's sister had been turned down by the British for admission to Hamburg University medical school because she was titled. I was able to help. She became a doctor and practiced until last year. Others I sent away — "friends" on whom it had not dawned how bitterly hurt and disappointed my parents had come to feel about them.

As soon as I could I visited Thekla Hübner, sister of Guido Möhring, our "radio doctor," and widow of Otto Hübner who had been arrested by the Gestapo after the July 20 plot against Hitler and executed a few weeks before the war ended. The Hübners had been among my parents' closest friends. His business, Jauch and Hübner, was the leading reinsurance bro-ker in Germany. The Hübners were good-looking, elegant, wealthy, and cosmopolitan. I used to wish they had been my parents. They lived in an English-style country house on the Elbe, until it was requisitioned by the British military and Thekla Hübner and her two sons evicted. Her husband's death counted for nothing. It took them years to regain possession of their home. In my time two young British counterintelligence officers lived there in pomp and circumstance, waited on hand and foot by German personnel. Both were German-Jewish refugees. Their way of life and arrogant demeanor bothered me greatly. They drove around Hamburg at top speed in a requisitioned BMW, brakes screeching, horn honking, ignoring traffic lights. They were supposed to hunt Nazis. I doubt they caught many. I heard troublesome stories of their physically maltreating their suspects. I happened to know one of the pair, Ulrich Steiner, quite well prewar. The father had been general counsel of AEG in Berlin. The family had left Germany with some money and valuable art. Steiner's likeable brother Konrad still lives in London, retired from a career at Marks and Spencer. The brothers had long drifted apart. Ulrich led a vagabond life until he died in Bolivia, where he worked for the Patino mining group.

Otto Hübner was one of the few who had had the courage to visit my parents up to the outbreak of the war. He was convinced there would be a war, and that Hitler would lose it. He was first and foremost a businessman. Anticipating Germany's defeat, he continued to cultivate and befriend his old international connections throughout the war. The Gestapo arrested him for helping and sheltering business friends in occupied Europe rather than for personal involvement in the July 20 plot, though he was friends with a number of the conspirators. I wanted to help his widow. I got her brother the radio doctor post. I also transmitted, illegally, mail to her friends in England. When life returned to normal she often visited my parents in London. When too old for travel, she and mother telephoned at least once a month. Both her nice and able sons worked in the insurance industry. One became a client of mine.

Among Hamburg bankers, I saw the most of Dr. Rudolf Brinckmann who had been a partner in M. M. Warburg. When Max Warburg was forced to "Aryanize" his firm he turned to long-standing friends and colleagues to take over the business. It became Brinckmann Wirtz and Co.

The Warburg family received some money and it was always understood
the firm would revert to them if and when National Socialism ended.

The Warburgs never forgot or denied they were Jewish, but Max was
a fanatic right-wing German. He found it hard to accept that Hitler's Germany did not want him. Never mind that he had been close to the Kaiser
before 1918 — they treated him no differently from other Jews. He was
not the only German Jew who thought in 1933 that Hitler should be
given the benefit of the doubt, that he'd calm down and not put into practice all he preached. During the first years after 1933 Brinckmann must
have been a godsend for the Warburgs. He was an important non-Jewish
partner, not even remotely in sympathy with Hitler. The bank needed
someone like him in the early Nazi years when it tried not to be forced out
of business. When it became clear to Max Warburg he could not carry on,
Brinckmann and Wirtz were, given the circumstances, welcome buyers.
Brinckmann had made his career at Warburg and it mattered to Max
Warburg that he would continue business in the Warburg tradition.

In 1938 Warburg and his family emigrated to the United States. They
spent the war in straitened circumstances. They survived with the help of
Max Warburg's brother Felix who was married to Frieda Schiff, daughter
of Jacob Schiff, senior partner of Kuhn Loeb and Co., America's leading
Jewish investment bank. Under the umbrella of Kuhn Loeb, Max and his
son Eric had formed E. M. Warburg and Co. on a shoestring after they
came to New York. Eric later served as an intelligence officer in the
United States army. He made his way to Hamburg as soon as the city had
surrendered to the British and was assured by Brinckmann that once the
law and circumstances permitted, Brinckmann Wirtz should again
become Warburg property, though Brinckmann would retain a sizeable
interest in the bank. Some years later Eric returned to live in Hamburg.
Initially the firm was renamed Brinckmann Wirtz, M. M. Warburg and
Co., but later took only the old name. The original harmony turned into
acrimony. After Rudolf Brinckmann's death the family, including his son
Christian who was a partner in the firm, were bought out and had all connections with the firm severed. For a time the London Warburg house

held an interest in the Hamburg firm, but failed to obtain control and eventually gave up.

I always considered Rudolf Brinckmann a German who acted loyally toward the Warburgs. Otherwise I would not have wanted to have anything to do with him. He was helpful to me in my work. He was respected in the Hamburg business world and by the British. From our conversations I gained a better understanding of what kind of programs would be beneficial for Germans and British alike. He also provided me with an excellent secretary from the bank, Martha Bayer, an elderly spinster who had worked for Warburg partners in the "good old days." It gave her a job and food. The Brinckmanns had a lovely house in Aumühle, a Hamburg suburb in Bismarck territory. I spent many interesting and agreeable evenings with the family. With the sons I continue to this day a friendship started in the emotionally charged atmosphere of those first peacetime months.

I don't know what caused the rupture between the Brinckmanns and Warburgs, but the outcome does not sit right with me. Brinckmann kept the bank afloat during and after the war. Without him Eric Warburg would not have found a viable bank when he returned to Hamburg. I knew and liked Eric Warburg. As a young man he came to my parents' Hamburg home, primarily because Joan Parry, our pretty English au pair, had become a great flirt of his at a time when it had already become illegal for Jews to associate with Gentiles of the opposite sex. In later years I observed him as a banker and as a key figure in the Atlantic Brücke, the German opposite number of the American Council on Germany in which I have been active as a director and treasurer for over twenty years. I do not mean to underrate Eric Warburg, but he was no heavyweight. Had he not been a German Jew, a survivor, albeit financially — and probably emotionally — hobbled, the only one from a prominent German-Jewish family to return to prominence in Germany after the war, he would not have attained the influence or recognition he enjoyed. The proverbial Warburg charm and a pleasing appearance helped, but his influence stemmed from conscience-struck Germans who wanted to make amends. Post-Hitler Germany's relationship with the Jewish survivors was about restitution. Monetary restitution was the easy part. More subtle and complicated, there was the attempt to make amends for lives turned upside down, careers destroyed, a fatherland taken away. The Hamburg Warburgs benefited from tangible and intangible restitution, and Rudolf Brinckmann's caretaker role.

It was my responsibility to help Hamburg's first postwar Bürgermeister, Rudolf Petersen, with his broadcasts. The mayor of Hamburg is not any old Bürgermeister. He governs a Hanseatic city-state. He presides over a senate. The very size of the Rathaus, the city hall with its spire and imposing facade commands awe. Over and over, members of Hamburg's leading families have held the post. Rudolf Petersen came from a prominent Hamburg family. Two Petersens had been mayors before him. The family, typical for Hamburg's business elite, were in the export and import trade, well-to-do but not rich. Rudolf Petersen took on the mayoralty reluctantly. He knew his strength was soundness rather than genius. He made no bones of the fact he preferred business to public service. In the Nazi years he had kept a low profile. He was half Jewish, which made him persona grata with the British. His mother was a Behrens, from the bank in which father had been a partner. He was good-looking, with blue eyes and a white moustache. His suits were Savile Row look-alikes. His English was perfect. I had occasion one day to introduce him to Major General Bishop, who was responsible for media control in the British Zone of Occupation. The conversation seemed friendly enough, but when afterward I asked the general what he thought of Petersen, his comment was: "The fellow looks like an Englishman, dresses like one, speaks like one, but did you notice how he said, 'When I took power in Hamburg as Mayor.' Imagine the Lord Mayor of Liverpool saying he took power in Liverpool!"

Petersen had a difficult and delicate task. He had been appointed by the British, not elected by the Germans. The city administration had to be denazified, yet could not be stripped to the point where it no longer functioned. The British let him keep run-of-the-mill fellow travelers (Mitläufer) and thought he did not have his heart in denazification beyond a certain point.

He had to persuade the population that their hardships were self-inflicted, the results of a war Germany had started and lost, that food and fuel shortages were not caused by the British. That on the contrary Britain, though herself exhausted by six years of war, was actually a net helper in the British zone. His credibility depended on convincing the population he was doing his best to alleviate the situation, and standing up for them with the occupying power. Early during the occupation there was a huge protest rally in front of the city hall. It was on the verge of getting out of control. The police and fire brigade were called, but Petersen addressed the protesters from the Rathaus balcony and persuaded them to leave quietly.

The radio was his main means of communication. For me it was immensely interesting to assist him with his broadcasts. It was within my authority to censor the contents, but it never came to that point. When I disagreed, we had it out before he went on the air. It helped that he knew about me, had known Father, and appreciated my constructive intentions. He had never been near a microphone. My broadcasting experience was not much greater, yet the results were good. I'd sit with him before a broadcast, make him rehearse his text over and over again, and even stayed in the studio while he was live on the air. He did a good job. He was dignified, brief, and persuasive. His critics claimed he was brief because he did not have much to say.

Petersen's speeches and broadcasts reflect the events and atmosphere of those early months in Hamburg after the war had ended. On May 15, 1945, he addressed the Hamburg senate. He reminded the senators that he assumed office with the greatest reluctance, mainly to follow in the footsteps of his grandfather who had been mayor in good and happy times before the First World War, and his brother who had held the post in the days of terrible stress in 1918. He counted on God's help and Jesus Christ's, a name banned in Germany by the government on racial grounds these past twelve years. He firmly believed in Hamburg's recovery, even if it were to take years of hard work by the population, and in particular by the leading families in commerce. Since the days of the Hanseatic League Hamburg had been not only the world's trading partner but also the intermediary between German and Anglo-Saxon culture. Hanseatic entrepreneurship would lay the foundations for Hamburg's recovery, and with that, for the recovery of Germany. In conclusion, he felt he owed it to his predecessors to acknowledge that they had found the courage, if only in the last moment, to surrender Hamburg in defiance of Hitler's orders, and thereby to save lives of friend and foe alike.

On July 1, eight weeks after Hamburg's capitulation, a month after Petersen had become mayor, he broadcast his first accounting, saying that he had responsibility for many government departments formerly run from Berlin, such as justice and finance. He asked for understanding if everything was not solved right away. Only the most urgent problems could be tackled. Military government had dismissed the great majority of the leading officials on account of their close links with National Socialism. While this was imperative, it made work more difficult. New personnel had to be found and trained. Anyone who had joined the Nazi Party before 1933 was automatically discharged — two thousand in all. Those who had lost their positions on racial or political grounds during the Nazi years were given their former jobs back as far as possible. Petersen hoped the sort of decency in public service that had once been taken for granted in Hamburg would soon return. As for economic and labor conditions, most foreign workers had returned to their homelands. There was an acute labor shortage, and anyone who stayed at home or in his garden should find himself employment. The Nazi Party–dominated workers' councils had been replaced by newly chosen councils. Alas, there was little likelihood for foreign trade to revive in the foreseeable future and he advised looking for other employment — in the building industry, for instance. With British approval the port was being rebuilt and the first vessels had arrived. The housing shortage was desperate. Homes of party functionaries and pre-1933 party members had been taken over to meet some of the most urgent housing needs. Transportation was reserved for food and essential raw materials. Long-distance passenger trains were being slowly reinstated, but the occupation forces had security concerns and the tracks needed repairs. Elementary schools would shortly be reopened. High schools and universities would follow soon. There were no health problems. Concerts and the circus had reopened. Theatres and movies would follow shortly, though only a few days each week. Conditions in Hamburg appeared better than in other parts of the country. "I would be less than candid if I did not say here that the understanding attitude of the British military government is making my task easier. Let us all work together. With God's help we will succeed."

On September 12 Petersen spoke on the radio about his concerns for the coming winter months:

> With fear the population is anticipating the coming winter. . . . It is hardly surprising that people are wondering whether all possible preparations are being taken. First, as far as food is concerned, I am well aware that the present rations are insufficient for older people, for children, and for anyone engaged in heavy manual labor who for one reason or another does not receive the supplementary rations to which his work entitles him. I hardly need to mention why it is difficult to improve daily rations. Part of our Hamburg and Holstein food production we must ship to other regions of our country where conditions are even worse, particularly Berlin and the Ruhr. I trust you share my opinion that this is something we must do. The English occupation force is helping to meet our most urgent needs to prevent the outbreak of hunger diseases. It is our moral duty to do everything within our power to overcome the crisis by all possible means to raise food production and industrial output. Part of our own effort has to include fighting the black markets ruthlessly and without mercy, especially the food marketeers. Any means of fighting them is fine with me. The survival and health of our fellow countrymen is at stake. We will conduct more raids and I hope the results will soon be felt.

Petersen went on to talk about the shortage of housing, the difficulty of getting building materials and coal, and the increase in the city's population — since June an additional 112,000 people had moved to Hamburg.

Two questions much on people's minds are how to deal with our
political past and how to participate in future party politics. It is
widely felt that the political cleanup process is going too slowly. I
agree. For me it is also too slow. . . . I would like to make it un-
mistakably clear, however, that denazification is the sole responsibility of the military government. It is up to them to decide who
to discharge from the public sector, private business, or the professions. This way of proceeding has the merit that it may help
avoid unfair dismissals which only place still further strain on our
already overburdened administrative machine.

It is difficult to come up with sensible answers. The military
are gaining confidence that we truly mean to break radically with
National Socialism. This makes me hopeful that the detailed
implementation of the denazification process will soon be left to
us. In my opinion what matters is to remove those elements from
influential positions who cannot be expected to make a clean
break with their National Socialist past. The great majority must
be integrated as quickly as possible into the process of rebuilding
our economy and society.

Now for the revival of party politics. As was true after the
First World War, conditions to create a true democracy could not
be more unpropitious. In the midst of an economic and spiritual
crisis the population can hardly be expected to be thoughtful and
sensible, two characteristics without which true democracy is un-
thinkable. True democracy is not possible unless we concentrate
on the immediate and tangible goal of rebuilding our country
without regard to different systems or philosophies.

Notwithstanding all obstacles I am not despondent. There is
some progress almost daily. Trains and mail are working better.
The streets are being cleared. The number of people at work is
growing. Schools, universities, and the law courts either have
reopened or are about to do so. The will to live, discipline and
order are coming back. Zonal government, at least in the British

zone, is beginning to take shape. The time seems to be approaching when we can reorganize our finances.

As winter came closer Petersen's warnings became more urgent:

Winter with all its horrors is on our doorsteps. The seriousness of our situation is underrated. I must disillusion you. There is a widespread assumption that things in Hamburg have gone better than anticipated. . . . Please prepare yourselves and mark my word, as things now stand there will be absolutely no coal for home heating this winter.

With this as background you will understand why I want to fight the black market as well as any theft of coal and wood from our depots with all means at our disposal. Similarly we will enforce strictly the regulations that limit us to one light per room. We must restrict electricity wasted for entertainment, or the manufacture of nonessential products. Don't you agree with me that we must at all costs prevent people who are not native here from moving to Hamburg? We have to create room for the population now living here, those sleeping in cellars or unheatable summer huts. Don't you agree we should avail ourselves of the opportunity provided by the English to evacuate to Holstein non-Hamburgers living here who are not engaged in essential work? There is room there, living conditions are relatively satisfactory, and families can be kept together.

These measures must strike those affected as harsh and even incomprehensible. It cannot be helped. We must use all the means at our disposal to prevent the outbreak of epidemics this winter, something that could easily happen, considering the years of wartime deprivations, the lack of heat and insufficient food that have undermined the strength to resist disease.

My conviction that we had to allow officials like Petersen to speak freely, to nurture some self-respect, to complain — even about the British —

was not shared by all my superiors. I felt that such a policy was not only laying the foundations for free speech, but provided a safety valve. Ralph Poston shared my belief and backed me, though sometimes it got him into trouble with his higher-ups.

The Petersens had me to dinner from time to time. At home he made no bones about the fact that he'd much rather rebuild his business than be Bürgermeister. As a family the Petersens had sought survival rather than opposition to National Socialism. Only one of his sons, Gustav, wanted to have nothing to do with Nazi Germany and emigrated to the United States. He and his wife were on the same ship with Mother, Bridget, and myself when we left Hamburg in 1936. He was married to a descendant of Eduard von Simson, the (baptized) Jew who had presided over the National Assembly in Frankfurt in 1849 and had offered Frederic William IV the Imperial German crown.

Some of Father's erstwhile banking friends made an overture of reconciliation by inviting me to a formal dinner in the basement of the Rathaus. They came with a long list of favors to ask! The dinner, well intentioned or not, was a disaster. It was winter and bitterly cold, which was hardly their fault. The ambitious printed menu, with the Hamburg crest in gilt letters, read better than it tasted. I do recall good wine. The trouble was the conversation. Each person, of whom there were perhaps ten, was anxious to explain away his Nazi years, lay claim to gestures of loyalty to Jewish friends, to opposition here and there, and so on. However, it turned out that everyone had been a party member — inactive and reluctant, of course, only to keep their jobs, or to exercise a moderating influence — and, by the way, couldn't I ask Father to write a letter on their behalf? I became visibly annoyed and inquired of the dignified, elderly butler whether he, too, had been a party member. Embarrassed and apologetic, the butler turned to Baron Schröder and, bowing, asked Herr Baron to please have understanding for the fact that he never joined the party. The evening broke up early. None of father's real friends had come that night.

It would be silly to pretend, over fifty years later, that I got neither enjoyment nor satisfaction from wearing a British infantry officer's uniform, being a field officer in a prestigious regiment with a handful of medals on my chest, and a wound insignia on a sleeve. But I hated it when any of our German staff, especially those who had been in their army, made an obsequious fuss over the "Herr Major." I hated it even more when the approach was "we who served as army officers, even if on opposing sides, surely understand each other." Then there was the expression *"dieser unseelige Krieg,"* — this dreadful war — that implied it had been wished upon all of us by some extraterrestial power, not started by them. Another line often heard was that of appealing to us of the "Christlichen Abendland" — we Germans and English of "the Christian West." I felt deeply committed to building a democratic, free society, but when anyone complained more than I was willing to accept about their miseries and fate my standard response was simply: "Fellows, you started it, please don't blame anyone but yourselves."

Most of us were loyal to our Russian ally. Many Germans found this hard to understand. I became quite angry with any who expressed anti-Russian sentiments. I'd say it was their own fault that the Red Army was in Berlin. If they had not attacked them and been beaten, the borders would still be a thousand kilometers to the east. In 1945 Nazi atrocities and Stalin's horrors were not considered similarly awful by the average British soldier or civilian. Perhaps we did not know enough about what had gone on in Soviet Russia. The Russians were not unpopular in Britain. Uncle Joe Stalin smoked a pipe, looked benign. Without Russia we probably would have lost the war. For my generation Communism held some appeal. We were in school or college during the Depression and had seen poverty around us and in our families. We did not realize the goal of economic equality meant equally little for everyone, or that state planning and state ownership were even more capricious and less efficient than capitalism. The West had to make the attempt to befriend Russia in the immediate postwar period. Without this effort the Western middle classes and intelligentsia would have argued that Russia had never been given a chance and that the Russians could not be blamed for their hard line and suspicion, that the West was to blame for the Cold War, not the Russians.

The high point of my time at the NWDR was a trip with Peter von Zahn to cover the Nuremberg tribunal. I spent several days in court, saw the accused, the justices, the helmeted American military police, the prosecutors, and the German defense. I tried to obtain autographs from the accused and invested many cartons of cigarettes bribing one who claimed he could deliver. Needless to say I failed.

The justices from all four nations — American, British, French, and Russian — lived up to the occasion. They, and the prosecutors, represented the best of their countries' legal systems. The famous became more famous, and many of the younger were launched on the path to the pinnacles of the legal profession. They were immensely hardworking and conducted themselves with decorum. None were Jewish, which was probably not accidental.

The numerous Allied hangers-on who (over)staffed the tribunal seemed less impressive. They lived in comfort in a ruined starving Nuremberg. There was something unedifying about having a merry time in the shadows of this trial. Many, too many, of the support staff were German-Jewish émigrés, which played into the hands of those who discredited Nuremberg as nothing more than an act of retribution.

Journalists, commentators, and cameramen from all over the world had descended upon Nuremberg. The opening sessions and the sentencing, the lengthy pleas by the defendants, Göring's suicide and Ribbentrop's disdainful scowls and wry smiles, the you-surely-cannot-mean-me expression and starched white collar attire of Hjalmar Schacht, the stoic inscrutable faces of the admirals and generals in their tunics stripped of all insignia — each and every nuance made front-page news everywhere. It was the end of the newsreel age, but too early for television.

For Zahn and his colleagues Nuremberg was the assignment of a lifetime, but not an easy one. Full radio and newspaper coverage in all four occupation zones was mandatory. In the Allied world the trial preached to the converted. For Germans, especially those who claimed ignorance, Nuremberg was the centerpiece of the victors' attempt to open German eyes to the Nazi years and stuff their past down reluctant throats. The charge of "crimes against humanity" broke new legal ground, but then, so did the crimes. It was futile for the defense to deny what had taken place and to argue that their clients had broken no laws because before the indictment there had been none to break.

Zahn, Rezzori, or Eggebrecht had no problem accepting the guilt of the accused and broadcasting accordingly. They saw for themselves that the trial was being conducted fairly. Still, they were in an invidious position. The tribunal press officers treated them as second-class citizens. They were denied the creature comforts of the international press corps. Inside the tribunal they had the poorest seating. Their audience was skeptical. Barely a year ago, the accused had been their leaders. German military tradition was based on a loyalty oath but Hitler, the Führer to whom they had plighted their troth, the ultimate authority, had evaded judgment and responsibility by suicide. No international law before this had decreed that it was illegal to execute an illegal act, that such orders not only relieved an officer of his oath to obey orders, but that disobedience to such orders was his duty. Total war had been waged on both sides. German skeptics asked whether, if Coventry and the Blitz were part of the indictment, what about Dresden?

Last but not least, few in the West were entirely comfortable with the Soviet Union on the tribunal. It was inconceivable in 1945 to deny the Soviets their place, yet it would have invited even more German skepticism and cynicism if German reporters had been denied the right to raise the question. My attitude was then, is now, and always will be: "Fellows, you started it. Live with, and put up with, the consequences."

Nuremberg was not all work. Zahn took me to the Stauffenbergs at Wilfingen. We huffed and puffed up the Watzmann near Berchtesgaden. We sheltered from a storm inside the lovely baroque Wiess church listening to an organ recital. On our way to Nuremberg we stopped in Frankfurt, where I saw my father's sister Maria Schaefer for the first time since before the war. There was not a second of awkwardness. There was so much to talk about. She was my favorite relative. I had been drawn by my parents to admire her courage, her self-sufficiency, her ability to live a full life without a penny in the world. No wonder she had friends throughout the Nazi years who stood by her and helped her survive, if barely. When told her arrest was imminent, she hid with friendly farmers in a village in the Rhön region a couple of hours by train from Frankfurt. Her sons, who had been drafted late in the war into forced labor camps, had also survived. Her sons had managed somehow to come and see me in Hamburg almost as soon as the war ended. They had begun to put their lives together, which included rebuilding their mother's badly bomb-damaged house. In Frankfurt I tried to discover the whereabouts of my grandparents Flersheims' chauffeur Nikolas Müller, a devout Catholic loyal to them. I found he had died in the last year of the war. Until his death he went regularly to the Jewish cemetery to tend to the grave of the Flersheims' only son, my Uncle Hans, who had died a young man in 1933. This required courage! I found the Flersheims' Myliusstrasse home intact but the Flersheim-Hess Mainzer Landstrasse office and warehouse had been destroyed in the air raids. I met several of Grandfather's former employees. Some had become Nazis and tried to explain they had never meant it, had only done it to protect the business, and wasn't it wonderful to meet a Flersheim grandson? I was not exactly friendly, especially when they asked me to intervene on their behalf with the American military. Others had never compromised with the regime. To them Ernst Flersheim had been a respected and loved fifth-generation owner of the business and they were shattered when they heard he and his wife had died at Bergen-Belsen.

Soon after the Nuremberg trip I was faced with decisions about my future. Military government wanted me to stay beyond the time when I was due to be demobilized. It was tempting. Was it possible I had rediscovered *Heimat* feelings for Hamburg and Germany? I had an influential and interesting job. Apparently my work was well thought of. I was promised a promotion with more pay. I could see ways of ultimately leveraging my NWDR experience into a civilian career in broadcasting or journalism without starting at the bottom. But in fact I had had one wish from the day I joined the army — to be demobilized the day it was my turn. I wanted to get home. England had become my country, even if the wretched British had not yet troubled to naturalize their loyal enemy aliens. In particular I wanted to go back to Oxford and get a degree. I was not sure what I wanted to do, but probably something in the City.

There was one final army assignment — to work a couple of months for information control in the British sector of Berlin, jointly with the other occupying powers. I traded places with Walter Wallich, a son of Father's Dreyfus banker colleague Paul Wallich from the 1920s. Wallich had agreed to serve on as a civilian after demobilization and in fact turned his NWDR years into a successful career at the BBC in London. I had a ball in Berlin, with little work, lots of social life, in particular with one very nice lady, half French, who was married to a Jewish concentration camp survivor who was in the process of becoming a minor movie mogul.

Socially I saw a lot of my parents' close friend Susy Werner Stanley. Her life and survival are a Nazi-era saga. She was born into a Jewish steel family, the Neumarcks of Herrenwyck, outside Lübeck. In pre-Hitler Hamburg she was a free spirit. She was divorced from Victor Werner, a successful, non-Jewish construction contractor on whose financial support she remained dependent. He, however, could only take care of her provided she lived in Germany. To survive safely in Germany she acquired British nationality in 1938. With the assistance of my parents she married and almost immediately divorced an obliging English homosexual artist. Protected by her British passport and supported by her ex-husband, she and her three children, who had all been close childhood friends of mine and my Schaefer cousins, survived the war relatively comfortably in Berlin. We had excellent parties at her home, especially with my Berlin lady friend to whom Susy had originally introduced me. On the other hand, Susy made me promise that I would have nothing to do with another childhood companion who, like her father, had turned into a horrendous Nazi. A pity, because I heard she was a beauty.

In Berlin I was billeted in a lovely Grunewald house, not far from the Werner- Stanleys, that had belonged to a German SS officer named Nebe. He had been on the staff of Admiral Canaris and General Oster, two high-level German officers implicated in the plots against Hitler. Two of Nebe's servants who had stayed on to become our servants told me that near the end of the war Nebe had gone for a walk one evening and was never seen again. The servants believed the SS killed him for his complicity in the Canaris affair.

I worked with my Russian opposite numbers on matters such as sharing and exchanging radio programs. In reality all they wanted was air access to the British occupation zone. As people they were interesting, and pleasant enough to get on with. They looted whatever they could lay their hands on. Zahn came to open a studio for broadcasts about Berlin from the British sector.

In his memoirs Zahn has described our daily routine in Hamburg, the lack of most amenities and comfort that both British control officers and German colleagues suffered from. Zahn claimed that we British liked to invite the Germans to our officers' mess because that was the best way for us to get a decent dinner — the kitchen staff, he pointed out, were willing to make a good dinner with plenty of meat only for the benefit of their hungry fellow Germans.

Back in Hamburg everyone was shivering. Christa von Zahn's hot water bottle sometimes froze in her bed. Their four-year-old daughter came to the office and huddled under Zahn's desk. According to Peter Bamm's memoirs I appeared on one occasion at midnight in the radio station to find four motherly ladies huddled together. One was knitting socks, another patching a pair of pants, another editing a manuscript. Officiously I asked what they were up to at such an hour, only to be told they were looking for a bit of warmth.

Zahn thought the main advantages he and his colleagues had over the general population were warm offices and exciting stimulating work. But they paid a price. The average listener, at least to begin with, disdained their programs. They received anonymous death threats. They were called Quislings, traitors, toadies. The Hamburg upper crust accused the broadcasters of being apologists for "vindictive" British measures, of Communist sympathies, and left-wing economic theories. Zahn wrote that I had to lecture him on the economics of the black market until he understood and accepted that it, and not planning or controls, were the reality of supply, demand, and pricing.

Peter von Zahn went on to become one of Germany's leading television producers and commentators. When he and his family moved to Washington and he began to cover the United States, he became the

"Alistair Cooke of Germany" for many years. Zahn has a perfect ear for the word and a perfect eye for the visual. He left the NWDR eventually, came back to Hamburg where he still lives and established his own production company which makes TV films all over the world. We see each other frequently on either side of the Atlantic. Our friendship has been a major factor in my life.

I prepared for my return to England and to Oxford. Zahn's words about me personally and my work, in his memoirs published in 1991, still give me satisfaction and pleasure:

By no means all of the journalistic attainments of which we were so proud were our own doing. Much was suggested by the English. The most creative among them was Captain Everitt. His real name was Walter Eberstadt, raised in Hamburg, the son of a well-known banker. He and his parents managed to emigrate to England before it was too late. If banking had not been in his blood, he might well have become a first-class financial journalist. He had limitless hunger for facts and information and an unerring sense of what an audience wanted and what would affect them. He could not bear pompous language or bombastic phrases. He was bilingual in German and English which put him in a position, especially when it came to political commentaries, to spot nuances that escaped others. He had not forgotten that on account of Hitler and his henchmen he lost members of his family and part of their possessions, but never with as much as a gesture took it out on the Germans with whom he worked. If there was something he did not care for he did not mince words, but if he liked someone he went to almost any length to help. Our friendship remains close to this day. He has long reassumed his original name and is a partner in one of the most prestigious New York banking firms. I can thank Walter Eberstadt for the fact that I was able to start my career more or less at the top rather than first spending long years of tedious grinding away. Nor will I forget the fortitude with which he opened his tobacco pouch without as much as a murmur while all the other control officers fled as soon as they saw me.

Hamburg and six years in the army came to an end with my demobilization in July of 1946. I was not quite twenty-five years old. The war had taken up over one-quarter of my entire life and well over half of my days in England.

16

Postwar England

With my demobilization in July of 1946 I needed a while to get accustomed to civilian life, but the adjustment was not the traumatic event it was for some. Major Everitt posed as the newly retired army officer, not, I hope, to the point of making a fool of himself. I walked at times with the symbolic officer's ash cane. For some probably silly reason there were nights when in Normandy fashion I slept outdoors on my camp bed in the garden under the stars.

Life in England continued to be austere. Food, gasoline, clothing and foreign currencies were rationed. Demobilized personnel, regardless of rank, were given one suit, not exactly Savile Row but indestructible. I wore mine for years. We also were given a hat, coat, one pair of shoes, underwear, a tie, and a couple of shirts. There was a tiny postwar gratuity, partly in cash, mostly in a savings bond, which became almost worthless in the postwar inflation. The entire amount was less than £100, which was not a lot even in those days. Fortunately I had no financial worries. I lived at my parents' home. For Oxford I received a government grant of £300 annually, which covered tuition and board during term time.

Thanks to my experience in Hamburg I obtained a part-time post at Wilton Park in Buckinghamshire, a center run by the Foreign Office, to give a crash course in democracy to German officers before they were sent home. It paid quite well and was interesting. I made enough money to be independent from my parents, which, at age twenty-five, mattered to me. Father was not well physically. He suffered from asthma, which very nearly killed him. He needed round-the-clock nurses at home. His illness could not have come at a worse time for his business. He had formed G. Eberstadt and Co. in part with capital from Siegmund Warburg who had a high regard for him and who also wanted to create a place in the City for his cousin Charles Warburg, for whom he did not have a high regard. Eventually there would be enough money for my parents to live comfortably when my Flersheim grandparents' estate was freed from the alien property custodian in the United States, but it took a while.

We celebrated my parents' silver wedding at Carlyon Bay in Wales, we celebrated peace and our own survival even if Mother's parents and sister's death were never far from her thoughts. Bridget had another year in the WAAFs before she was demobilized, but we all could begin to plan our future.

I started Oxford in the autumn term of 1946. Returning soldiers were given every consideration despite the really terrible shortages of almost everything. I was allotted lovely rooms — a bedroom and living room all to myself, on the ground floor of Peckwater Quad. There were a few others from my year — 1939 — who had come back. One was Adam Stainton, to finish his law degree. Nearly all had been in the war. Some had managed a year at Oxford before being called up, but many had joined the forces straight from school. Friendships struck then have continued to this day, even if I came to have little contact once I moved to the United States. *Nomen est omen*. Walter Everitt was more English — and Anglican — than the erstwhile Walter Eberstadt. What a blessing I had picked a nondescript name from the London telephone book rather than something out of *Burke's Peerage*, which many of my erstwhile Pioneer

Corps cohorts had chosen. Everitt caused me sufficient turmoil, some Scottish laird's name would have caused havoc. I could have reverted to Eberstadt the moment I was out of the army but did not really feel like it. I wanted in those days to distance myself from my origins and, given the events between 1933 and 1945, that was perhaps not surprising.

The social background of my friends mattered to me — unduly. I was accepted, I hope, without too much murmuring behind my back. I had had, as they said, a good war, and that mattered, as it would have continued to matter had I lived out my days in England rather than America. Few of us were particularly scholarly. We wanted a degree to get a job. The civil service and the Foreign Office were recruiting. Their selection boards looked at one's war record more than at academic qualifications. Some of us became schoolmasters or went into the Church. Not many were good enough for an academic career. Very few, unless they had family connections, chose the City, which was still hamstrung by the aftermath of Depression and wartime restrictions, in particular continuing foreign exchange controls. Some went into family businesses. Typically for Christ Church there were numerous links with the old landowning families. There was a future Duke of Buccleuch. Another was Bill Birch-Reynardson, from an Oxfordshire family with close links to my wartime regiment. I came across Bill in later years in the City. There was the engagingly bright (future Sir) Francis Dashwood with whom I shared Roy Harrod's tutorials. His forebears in the eighteenth century had founded the Dilettanti Society and the infamous Hellfire Club. They still owned West Wycombe, where I attended one of the first postwar balls, one of the grandest parties of my life. Dashwood successfully rebuilt a somewhat diminished family fortune. I cannot today recall many contemporaries of mine who already as undergraduates seemed determined to make a fortune.

Adam Stainton was one of the few I had known well since 1939. He had seen more active service than most of us, as a platoon commander in the Scots Guards. He had served in the Middle East, Italy, and Western Europe. By sheer luck — sickness — he missed a couple of battles that probably would have cost him his life. He did not much care for postwar

Oxford. The war was still very much in his system and never really left it. His younger brother Andrew, who had also been in the Scots Guards, came up a term after me, a pleasant man with conventional interests but a particularly delightful unconventional wife. He worked later for Dewar's, his family's whisky business. We still see each other. Another good friend was Anthony Birley, a contemporary of Adam's at Winchester where fathers Stainton and Birley had been contemporaries. Father Birley was a stockbroker, supposedly not a particularly good one. Anthony became a House of Commons clerk, a pleasant, prestigious, poorly paid and not very demanding job. The working hours were awkward but left Anthony time for bridge, at which he excelled. He and his wife, a Ponsonby, now live in retirement in the Cotswolds.

I continued to have contact with Peter Giffard. He lost a leg as a platoon commander in the Grenadier Guards. He became a barrister and later served as Lord Lieutenant of Staffordshire where the family had a beautiful quite grand home. After we went down from Oxford we had neighboring apartments in London in the basement of 35 Wilton Place, right underneath the future Berkeley Hotel. In 1946 I paid £4.10 a week, breakfast included; at the Berkeley in the year 2000 it is £220 a night, breakfast excluded.

When Peter Giffard got tired or a little drunk, he'd detach his wooden leg and brandish it in the air. I also came to know his brother-in-law Airey Neave, a wartime intelligence officer who played a prominent role at the Nuremberg trials. At the age of twenty-nine Neave, who subsequently wrote two famous books, one about his escape from a German prisoner-of-war camp and the other about Nuremberg, served the Allied indictments on the twenty-one top Nazis awaiting trial in the Nuremberg jail. He later lost his own life when, as a member of Parliament and one of Mrs. Thatcher's closest associates, he was blown up in his car by the IRA.

Another friend from those days is Dermott, now Sir Dermott, de Trafford. He followed his father into the City where our paths crossed from time to time. He was one of the first of my contemporaries, while still at Oxford, to marry. My two Howard cousins were back at the House. Denis returned after an arduous war as a gunner in the Far East. Michael had earned a Military Cross as a subaltern in the Coldstream Guards. His wartime experience became the start for a career as one of Britain's most distinguished military historians. It led for him to a Chichele professorship and a knighthood. In fact, I can claim two university professors of history as cousins, Sir Michael at Oxford, and Sir Geoffrey Elton, the Tudor historian, at Cambridge. Last but not least there was James Collier, who married my sister Bridget. James, an only child whose father had been the chief forester of a Nepalese king in the interwar years, went to Harrow and spent the war as an artillery officer in the Far East. After Oxford he had a distinguished civil service career. Bridget appeared at Oxford when she was demobilized to attend a good secretarial college. We tried to produce members of the opposite sex for each other, for me with limited success, but eventually for her there was James Collier. I also became friends with Evelyn Joll who was at Magdalen. He married into the Agnew family and for many years was chairman of Agnew's. The few good paintings I own have all come from him. I must have been one of his least lucrative clients compared, for instance, with Paul Mellon for whom he put together the wonderful collection of eighteenth Century English painters at Yale. Evelyn became perhaps the leading contemporary expert on Turner.

Considering most of us were grown-ups, not boys straight from their public schools, women did not play that much of a role for most of us in our term-time lives. There was Pamela Maxwell-Fyfe, Joanna Money-Coutts, Vicky Reynolds, Celia Buxton. We partied and flirted, but I don't think many friendships were fully consummated. The promiscuous war years were over and the English sexual thaw was yet to come — though I could be very wrong with this hypothesis!

I was never much of an athlete. I stroked the Christ Church Eight in the winter Torpid races, and the Second Eight in the summer Eights Week. I played a little golf — poorly. I loved the Oxfordshire countryside and most Sundays we'd walk somewhere, ending with a beery pub lunch. Adam Stainton was in great demand as a walking companion. He was one of the few with a car and a petrol ration just about sufficient for these Sunday expeditions.

My social life was active but the postwar shortages limited entertainment. I generally dined in Hall, which was convivial and beautiful. I was a member of the Canning, a Conservative eating club. Living conditions were harsh, especially in the winter of 1946. It was the coldest on record in the century. There were shortages of everything, in particular coal. We had enough to lay a fire two nights a week and took turns seeking warmth in each other's rooms. Electric fires were not allowed. Hot baths were rationed to one a week. Due to the cold, railroads had come virtually to a standstill. Food and clothes rationing was almost as strict as during the war. There was an annual allowance of £75 in foreign exchange for holiday travel abroad.

As far as work was concerned, I was greatly interested in Economics and did well. I graduated with a Second Class Honors degree in Modern Greats, the formal name for PPE (Philosophy, Politics, and Economics). Harrod generously wrote it was a good Second. I started the Christ Church Economic Society, less as a vehicle for acquiring knowledge than as a platform to invite prominent City figures and economists to dine and speak in the hope they might prove friendly after we graduated. None offered me a job but several became useful contacts once I was a financial journalist. The Christ Church Economic Society continued for many years after my time.

I enjoyed Politics, the second *P* in PPE, but had a hard time with Philosophy, the first of the two *P*'s. My Politics tutor was Bobby Blake who became Lord Blake, one of the postwar period's most distinguished constitutional scholars and writers, whose works include a masterful Disraeli biography. We had a good relationship that has endured, albeit sporadically. He had been captured at Dunkirk. For over five years he had been a prisoner of war. He made no secret that what he taught he sometimes read up on mere hours before a tutorial. Philosophy was in the hands of Gilbert Ryle, an eminent scholar wasted on me. We did Hobbes's *Leviathan*, Aristotle, John Stuart Mill, and others I recall not even by name.

For most of us Oxford was an anticlimax after having been "someone" in the war. It served as a decompression chamber. Few had great scholarly ambitions. We had to make up for lost time. We needed a degree to make a living. In addition I wanted something else. I wanted Oxford to put more distance between the prewar Walter Eberstadt, German refugee, and the postwar Walter Everitt, striving to be part and parcel of British life. It seemed to work quite well. I contributed articles to the *Manchester Guardian*, wrote the odd letter to the *Times*, mainly on subjects to do with my role in Hamburg, and hobnobbed wherever I could with the "establishment."

The Stainton family was friendly. Adam's father, Sir John Stainton, planned a well-remembered walking weekend for us on the Wiltshire Downs, almost step by step where he had walked a generation earlier with Anthony Birley's father. He helped Adam and me plan a summer trip to France and Italy, more or less to the same places where he had gone in his undergraduate days. For me this trip became the most important cultural experience of my life. It opened my eyes and mind to a legacy ingrained for generations in the English. Harold Nicolson and Vita Sackville-West invited me to Sissinghurst. He and I had struck up a correspondence about postwar Germany. He offered his help should I want a career in politics. Roy Harrod and his wife, Bella, were hospitable beyond a tutor's obligation with invitations to tea and sherry parties. I was invited to country homes, in particular my friend Anne Coventry's Croome Court. I was laying foundations on which I might build something enduring one day, but to what extent was my heart in it? My links continued with my refugee parents and their ways, their friends and many of their friends' children.

With Father I had discussions about my future. He wanted so badly to assist me with the right start and felt that he was no longer well connected. He thought I should find a way to avoid starting on the very bottom rung of business. Financial journalism seemed a means of eventually going into business or finance, if I did not want to make journalism a life career, and that is how I came to apply for a job on the *Economist*. Roy Harrod favored the idea. I had shown a flair for writing in Luxembourg and Hamburg and had a sense for the newsworthy. Harrod set me up with Geoffrey Crowther who hired me there and then to start on January 1, 1948. He wanted me to cover business, in particular the City. I was in seventh heaven. The *Economist* was prestigious, my colleagues would be interesting, and the pay by the standards of England three years after the war was not too bad — £400 a year.

On the strength of the prestige of being on staff at the *Economist* one was expected to supplement one's income from writing part-time for other publications, lecturing, consulting, and so on. One colleague, Jack Horsfall, wrote a weekly market letter for a firm of stockbrokers. Another, Ronald Brech, was an expert on commodities and an adviser to Unilever. The well-known senior editors, such as Crowther, Barbara Ward, Donald McLachlan, Wilfred King, Paul Bareau, and several others were in demand everywhere for everything. On what he earned as a financial journalist Paul Bareau managed a house in the country, a home in London, and sons at Eton and Oxford. He was a genius at recycling the same stories over and over. First he'd write the daily financial column for the respected, Liberal *News Chronicle,* next he'd adapt the material for the weekly *Economist,* then, in greater depth he'd cover the subject in the monthly *Banker* of which he was joint editor with Wilfred King. There'd be the occasional article in a bank quarterly publication, broadcasts on the BBC — Home and World services — advice to his fellow Belgian, Louis Frank, head of Samuel Montagu, all seemingly effortless and with charm. He even found time for four-handed piano with his wife. He died only recently, aged almost a hundred. His son Peter later worked for me in New York at Model Roland, a gifted violinist who preferred his fiddle to finance. I was indirectly responsible for Peter's New York marriage, which ended badly. He was very English and was blindsided by his bride-to-be who came from a cosmopolitan moneyed, pretending not-to-be Jewish background, which probably fascinated him because it was so different from his own.

It took me a while to understand that the *Economist* wanted facts rather than opinions from me. I was assigned minor stories and was never sure whether they would appear in print. Eventually I wrote worthwhile pieces. I became somewhat of an expert on the Rhodesian Copperbelt and its complicated ownership structure. I became interested in the economics of the art market. I was the first financial journalist to write about the infamous "Ring" of London dealers who rigged the market at provincial art auctions rather than compete against one another. I gained the confidence of Simon Marks, then head of Marks and Spencer, enough to let me write about his company. They were then in the early stages of entering the food business and the public was showing some resistance to buying food from what till then had been primarily a clothing retailer. Apparently I found the right language to convey his pride in high quality at low prices. The editorial staff was used by the incipient *Economist* Intelligence Unit to work on reports that sometimes required weeks of research. The extra money was welcome and the work interesting. A leading firm of London stockbrokers, McAnally Little and Ingeljohns, commissioned a report on the impact of inflation on French share prices during the interwar years. I obtained the assignment and had a fascinating week in Paris collecting material. Much of the time I spent at the Paris Lazard firm, which was just awakening from its enforced wartime skeleton activities. Decades later, when I worked at Lazard in New York, some of my then contacts were still there. The McAnally senior partner, Ian Hill, was confined to a wheelchair, crippled by arthritis. His sister brought him to a spartan Victorian office each morning. We became good personal friends. He used my study to promote business, especially with his clientele in Scotland. Some years later, when I had moved to New York, his firm became an important client of mine.

One of Father's friends was David Sachs, the only Jewish senior executive at Guinness Mahon. From Guinness he had moved to the *Investors Chronicle* as a stock market editor. The *Investors Chronicle* paid better salaries than Guinness but still hardly enough to live on. As a second job Sachs was financial editor of the Liverpool *Daily Post and Echo,* which involved writing each evening from their Fleet Street office a column on the day's London Stock Exchange activities. For the amount of skill and time required it was well paid. Sachs passed on the Liverpool *Post* job to me when he became a partner in Rowe Swann, a well-regarded London Stock Exchange firm, and had to give up journalism. Each evening, after I was finished at the *Economist,* I'd take a number 9 bus down Piccadilly and the Strand to Fleet Street to dash off my market column. Often, afterward, I had a few beers with other journalists in one of the many Fleet Street pubs. The Liverpool *Post* was a first-class provincial paper owned by the Jeans family, best known for their astronomer kinsman. Alan Jeans, the paper's publisher, became a friend and in later years I was helpful to him when the family bought a newspaper in Canada. With my *Economist* salary, the Liverpool *Post,* the Intelligence Unit fees and the alas short-lived income as editor, together with Ronnie Grierson, of a travel magazine, I had a good income, but not enough to accumulate a little capital. Even though I wrote about money and rubbed shoulders with money, I lacked experience, desire, or ambition to become a "capitalist." I lacked confidence in my own judgment to back ideas with the few hundred pounds I could have spared. Nor did it seem to me that Father, whom I loved and admired, had demonstrated that stock market speculation could make one rich.

Probably my most influential articles covered the negotiations leading up to debt settlement in 1951 of Germany's interwar debts. The most important were the Dawes and Young loans — issued in different tranches and currencies in Europe, Britain, and the United States to help fund Germany's World War I reparations debts. In addition there were municipal borrowings and the Potash loans. Interest payments were suspended or reduced beginning in 1931 and transfer into foreign currencies all but ceased with the imposition of exchange control after Hitler came to power. A debt settlement was needed to reopen Germany's access to the international capital markets. The negotiations had been placed in the hands of Herman Abs, who eventually became Germany's most important postwar banker as head of Deutsche Bank. As I happened to know Abs slightly, the *Economist* asked me to write about the newly emerging banking structure in Germany and the debt settlement. It became a fascinating assignment for me. Abs realized the *Economist* was an ideal vehicle for airing his ideas, and that I was a good conduit for his views. It was a complicated subject and I was not up to understanding it properly without the expert guidance he was more than willing to supply.

According to the Deutsche Bank history (English edition, pages 440 and 441):

The public relations campaign for recentralization of the German
big banks began in the Anglo-American countries in March 1949.

A British editor from the *Economist*, Walter A. Everitt, visited the Western zones, accompanied for part of the trip by the renowned German radio commentator Peter von Zahn. Everitt was gathering material for a major series of articles on the German economy and banking system. E. W. Schmidt from the Rheinisch-Westfälische Bank supplied him with an extensive exposé on the negative effects of bank decentralization. When Schmidt told Abs this, the latter replied: 'Last week I had a three-hour talk late at night with Mr. Everitt about the financial situation in West Germany in general and am now curious to see how the series of articles in the *Economist* will turn out.' Before the article entitled 'The German Banking Reorganization' appeared in the *Economist* on October 29, 1949, Everitt published a similar one entitled 'Germany's Capital Needs' in the London journal *The Banker* in July 1949, which dealt with the weaknesses of the decentralized German banking system. Abs was pleased: 'I noted with interest that the night hours I spent with the author were not wasted.'

In the course of my writing assignments I made friends in the City, especially among the merchant banks. At Schroder's I became friendly with Henry Tiarks and Ashley Ponsonby whom I had known at Oxford. My later business links with Helbert Wagg went back to my having become acquainted with Lionel Fraser and Michael Verey during my journalist years. My best contacts were at Kleinwort's. Cyril Kleinwort helped me write about the German standstill agreements that had hobbled his firm in the 1930s. The managers under him were helpful and often invited me to lunch. The gulf between partners and managers was immense. The Kleinwort partners lunched in a paneled, country house–style dining room, the managers in the damp basement of 20 Fenchurch Street, water condensation dripping from the ceiling and whitewashed walls, food mediocre, wine too plentiful and good but still not making up for the lack of other amenities. The managers did the work but were paid poorly for the privilege of a position at a prestigious house. One, Walter Michaelis, had come to London soon after the First World War. He was the son of a colonel in the Kaiser's army. After the Versailles Treaty he became a trainee at Lincoln Manny Oppenheim, a well-regarded Jewish bank in Frankfurt as a thank you to the colonel for having kept a son Oppenheim safely out of the front lines in the war (he peeled potatoes). The other manager was Leonard Steljes, highly intelligent and the unofficial agent at Kleinwort's of Juan March, the hugely wealthy Spanish financier and Franco friend. For years part of Kleinwort's working capital came from deposits March kept there. Eventually Steljes tired of his second-class status and joined March. Steljes helped me with an *Economist* Intelligence Unit report I wrote on Barcelona Traction, March's public utility holding company. The report had been commissioned by Model Roland and Stone, the New York stockbroking firm I joined in 1954.

At Barings father had introduced me to Leonard Ingrams, an elegant and well-connected "establishment" figure with excellent connections in Central Europe. One of his sons became the founder and editor of *Private Eye*. At Lazards' I got help from their economist, a nice man but of little consequence by the name of Cuthbertson. He complained about the pittance he was paid but dressed elegantly and came to work with a red rose or carnation boutonniere. Crowther himself was so close to Lazards' leading figure, Lord Brand, that there was no room for me, sadly so because Brand and Father used to know each other well. My most helpful friends in the City were at the Prudential. I had become the *Economist* insurance expert, a subject of which I knew even less than the other fields I was meant to cover. I had to compile an annual insurance supplement, which would never have seen the light of day without much help from the "Pru." After I had written it a few times I became quite knowledgeable about the investment policy of the British insurers, which differed radically, as I discovered when I lived in New York, from their American counterparts. British companies invested between a third and two-thirds of their assets in common stocks, which proved immensely beneficial to their policyholders. American life companies, by contrast, were still stuck in the aftermath of the Depression. Until the 1960s they were limited by law to invest in little else other than bonds and mortgages, which left their policyholders unprotected against inflation. The origins of my subsequent business dealings with the Pru, which later became my single most important client, go back to my days on the *Economist*.

Although I worked for a prestigious paper, had a decent income, and an active social life, by 1950 I had become restless in England. I felt it was time to marry, but since Hamburg I had not been really deeply involved with anyone. I did not see England going anywhere, nor myself in England. I had never meant to make the *Economist* my long-term future. The City interested me greatly, but I lacked the imagination to see that only a handful of years later it would regain its international importance and that those who had started work there at the end of the war would shortly be lifted by a rising flood tide. Father had a nice little business, but it was little, and neither of us thought I should join him. On account of mother's Flersheim inheritance I had been to New York in 1948 and had absolutely loved it. To cut a long story short, I made up my mind I'd like to try my luck in the United States. Bridget had married in 1950. A brother's responsibilities toward an unmarried sister had been fulfilled, the more so as I was the one who had introduced her to James Collier. It troubled me that I would be leaving my parents in the lurch. They did not get on particularly well. Mother was still mourning her family. Father was quite dependent on me for companionship. However, I had developed increasingly ambivalent feelings about England. I considered myself English in many respects but did not think I would ever truly belong, was not even sure I really wanted to be totally part of them. Since internment I felt like a rejected lover. It still makes my blood boil when I think of the way in which the British government, under the pretext of the Trading with the Enemy Act, had stolen the Flersheims' assets in England. Before I was demobilized Father and the senior partner of our solicitors, Slaughter and May, took me to the Alien Property Custodian in the hope if they saw one of the heirs, a British officer in uniform, they might change their mind and release the money. It really was obnoxious that the British had us serve as German nationals in their army and were unwilling to naturalize us until 1946. Probably the Pioneer Corps cook whom I happened to meet after the war, still a cook, in a dingy restaurant off Piccadilly was right when he said England was a "country for water fowl, but not for the likes of us."

PART FIVE

WHERE WE WENT:

AMERICA

17

Life in America

A nd thus I sailed for New York on the *Isle de France*. Father urged first class, but the cheapest cabin. "You might meet someone who will offer you a job." I left with introductions that proved more effective than networking in cabin class. I landed in New York on January 2, 1951. A month later I started work at Lehman Brothers. I had looked at several opportunities. Father's friend Henry Sonnenberg offered me work at Hunter-Douglas, where he was making a fortune with a continuous casting process for aluminum venetian blinds. Father had introduced me to Stanley Yassukovich at White Weld, then a leading international Wall Street house. They offered me a job on their foreign trading and arbitrage desk, but I had come to the United States to work in American, not international banking. Father's friend Arthur Guinness had introduced me to Ladenburg Thalmann, whose founders had come from Frankfurt to New York toward the end of the nineteenth century and become wealthy and respected. However, after seeing their office, I realized they were respectable but dead.

Guinness had also given me an introduction to Francis Callery, who had recently moved from Ladenburg to Lehman Brothers to head up their oil department. Callery was a successful Texan, likeable, ruggedly handsome, Anglophile, and willing to assist a "greenhorn" such as myself. He had come to New York on a shoestring and liked my attitude. A Lehman associate who knew Siegmund Warburg checked me out, evidently with a positive response, and they started me at $100 per week plus the assurance of a small Christmas bonus. I was hired for the industrial department, which worked on mergers and underwritings. An Oxford degree and the *Economist* were considered attractive qualifications; an M.B.A. was not yet all-important. From the day I arrived I was given interesting assignments. At the senior partner level I worked for Paul Mazur, through Herman Kahn and Morris Natelson, the partners who ran the industrial department. My colleagues were hardworking, ambitious, mostly Ivy League, friendly and hospitable, with none of the English upper-class dilettante attitude that looks down on the business world. I was glad to have moved away from what I had once wanted to emulate in England, and which probably would have ruined me.

Lehman was a Jewish firm, though with many non-Jewish partners and associates. The non-Jewish mostly had an Ivy League, East Coast background. Still, they were hungry for money and success. They were children of the generation that had lost its money in the 1929 crash. The Jewish element, the Lehman family and their connections aside, were Lower East Side, able, and very hardworking. They took pride in being at Lehman Brothers — the Firm, as it was called.

I became totally focused on work. I had to make a success of it. I had taken a considerable chance uprooting myself from England. I was about to have my thirtieth birthday and as yet had no capital. Going back to England would have been an admission of failure. Luckily it did not come to that. Within a few weeks of working at Lehman I was sent, for instance, to Kalamazoo in Michigan, where Herman Kahn had obtained a mandate from the Sutherland Paper Company for a private placement. I was to do the due diligence and write a private placement memorandum. Rather than fly, I took the New York Central. The train left in the afternoon and traveled along the Hudson River Valley as the sun was going down. In the diner I had a martini, a T-bone steak, and watched the sunset. I could hardly believe my good fortune.

In Kalamazoo I made friends with Lew Sutherland and his son-in-law, an English expatriate who ran the business. Herman Kahn seemed pleased and gave me other assignments. The most challenging was a private placement for what was then called the Burroughs Adding Machine Company. Burroughs had lost its preeminence but still had a well-known name and a fairly strong balance sheet. In Ken Tiffany they had a first-class CFO. My memorandum seemed convincing. Herman Kahn and Tiffany were great salesmen and we got more than twice what we had set out to raise. I think it was $100 million, in those days a lot of money. Decades later when Michael Blumenthal (mis)managed Burroughs (re-named by him, God knows why, Unisys Corp.), I showed him my old memorandum. He claimed it gave him, for the first time, a perspective on the company's origins.

Some of the associates more senior and more experienced than myself used me for analytic and writing work. With Gordon Calder I worked on the Monroe Calculator Company, with Bill Osborn on Litton Industries, and with Frank Manheim on a number of his deals. Frank was brilliant to the point where it verged on insanity, charming yet ruthless. My friend-ship with Arthur Altschul and with Jimmy Leonard, which has lasted to this day, started on the ninth floor at One William Street. The Mazurs were nice to me and had me at their Gracie Square apartment to dinner from time to time. Mazur had an almost fanatical faith in the American economy. He liked to try out some of his theories on me. The Lehman economist Charlie Broderick was used to good effect as a new business tool. I greatly enjoyed his new business dinners at the Gramercy Park Hotel. Charlie Broderick, Brooklyn Irish, took me to my first baseball games at Ebbets Field. I followed his economic theories more readily than his explanations at the ballpark.

Mazur made me part of a team that handled the formation of General Dynamics. Merging the Electric Boat Company with Canadair created it. The deal was in part tax motivated. The Korean War was on. There was an excess profits tax on defense-related profits, which did not apply to orders in Canada. The driving spirit was Jay Hopkins, first head of the new company. A big, handsome, hard-drinking man, Hopkins was a politically well-connected promoter, devoid of interests other than business. He lived in an impersonally furnished hotel apartment at the Pierre, lined with walls of empty bookshelves. It was early days for nuclear energy. Hopkins thought a nuclear angle would play well with the financial community. He considered Electric Boat to have nuclear expertise, though in fact all it did was to install in a submarine a nuclear-proof shield around a generator supplied by Westinghouse. Mazur wanted a sense of what we all thought of General Dynamics as a name for the new company. With trepidation I said it seemed rather promotional, only to be told in no uncertain terms to keep my stuffy thoughts to myself. With my usual lack of imagination I failed to foresee it had the makings of a great corporate logo.

Mazur once took me to a brainstorming session with David Sarnoff, the legendary head of RCA. The General was by then elderly but still brimful of ideas. On this occasion he summoned some of his technical staff and ordained the development of a totally silent air conditioner without moving parts, which he deemed technologically feasible. Obediently but without success they went off to work on the General's latest project.

In my personal life I saw a lot of the Sonnenberg family, especially their daughter. I was fascinated with Henry Sonnenberg's boundless energy and success in business. He was my first exposure to a major self-made success story. In my own family I had met few practicing Jews and while the Sonnenbergs were not particularly devout they celebrated the Jewish holidays and supported Jewish causes. I liked their lifestyle, which was focused on work, family, and horseback riding. Henry Sonnenberg's father had been a horse trader in Germany; hence perhaps the family's love for horses. I learnt to ride without ever taking a lesson. We rode on the gorgeous Rockefeller bridle paths at Pocantico Hills.

Arthur Altschul was still a bachelor. He had frequent parties to which he invited me. At his home I became acquainted with "Our Crowd," the New York Jewish establishment. At a dinner party to eat saddle of venison from a deer I had shot at Andy Sage's family place in the Adirondacks, I met the lady who later became my first wife. It turned out to be a costly deer.

I got to know Father and Mother's New York refugee friends. Most of them had become successful. I knew I should not make it comfortable for myself by accepting their hospitality. Father urged me to "play the English card," join one of the more exclusive country clubs, whether I could afford it or not, and stay away from the émigré crowd. It was well-meant advice, easier said than done, but not really what I wanted. I liked the erstwhile Europeans. My friendship with Henry and Sissy Arnhold goes back to the year I came to New York. Alfred and Katrina Romney were hospitable. As Alfred Rosenfeld he had worked with father at Dreyfus in the early 1920s, so successfully that Willy Dreyfus described him as someone who would one day occupy his office. Rosenfeld, however, was distrustful of the times, moved to Amsterdam in the 1930s, where he started an investment and trading firm with Ernest Gottlieb, another Berlin banking émigré. The two did well financially and left the Netherlands in time to settle in New York. There Rosenfeld changed his name to Romney (it was suggested to Gottlieb that he become Gainsborough). The Romneys had a lovely brownstone on East 78th Street and spent their summers on Martha's Vineyard.

Katrina de Hirsch was his second wife. She was a well-known speech therapist, good-looking, bright, ambitious, and she humanized her husband. With her personality and his financial backing they opened interesting doors for themselves. Katrina's sister Ruth was married to Father's G. Eberstadt and Co. partner Henry Blunden. He, born Heinrich Blumenthal, had been steered to father by Siegmund Warburg. Blunden was pleasant, had some money and quite good connections. He had expected a significant inheritance from his American uncle George Blumenthal, onetime senior partner of Lazard Frères in New York, and a major art collector and benefactor of the Metropolitan Museum. Blumenthal was so successful as a speculator that it was said he could find a gold watch if he reached down a sewage drain. In the 1920s a Venetian palace was dismantled and reassembled as his home on East 70th Street. After his death, the stones were stored in the basement of the Metropolitan Museum and eventually used for the Blumenthal Patio at the Met. Most of Blumenthal's money eluded Blunden. Late in life he remarried and his widow became the heir.

George and Elsie Griesbach as well as their daughter Dorothy became good friends. He traded with South Africa and Japan, played the violin, and was well read; though a successful businessman, he was at heart a scholar. Elsie was a handsome man-eater, disliked for personal reasons by my mother. They had a lovely hospitable weekend home in Pomona, New York.

I regularly saw mother's cousin Fritz Flersheim, a lifelong bachelor, historian, bookworm more than banker, loath to breathe more fresh air than essential for survival, afraid of almost everything yet an inveterate traveler. He returned to places familiar since his Frankfurt childhood, but also traveled to distant lands only the more intrepid see. Whenever he came home from something new he crossed it off his travel list, relieved he would not have to go there again. He had sufficient money to live comfortably, but not so much that he took his comforts for granted. He lived in two rooms at the Hotel Elysée on East 54th Street. He had a small interesting circle of fellow émigré friends. He had a brain that was better at memorizing than evaluating. In the morning he went downtown to H. Cassel and Co., a small, well-to-do stock exchange firm where he had a desk. After lunch he slept and after waking up, read into the night. We dined together once a month, an occasion to go to a decent restaurant. We always went "Dutch." After dinner each put cash on the table. The change was divided fifty-fifty to the last penny. I learnt much from our dinner conversations — history, Frankfurt, the Flersheims.

He was incapable of discarding the printed word. Stacks of the National Geographic from the year he arrived in America lined what little wall space was free of bookshelves. As co-executor of his will I had to dispose of the apartment contents. To my horror as I opened drawers and closets I found them brim full of pornography, not Playboy or the like, but really nasty stuff. I had always assumed sex was no factor in his life. I hope he stopped short of practicing what he read. His collection of high-quality classical pornography was willed to the New York Public Library. For the good of his reputation at the Elysée, where he had lived four decades of a seemingly blameless life — the owners of the hotel planted a forest in his memory in Israel — I had somehow to get the magazines out of his apartment. I stuffed them into garbage bags (after a little browsing) and loaded them in my station wagon. Luckily a garbage truck happened to drive by to relieve me of my compromising cargo. I wonder what all his elderly friends who attended his funeral at Frank Campbell knew of this side of their scholarly friend.

Early in my New York days Flersheim took me to a cocktail party given by Helene von Kuffner for her brother Paul Dreyfus, who was visiting from Basel. That evening I first met (her daughter) Vera, who a dozen years later became my wife and then the mother of George and Michael. We right away liked each other. We went out for several months. She even made a sculpture of my head but got so mad when we broke up that she took the cast and smashed it on my doorstep. It is sad I wasted years until we married. Alice Lubin, whom I did marry in 1953, came from a background not unusual in New York, but not familiar to me. Her father, Isadore Lubin, had modest beginnings in Worcester, Massachusetts. His father, a first-generation immigrant from Eastern Europe, had a clothing store, which he expanded into a regional chain in the 1920s that went under in the Depression. My father-in-law had ambitions and ability. He was an economist who became part of FDR's New Deal "brain trust" in Washington. He was on the left wing of the Democratic Party, so much so that it created absurd problems for him in the McCarthy years. He was deeply patriotic, a believer in the American way of life, honorable, and very likeable. Under Roosevelt he succeeded Frances Perkins as head of the Bureau of Labor Statistics.

After the war he was associated for a while with Leon Henderson, who had been price controller in the war. By the time I knew Henderson, he seemed a little shoddy, overweight, hard pushed for money. "Lube," however, was devoted to him. They tried something together, I forget what, in the movie industry. Lube was not a businessman, but he became an economics professor at Rutgers and joined Averell Harriman when he became governor of New York State, as Harriman's labor commissioner. Alice was a daughter by his first marriage. With his second wife, who died in childbirth, he had another daughter and eventually he married a third time. I failed to grasp the extent to which family turmoil had affected Alice. When we met she worked for the International Ladies Garment Workers Union, and had gone to Bennington, a flaky college. She was talented but with no follow-through, and was socially gregarious. She had a comfortably off but spendthrift mother, a decent but limited stepfather, and a father for whom she was the child of a failed marriage. For me her métier was interesting and she liked my Anglicized background, war record and all that sort of stuff, and the albeit tenuous but promising hold I had established on life in the United States. The day I asked her to marry I knew it was a mistake. My parents were skeptical, though they had never met her and tried to dissuade me from the marriage. They did not come for the wedding, which was performed at the Lotos Club by a judge. We honeymooned in style at the Balmoral Club in Nassau. Near us on the beach I first met Eliot Janeway, who was to become an interesting friend and client. When Eliot saw me reading a history of the Third Reich he told me the marriage of anyone reading that book on his honeymoon would fail.

I could not afford to marry on my Lehman salary and could not expect any substantial increase for several years. I had become acquainted with Leo Model who headed Model Roland and Stone, a young successful member firm of the New York Stock Exchange. We had had indirect contact earlier when I did a study on Barcelona Traction at the *Economist* Intelligence Unit. He knew about Eberstadts and Flersheims from his days as a young broker in Frankfurt. He really wanted me and offered me three times the income I had at Lehman. He thought I could work on the deal ideas he had, and generally be useful. I accepted, which was a huge mistake. I liked him but did not care for the other name bearers in the firm, and made no effort to win them over. Financially it worked out well, but on most counts I was frustrated. It took longer than it should, six years, until I became a partner. It taught me important lessons. It made me a self-starter. I came to comprehend that nothing would be handed to me. If I did not create my own business, no one else would. The *Economist* had a world-class name that opened any door. Lehman Brothers was in the major leagues. Connections came to us. Once out of the mainstream it was hard on Wall Street to get back in. I started work at Model Roland and Stone in 1953. In 1969 I made the transition back to where I thought I belonged and joined Lazard Frères — late in my work life but, miraculously, not *too* late.

Leo Model made a virtue out of necessity. He was a foreigner, a German refugee who brought with him European stock market credibility. There was no reason for an American investor to heed him rather than any number of American stockbrokers on American investments, but he was one of the few who knew foreign securities. Moreover, he was a superb salesman. Americans in the early postwar period were conscious of international risks rather than international opportunities. Blue chips on Wall Street were not expensive, but leading European companies sold at maybe half the American valuations. Exxon, still Standard Oil of New Jersey, sold at seven times earnings and yielded 5 percent, but Royal Dutch shares were valued at under four times their profits and yielded 7 percent. High-quality American consumer goods stocks stood at under ten times earnings, Unilever at only five times. Dupont was valued under ten times earnings but the German chemical industry under five times. Foreign bonds, no matter how creditworthy, were treated with suspicion and yielded two or three times the return on U.S. government or corporate bonds.

European accounting was conservative. Its objective was to minimize taxable profits but to maximize cash flow. Nearly everywhere outside the United States currency controls restricted the international flow of capital, which created dual exchange rates, one for foreign trade, another, usually cheaper than the official rates, for capital transfers and other securities transactions. Circumstances were ideal for profitable international currency and securities arbitrage at which Model's partner Rolf Roland — the two had already been in business together in prewar Amsterdam — excelled. By the time I joined, Model had taken aboard a number of well-connected stockbrokers and investment advisers, Europeans and

Americans, to manage clients' money and to market the firm's expertise to third parties. He had put together a small research department for American stocks, which were marketed to clients in Europe. This two-way traffic was a good business formula. We gave brokerage orders to European banks and brokers in European stocks, which we then sold to our American clients. The European banks reciprocated for the business we gave them with brokerage orders in American securities. Those were the days before negotiated commissions turned brokerage into a cut-throat business.

I missed the corporate finance work at Lehman Brothers but caught on without great difficulty to how to make money for Model Roland and Stone. I started to do business in American stocks with many of the people I had come to know in the City while I wrote for the *Economist*. My first major client in London was the Prudential Assurance Company, Britain's biggest institutional investor. I had originally come to know them when they helped me write the *Economist* annual insurance supplement. When we started business they did not telephone or cable their orders, they did not even send them by airmail. They came by sea mail! I had thought up for them an effective way of investing in the American market without incurring the onerous costs of trading in so-called premium dollars. In common with most European countries Britain was short of foreign exchange and placed severe restrictions on capital transfer abroad. The only funds available were in the premium dollar market, which fluctuated between 15 and 35 percent above the official exchange rate. Each time a foreign security was sold the owner had to surrender 25 percent of the proceeds at the official exchange rate, which made the cost of switching almost prohibitively expensive. I gave the Pru the idea to buy first-class American investment trusts that did their portfolio switching outside the British exchange control and thus saved British holders the premium dollar surrender expenses. This became excellent business for me. The Pru kept the trusts for about twenty years and eventually sold them through me at Lazard Frères when British exchange controls finally had been dismantled and the trusts had served their purpose.

International investing, indeed any investing, was more interesting than it is nowadays. There were demonstrable bargains, in the sense that you paid for a proven record rather than future hopes. I did a report on some leading international, nowadays called multinational, companies. Colgate and National Cash Register, for instance, in those days did not consolidate their overseas assets financially. Their worldwide businesses were carried on the parent company books at one dollar. In the profit and loss account, earnings retained overseas did not appear. Only dividends actually remitted home were shown. With a few notable exceptions the American business community had limited interest or confidence in its overseas empire in the postwar days.

We analyzed the Hoover Vacuum Cleaner Company. The entire business was priced at less than the value of its highly successful British subsidiary. Similar calculations applied to H. J. Heinz. The British, who had been the most active foreigners on Wall Street before the war, were longing to come back, notwithstanding the hurdle of the dollar premium. But they needed really compelling ideas. Our British and continental banking and brokerage clients gave us Wall Street business not only because we had good ideas but, as I said above, to reciprocate for the orders we gave them in their own markets.

Another interesting business was the purchase of American shares from controlling stockholders in the United States who would otherwise have had to register any sales with the SEC. Instead we placed them abroad with a so-called investment letter. This not very onerous document blocked the foreign purchasers for six months before they were free to resell in the American market. I had become friendly with the Hoover family and a colleague of mine with Jack Heinz, and we placed large blocks of their shares in Britain.

I should, of course, have built on the American connections I had begun to make at Lehman Brothers. There was more money to be made in any one of a dozen of the states of the Union than in all of Europe, but notwithstanding my move to America I still had many ties with Britain. My parents lived there and I never ceased feeling I had deserted them. I was liked in the City. They liked to do business with a quasi-Brit on Wall Street who had gone to Oxford and served in their army. I understood their mentality and they trusted me. Model Roland had a London office, in Moorgate. Its main function was to work with Rolf Roland who was one of the important international arbitrageurs on Wall Street. The London staff were traders rather than client oriented. Because of the arbitrage business they knew the merchant banks and the internationally oriented stockbroking community, but at the trading rather than the investment level. Still, they opened doors and those of us on the investment side put the entrée to good use.

I'd travel to Europe, especially to England, numerous times a year, alone, with an analyst, or to present an American corporation we considered a good investment. The first company head I took to London was Joseph Grazier, then the CEO of what was still called American Radiator and Standard Sanitary. We considered it a substantially undervalued stock, selling well below book value, seven times earnings with a 7 percent dividend yield. It was a well-known brand name and a world leader in admittedly not a glamorous industry. For us the presentation was a success. We did substantial business in American Radiator stock but they were sell orders. Perhaps we had overrated the management. Mr. Grazier was not exactly eloquent. (In my experience eloquent, let alone spellbinding, management can be a menace. I feel safer with boring rather than scintillating business people). Perhaps we had overlooked that *pissoirs* lack investor appeal.

Other managements came across more successfully. I took Ken Hannon of Union Carbide and George Lesch of Colgate all over Europe. Neither at that time were exceptionally good companies, but they were safe. I hated to take much risk with clients or my reputation just for the sake of earning a brokerage commission. With this in mind the electric utility companies became one of my favorite industries. I could not go too wrong. I had become friends with Sanford Reis, head of Reis and Chandler, specialists in electric utilities research. Sanford spent most of his time negotiating rate cases on behalf of his utility clients before state regulatory commissions. For him a favorable regulatory climate and conservative accounting were far more important for future profitability than regional economic conditions. Growth in California mattered less to him than the hostile California regulatory commission, whereas the stagnant economy of the Midwest had helpful commissions. One of Sanford's favorites was Potomac Electric, the power company for the District of Columbia. Its pleasant and competent CEO loved to travel with us all over Europe. Power consumption in D.C. grew pari passu with government growth and the regulators allowed the company a good return on assets. Utility stocks paid good dividends, which were important in the days when income, not only capital gains, played a role in a portfolio. On our European travels we always kept a little time aside for sightseeing, especially museums.

Some of my competitors scored more spectacular successes but also suffered spectacular failures. I built my business on personal relationships, which endured over decades. I wanted to avoid making our clients, who were not entrepreneurs but salaried professionals, have to face their boards to explain a disaster bought on the advice of an idiot in a relatively unknown Wall Street firm.

Though I had moved away because I had not wanted to spend the rest of my days being all that English, and by the mid-1960s I had lived more years in the United States than in England, I still felt comfortable in my first adopted country. The names, the lore, the way of doing business in the City, appealed to me. I had more in common with a London stock-broker, a merchant banking director, or an Edinburgh investment man-ager than with my Model Roland colleagues. We had the same education, spent the war in the same army, and had common friends. It was the old conundrum. Leo Model and I were born in the same town in Germany, certainly a bond, though neither of us reveled in our origins. Though he had married the daughter of the chief of the Bad Homburg fire brigade he, unlike the Eberstadts, had stuck to the Jewish religion.

Had I remained in London but turned to work in the City from the *Economist,* I probably would not have met as many of the City hierarchy as I did from a New York base. I did business with the grandees among the stockbrokers, Cazenove, and Rowe and Pitman. If you worked in the latter firm and your surname was Smith, you belonged to one of the found-ing families. I used to look at the Rowe and Pitman internal telephone directory. Conforming with the cricket style of listing amateur players with surnames and initials but professional players with surnames only, the Rowe and Pitman partners' names were shown with initials; staff, no matter how senior, without. An invitation to lunch sent a signal one had been "accepted." Luncheon was an important, lengthy City ritual with good food, good wine, and during the first and main courses good conversation about anything but not about business. Over dessert/cheese, coffee, brandy and cigars, business was finally accomplished. The larger firms had waiters; in the smaller ones junior partners waited on seniors and guests. At the appropriate seasons there was trout, salmon, partridge, pheasant, grouse, venison, fished or shot by a partner. At New Court, the N. M. Rothschild office, there would be a pre-lunch business conversation in the partners' room. Lowering a green blind over the window of the door that led to the adjoining dining room signaled that lunch was about to start. The senior guest would be seated at the head of the table, a seat not occupied by the family since Natty Rothschild's death.

Few of the firms I dealt with survived "Big Bang" — the end of fixed commissions and the innumerable other changes that occurred in the 1970s and 1980s. "Big Bang" brought the end of business based on long friendships, on trust that you would never knowingly make a foolish, let alone dishonest recommendation. It was replaced by an impersonal if perhaps more professional relationship. In New York people moved from one firm to another. In London the character of the City changed. The smaller and even the large partnerships merged, were bought by foreign banks or went out of business. Simon and Coates were taken over after Sidney Simon died. He had been a good friend. He collected me for a morning walk on Constitution Hill from the Hyde Park Hotel in his chauffeur-driven Rolls-Royce. These morning walks, car following, always generated good business. Simon started at Nathan and Roselli, which had been Ricardo's firm. MacAnally Little and Inglejohns, old friends from my time on the *Economist,* disappeared. Sebag, at one time the premier Jewish broking firm with close links to the Montefiore family, was absorbed. Vivian Gray, George Henderson, Laing and Cruickshank, Montague Loebl, Kitcat and Aitken, Vickers da Costa, Simon and Coates, all were friends and clients. With the exception of Cazenove, none have survived.

Kitcat was my closest connection in London, primarily because of my friendship with Nils Taube, a brilliant investor who succeeded Victor Brooks, a leading figure in the City, as senior partner. He eventually sold control of the firm to Jacob Rothschild and joined Jacob as his influential and successful senior money manager.

Nils stood me to good stead as trustee for a modest sum of money I received from Mother, though it was blocked in England. After Father's death in 1963 she settled part of her assets on Bridget and me to avoid the then punitive English death duties. We invested my trust rather successfully. Thanks to a quirk in the law, it was free of tax anywhere.

Among the merchant banks Kleinwort Benson was my main connection. Leo Model had established a close relationship with (Sir) Mark Turner and I knew the firm, in particular Cyril Kleinwort, from my *Economist* times. He introduced me to his partner Ivo Ford and to Bobby Nicolle who invested the family's money. My friend Michael Devas, who joined Kleinwort's when M. Samuel merged with Philip Hill, was one of their senior investment directors, and I developed a good business with the Kleinwort-managed investment trusts. The real fun part, though, was the principal investing with Peter Wake, a brilliant, cantankerous but likeable Kleinwort director. His brother-in-law Mark Turner had brought him into the firm. On an earlier trip to Trinidad it struck me that the island had economic growth potential, somewhat akin to Puerto Rico's, even if on a smaller scale. It had oil and gas. Tar from the famous Pitch Lake was exported for road surfacing. Sugar cane was turned into well-regarded rum. Angostura was exported worldwide.

Trinidad was still quite British colonial and I thought — correctly — that I'd need a good City name as a partner to be accepted. Bobby Henderson, who later became a Kleinwort chairman, had Trinidad connections. We made two reasonably rewarding investments, but money aside, the experience was thoroughly enjoyable and interesting. The first, and smaller, was with Bob Skinner who owned a couple of oil rigs and needed capital to buy more and bigger equipment to drill offshore in the Gulf of Paria, the shallow waters between Trinidad and Venezuela. Bob's father had been Trinidad's financial secretary and he knew the two or three oil and gas companies, which held most of the reserves. Skinner was a powerfully built, hands-on manager who handled a drill as well as any of his riggers. We came to own 45 percent of the company, mainly in the form of a convertible preferred stock. We went on the board together with Ted Roper, senior partner of Hunter Smith and Earle, the leading local firm of chartered accountants. We held the investment for several years. There was a bad spell when onshore drilling slowed down before the offshore activity got under way. We discovered the hard way that few assets become as unsaleable or rust as quickly as an idle rig on a far away humid island. Once business recovered Skinner bought us out. I was a little sorry, but it was right for us and for him.

Our second investment was more substantial. We bought a sizeable minority interest in Canning and Company, the largest food retailer on Trinidad and Jamaica. It also owned the Pepsi-Cola franchises on the two islands. Gordon New, an American who had married into the Canning family, ran the business. He introduced supermarkets on both islands. Named Hi-Lo, they were shiny, spacious, air-conditioned, stocked with high-quality products. But it was a cash business, and though the local population was relatively well off by Caribbean standards, they still tended to be short of money before payday. They were accustomed to being extended credit by the traditional stores, owned predominantly by the Indian merchants who have lived and prospered on Trinidad for generations, people so well described by V. S. Naipaul in A House for Mr. Biswas. Credit mattered more than air conditioning, a next-door location, even if fly-ridden, more than European chocolates. Speaking of chocolate — on a trip at Easter I noticed chocolate Santa Clauses rather than Easter bunnies on the shelves, a warning signal that our merchandise turnover was a little slow. We had taken Red Owl Stores, a successful Minnesota supermarket chain in which Model Roland had an investment, into our group. Its able and likeable president, Erling Rice, improved Canning's efficiency, though at the cost of friction with Gordon New.

Trinidad was well governed. Its standard of living was rising. By Caribbean standards it was prosperous. The population developed a taste for air-conditioned shopping, for chocolate Santas and Easter bunnies.

Hi-Lo sales and profits improved. Eventually the Carling family in Minneapolis, whom Rice had joined, bought us out on quite satisfactory terms.

I have fond memories of Trinidad, Tobago, and Jamaica. When I have a Trinidadian or Jamaican taxi driver in New York I ask them whether they used to shop at Hi-Lo, a question that always makes them friendly. I experienced the tail end of Trinidad's colonial times. Port of Spain was a mixture of old and modern. The architecture and atmosphere reminded me of New Orleans. When I first went, there was only one hotel of tolerable standards, the Queens Park, which was built long before the turn of the century. There was no air conditioning, just cross-ventilation. The bedroom doors were louvered and opened into a wide, central, floor-to-ceiling well. I do not recall an elevator. A sweeping flight of stairs connected the handful of floors.

Usually I combined work with a weekend on Tobago, fifteen minutes away by plane. There was a full fare or cheap flight. The full-fare flight attained an altitude over land from which it could glide to the airport on either island in case of engine failure. Tobago was sugar cane and coconut plantation country with a few pretty guest houses in quiet leafy bays such as Arnos Grove. Much of the land was British-owned. Tobago has become expensive and nowadays is mainly about tourism. The British era is over, and most of the old-time English have gone. The oil and chemical industry has attracted the new colonizers from the United States. BWIA, short for British West Indies Airways (or Britain's Worst Investment Abroad) still flies. The airport has lost in significance. In piston engine days it had been a refueling post for flights to South America.

Early in our married life Vera and I vacationed on Tobago. It was a perfectly pleasant holiday but lacked the special interest of my Anglo-American business days. Traveling on business is so much more interesting than being a tourist. On business trips I have always managed to steal some of my employers' time by going to museums and sightseeing. Actually it was a good investment of their time. It ingratiated me with our local clients when they saw I was interested in their country and culture.

I worked agreeably with Kleinwort's and brought them other ideas. I had made a study of the dental industry and taken a close look at Amalgamated Dental, a British company, the world's leading maker of artificial teeth. Amalgamated had subsidiaries and affiliates all over the world. In the United States it owned over one-third of Dentists Supply Company of York, Pennsylvania, the largest American maker of teeth. Dentsply stock was publicly traded in the over-the-counter market. The value of Amalgamated's Dentsply holding alone exceeded the valuation of Amalgamated capital on the London Stock Exchange. My plan was to purchase a substantial holding in Amalgamated and persuade them to reorganize the company for the benefit of all shareholders. Amalgamated and Dentsply were not particularly well managed. The artificial teeth industry under the leadership of Amalgamated was a cartel, and, like many cartels, was inefficient. The constituent companies, chiefly in Britain, Germany, France, Switzerland, and the United States had combined in the 1920s to fight off a price war with China. The industry was then on the brink of failure. No less than a Royal Commission was appointed in Britain to investigate unfair competition from China. Since dentures were part of the British way of life, there was a good deal of sympathy for the suffering manufacturers — who claimed, naturally, that Chinese teeth were not good enough for British mouths.

Together with Kleinwort's we accumulated a sizeable position in Amalgamated. In a reorganization the shares would be worth at least three times as much as we paid. We needed Kleinwort Benson to negotiate with Amalgamated. A company as sacrosanct as the maker of teeth that were probably sitting in the mouths of the royal family and peerage would hardly deign to deal with New York Jews of German extraction. We found it hard to buy enough stock to lay down the law. The capital was closely held, much of it in the hands of the families that had joined the cartel.

We needed an inside ally. I suspected that Dentsply might be glad to rid themselves of the British, who in effect controlled them, and I befriended Bob Thornton, chairman of Dentsply, a job he held because his wife's family had founded the company. I met with Thornton and his number two, Bob de Trey, and found that, indeed, they would like to rid themselves of the British. In teeth the name de Trey is like the name Cabot in Boston. The de Treys were originally Swiss. They invented the modern enameled tooth. Bob de Trey was British; as it happened, we had both gone to Tonbridge. When he started he worked for the English de Trey company but then moved to York. He was intelligent, likeable but idle. Thornton was intelligent, not likeable, and also idle. We did not get their active support, but the tacit assurance that they would not oppose our plans. They were suspicious of our intentions. They were afraid that if we obtained control of Amalgamated's Dentsply stock we'd become their new taskmasters. We knew we ran the risk that they'd tell Amalgamated of our conversation and that Amalgamated, to get rid of us, would sell their Dentsply stock either to Dentsply or in the open market. We would have preferred they not do so, but if they did, at least it would trigger a major move upward in Amalgamated shares.

They did tell Amalgamated and the shares did rise substantially. We sold our holding but the subsequent reorganization, which we would have liked to handle with Kleinwort's, was instead executed by Lazards', the traditional bankers of Amalgamated. As a consolation prize, Dentsply let us handle the sale of their stock in the United States, which was a sizeable transaction. Eventually Dentsply obtained excellent management. They took over some of Amalgamated's businesses. I should have continued following the stock, and all I have to remind me of this interesting adventure is a handful of molars and the 1922 report of the Royal Commission.

My most interesting and rewarding investment banking activities at Model Roland were with the General Railway Signal Company, a relationship that grew in importance for me once I joined Lazard Frères. When I first came across General Signal, as it later became named, it was controlled by J. H. Whitney and Co., one of the early high-technology venture capitalists. It was run by Nat Owen, a Whitney partner. The Whitneys wanted to sell their interest gradually, without an SEC registration. They considered the company too tame for venture investors. Over time I placed large amounts of the stock in London, Scotland, and on the Continent. The main buyer was the Prudential in London, in part at least because the then head of the investment department was a railway buff with a large-scale model railway in his garden. General Signal was the world leader in railroad and rapid transit signaling equipment. It built, for instance, the rapid transit systems in the District of Columbia and the San Francisco Bay Area. Owen broadened the product lines with a number of high-tech acquisitions, not all successful, but he really had his eye on a major move, to buy New York Airbrake, an asset-rich company which he considered a good fit with the signaling business. He made me privy to his plan and I became aware that someone else was about to step in before Owen was ready for his move. With his tacit approval I started to buy New York Airbrake shares heavily for a few institutional friends of ours, particularly in Boston. I was in a position to virtually assure them of an early profit, either from General Signal or the competition. By "warehousing" the stock for General Signal, Owen was able to do his deal and with it became my good friend. Nowadays this transaction would not be possible.

We were never paid a fee, but at least it was a lucrative investment for us. Owen used White Weld for the tender offer. He was candid. He did not think the Model firm was qualified for the business but he felt bad toward me personally. It made me realize that I really had to find a better platform for myself. At my suggestion he probed whether White Weld might take me into their firm, but that did not work, which was quite lucky because they lost their independence a handful of years later. A prize possession in our New York apartment is the engine room telegraph made by Henschel Corporation of Amesbury, Massachusetts, a New York Airbrake subsidiary. We found it unassembled in an attic. It was the last ever of a pair of mechanical engine room telegraphs — destined for a Liberty ship never launched because the war ended before it was finished. Nat Owen has the matching pair in his home. When I joined Lazard we got most of the General Signal investment banking business. Their pension fund became one of the largest investors in my "Fund of Funds" (Scottish and English) limited partnership, and we continue to look after the Owen family money to this day. We traveled frequently together in Europe on business. General Signal shares came to be held from north of Scotland to Edinburgh, south to London, across the Channel in Amsterdam and Rotterdam, in Frankfurt, and in Switzerland.

Model made the effort to attract younger people into the firm, but the better they were, the shorter their stay. Wall Street paid far better than industry, and we got two bright young men from Owens-Corning-Fiberglass, Tom Keresey, who went on to head a trust company in Palm Beach, a position for which he was tailor-made in the literal sense, and Carl Menges who later made an excellent career at Donaldson Lufkin.

I recruited Alan Blinken, who became a good institutional trader. He, in turn, brought Kenneth Oberman as the firm's widely respected, well-liked, head of research. Oberman eventually moved to Oppenheimer and Alan Blinken joined Wertheim; he became active in the Democratic Party and U.S. ambassador to Belgium. The Blinkens were an interesting family and for many years we were good friends. The father, self-made, of Russian-Jewish origin, became well-to-do reorganizing the Sherry-Netherland Hotel in the Depression. He had a textile machinery business, which during the Cold War he converted into a profitable supplier of tele-type equipment for the military. His Zionist activities opened influential doors for him in Israel and New York. Another son, Donald, became the U.S. ambassador to Hungary. In business he helped join Lionel Pincus with E. M. Warburg. The latter needed the former to become a successful rather than marginal Wall Street firm, and for Pincus in his early days the Warburg name was helpful. Bob Blinken, the most down-to-earth of the brothers, limited himself to business and golf. At Model Roland we raised money for his company, jointly with Kidder Peabody.

The London office was largely my bailiwick. Roland used it for his arbitrage business. I used it to build up the firm's institutional sales in Britain. Alan Corner headed the office. He had worked in the City since the war, solid, reliable, sensible British middle class, but not City establishment. We experimented with two establishment bankers. One turned out a crook, the other too intelligent to make a good stockbroker (a nephew of Sir Oswald Mosley, hardly his fault, but it caused him self-inflicted mental turmoil in a Jewish firm). We found the right person with David Russell, who had the City and stockbroking in his blood. His father was senior partner of George Henderson and Co., London stockbrokers, whose wife's family had founded the firm several generations earlier.

David's older brother Tony, a good friend of mine, brought David to us. Tony trained in our New York office before he joined the Henderson firm but died suddenly, soon after he had married a daughter of Sir Vansittart Bowater, onetime London lord mayor and member of the newsprint and pulp family. David did exceptionally well but went on to Rowe and Pitman as a partner — proof we had lost a first-class man. Leo Model had a predilection for non-Jewish associates, preferably tall and blond. Andre Meyer at Lazard Frères was the same way. He liked them best if they were Kennedy connections.

Over the course of my years at Model Roland, Frits Markus and Herman Stone, two of the founding partners, left to set up their own firm. Markus, a Dutch Jew with good connections and common sense but an inferiority complex, opened many doors for Model, in particular the Rothschild door. In order to have a foothold in the United States, the Paris and London Rothschilds, in combination with Pierson, Heldring and Pierson of the Netherlands, had formed Amsterdam Overseas Corporation, a finance and money management company. It was run by Peter Fleck, an able Dutch-German-Jewish émigré, lay preacher and ultimately ordained Presbyterian minister. Markus knew Fleck through his father-in-law, who had been a partner in Pierson, Heldring and Pierson, but it was Model, a brilliant idea person with great sales skills, who had the talent to fully develop the potential of the Markus connections. Model failed to give Markus what he considered sufficient due for the role he played in the firm, and the wealthier Markus became the more he could afford to resent Model.

Stone's reason for leaving was different. Once Maurice Wertheim's personal assistant at Wertheim and Co., he did not create business but was skilled at processing Model's deals. He was the English linguist in the firm and knew the ways of Wall Street. As Model's English improved and he became less in need of Stone's talents he began to show his disdain for Stone's limitations. Eventually Markus and Stone had had enough and formed a small, not particularly successful firm of their own. After a while Markus linked it with Sandy Gottesman, whom he had first known at

Hallgarten. It became First Manhattan, an outstanding success story that made Markus a very wealthy man.

The Model firm was best known for its work in foreign securities at a time when such work was the specialty of only a handful of houses, such as Burnham and Co., Arnhold and S. Bleichroeder, and New York Hanseatic. Initially the buyers of foreign securities were mainly on the East Coast. With introductions from a Los Angeles friend of Model's I was one of the first to introduce foreign investing to the California market during the 1950s. It was interesting and enjoyable work. I made friends with leading local houses such as Mitchum Jones and Templeton and Hill Richards in Los Angeles, J. Barth and Co., Schwabacher, and Shuman Agnew in San Francisco. They would assemble their sales staffs and I would propagate the merits of leading European companies such as Royal Dutch, Unilever, Siemens, and numerous others. The thesis was simple. European markets were cheaper than Wall Street and European economies were growing faster than the American. The California houses liked over-the-counter ideas, which were more profitable to sell to their customers than listed securities. The European brokers from whom we bought the stocks earned a commission and in return gave Model business on the New York Stock Exchange. The Model firm made a good profit marking up the securities before we sold them to the California houses, which marked them up further before they retailed them to their clients. Fortunately the stocks went up so much in price that even the retail customers made a profit. For me it was a great way to gain insight into the West Coast, something I never could have done as a tourist. Dick Jones and his wife, Cynthia, early Angelenos, remain friends to this day. Through them I became friends with the Bliss family and their beautiful camp on Lake Tahoe where Vera and I vacationed the summer before George was born. I have lost track of Bob and Beth Hill. Al Schwabacher died a long time ago; he was wild and lots of fun. Micky Hellman of J. Barth is also long dead; his family were German-Jewish-California "aristocracy"going back to the last century. His son Warren has become one of the leading San Francisco investment bankers.

In the 1960s I spent a good deal of time building up the British and continental institutional business to which I referred above. I worked well with Tony Wallis and David Russell in London but never got on with Pierre Feuchtwanger who ran the Paris office. It took a while but eventually we developed a good business with the fabled Scottish investment trusts. To begin with I was helped by "Chip" (Manice de Forest) Lockwood. Chip had made his name at Lawrence Marks and Co., at one time a highly regarded research firm, as an expert on stocks such as IBM and Gillette and had a good following in Scotland since his Marks days. On our first trip he made appointments mostly with people I had never met before; the first meeting I had to sell them on myself and on Model Roland. In Edinburgh I came to know Baillie Gifford, Martin Currie, Investors Capital, Ivory and Sime, Scottish Investment Trust, Edinburgh Investment Trust, and others; in Dundee the Alliance Trust; in Aberdeen Paull and Williamson's. Lockwood was initially an asset, but it became apparent that he was rather erratic and eccentric, and no longer up to date on the companies that had made his reputation. It was awkward to leave him aside, but we did not develop a real business in Scotland until we brought other Model research analysts into the picture, in particular my electric utility friend Sanford Reis.

Scotland was enjoyable and profitable work. The trust managers were loyal, agreeable clients once one gained their confidence. I usually stayed at the Caledonian Hotel in Edinburgh, a Victorian-Gothic monstrosity with large, sky-high-ceiling bedrooms, electric fires, cozy beds, lots of blankets, huge bathtubs, drafty corridors, views of the castle, good service, bad food, character, and a long history. "One" stayed at the Caledonian and hosted business luncheons in a private dining room. It obviously mattered to have a good turnout at a lunch and it made me nervous to see the names of competitors in the entrance hall who had a lunch the same day. The Edinburgh financial community was polite and would see to it that someone attended, but it was a blemish if he was a junior analyst and your partner pal lunched with the competition. Much planning and juggling of dates went into an Edinburgh visit. A lunch was insufficient for producing business. The client expected a one-on-one visit in his office, fifteen minutes of generalities, a five-minute postmortem on what had been said the last time, a hauling over the coals if the stock they had bought had failed to do as promised, fifteen minutes for new ideas, five more minutes of nothing much at the end — maybe to make a date in New York or to arrange visits to companies in which they held stock — then a peek on the way out in the waiting room to see a competitor sitting there, a handshake outside on the doorstep . . . and on to the next appointment (if well planned, in Charlotte Square, where the majority had their offices). Sometimes business came right away but generally they would first have a think. Donald Fortune of Investors Mortgage used to say, "If in doubt, do naught."

When I first went to Scotland I'd take the night train from London, breakfast in the dining car with an early edition of the London morning papers which had traveled with us (embargoed in the mail van until 6 A.M.), check in at the hotel and go to the first appointment. To save money we rarely rented a car, let alone a driver, but took the train to Dundee and Aberdeen. Eventually I hired Mr. Haldane, a driver whom I have now used for thirty years, and took the air shuttle rather than the train.

I was especially close to Baillie Gifford and five successive senior partners. The firm, like many in Edinburgh, were originally lawyers — "writers of the signet," as they are called in Scotland. They took up investment management under Carlyle Gifford, a legend in the Scottish investment world to this day. He was still living but had retired when I started to go to Scotland. George Chiene, the first Scot to give me business, succeeded him. We saw eye to eye about investments and the world in general. Chiene was a handsome man, cautious, an incessant pipe smoker. He spoke English with a slight Scottish dialect. In the war he commanded a Scottish infantry battalion. Like Carlyle Gifford he believed in the American economy more than the British. For me the most important partner was Angus Millar.

My divorce in 1961 was upsetting but liberating, and a stimulus in many directions. I had just turned forty, was comfortably off, a bachelor in New York. I rented a small apartment in a new building on 87th Street between

Park and Lexington. I found a housekeeper, a survivor from the *Titanic*. She had previously worked for one Billy Bristol, as in Bristol-Myers, and considered me a comedown. I led an active social life but worked hard and quite successfully, even though I became increasingly conscious that Model Roland had limitations that could not be overcome. I had two girl-friends, one an architect, short and dark with a good figure and lovely eyes, earnest, from a Frankfurt Jewish refugee family. The other was tall and blond, a Californian, divorced, worked on Wall Street, cosmopolitan, gregarious, and a lot of fun. I never seriously considered marrying either, though Father, sight unseen, thought the former would make a good wife. With all the talk about the Eberstadts not wanting a ghetto life, we never strayed that far away from it.

For summer vacations I kept going back to the Engadine. My parents had forever gone to the Waldhaus at Sils Maria, but in the 1950s I had started staying at the Saratz in Pontresina. The same people came each year. My friend Paul Lichtenberg, chairman of Commerzbank, had a house nearby. Lots of Petscheks stayed at the Saratz. Leo Model was at an-other hotel in Pontresina. The Wymans were in St. Moritz. My Schaefer cousins visited. They were good holidays. One summer I climbed Pitz Palu with the Schaefers, my only 4,000-meter mountain and the pinnacle of my alpinist achievements. I rode horseback all over the Engadine, some-times with my Zurich banker friend Nicky Bär, sometimes with a German lady friend who also stayed at the Saratz.

In December of 1963 Father died, at the age of seventy-six. I happened to be in London. I had organized a meeting jointly with Rothschilds for Joe Swidler, head of the Federal Power Commission in Washington. It was a big affair. Father came; I thought he would enjoy seeing me mingle with the City establishment he so much wanted to be part of. He was no longer well. He needed a car and driver and came in slippers. Two days later he died in his sleep. The times had not dealt him an easy hand. He got us out of Germany. He provided Bridget and myself with a good education. Notwithstanding adverse circumstances he earned enough money in England for us to live better than the majority of refugees.

There were even occasions for my father to revisit Germany to renew ties with former business associates. George Behrens, who had escaped detention in the South of France in 1941 to spend the rest of the war in Cuba, had returned to Hamburg, where L. Behrens und Söhne was reactivated by former employees and Henry S. Willink, a friend of George Behrens and member of a prominent old-line Hamburg merchant family. The firm did not go back into banking but became reasonably successful, mainly as food importers. They owned a handful of freighters. In 1955 the company celebrated its 175th anniversary. Father was invited to speak at a black-tie dinner. He went with mixed feelings, but he loved it.

In England my parents had been able to live comfortably. Mother had come into her parents' inheritance. Father received a small pension from Dresdner Bank and a rather more generous restitution pension from the German government. The payments helped, especially because they came in German money in the years when the pound was weak. They were able to travel. Oakwood Court was a spacious, hospitable home. He had his own business, profitable, albeit modest. It had a good name, and he, personally, had a good name. He deserved a more distinguished career. He had longed for it but it was not to be.

Mother was beside herself when he died, was sure she would not survive, but managed well. She lived another thirty years, missed him, spoke of him daily, but became more a person in her own right than she had been in forty-three years of marriage. The funeral was at the Golders Green crematorium. I spoke. There was no clergy. As a baptized Christian Father could have had a priest, but Mother considered a priest as inappropriate as a rabbi. Many attended — London friends and family, our German family, flowers and tributes were sent from his old Hamburg friends. Complimentary words about him waited for me when I came back to New York. By then I had lived twelve years in the United States. New York had become my home. Father was fond of Latin tags, one was "Ubi bene, ibi patria" — your home is where you are doing well. Another of his, explaining baptism, was "Cuius regio, eius religio" — in whose land you live, his religion make your own.

Father left more money than had been apparent. He had carried the money the Flersheims had given Mother to settle his obligations at Behrens as an intramarital debt. It saved taxes on his death but did not solve what to do with G. Eberstadt and Co., of which Mother and he owned 60 percent. The rest of the capital belonged to Charles Warburg and Henry Blunden. Both wanted to continue, to which I had no objections as long as they bought Mother out and changed the name of the firm. I was in the financial business and did not want someone else to have control over our name. Anyhow I was sure Father would have wanted it that way. Warburg and Blunden had the means to buy Mother's holding but wanted to find someone with money and the ability to expand the business. They came up with several ideas, but none made sense. I became embarrassed to be the perpetual naysayer.

They introduced me to a Mr. Gerald Caplan who according to them had made a great deal of money and wanted to establish himself in the City. I took one look, was appalled, but felt I could not go on being an obstacle. If they wanted Caplan, so be it, provided he bought Mother's shares and the firm was renamed. First Caplan quibbled. He'd eventually name the firm London and County Securities, but he wanted to keep the Eberstadt name, at least in parentheses, for the first two years. Fortunately we remained adamant. At first I felt foolish and a little envious. Caplan took the firm public, the share price multiplied manifold, but the business soon got into trouble. London and County Securities became the first of the secondary banking crisis casualties in England, a crisis that seriously damaged the City. To avoid a widespread credit collapse the Bank of England's official "lifeboat" rescued dozens of firms. Caplan escaped criminal prosecution by fleeing to Florida. The episode was a reminder that the one irreplaceable asset is one's name. The end of G. Eberstadt and Co. severed another link with my English life.

Less than a year after Father's death, in October of 1964, I married Vera. The marriage began a fulfilled family life and from it all else stems since. There had been too much discontinuity, even if not all of my making. A German childhood ended with Hitler, followed by an English upbringing, six years of soldiering, and the early postwar years in England. Finally there was a break, wholly of my own making, leading to fifty years in the United States. My pre-American life was not all of my choosing, but what I have done with it since has been my responsibility.

By 1964 I had been divorced for almost three years. I wanted to remarry. I wanted children. I was well off and tiring of late nights and too much social activity. No one I had gone out with seemed quite the right person to marry. That spring I chanced upon Vera, on Madison Avenue outside the new Whitney Museum. We had not seen each other in years, but she was unchanged in looks and manner. We were spontaneously pleased to see each other and had a prolonged cup of coffee at Stark's on Madison. We soon started spending time together. There were happy visits to the pretty apartment of which she was so proud, at the corner of 77th and Lexington, nicer than where I lived on 87th Street.

Though we took each other seriously almost immediately, I stuck to earlier plans to travel that summer to Russia, India, Kashmir, and the Middle East. I had arranged to meet my old Oxford friend Adam Stainton in Delhi. He had organized guides to take us climbing and hiking in Kashmir. India was his territory. After abandoning the bar he spent almost half of each year in the Himalayas as a botanist. He had become an expert on Alpine but particularly Himalayan plants and flowers. He worked with Kew Gardens and was in the fortunate position that he could afford to pay his own expenses. His books became standard works. I could not have had anyone better able to make this Kashmir holiday a highlight of my travel days. We did it in style, with cooks, porters, and ponies. We started on a houseboat in Srinagar. We fished and washed in ice-cold streams. We sat out heavy rains in a small but adequate tent. We were attacked by wild dogs, which probably would have eaten me alive if the experienced Stainton had not kept his cool and warded them off with well-aimed stones. We crossed snowfields and glaciers and made it up easy peaks, but of respectable altitude. After Kashmir I traveled alone through northern India. On my way home I went to Lebanon and Jerusalem. The fleshpots of Beirut felt good after primitive weeks in Kashmir and India.

Vera meanwhile was holidaying in Europe. I came back to New York on September 6. By October 21 we were spending the first night of our honeymoon at the Williamstown Inn. Her mother gave us the best of

weddings in her home. We might have hurried less, but my mother happened to be in New York on a long-planned visit and I very much wanted
her to be at the wedding. She was totally pro-Vera. Vera was her kind of
person — and a niece of Paul Dreyfus, who supposedly was the first person
other than my parents to hold me as a baby in his arms. My niece Caroline
came from London and was one of the bridesmaids. Vera's cousin Tania
Blum came from Paris. My cousin Fritz Flersheim was given a place of
honor; after all, he had introduced us in what Vera calls our first life.
Henry Arnhold was our best man. We found a rabbi in Greenwich Village
who was not put off by the religious blemish of my baptism and officiated
enthusiastically. Vera has never been a collector of people but had a handful of good friends. They all came — and remain good friends to this day.
Christmas 1965, George was born. Michael came fourteen months later.
It is now thirty-six years that we have lived in our present home on Fifth
Avenue.

For another five years after we married I worked at Model Roland, increasingly concerned about the firm's longer-term viability. Eventually my
concerns got to the point where I believed I had to make a change. I heard
that Rainer Gut wanted to leave Lazard, where his responsibilities included
work for which I was well qualified. (He moved back to Switzerland,
where he eventually became chairman of Credit Suisse.) News of this
opening prompted me to telephone Andre Meyer and ask if I might come
to see him. "If you want to talk about joining my firm I can't see you. I
consider Mr. Model a good friend." Pause. "But why don't you come over
anyhow for a talk tomorrow morning?" We had met a few times, but he
did not know me at all well. I suggested he should talk about me to Vera's
Dreyfus family in Basel and to Ben Buttenwieser at Kuhn Loeb. He had
me meet Felix Rohatyn, with whom I had been acquainted for years.
Andre said he could not take someone from a "second-line" firm such as
Model Roland right away as a partner, but if I fit in there would be a partnership in six months. I agreed, even though Andre had the reputation of
changing his opinion about people. Leo Model was enraged. He wor-
shipped the ground Andre Mayer trod. If he could not be a Rothschild he

at least wanted to be another Andre Meyer. Model had brought Lazard deals, some of which I had worked on. He threatened to call Andre, warn him that I was a no-good so-and-so and have me legally restrained from doing business with any Model Roland client. I was told by a former colleague that after thinking about it further he decided it would not be in his interest to have a fight with Andre Mayer over someone as unimportant as myself.

Luckily it worked out at Lazard as promised. I got my partnership, though many a day Andre was to make my life difficult. It made me feel better that I was treated no worse than others, and then there were the redeeming moments — Andre's fascinating business acumen, his enormous warmth and charm when he was not being beastly. My income had risen considerably, which eased the pain of his outbursts. The partners participated in the firm's lucrative private deals through a simple device: Andre debited our firm accounts for what he considered an appropriate amount.

In my daily work I was saddled, as I knew I would be, with the international distribution of Lazard's Eurobond and equity underwritings. I had not realized when I took on the assignment, however, how little placing power the firm had. I have always had ambivalent feelings about underwritings, even if they are at the heart of the investment banking business. The underwriter is paid by his corporate client for selling his securities to institutions or individuals. You dance to the tune of the piper who pays you. Yet shouldn't the banker be on the side of the provider of the money, obtaining for him the most advantageous terms?

My clients had been institutions in Great Britain and on the Continent. I had sold them securities researched for their merit, not because Model Roland was the underwriter. At least at Lazard the dilemma was not about quality, but about pricing and timing. Soon after I joined the firm we did a large convertible bond offering for a newly established mortgage real estate investment trust affiliate of Connecticut General, a blue-chip life insurer. My old Scottish and Continental friends wanted to support me personally, and thanks to them the underwriting became a success. However, all involved failed to understand that the concept was flawed. Connecticut General got their capital, but it took years before our customers made a profit. Underwritings for other Lazard clients such as Pfizer, Owens-Illinois, or Corning Glass generally were more successful.

One Pfizer transaction was perhaps the single most interesting deal in which I was involved. Pfizer wanted to buy a major, privately owned pharmaceutical company in Germany. The selling German family was divided. Half of them were willing to accept and keep Pfizer stock, but the other half would not go along unless we guaranteed them the sale of their Pfizer stock, and remittance of the proceeds in deutschmarks simultaneously with the closing. At a gathering at the Dolder Grand in Zurich, it became up to me to persuade the timid, unsophisticated, suspicious family members that this could and would be done, without — and this was our problem — compromising certain tax aspects of the transaction for Pfizer. The arrangement worked, which gratified me immensely and pleased Pfizer. True to Lazard culture, however, the achievement was barely acknowledged by my colleagues.

My single most disagreeable experience was an initial public offering of Avis, the auto rental company owned by ITT. It looked like a difficult transaction. "We Try Harder" Avis was a poor second after Hertz. Andre, who was only interested in "hot" underwritings, wanted no part of it for his clients. Somehow, we got sufficient commitments to make the deal possible, and suddenly, when it looked as if Avis would after all be "hot," Andre insisted on stock for his clients. This was bad enough, but then it turned "cold" again, and he expected myself and others to find a home for the stock he had released. Andre literally drove me close to tears with his not very veiled threats about how dumb and inefficient we all were and how we should be got rid off. I restored my equanimity that day by lunching by myself at La Grenouille with a book and half a bottle of wine. We began the so-called road show for Avis in London with lunch in one of the Gilbert and Sullivan Rooms at the Savoy the day President Nixon sacked half his cabinet. The Scots in Edinburgh rarely participated in underwritings and had too many questions about the Avis financials. We presented the company as a way of participating in the growth of business and leisure travel. In reality the profits depended largely on the profitability of selling their older car fleets in the secondhand market. In Paris the French Lazard firm invited a high-class audience at the Ritz, but they didn't look like potential investors. Pierre David-Weill hosted a splendid dinner at his home, a footman behind every chair, but even that did not bring in buyers. Somehow the deal got done but after checkered years Avis was eventually taken private again.

Another difficult deal was taking the *Washington Post* public. Katharine Graham, the daughter of Andre Meyer's friend and namesake Eugene Meyer, had been running the paper for only a short time since her husband's death. For years Andre had cultivated Eugene Meyer, a prestigious name in the private and public sector. He owned the *Post*, put together Allied Chemical which became a Lazard client, and had been the first head of the World Bank. Half of Wall Street wanted to take the *Washington Post* public. Andre was determined Lazard should have the deal. He succeeded, but only by overpricing the offering. We left no stone unturned to find purchasers for the stock. It was put into accounts over which we had discretion, something that would not be tolerated nowadays. Inevitably the shares did not do well, and our clients started to sell once the shares had recovered to their purchase price. The buyer for the shares sold by the irritated Lazard clients turned out to be largely the famed Warren Buffett, who has kept the stock ever since. He made a fortune on his holding and became Katharine Graham's business mentor.

Prestige transactions tend to be the least profitable. The money is made on deals best forgotten. Andre Meyer was hungry for prestige and money. In my first years at Lazard the most prestigious business was still to be in the management syndicate for foreign government bond issues and international agencies such as the World Bank, the European Investment Bank, the Coal and Steel Community, and others. The Paris and London Lazard houses had long played a leading role in their financial communities, but the New York firm had not been particularly prominent on Wall Street until Andre Meyer's days. Through sheer willpower and the cultivation of friendships with Jean Monnet, the "father" of the European Common Market, and Eugene Black, head of the World Bank, he obtained for Lazard Frères an important position in these prestigious underwritings, which at one time had been the almost exclusive domain of firms such as Morgan Stanley or First Boston. The traditional houses had big bond departments and a large sales force. Lazard had three or four domestic salespeople, and I was supposed to take care of the international distribution single-handedly. It was a nightmare. Andre Meyer wanted Lazard in the underwriting "tombstones" but was unwilling to incur the expense of a real sales force, let alone an overseas office or providing the capital to carry unsold inventory. When there was a deal I'd fly overnight to London, spend the day in the City, host a lunch at the Savoy, fly the same evening to the Continent, spend three days in four different countries, and fly back to New York, at best modestly successful. Some deals we managed single-handed, some we co-managed, quite often with Goldman Sachs, with whom I worked well.

Gradually I evolved ways of placing our participations, none particularly elegant or profitable. I had friends at the Union Bank of Switzerland and Swiss Bank Corporation. They wanted to be co-managers of the lucrative and prestigious syndicates of Eurobond and equity issues made by American corporations. Lazard had the corporate clients, but they had the placing power. They had discretion over the numbered accounts of their global clientele. By ceding them most of our own quota we gave up a large part of our potential profit but reduced our risk and saved the expense of a proper sales force. Union Bank and Swiss Bank wanted to be in these deals so badly that they gave us sizeable stock exchange business in return for being invited into Lazard syndicates. Nowadays this would no longer work. The European banks established their own connections with American corporations. They have become competitors rather than clients. Instead of giving out their brokerage business, they have their own seats on the New York Stock Exchange.

Work became much more interesting for me when Michel David-Weill took over as head of the New York and Paris houses. Andre Meyer had unsuccessfully tried to replace himself without giving up completely. He appointed Donald Cook, retired chief executive of American Electric Power and former SEC commissioner to head a Lazard management committee, together with Siem Alderwereld, formerly chief financial officer of the World Bank, and Robert Rivel, who came from a senior position at Chase. Michel's arrival was not a minute too soon. The firm was in need of new leadership. He and Felix Rohatyn had known each other since their earliest days in the business and complemented each other. Michel brought in a group of well-connected senior investment bankers from Lehman Brothers. From Morgan Stanley he hired Damon Mezzacappa, who became the partner responsible for building up sales and trading departments. At Oppenheimer Michel found a team that in a handful of years made Lazard a major factor in money management.

With Michel's encouragement I hired a couple of people I had worked with at Model Roland. One became an embarrassment, the other a winner. The headache was Tony Lockhart, a Canadian who had been an early Eurobond expert. I had hoped he would be able to place our Euro underwritings, but he failed to integrate himself into the firm. The other was Alex Zagoreos, with whom I had been good friends at Model Roland where he had become quite senior working closely with Leo Model on the international money management side. At Lazard he and I enjoyed a good deal of autonomy, which had its good sides but also left us betwixt and between departments. The ex-Lehman partners brought new clients, including Halliburton and Transco from the energy industry, whom Alex and I took around Europe.

Gradually I extricated myself more and more from the sales side of the firm. Michel gave me leeway to create some investment vehicles jointly with the Paris and New York houses. They never became very big, but earned good fees for the firm and made good money for the clients. One was the Lazard Capital Growth bond fund, which invested exclusively in zero coupon bonds. It was highly tax efficient in that it converted interest into long-term capital gains. I did rather well with it for myself, and enjoyed the satisfaction of having invented something novel. We also created several multicurrency bond funds, which did quite well. There had never been much love lost between the London and New York firms, but these vehicles, which were managed by the London bond department, brought us closer. The funds suited the tax and investment needs of the Paris firm, which placed a considerable amount with their clientele. I was chairman of the funds and helped raise the capital. Their legal residence was in the Channel Islands. I enjoyed going there a couple of times each year. Other board meetings were in Switzerland, France, Germany, and Britain, where we had directors as well as many of our shareholders.

I take considerable satisfaction from the Scottish and English partnership that Alex and I created. In 1983 my old Edinburgh friend Angus Millar of Baillie Gifford gave me an idea that changed my work life. Instead of selling American securities to the British trusts, he suggested, why don't you form a vehicle to invest in them? The trusts had fallen out of favor in Britain for a variety of reasons, and their shares were selling at discounts of up to 30 percent from the underlying values. For Americans they had tax advantages. They had well-managed portfolios with worldwide diversification and possessed a mystique, which made the concept of investing with the canny Scots very saleable.

Together with Alex I formed "Scottish and English," a limited partnership backed by private and institutional clients in the United States. I don't think either of us ever worked harder or with more determination and enthusiasm. I personally, Vera, and her mother put money into it. Our timing was fortunate. It became a profitable investment. More important, it gave Alex and me work satisfaction. We both were thoroughly enjoying ourselves. We were creating something original. We had come to know the trusts and their managers over the years, the sound and the flaky. We knew enough to avoid a manager who used to attend our institutional luncheons at the Caledonian, dozing during the investment presentation, had more than two glasses of wine, and walked away with a couple of Havanas. There are few geniuses in Charlotte Square (or, for that matter, elsewhere in the investment business), which suited us well. It obviously is not good to be really dumb, but genius as often as not ends with unpleasant surprises. Scottish and English never became enormous in size, but it was solid. Growing too large or too fast would have cost us our flexibility to perform well for our clients. Still, we soon had over $300 million, which in the early 1980s was a respectable sum of money. We lost very few partners over the years but added some new names most years.

Among our earliest backers were the Rockefeller family and several of their charitable endowments, such as Rockefeller University and Colonial Williamsburg. The U.S. Steel and the General Signal pension funds were early major participants. If quality of partners confirms quality of the product, ours was good.

In a sense I had known something about investment trusts since my youth. At Oxford I had become interested in the workings of the City. The books I read avidly were not Hobbes or Locke, whom I had to read for Gilbert Ryle's tutorials, but Truptil's *British Banks*, Geoffrey Crowther's *Money*, Bagehot's *Lombard Street*. The merchant banks, almost mystically enshrined and glorified by Truptil and Bagehot, managed many of the investment trusts. In my undergraduate days I memorized the names of the City grandees who sat on their boards and fantasized I might become one of them. On the *Economist* I analyzed the — sparse — data in their parsimonious annual reports. Father's interest predated my own. In the 1920s he had become an authority on the Anglo-American and especially the Scottish trusts. He was a frequent speaker at German bankers' meetings on the subject. He was attempting to popularize the diversified risk approach of channeling private savings via the stock market into German industry. In the 1920s British and American trusts were also investing in German securities and had become clients of his at Behrens. When we were marketing Scottish and English it was a nice ploy to point out that the subject ran in my blood.

Both in my Model and Lazard days I was friendly with Henry Wallich, who had emigrated to the United States before me and enjoyed a distinguished career. He started with a New York stockbrokerage but did not like it. He first made a name for himself as an international analyst at the Federal Bank of New York. Subsequently he became a respected economics professor at Yale. Under Nixon he joined the Council of Economic Advisers. In his last post he was for over a decade one of the most visible members of the Federal Reserve Board in Washington. He was conservative in every respect — lifestyle, politics, and economics. He was a prolific writer. The enemy for him was inflation. He never forgot the German inflation and its political aftermath. He warned ceaselessly against its dangers, in scholarly journals and the popular press. For years he had a column in *Newsweek*. I envied his fluent pen, although Arthur Burns, who chaired the Federal Reserve Board in Wallich's time, once told me he considered him relatively ineffective because he was too much of a publicist: someone who preferred the academic polemic to the less visible boardroom role of implementing policy.

Henry was always quite friendly to me. For many years I looked after some of his personal investments, which was no easy task. He accepted the unavoidability of owning equities in an inflationary era, but did not believe it was possible to beat the stock market. A couple of times a year he'd invite me to lunch in a private dining room at the Federal Reserve Bank. Nothing remotely to do with Fed policy was ever discussed. Earlier, while he was on the Council of Economic Advisers, we'd lunch more modestly at a restaurant. One time, when I was still a cigar smoker, I brought him two good Havanas from New York, which he loved but considered too expensive to buy. I knew we would split the lunch check because he considered it inappropriate to accept hospitality from the private sector, but it seemed a bit exaggerated to decline my Havana and instead smoke his own cheap cigar. This self-sacrifice was typical of the Prussian side of this son of a Potsdam-worshipping father.

If the 1970s at Lazard were rather a struggle for me, the 1980s became enjoyable years. I had created something that worked and was respected. The firm flourished. Was it Michel David-Weill or the times? Probably a bit of each. My partnership participation became increasingly profitable. There were years in the 1980s in which my income exceeded a million dollars, decidedly more than my $5,000 salary at Lehman Brothers in 1951. I am not a particularly imaginative or daring investor. It took years to discipline myself to run profits but cut losses, to implement the truism that you can never lose more than a hundred percent, but the potential on the upside is infinity. Thanks to Ronald Reagan's bull market our family assets prospered without having to stray from financial terra firma. I had seen enough when young to appreciate that the difference between some money and none is infinitely more important than the difference between some and lots. Once you have a "critical mass" of capital it is not all that difficult to make it into more, given reasonably propitious general conditions. The arithmetic is obvious. If you have a million and make 10 percent, it's an additional hundred thousand. If you have ten thousand, the next 10 percent brings you only to eleven thousand. Yes, but 10 percent of ten million is another million. "God," said Napoleon, "is on the side of the biggest battalions." "The devil," said a Hamburg waterfront business friend of Father's, "shits only on the biggest heaps."

I was fortunate in that Vera and her mother were comfortably off, and very fortunate that neither, unlike some well-to-do New York ladies, was ever a pain in the neck to me about money. Even if I say so myself, they could have done worse than to have me in the family. There is a temptation for Wall Street husbands/sons-in-law to prove their macho-cleverness and in the process to lose the family wealth. Much of Vera's money is in the same securities she had when we married. It turned out to be not the worst way of handling things.

At the end of 1986 I became a limited partner in the firm, which suited me well. I no longer had an obligation to work but was in a position to continue with activities where, seemingly, I was welcome and considered useful. My profit participation was reduced, but it provided a nice addition to my other income. As a limited partner I still was able to participate in Lazard-sponsored investment opportunities on advantageous terms. I kept an office and, blessedly, a secretary. Alex Zagoreos took on the prime responsibility for Scottish and English, and created similar additional vehicles. I became chairman of the Lazard World Trust Fund, which trades on the London Stock Exchange. It is the most visible of our "Fund of Fund" activities. I also joined the advisory board of Corporate Partners, a Lazard-sponsored limited partnership, which takes strategic stakes in public as well as private companies. I continued to keep an eye on the affairs of several Lazard clients, in particular one member of the Engelhard family and my old General Signal friend Nat Owen. In Germany I saw to it that our relationships with a number of banks such as Dresdner Bank were kept alive. I also was able to help the London house to build up its institutional business by introducing them to some of my old friends in Scotland, in London, and on the Continent.

My main reason for visiting England ended with Mother's death in

1992. It was she as much as business that continued to bring me across the Atlantic. Unlike the Eberstadts, she had never had any desire to be baptized. She never went to a synagogue but drew the line at being herself baptized though she went along with it for her children. When she and I spoke of death I said I would find a rabbi for her funeral, which is what I did.

Though my father had appeared to others as the dominant partner in my parents' marriage — and he was — she had managed perfectly well for twenty-eight years of widowhood. Friends would tell her she could be her own worst enemy. She had relied on Father to make most decisions and deferred to his way of living, yet he often told her she was the wiser of the two. If he had short-changed her at times, even in front of others, it was because she short-changed herself. She did not need advice from others half as much as she thought. She would telephone me in New York, one of many similar calls: "Charles Warburg's stepson is getting married. Should I spend fifty or seventy five pounds on the wedding present? Make it seventy-five, Mother. No, Walter, I think fifty is enough. All right, Mother if you think fifty is enough, make it fifty. No, Walter, I will make it seventy-five, if you think so." This was not the end. Ten minutes later she called again, just to say she had decided after all to stick with her idea of fifty pounds. The cost of the phone calls far exceeded the twenty-five pounds she was saving!

In many respects she had been meticulously organized, in others the opposite. She mislaid or lost jewelry, gloves, scarves. She was never on time, and it was never her fault. She often underrated herself, but not so when it came to driving. Miraculously she never had a major accident, which was solely attributable to the considerate and cautious driving habits of the English, but her car rarely had four undamaged fenders.

The tragedy in her life was the concentration camp death of her parents. She never got over it, in part because she blamed herself for not having forced them to leave Holland in 1939 and come to England. She actively supported people suffering from multiple sclerosis because she believed, no doubt correctly, that if her sister had not suffered from MS she might have escaped from Belgium before the country was overrun by the Germans in 1940.

18

From Wall Street
to Main Street

Nothing connected me as much with America, and with my becoming to all intents and purposes American but for citizenship, as our participation in George and Michael's school life, meeting their friends, and the parents of their friends. It began at Park Avenue Christian, their kindergarten. The real involvement started with St. Bernard's School on 98th Street in Manhattan, where they went from first to eighth grade. Both boys were happy there and still consider it the place where they learnt most of what they know. The school goes back to the early years of the last century. It has many links with England, and its founder and many of the teachers have been English. The curriculum might have been taught at an English school. A Shakespeare play was the highlight of each school year.

When we put the boys' names down for the school it was Bill Westgate, the headmaster, who interviewed us, rather than the other way around. We passed muster with him as much as he did with us. Vera became friends with many of the mothers, and is so to this day. I became a trustee of the school when George was in the second grade. I chaired the school endowment investment committee and headed up a capital campaign. The sums were trivial by present-day standards. Still, we raised more than in any previous campaign. Bill Westgate himself was a marvelous fundraiser. He had a handful of loyal friends, generally alumni, who frequently had children or grandchildren of their own at the school. One of the staunchest supporters was Al Gordon, senior partner of Kidder Peabody and a Wall Street icon. He would give money wherever needed, preferably for sports. He held one threat over our heads: my support will cease if you ever install an elevator. Today there is an elevator and the Gordon family's support has not ceased.

The parent body reflected the New York professional and social upper crust. Many of the fathers were New York's Brightest, from the law firms, the financial world, medicine. Mothers having their own careers was not as prevalent as it is nowadays, nor was divorce.

Trustee meetings were interesting and collegial. In my years the major emphasis was on raising faculty salaries, improving and enlarging the physical plant, and student body diversity. It used to be almost impossible to live on a New York private-school teacher's salary, yet the quality of the faculty, to their undying credit, was superb. The young somehow managed, but once they married they had to look elsewhere unless they or their spouses had another income.

We discussed starting a nursery school, but it came about only a quarter of a century later. On my watch we had three headmasters. The time had come for Bill Westgate to retire. He was succeeded by Esty Foster, pleasant and well educated, but after a while he found that teaching was more to his liking than headmastering. I found myself much involved in the search for his successor. Some of the more (perhaps excessively) Anglophiles on the board had their hearts set on the chaplain to the royal family, a traditional Anglican, an amateur theatrical producer of some standing, personable, but, at least so it seemed to some of the board, hopelessly unsuited to be headmaster of a New York private school at the end of the twentieth century. We were firmly convinced a New York parent body such as ours would make mincemeat of the poor man. Still, an offer was extended. Mercifully for him and the school, at the last possible moment his bishop advised him against accepting — for the good of the Church. On short order we then found Amos Booth, English with a French wife, who had been head of the French department at Groton. He was a good head even if he and his wife never felt entirely at ease in New York and in the end they went to run a school in France. After my days Stewart Johnson became and still is St. Bernard's superlative headmaster. Lately, to our great pleasure, our son George has become the school's youngest trustee ever.

As my work obligations at Lazard Frères diminished I had both the inclination and time to increase my involvement in the New School for Social Research. I first became a trustee in the mid-1970s. My interest started with the Graduate Faculty, which had its roots in the University in Exile founded in the 1930s to provide a new start and intellectual home in the United States for émigré scholars from Europe such as Hannah Arendt. My first official function as a trustee happened to be her funeral. It was, fittingly, at the Riverside funeral parlor on Amsterdam Avenue. (The Riverside was the funeral home of choice for Jews not closely affiliated with a synagogue but reluctant to bid this world farewell at Frank E. Campbell's on Madison Avenue where not long ago the Semitic deceased would not have been welcome; not to mention the higher costs of an East Side funeral.) Arendt's close friend Mary McCarthy delivered the eulogy. The New York intellectual world was there. I loved the occasion, the first of over two decades of captivating and enjoyable New School events.

In Manhattan you are nobody without an involvement in non-business activities. Since I never became a Wall Street tycoon I wanted all the more to be "somebody" away from work. The foundations for that could be laid only while I was active in business.

My first substantial commitment to a truly non-business activity came in 1961 when I joined the board of Northside Center for Child Development. Drs. Kenneth and Mamie Phipps Clark founded the Center in 1946 in Manhattan. It provided psychiatric help for minority, mainly black, children from troubled Harlem families and assisted them with reading and writing problems. Kenneth Clark, a prominent black psychologist, had become known and respected for the testimony he submitted in the famous 1954 U.S. Supreme Court desegregation case, *Brown v. Board of Education*, on the effect of prejudice on black children. "To separate them from others of similar age and qualifications solely because of their race," the Court decision read, "generates a feeling of inferiority as to their status in the community that may affect their hearts and minds in a way unlikely ever to be undone."

It does not require much imagination to see why I jumped at the opportunity to help Northside. Though Father had at first adopted a wait-and-see attitude in Germany when Hitler came to power, he decided the time had come to leave with the promulgation of the Nuremberg racial laws in 1935 which formally made Jews outcasts in their country. Aside from the implications for his own career, he and mother concluded it would damage Bridget and me to grow up in a society that officially declared us inferior. As Kenneth Clark argued in *Brown v. Board of Education*, "Segregation, prejudice, and discrimination, and their social concomitants potentially damage the personality of all children."

Many Jews considered themselves natural allies of blacks. The bond was discrimination. I came to learn that blacks empathize with Jews and their history, but only up to a point. Blacks consider present day anti-Semitism trivial compared with the unresolved civil rights and equal opportunity struggles. Jews (or Gentiles) who champion the place of African Americans in our society should not expect gratitude. If I fall in the water and someone pulls me out of the ocean, that person is entitled to expect my gratitude. But should anyone expect gratitude for helping to right wrongs? That it is politic to say thank you is a different matter.

The early money for Northside was largely German-Jewish. It came in particular from Marion Ascoli, a daughter of Julius Rosenwald, founder of Sears Roebuck. She was more than merely a financial supporter. She involved herself in all aspects of Northside and became close to the Clarks. Ascoli, influenced largely by her brother-in-law David Levy, a prominent New York psychoanalyst, believed in orthodox Freudian psychiatry. The Clarks were of the same opinion to begin with and thought that Northside children would benefit from orthodox psychiatric treatment. They wanted to prove that, contrary to white skepticism, psychiatry could help black children just as much as white. In the end, however, after prolonged disagreements the Clarks and Ascoli (and others she had brought on the board or staff of Northside) parted company. The issues had become twofold. The Clarks concluded that given the economic and family misery in Harlem, Northside's children would benefit more from social workers with therapeutic skills than from orthodox Freudian doctors. Ascoli's German-Jewish refugee husband failed to comprehend the dynamics of Harlem. The other issue was over control. Ascoli had a powerful personality and expected the recipients of her philanthropy to dance to the tune of the piper that paid them. In any event, she resigned together with other early supporters, though her daughter-in-law Joanne Stern remains a board member to this day.

Howard Sloan succeeded Ascoli as Northside's president. Sloan, a friend of mine, recruited me. The Clarks gradually replaced the Rosenwald money with smaller amounts from a wider circle. Most important, they secured support from New York City and other public sources, in particular the New York State department of mental hygiene. Northside remained a nongovernment agency even though 90 percent of the budget was publicly funded and only 10 percent raised privately. Jim Dumpson, who had Harlem roots, replaced Howard Sloan in 1960. I became treasurer. Dumpson had to resign as president when he was appointed New York City Commissioner of Human Resources. He stayed on the board and I became president jointly with Robert Carter, a prominent New York attorney and later a judge on the Southern District Federal court. As a young lawyer Carter had been on the NAACP staff and played a leading role in the *Brown v. Board of Education* case. For me it was a wonderful opportunity to make friends with the Clarks, Carter, Dumpson, and others from the early days of the civil rights movement. They accepted me. I tried to be useful and was devoid of personal ambitions or political agenda. Mamie Clark believed other Northside activities were secondary to helping children. I felt the same way.

I continue to support Northside financially but no longer attend many meetings. At the 1997 annual dinner I was the main speaker and was "honored" together with Wynton Marsalis. It is not difficult to speak reasonably fluently if one means what one says. I like the photo taken of me that evening with Marsalis. It goes with an earlier one of me with Jim Dumpson and Muhammad Ali — agreeable reminders of interesting moments. These occasions, even if thinly disguised fund-raisers, are pleasing to the ego.

Northside could hardly have been more of an eye-opener for me, but the board meetings did not give me the scope for the involvement I wanted in organizations with which I was associated. I would have liked to be more part of day-to-day operations, but Mamie Clark kept details to herself. The running of Northside — struggling with money, keeping up with her other boards such as the Museum of Modern Art, with Kenneth's life — left little time for cultivating the board. I could not blame her. Few board members gave significant money. While well intentioned, not many made an important contribution by virtue of their name, expertise, or connections. To be on the Northside board was a labor of love. Compared with museums or hospitals, it offered little social cachet or business networking, though I would not have got the Seagram pension fund for Lazard had I not become friends at Northside with Jack Yogman, the company's then chief financial officer.

One of the more interesting responsibilities of being a board member is to recruit others. I was quite successful at getting good people for Northside. Among others I found Susan Patricoff, who for many years has been the most effective president an organization could ask for.

Mamie Clark retired in 1979. She died of cancer in 1982. It is difficult anywhere to find the right successor to the founder. There were a couple of missteps before Mamie's daughter Kate Harris took over. She had never run an organization but did well, in part because everyone was on her side and wanted her to be successful. Kate and I enjoyed working together. She stepped down to move with her husband to Hong Kong, where he heads the Far Eastern business of Philip Morris. Since Kate's departure the center has been run by Dr. Thelma Dye, a longtime staff member. She was Kate's and Kenneth's choice, is doing very well, and has stabilized Northside's finances.

I wanted to do more than Northside, and two interesting opportunities came my way. I joined the board of the American Council on Germany and soon became its treasurer. The council was founded to foster relations between the United States and the Federal Republic. Elizabeth Midgeley, wife of my old London friend and erstwhile *Economist* colleague John Midgeley, who meanwhile had become the paper's Washington correspondent, brought me on. Elizabeth had been Walter Lippmann's assistant and through her first husband, Tom Farmer, had German connections.

The American Council was a way to continue what I had started in Hamburg after the war. Even then it had seemed to me neither just nor wise, however understandable, to reject anything to do with Germany. Be that as it may, I have had an interesting time with the American Council. It has a well-connected board. It provides a platform in the United States for German politicians and can open almost any door for Americans over there. My early years at the Council during Arthur Burns's tenure as U.S. ambassador in Bonn were particularly interesting. After his death the American Council initiated an annual Arthur Burns memorial lecture. I funded the first, at which Paul Volcker was the speaker.

In my time as treasurer the Council's endowment increased from one million dollars to just over ten million. I credit this quite remarkable growth to three factors: the fund-raising and management skills of Carroll Brown, the Council's effective and popular president, and to kindly treatment by Messrs Dow and Jones. I oversaw our investments together with the Fiduciary Trust Company. I never allowed myself to be carried away by a roaring stock market, but made sure the portfolio had plenty of (short-term!) bonds and a safe income.

My primary interest, though, was and is the New School for Social Research, now named New School University. It started for me in Central Park on my regular morning walk with my friend Roy Neuberger, the art collector and founder of Neuberger and Berman. "Walter, I have been too long on the board of the New School," said Roy. "It's time to get off. I told them to put you on. Think about it." It did not take me long to conclude I was interested. I knew of the New School as a pioneer of adult education in Greenwich Village. I had often participated in its annual Wall Street conference, an interesting and enjoyable way of spending a winter Saturday, but was one of the rare New Yorkers who had never taken a class. I was well aware of the Graduate Faculty composed of refugee scholars from Hitler. Household names in their home countries, especially Germany and Austria, they had created a faculty of brilliant scholars.

In my early years the New School was smaller and less structured than it is now. I was interviewed by Jack Everett, the president. We found we had common interests and took a liking to each other. He understood that the erstwhile University in Exile would be of special interest to me. I liked its scholarly links with pre- and post-Nazi Germany, and the renowned economics department in which my good friend Robert Heilbroner, author of the famed *Worldly Philosophers*, was the star professor. Dorothy Hirshon interviewed me on behalf of the board nominating committee. A few weeks after our Central Park conversation I replaced Roy Neuberger, and ever since the New School has been a major commitment for me, financially and time-wise. I had no obvious links to other organizations that might have interested me, such as a museum or an Ivy League university. The money I was in a position to give would not have given me much of a voice at the Metropolitan Museum, but at the New School it was meaningful. We were a New York institution. The board and visiting committee members were New Yorkers. We met constantly — breakfasts, luncheons, dinners — unlike the typical college board, which consists largely of far-flung alumni who meet just a few times each year.

Jack Everett was an imaginative academic entrepreneur and a good if somewhat ad hoc fund-raiser. The board under him was a bit of a hodge-podge — in fact, everything was. He did not sufficiently go after the board as a whole for money, but cultivated a few families, especially Albert and Vera List and Jacob Kaplan. Money had not yet become quite the crucial factor it is today. The adult division was profitable. Its surplus financed the deficit of the Graduate Faculty. Under Everett the New School took over the Parsons School of Design which, notwithstanding its illustrious history, had fallen on hard times and was on the verge of closing down. Once in the New School fold it soon flourished again under the brilliant leadership of David Levy, who later became the highly succesful president of the Corcoran Gallery in Washington.

By the time I came to know Everett his tenure was coming to its close. His health was not the best and was beginning to affect his energy level. A search committee headed by Dorothy Hirshon found Jonathan Fanton, whose five-year terms were renewed three times: no better tribute could be paid to a successful academic leader. He had previously been at Yale under the great Kingman Brewster and then at the University of Chicago. He set out to fashion the New School more in the image of the degree-granting universities he was used to, rather than content himself with building on what he found. He had been a senior member of large hier-archies and probably saw no imminent opening there in a top slot for himself.

He took the New School post because he wanted to be boss some-where worthwhile. The New School was not Yale or Chicago, but an in-teresting institution with sufficient standing to make him feel it was not a comedown from the major league. Yet, would he really be satisfied presid-ing over a not-for-degree adult division offering courses on everything from the trivial to the substantive? Preside over a design school renowned for its fashion shows more than the arts?

In fact, the New School recognized the need for growth and change, and the mandate for the new president was to be enterprising. Jonathan proved a great choice. He had ambition, energy, ability, and was enor-mously likeable. From his first board meeting on he set out, successfully, to make the trustees his partners. The most urgent need was to rebuild the Graduate Faculty. The University in Exile faculty was the Past. The Future was uncertain. With a few important exceptions the faculty had not been rejuvenated all that successfully. Just before Fanton's arrival an en-abling committee, convened to revive the Graduate Faculty, had engaged Ira Katznelson, a prominent University of Chicago political scientist, as the new dean. Fanton and Katznelson had been friends in Chicago and made it their first priority to rebuild the faculty. This was not only worth-while per se, but it was the core that lent academic credibility to the whole of the New School. I agreed to chair the visiting committee and to head a $20 million capital campaign, the first in the New School's history. Ira Katznelson and I enjoyed working together. He had the substance, style, and looks to recruit a new faculty almost from scratch. We could not afford many appointments: each had to count and, ideally, be a Toscanini in his or her field.

It needs a good student body to attract a good faculty, and a good faculty to attract good students. The goal is academic success, but it can take a decade to know whether anything sufficiently outstanding has been produced to attract still higher quality. It is a slow process, testing faith and patience. As everywhere, success breeds success. At Harvard the pipeline at any given moment is full of the best, at the Graduate Faculty it first had to be filled. As I write I question that the Graduate Faculty is making it. Many professors enlisted by Katznelson have left. First-class replacements are hard to find. The financial situation is precarious. Subsidies from the profitable New School divisions such as Parsons have been reduced. As a partial solution faculty members will take on some of the teaching load at Lang College, the undergraduate school, which will benefit from — much needed — improved teaching. I have a vested interest in the Graduate Faculty's survival. I want the spirit of the University in Exile kept alive. They had been fellow refugees. I understood what they had given up, understood their struggle to reestablish their lives and careers. I put as much effort into the Graduate Faculty endowment campaign as I did into my business, solicited friends who gave generously, and personally endowed a professorship and scholarships. I'd be sorry if the one time something was named after me were to end a disappointment. However, I should not complain. It was all enormously interesting and enjoyable.

In business I missed that I never had significant management responsibilities. I suppose I could have started a firm of my own, but I could not get myself to give up the reflected glory of an association with the *Economist*, Lehman, or Lazard. It is in the nature of the professions, be they the law, finance, or medicine, that most practitioners are doers rather than managers. The New School board and its numerous committees gave me the opportunity to be part of the planning, decision-making, hiring, and criticizing processes. Jonathan Fanton was good at involving the trustees.

Perhaps it was also a bit devious — seek their advice, and thus make it more palatable to seek their money.

I joined the board when Henry Loeb was chairman, a good human being and a first-class chair. His name carried weight in New York. His family owned Carl M. Loeb Rhoades and Co., a well-regarded, wealthy investment banking firm. The Loebs were quintessential German-Jewish establishment. Their father, Carl, had come from Germany before the first war as a young man. He had become wealthy in the metal trade and finance. Henry Loeb's older brother John married a Lehman and became the ambitious successful head of the firm founded by his father. At the New School, Henry operated outside his brother's shadow, and he thrived on it. Before Henry arrived the board, with one or two notable exceptions, had never been challenged to give meaningful money. Persistently but politely, he made trustee giving by those who could a condition of board membership. He was able to set an example. Over the years he gave many millions of dollars.

For a short time he was succeeded by Dorothy Hirshon. She had a razor-sharp mind (and tongue), great taste in the arts, was politically a liberal, almost intuitively on the "right" side of issues that mattered, greatly admired and loved by Jonathan Fanton and the board. She had been married to William Paley, the founder of CBS, who left her comfortable but not rich when they divorced. Over the years she gave the preponderance of her money to the New School. My friend Malcolm Smith, whom I had recruited for the board, succeeded Dorothy. I would have liked to succeed Dorothy, but the board thought otherwise. I chose to stay on. Jonathan was skillful in maintaining his friendship with me. I accepted the rather meaningless title of first vice chairman but carved out an interesting and satisfying role for myself. I greatly enjoyed chairing the Graduate Faculty visiting committee. I also recruited some of our best board members, mostly personal friends, in my capacity as chair of the nominating committee.

Malcolm Smith, conciliatory, even-tempered though quite stubborn, ran good meetings. All people were given their say without allowing a discussion to get out of hand. He said little himself. He was an endlessly diligent chair who actually read the reams of paper that emanated from Jonathan's office. His extraordinary devotion to the New School still did not quite compensate for what he lacked — name recognition, eloquence, charisma, or wealth to attract the prominent in New York to a board that does not carry the prestige of Columbia, NYU, the Opera, or the Metropolitan Museum.

Jonathan and his able, nice wife, Cynthia, entertained almost nightly at their Greenwich Village brownstone on Eleventh Street, the modest official university residence. The evenings were built around a guest of consequence who might have lectured to a broader university audience earlier in the evening, someone from Washington, a foreign visitor of note. The evenings were a thank you for trustees and other donors, a way to attract prospective supporters. They were lively, the conversation stimulating. The guests were a mixture. The less interesting tended to be the better fund-raising prospects. Food and drink were good, though on the plentiful side. For the Fantons it was a tough way to make a "living." Jonathan was a great impresario. He managed to be spontaneous and upbeat night after night. The evenings provided his interface with a constituency the New School needed to cultivate.

19

Martha's Vineyard

Even if at times it hardly seemed so, there was more to life than the New School! Martha's Vineyard became far more than a summer home. We first went in 1966 when George was eighteen months and Michael four months old. Almost everything that has happened to us there turned out well. We were fortunate to be able to rent the same lovely house, heaven on earth in our mind, for a dozen or so summers. It belonged to John Tuthill, "Tut," the well-to-do, ubiquitous, talented doctor at Phillips Exeter Academy where our sons later went to boarding school. The Tuthill property was on Eel Pond, an ocean inlet on the outskirts of Edgartown. We treated the house and garden as if it had it been our own.

After a few summers we knew Edgartown was the right place for us and looked for land to build a house. It came our way — on the same Eel Pond we had come to love. We started with a one-acre lot, barely big enough for the house that Bruce Fowle, our architect, designed in 1977. He "moonlighted" while working at Edward E. Barnes on the IBM building at the corner of Fifty-seventh Street and Madison Avenue in New York. Today he is one of the country's leading architects. We gradually acquired neighboring properties and now own eighteen acres of fields, woods, and a beautiful salt marsh. I derived much satisfaction from helping to clear the land from pernicious vines and bittersweet. However colorful in the fall, it obliterates and strangles fields and trees. We gained the upper hand, but there is no permanent victory.

After a couple of summers we joined the yacht club. I took up one-design racing. In Andre Meyer's days, really not until I became a limited partner at Lazard, it was difficult to have a long summer vacation on top of other time off here and there, such as Sun Valley over Christmas and New Year's or travel in the boys' spring vacation. The Vineyard is not all that accessible from New York, too far for a satisfying two-day weekend. Instead of a longer vacation I took most Fridays plus bits and pieces here and there. Mondays at 6 A.M. "Air-Eberstadt" took off, a charter I put together for a few of us who worked in New York. I was in Rockefeller Center before 8 A.M. after coffee, juice, and two poached eggs for $1.25 at a counter on 49th Street. (The price increased eventually to $1.65.)

Edgartown and Martha's Vineyard, more than anything else, "bonded" us with America. We made friends with "summer people" and year-round islanders. Vera came to know everybody and was known by everybody. For years she immersed herself in the summer lives of the Edgartown Yacht Club children. Her organizational and leadership skills are a legend in the club. Her committee reports at the annual meeting were eagerly awaited, loudly acclaimed, and charmed the membership.

Edgartown at one time had the reputation of being stuffy. If it was, it has changed since we came in the early 1960s. Our own background never seemed an issue. I have served two terms as a trustee of the club and one term as treasurer. Still, Edgartown is more conventional than Chilmark. At cocktail parties the women are elegant and the men wear ties and jackets. The Race Committee dress code is out of the Royal Yacht Squadron at Cowes or the New York Yacht Club. We rise to stand when the American flag is lowered, preceded by a cannon blast, at sunset.

Edgartown homes are in town or on the harbor, have gardens but little land. Many have been in the same families for generations. The owners work in the law, in — not overly prosperous — family businesses or have some money of their own. They are commercial rather than invest- ment bankers. They are third- or fourth-generation Princetonians more than Harvard men. Quite often there may have been more money in their grandparents' days. They are Republicans, though not all. They go to church, though not all. My generation served in the war, the navy more than the army. They are understated and there is usually more to them than meets the eye. They are the America I would not have met without our decades of Edgartown summers. They are no more the "real" America than cosmopolitan New York, but they are the foundation to which the diverse elements that make up this wonderful country are grafted.

Up-island Chilmark in the summer is different. They teach at Har- vard, are journalists on the *New York Times* or the *Washington Post*, write books, collect trendy art. They make a point of not wearing a necktie at their (innumerable) cocktail parties but dangle gold chains over hairy suntanned chests. They are old-fashioned liberal Democrats, champions of the underdog, champions of "socially responsible" causes, none of which inhibits them from championing the stock market. They have summer homes from the simplest in the stifling midst of mosquito-infested jungly woods to gorgeous houses on dozens of acres near the up-island beaches or on hilltops overlooking the ocean. In recent years more and more have come from New York and work on Wall Street.

Edgartown or Chilmark? We, in the spirit in which I had been raised, and in which Vera in her Viennese childhood had grown up, chose what Edgartown stood for. We are quite content without some of the more extreme up-island fiddle-faddle. Chilmark rehashes the *New York Times* op-eds, Edgartown the afternoon's sailing.

I became quite passionate and reasonably skillful at one-design racing. We started with a sunfish and a Boston Whaler on Eel Pond. George named it *Macaroni*, as in "Yankee Doodle Dandy." Thirty years later we still have the same boat. The year we joined the Yacht Club I bought a Rhodes 19, which we named *Yellow Bird* after the yellow birds of the long defunct Northeast Airlines, which serviced the Cape Cod region. When

I started I knew nothing about racing but befriended experienced club members, especially the Hufstader and Warner families, who took pity on me and taught me the essentials. Before too long I began to do better and won some silver.

After a couple of seasons I sold *Yellow Bird* and at the urging of my friend Jim Cannon bought, secondhand, a Shields, sail #52, a 30-foot sloop in an entirely different league from the Rhodes. It was much more boat, with graceful classic lines. It needed myself and three others, preferably strong and knowledgeable, to race. The class had been designed by Cornelius Shields with a fiberglass hull to replace the wooden Internationals that had dominated Long Island Sound racing in the interwar years. In the first seasons there were only three of us on the line — Hugh Bullock who usually won, trailed distantly by Jim Cannon and myself. The fleet grew to twelve boats and I gradually got better. I found myself more often than not among the first three or four to cross the finish line and even managed the occasional first place.

My most regular crew member was Bob Hayman, a good sailor and good companion. Alas he died young. Bob could have done anything well, anywhere. His love was the sea, especially fishing and sailing. He made a good living as a shrimp broker. He bought shrimps all over the world and sold them to supermarkets, food wholesalers, and caterers. We raced together in Edgartown and in Shields regattas in Newport, Marblehead, Marion, Patanaram, and on Long Island Sound. Newport was the grandest; Marion, which is on Buzzards Bay, the most intimate. We'd encounter every kind of weather. The wind and seas off Newport and on Buzzards Bay could be quite a challenge. In the regional regattas I managed to stay in the middle of the fleet, but in the nationals I never got anywhere. In a couple of the off-island regattas I crewed for Jim Cannon. Sailing was his great love. Even if we came home empty-handed we had a good time and made many enduring friendships. Shields sailors are from an America I relished being part of, and never would have come to know without sailing. I seem to end up as treasurer of organizations in which I am active, and so it became with the national Shields Association. They may have been fast sailors, but they were slow payers.

If there was one occasion that should have opened the eyes of the business world to my organizational and people skills and eminently qualified me to run Lazard Frères, General Motors, or, at a pinch, both together, being in charge of the Shields Nationals Regatta in Edgartown in 1987 was the test. It needed foresight, planning two years ahead; the instinct to sense pitfalls before falling in the pit; the ability to motivate, persuade others they were wrong and I was right, and to accept when they were right and I was wrong, to threaten, flatter, cajole, give credit, take blame, be flexible, stubborn, stay cool, stick to a plan, change it. And to be lucky with the weather. At my nationals, we had the right weather and winds. I even wangled a berth for myself on a good visiting boat and ended up actively participating in what we had put together over a couple of years.

Most of the winning Edgartown boats were raced by the young. They never begrudged me the occasional triumph — in fact, could not have been nicer or better sports about it. Among the best were Robert Whittemore, son of our Edgartown friend Susie Whittemore and the chaplain of the Seaman's Institute in downtown Manhattan (where I sometimes lunched for 40 cents when I first came to New York; the only lunch still cheaper was gate-crashing the ITT cafeteria on Broad Street), and the grandchildren of Cornelius Shields. Hugh Bullock, an American grandee, continued to do well until he withdrew from racing in his high eighties on account of failing eyesight. In all the years we raced in the same fleet, no matter what, he never once protested a competitor. In business he ran, equally gentlemanly, the Calvin Bullock mutual funds founded by his father. He was an ardent Anglophile, chaired the Pilgrims, was awarded the KBE (Knight of the British Empire), and had a fascinating collection of Napoleonic memorabilia. He and his wife were very nice to Vera and me; in New York they lived next door to us.

Summer weekend moods mirrored racing scores. I took my results seriously. If I sailed badly I could count on George and Michael to uphold the family reputation. For several summers George was a sailing instructor at the yacht club and later he was on the Harvard sailing team. Michael became the "boat boy" on *Madcap*, owned by Charlie Leighton, commodore of the New York Yacht Club and one of the most successful off-shore racers on the East Coast. For several summers Michael operated one of the Edgartown harbor launches, a responsible and lucrative summer job, especially with the tips during a New York Yacht Club cruise layover. The boys did well at sailing and tennis. The Edgartown house and the New York apartment are full of their trophies, with enough silver of my own not to feel left out. I now sail *Persephone II*, a sixteen-foot Herreshoff, gaff-rigged with brown sails, one of his most graceful classic designs. In 1999 I had my best racing season. In my Herreshoff I won the Club championship, with my friend Carol Berwind as crew. Twenty years earlier Michael had won the same cup.

Father was seventy-six when he died. I am conscious of my good fortune. At the age of eighty I enjoy racing and the comradeship that goes with it as much as ever. I seem to do better in heavy air than light breezes and don't mind getting wet. The nice and skilled Carol, who has now sailed with me to my advantage and pleasure for many summers, would probably point out that she sits forward and gets a lot wetter.

The other cocktail party conversation staple besides sailing dealt with travel dramas — fog, canceled or delayed flights, last-minute switches from planes to ferries, don't-spare-the-horses cab rides from Hyannis to Woods Hole, martinis and chowder at the Land Fall bar before catching the last boat. Summer was about shared adventures, parties, old friends, new friends, smiles and hugs from children and wives when the dads finally got there. It was about hot plane rides and welcoming cool evening breezes.

For Vera, Edgartown healed a childhood destroyed at the age of ten with the death of her father; being hounded out of Austria with a newly widowed mother by Hitler weeks later; a lonely interlude with her Swiss grandparents; mother and daughter on their own in wartime England en route for America; growing up in wartime New York in an alien land. Vassar, Columbia, and the Art Students League made her American. Two American-born sons, their friends, our friendship with their parents and teachers, cemented the links. It was the more than thirty years on the Vineyard, though, which made us truly part of this wonderful country.

With Arthur Burns, American Ambassador to Germany and
ex-chairman of the Federal Reserve Bank, and John J. "Jack" McCloy,
Chairman of the American Council on Germany and
post-war U.S. High Commissioner in Germany.

With Alan Greenspan, Chairman of the Federal Reserve Bank, at an Arthur
Burns memorial lecture sponsored by the American Council on Germany.

2 Are Attendants Of Vera Kuffner At Her Wedding

Sculptor Is Married to Walter A. Eberstadt, a Stockbroker

Teri-Larkin

Mrs. Walter A. Eberstadt, formerly Vera Kuffner.

Miss Vera Kuffner of 150 East 77th Street and Walter A. Eberstadt of 125 East 87th Street were married yesterday afternoon in the home of the bride's mother, Mrs. Ignaz Kuffner, at 49 East 86th Street. Rabbi Charles Davidson of the Village Temple performed the ceremony, and there was a reception at Mrs. Kuffner's home.

The bride is also the daughter of the late Mr. von Kuffner of Vienna. Mr. Eberstadt's parents are Mrs. Georg Eberstadt of London and the late Mr. Eberstadt, who was a banker in London.

The bride wore white silk with a lace veil and carried small sweetheart roses. Miss Caroline Collier, a niece of the bridegroom, and Miss Carol Eaton attended the bride. Henry H. Arnhold was the best man.

Mrs. Eberstadt, a sculptor, studied with Jean Arp and William Zorach. She is a member of the National Arts Club and the Art Students League of New York.

The bride holds an A.B. degree from Vassar College and an M.A. from Columbia University. Her grandparents are the late Mr. and Mrs. Moritz von Kuffner of Vienna and the late Mr. and Mrs. Jules Dreyfus-Brodsky of Basle, Switzerland.

Mr. Eberstadt, a partner of Model, Roland & Co., members of the New York Stock Exchange, was previously married and divorced. He studied at the Gelehrtenschule des Johanneum's in Hamburg, Germany, and graduated from the Tonbridge School in England. He also attended Christ Church of Oxford, graduating with an M.A. degree.

The bridegroom, who served with the British Army from 1940 to 1946, was a major in the Oxfordshire and the Buckinghamshire Light Infantry.

Wedding announcement in the *New York Times*.

Our wedding on October 20, 1964.

Opening of Stephan Blaut Library at Northside Center for Child Development, February 1975. (*Left to right*): Jim Dumpson, Administrator of Human Resources and Commissioner of Social Services 1974–1976; Percy Sutton, Manhattan Borough President; Dr. Mamie Phipps Clark (executive director); WAE (president); and Dr. Kenneth Clark.

With David Dillard, climbing to Bara Pokhari. In the background: Annapurna II (26,042 feet) and Lamjung Hind (22,740 feet).

Deer stalking in the Scottish Highlands, 1997.

Jürg and Klaus Schaefer, and me, on top of Piz Palü, 1962 (Kitty Schaefer is not shown). At the left is Caspar Grass from the famous guiding family with whom I climbed many Engadine peaks.

Camp at Vishenar during a trek in Kashmir 1964,
with my Oxford friend Adam Stainton (*far right*).

George's Harvard graduation, 1989.

Alpha Kai fraternity president Michael Eberstadt, with Vera,
during his Dartmouth graduation, 1989.

Michael at his Dartmouth graduation, 1989.

Vera, George, and Michael in front of Cawdor Castle, 1989
(where Macbeth murdered Duncan).
Our Scottish trip celebrated the Harvard and Dartmouth graduations.

At the helm of Bermuda "40" yacht, *Caroline*, on Penobscot Bay, 1993.

A day off on the Great Wall during the Lazard World Trust Fund board meeting in Hong Kong and China, 1994. *Left to right*: Lazard Paris partner François Voss with his friend Corinne Droit, Vera, and me.

Alex Zagoreos, friend, colleague, and partner for over thirty-five years, at a Lazard World Trust Fund board meeting in Prague, 1995.

Jenny Lake in the Grand Tetons, 1998.
The trip was a seventieth birthday present for Vera from George and Michael.

(*Above*): Our house on Planting Field Way;
(*below*) George and Michael, on edge of Eel Pond, 1999.

The Flower Garden on Martha's Vineyard

Seventieth birthday lunch in our Edgartown garden, 1991.
Left to right: Me, Michael Gellert, Mary Gellert, Henry Arnhold,
Bill von Bredow, and Walter Levy.

(*Foreground*): *Persephone II*, Herreshoff "12" Class, leading at windward mark on a breezy day, 2001, me at the helm with Carol Berwind crewing.

Now that I stay on the Vineyard most of the summer rather than commute back and forth to New York I have become involved with the Martha's Vineyard Preservation Trust. It takes time and money, both of which I give happily. I became president of the trust in 1996 and chairman in 1998.

The trust was started in 1946 for the preservation of historic buildings on the island. The board is a mix of year-round islanders and summer residents. It owns the Old Whaling Church on Main Street in Edgartown, which it acquired for one dollar but spent one million dollars to restore. The last members of a once thriving Methodist congregation still worship there on alternate Sundays. It is used for weddings, funerals, concerts, lectures, town meetings, an overflow courtroom, and the like. The Trust also owns, and restored at great cost, the Dr. Daniel Fisher House, which adjoins the Whaling Church. It is the grandest of the Edgartown homes, dating from the days of whaling prosperity in the middle of the nineteenth century, and is set in beautiful grounds. The Trust has its office in the building, some space is rented out, and the magnificent downstairs rooms are in great demand for weddings and other receptions. Our friend John MacKenty and his family donated the Vincent family's home, the oldest surviving house on the island. It was moved to the Fisher House grounds where it has become a popular tourist attraction. In 1985 the trust bought the Flying Horses in Oak Bluffs, a landmark protected by the National Parks Commission. It is the oldest merry-go-round in America.

In 1994 it purchased and restored Alley's General Store at West Tisbury. The store, which had fallen on hard times, is a landmark building and the oldest retailer on the island. It is now operated by the Wampanoagh Indians, who are the earliest known inhabitants of Martha's Vineyard. To make the lease with the tribal council legally enforceable, the tribe had to abandon its sovereign nation status!

In 1996 the Preservation Trust acquired from the town of West Tisbury the old Agricultural Hall, which was urgently in need of major restoration work. It is a classic handsome building, dating from the middle of the nineteenth century, set in four acres of beautiful open land. The grounds had become too small and the hall too rickety for major events, in particular the annual agricultural fair which was moved to a much larger new building with lots of land. The West Tisbury Town Council sold the site and building to the Preservation Trust for $300,000 on condition the trust would restore it and use it only for purposes considered appropriate by the West Tisbury Town Council.

The immediate challenge was to raise close to three-quarters of a million dollars. While most of the Trust's earlier projects had been partly financed by bank loans, the board agreed to the Agricultural Hall acquisition only on condition none of the money be borrowed. Chris Scott, the trust's executive director, is competent and well liked. He and I enjoyed working together. Between us we were able to raise the money. He got $100,000 from the state of Massachusetts. It seemed incumbent upon me to make a major personal gift. The times were good and I was happy to do so, which in turn put me in a position to solicit friends and others on the island. We raised what was needed. It is again the Grange Hall, its original name. Other than in midwinter it is in almost constant use — for the Farmers Market, movies, weddings, art shows, auctions, dances, lectures. It has been back in business for only two years but is already paying its way.

I count myself fortunate to have linked with the Preservation Trust. It has been my most "American" involvement, even if once in a while I fantasize it is England's National Trust, with a knighthood in store at the end of the day.

20

Winding Down and Sorting Out

It is high time for me to sort out the role of religion in my life. Is man God-made, or is God man-made? I don't consider it sacrilegious to believe the latter. What greater compliment can we pay to the nonexistent God than that our need for Him is so great that we had to invent Him. The Greeks and the Romans, the Egyptians and primitive tribes, had gods and goddesses for every facet of life and natural phenomena. The monotheistic creeds — Islam, Judaism, and Christianity, still need man-lookalike images to help us believe there is a God. "And He sitteth on the right hand of God, from where he shall come to judge the quick and the dead." If it needs for Christ to be deemed the Son of God to give greater plausibility to God the Father on whom we count to give meaning to Life, so be it. If it needs the Scriptures, the Old and the New Testament, the Torah and the Koran, needs popes and archbishops, garments and crosses, incense and church bells, Canterbury Cathedral and St. Peter's, rabbis and synagogues, parish churches and parish priests to give meaning to why we are on earth, hell or life eternal, ritual, prayer, baptism, and confirmation, circumcision, confession, incense, and communion, let us have it all. Belief is a self-fulfilling prophecy. It has all been around for so long that it is best taken as Gospel truth. Let us pray — and pretend — say the Lord's Prayer, heed the Ten Commandments. Theirs is the authority of millennia. Let us fulfill the Will of the God we made. Let our spirits be lifted by hymns and psalms, Bach and Fra Angelico, by stained-glass windows, by the Gothic of Europe or the ravishing colors of Isfahan and Shiraz mosques. Location, location, location, whether the parish church in a Cotswold village or the white steeples of New England, Chartres, or St. Paul's. They are our history. We need the ceremonial, to marry and bury, wage war, or celebrate the holy days.

For heaven's sake, though, let us not think one religion is better than another. If there were a God, He would surely not tolerate prejudice, while man is — and always will be — suspicious of the different and unfamiliar. One can well question whether religion does more good or harm. The fear of God is man's most effective fund-raiser, and sinful sex the clerics' futile threat to contain illegitimate births and syphilis.

I rarely take Communion. It seems not fair to the devout. I rarely go to church. I miss it, but is it fair to my forebears to pray to the Christian god? I am too old to revert to the Jewish god, and anyhow don't really like minority religions. Like small nations, they carry a chip on their shoulder. As long as there is anti-Semitism I won't walk away from my origins. Since Jew and Gentile between them are doing their best to keep it alive I will just have to muddle through best as I can.

As I write I am looking at the pines and oaks next to our Edgartown house. The evening sun is casting long shadows. The flower garden to the left could come out of Country Life. On the right the lawn slopes to the edge of Eel Pond. Beyond lies Nantucket Sound. Vera's mother and mine lived to share many Vineyard summers with us. It made them happy to see our ship had come home safely. Father would have loved our island life, to see us as part of a settled community and own what had eluded him — a country home. He would be relieved, but I hope not too surprised that I seem not to have altogether squandered my life, considering in my schoolboy days he despaired that I would end up at best a street sweep — not even a streetcar conductor: "For that they don't take the likes of you."

Fifty out of my almost eighty years I have lived in New York, thirty-six of them in the same home. I have been married to Vera for thirty-seven years. Our sons are in their thirties. There is Max, our little grandson, and Zoe Helene, an even littler granddaughter. I have been in the financial field for fifty years, thirty of them in the same firm. After an uncertain start — not only Hitler's doing — mine became a stable life. Without Hitler it might have had greater continuity, but it might also have been less interesting. The only balance sheet that really counts is ultimo, which I hope is still a little down the road. All our lives we work for our obituary. For me life has become progressively better, which is reason enough to be fearful of all that could still go wrong.

Much as we love the Vineyard, the New York apartment is our real home. Vera has kept it uncluttered, too uncluttered for my liking! The walls might well have remained bare if we had not long ago decided we both like Calder, whose tapestries in our living room, dining room, and bedroom give both of us pleasure. Square foot by square foot, inch by inch, I have annexed wall space for the handful of pictures I have bought. Expressionists, too obviously pleasing, never appealed to me in the sense I wanted to own them, not to mention I could not have afforded what I might have wanted. But — and this goes back to museum visits before the war, especially with my Grandfather Flersheim, and after the war with my Oxford friend Adam Stainton — the European masters, whether of the Quattrocento or the Victorian era, never fail to give me pleasure. I really know Italy quite well — the churches or galleries of Florence, Venice, Padua, Verona, Vicenza, and, though not well enough, of Rome. In London I go to the museums I have known since my English days. In New York I cross the street to the Metropolitan, not only to see the crowded blockbusters of which there are too many, but to the peaceful permanent galleries. I traveled a lot in my work, and what fun it was to sneak off to do some sightseeing rather than to call on every last client.

The small handful of good paintings I own, partly by chance, partly by design, reflect the European culture and history that has made us into who and what we are. My old Oxford friend Evelyn Joll, who for many years headed Agnew's in London, advised me well. A seascape of William of Orange arriving on the English coast, by the younger van der Velde, appeals to my love of the sea, of clouds, wind, and ships, and English history. It gratifies my mercenary instincts that I bought it and other paintings before the artists were rediscovered. *The Adoration of the Magi* triptych by Ysenbrandt, which I bought in 1985, has received compliments from people in the art world whose taste and judgment I trust more than my own. Anyone with an interest in old masters has to own some religious works of art. Almost the first picture I bought is the fragment of a Madonna by Neri di Bicci — too heavily restored to be very valuable, but she has a loving calm smile of which I never tire. Giotto might have painted her. Soon after I joined Lazard I bought for relatively little money a portrait by Romney of an elegant young eighteenth-century Englishman, similar to his famous Eton leaving pictures. When I showed it to Andre Meyer, his only reaction was: Make more money before you buy art.

One wall in our living room and one in the hallway is covered with the books that reflect our intersts. Vera's are about sculpture and literature, including French. The largest number of my shelves is devoted to art. Next come the biographies of nineteenth- and twentieth-century English politicians, First and Second World War generals, George V and VI, Edward the VII, books by and about Winston Churchill, and, last but not least, American history, mainly of the nineteenth century. The German generals and others who resisted Hitler and almost killed him on July 20, 1944, are heroes of mine, and there are many books about them.

There are lots of Baedecker guides, from the mid-nineteenth century on, in German and in English. The height of the Swiss mountains has not changed, but the glaciers have shrunk and hotel prices have risen. Before the First World War a good hotel in Switzerland cost less than five Swiss francs a night, breakfast included. Nowadays there are better guidebooks than Karl Baedecker's.

If you looked at my shelves you would find several rows of financial history, especially of the City — the merchant banks and old established stockbrokers, Rothschilds, Morgans, and Warburgs, Deutsche Bank and Dresdner. Who will keep them together after I am dead? Almost needless to say, there are many, many books about German Jews; Vera would say too many, and she may be right.

From my writing desk I can reach for Keynes's *General Theory*, Bagehot's *Lombard Street*, selected essays by Emerson and *Tom Sawyer*, which Michael once gave me, Theodor Fontane's *Effi Briest*, Goethe's *Faust*, Part I, Heine's *Deutschland, ein Wintermärchen*, and the Edgartown Yacht Club Yearbook. Also an anthology of English poetry, which I bought as a schoolboy at Tonbridge but reach for too rarely.

I have worked on this book on and off for almost ten years. It has helped — and forced — me to remember. It made me think about loose ends that needed tidying up before it is too late. For instance, there is now a plaque affixed to the old Flersheim home in Frankfurt to commemorate the years they lived there. I am deeply grateful to its owners, Peter Fischer and his wife Christiane, that they had the generosity of spirit to saddle themselves, day in, day out, with a reminder that they live in a house whose erstwhile owners perished in a concentration camp.

I spent weeks going through mother's photo albums and had four sets of copies made of family pictures for George and Michael, and my sister's children.

After three years of an intensive, costly, legal and public relations effort I have succeeded in recovering the ownership of one of the works of art in the Flersheim collection confiscated by the Gestapo in 1938. It was one of Ernst Flersheim's favorite pictures, a pastel drawing by his good friend, the important nineteenth- and early-twentieth-century Dutch artist Jan Toorop, of a farmer named Pieter Provoost in Domburg in the Netherlands, where the Flersheims used to summer before World War I. Toorop, as Ernst Flersheim writes in his memoirs, was deeply religious and engaged him in wide-ranging conversations.

I shall never know how the picture found its way to Holland during World War II. In 1943 it was sold by a member of the German occupation forces to a Dutch art dealer who in turn sold it to two prominent

Rotterdam businessmen who acquired it on behalf of the Boijmans van Beuningen Foundation, which owned much of the art displayed in the municipally owned Boijmans Museum in Rotterdam. By chance a cousin of ours saw the drawing — its title was *Faith in God* — hanging in the museum after the war.

In 1954 Father's request to have it returned to Mother as the rightful owner was turned down by the Foundation, though the museum director at that time thought it should be given back to her. By then I was living in New York. I then forgot about *Faith in God* until I started working on this book and began reading old family correspondence. In 1998 I approached the Boijmans Foundation to have it returned. By then in many countries "looted" Jewish art was being returned to its rightful owners or their heirs, though not in the Netherlands. It never dawned on me that I would be faced with years of obstruction over a picture called of all things *Faith in God* — especially given its history. I had assumed that the Foundation would hand it back to me the next day. The outcome is fairly summarized in the joint press release by the Foundation and myself when we finally reached an agreement in November 2001:

Rotterdam, November 2001 — The Museum Boijmans Van Beuningen Foundation of Rotterdam and Mr. Walter A. Eberstadt of New York have reached an agreement under which ownership of the drawing *Faith in God* by the Dutch artist, Jan Toorop, will be transferred to Mr. Eberstadt, grandson of the original owners, the late Ernst and Gertrud Flersheim.

The drawing was acquired in 1943 by two board members of the Foundation from an art dealer in The Hague and donated to the Foundation which makes its works of art available to the Boijmans Van Beuningen Museum in Rotterdam.

The Flersheims were close personal friends of Jan Toorop. Already at the end of the nineteenth century they owned some of his artworks. In Mr. Eberstadt's words: "If Toorop, the Flersheims, or my parents could know that after all these years the *Faith in*

God is in the possession of our family, they would be enormously gratified." Mr. Eberstadt's sister and Flersheim granddaughter, Mrs. Bridget Collier of London, said: "I am proud of my brother's efforts and happy for him. He deserves to own it."

Ernst Flersheim was a German-Jewish businessman and art collector in Frankfurt on Main who fled with his wife from Germany to Holland in 1937. In 1943 they were arrested in Amsterdam and detained in the Dutch camp Westerbork. From Westerbork they were sent to the German camp Bergen-Belsen where they perished in 1944.

Mr. Eberstadt recently had claimed the drawing, stating it was family property. The Museum Boijmans Van Beuningen Foundation initially had some difficulty in finding legal grounds for yielding ownership. No details were disclosed but "the terms under which the Boijmans Foundation offered me the *Faith in God* are acceptable to me. I am glad that even if it was a lengthy process, my belief in the fair-mindedness of the Dutch has been vindicated," stated Mr. Eberstadt.

According to the chairman of the Foundation board, Mr. J. van Caldenborgh, "We had to make a gesture, ownership or no ownership."

There is more work for me to do but I doubt I have the energy to fight the way I did for *Faith in God*. Two other paintings confiscated from the Flersheim collection are in Dutch museums. In 1937 the Boijmans Museum — not the Foundation — purchased Toorop's *Thames at Tower Bridge*. In 1981 the Zeeuws Museum in Middelburg bought Toorop's *Mealtime Prayer*, one of his most important works, without having troubled to research its provenence. The museum at first took the position I had neither a "legal or moral" claim to have it returned to me. I believe, though, that we will eventually reach a compromise and it will be returned, but then given back as a gift from my sister and myself, with the Flersheim ownership and their death commemorated in a plaque.

Two major — and valuable — works by the Swiss painter Ferdinand Hodler have disappeared without a trace, but with professional help I am continuing to search for them.

I have recently obtained the official German records detailing the expropriation of the Flersheim assets and the loss of their German nationality. Should one laugh or cry? On March 22, 1938, the Gestapo in Berlin applied to the Reichsführer of the SS and chief of police in the Ministry of the Interior (Ref S-PP (II B) for permission to deprive the Jew Ernst Karl Flersheim and his wife, Gertrud, née Baroness von Mayer, "apparently of Jewish descent," formerly of Frankfurt on Main and now of Amsterdam, of their German nationality. Steps were taken to confiscate all assets remaining in Germany, after payment of Reichsfluchtsteuer — tax previously paid for permission to leave Germany. The confiscated assets were in excess of RM 1,000,000. Flersheim is described as the owner of a family business but "details regarding his life are not known." However, "it is known that Flersheim and his family gave financial support to Marxist political parties and that his late son Hans was a member of the Reichsbanner [Social Democratic Party]." Further, "Flersheim was fined RM 4,000 on August 20, 1937, by the Reich Economics Ministry for contravening a currency regulation." This is the first I ever heard of the Flersheims' politics. I am convinced it was a piece of fabricated nonsense, and anyhow, so what! The German Embassy in the Netherlands was asked whether it could have adverse international repercussions. The ambassador, Herr von Bülow-Schwante, saw no reason not to go ahead.

On a more cheerful note, also part of tidying up, it occurs to me that I mention nowhere the handful of honors I have collected. "Elizabeth the Second, by the Grace of God of the United Kingdom of Great Britain and Northern Ireland and of Her other Realms and Territories, Queen, Head of the Commonwealth, Defender of the Faith and Sovereign of the Most Excellent Order of the British Empire appointed our trusty and well-beloved Walter Albert Eberstadt Esquire" in 1986 to be an "Ordinary Officer of the Civil Division of our said Most Excellent Order of the British Empire." The award was given for furthering British financial interests in New York over many years.

President Richard von Weiszäcker awarded me the Verdienstkreuz First Class in 1987 "in recognition of special services rendered to the Bundesrepublik." It was really for my work at Radio Hamburg in postwar Germany. Peter von Zahn was the "proposer."

The New School gave me an honorary degree in 1996: "Walter A. Eberstadt — investment banker, citizen of the world, dedicated Trustee. Your unpredictable wit, fused with unfailing charm, your mastery of international capital markets and your humanitarian instincts are well known. You impart elegance and grace to every activity. And you find the right balance: you work, hike and sail with equal zest, knowing what you value and why it matters. Your long support of the Northside Center for Child Development in Harlem is exemplary of your concern for this City and your willingness to give of yourself. Through your service as a New School Trustee you invigorate every part of the University in which you are involved. You embody its best characteristics: an openness to new ventures and vistas, tenacity in the defense of principle, and the courage to ask uncomfortable questions. As a discerning and imaginative ambassador, you widen the New School's sphere of acquaintance and circle of friends. Because of your spirited commitment, a steady surge of outstanding additions has transformed the New School's leadership: you raise the trend line. Recognizing that you have served New York and the University with distinction, the New School for Social Research is delighted to confer upon you the degree of Doctor of Humane Letters, honoris causa."

For my seventieth birthday Vera redecorated George's old room into my study. There is no place where I find myself as content and comfortable. Much of the furniture and paintings come from my parents' London home. Many hours have been spent there working on this book. I am surrounded by my animal bronzes, the Barye lions and the Barye elephant, the Bugatti and the Pompom pumas, a Giambologna and a Susini, the Barye centaur, his Turkish horses, and Herbert Hazeltine's bronze of King George V's favorite horse. I spend more time at home and relish our neighborhood. I still buy more books than I read, but I am catching up a little. I struggle to avoid being swept away by uncertain financial times. Increasingly I want my peace and quiet, without becoming isolated. I struggle to delay the onset of old age in the gym and by keeping company with the young.

Not only Mother kept a travel diary. Mine is not in her league. Still, browsing through it brings to mind good times:

- At least a dozen Christmases with Vera, George, and Michael in Sun Valley, the very, very best of holidays, cross-country skiing at Galinas and Busterback below the headwaters of the Salmon River in the Sawtooth Mountains, Vera skating on Sonja Henie's rink, steaks at the Ore House, marketing at Albertson, oddly enjoyable delays at the Salt Lake airport.
- Innumerable stays, first at the Hyde Park Hotel, later the Berkeley: invited by the Queen and the Duke of Edinburgh to a ball at Windsor Castle to celebrate my friend Angus Ogilvy's marriage to Princess Alexandra of Kent.
- Pebble Beach and San Francisco while we expected George.
- The Hotel de Bergues in Geneva, the Suvretta in St. Moritz in winter and summer, innumerable times at the Baur au Lac in Zurich or that unique Schloss Hotel in Kronberg outside Frankfurt (Room 402 with views in all directions and birdsongs at dawn), many times at the Hotel Vier Jahreszeiten in Hamburg overlooking the Alster.
- At the Ritz in Paris on the Rue Cambon side, probably over-rated and certainly overpriced; I always feel a fish out of water in Paris.
- Our first holiday alone since the boys were born, in Nairobi, Capetown, animals at Mala Mala, lunch with Harry Oppenheimer, Victoria Falls.
- Cambridge Beaches in Bermuda with little George and Michael at each other hammer and tongue.
- An eye-opening first trip to the Far East, a World Bank meeting with that awful Marcos in Manila, and then Hong Kong; other years back to Hong Kong, to Singapore, Penang, and Bali with Vera.

- Parents' Days at Exeter visiting George and Michael (much much preferable to Tonbridge!)
- Three weeks trekking in Nepal in October 1984, aged sixty-three, with my Lazard partner David Dillard, the last fling with big league "adventure" by my admittedly rather tame standards. (I can refresh my recollections looking at photos on top of the bookshelves in Edgartown, certainly the trip merits more than this passing reference.)
- The very best of holidays in Scotland in June 1989 with Vera, George and Michael, after their Harvard and Dartmouth graduations: Skye, Thurso, Orkney, Culloden House Hotel at Inverness and the Culloden battlefield.
- Walking in all weather on the dykes at Colchester with Nils Taube, drowning a dozen or two of Colchester oysters — the best in the world — in appropriate quantities of white Burgundy.
- Staying in pomp with Arthur and Helen Burns at the American Embassy in Bonn.
- Spring in the Arizona desert at the Boulders.
- Chartering David Dillard's 75-foot yawl *Leonore* in the Caribbean with the New York Henry and Sissy Arnholds and the Edinburgh Gus and Julia Millars.
- Chartering a Hinckley Bermuda 40 with George and Michael on Penobscot Bay.
- Barcelona, Grenada, Cordoba, Seville, and Madrid with Vera, virtually camping out at the Prado.
- Nova Scotia with George, Baxter State Park in a lean-to with Michael, salmon fishing, meager results, with George and Michael at Susan and Roy O'Connor's on the Grand Cascapedia.
- Hong Kong, Beijing, the Great Wall, and Shanghai with Vera, also with her Patagonia, Santiago, Punta Arenas, Beagle channel, Parque Nacional Torres del Paine with condors overhead and Guanacos running around, Cape Horn, all in splendid

comfort aboard the German *Hanseatic*, Egypt, with Vera; Prague, many a time Vienna, a few times Berlin.

- Jackson and Yellowstone as a seventieth birthday present for Vera from George and Michael.
- Deerstalking (of course, strictly a business trip) with Alex Zagoreos, Gary Glyn, and a handful of other cronies in the Scottish Highlands at Roger and Jean Adams' Forest of Dalnaspittal, one year shooting that season's biggest stag.

On this braggart note I stop. Any more would be an anticlimax. But haven't I been fortunate, just unbelievably fortunate! May it last just a bit longer . . .

- A fourth Wagner "Ring," maybe in Seattle. I've never been to Bayreuth, but don't read politics into that; the Met Opera is so conveniently close.
- More Schubert lieder, not only at my memorial, when I won't be there to hear them.

In theory I am orderly, in practice there are untidy files and drawers filled with paternal correspondence and diaries on every facet of her long life kept by Mother — the books she read, the plays she saw, the parties she had, houseguests, Christmas cards sent and cards received, watercolors she made to celebrate anniversaries, her household expenses each month of her married life.

In 1921, her first married year, she spent RM 2,802 in January, but by December with the early impact of the German inflation, a month cost RM 8,744. The first months of 1922 were still in the four-digit range, but in October her cash expenses were RM 77,932, in November RM 122,953, and in December RM 252,080. The year, all told, cost RM 572,542 in cash and RM 366,906 paid by check. In 1923, in the month of November alone, it was RM 911,210,000,000,000, in December RM 1,397,005,000,000,000! In 1924 the inflation was over and her total expenses were RM 17,483.

If only to relieve George and Michael from a multitude of dilemmas of what to keep and what to throw away I vow herewith to tidy up loose ends before it is too late.

I could go on and on with snippets of this or that, of interest probably to none other than myself. Hence, as they say in the London *Times*, this correspondence will now cease.

George and Michael asked me to write about our family and my life. I was touched but at first I discarded the idea. Their filial loyalty overestimates me, but on reflection there seemed enough of interest to preserve about preceding generations. Lives that were made extraordinary by the impact on them of the Kaiser's and then of Hitler's Germany would have slipped away into the fog of unrecorded history. Is it an asset, or a liability, to know whence you come? Does it influence who you are, what you make or don't make, of yourself? We all stem from Adam and Eve, hence all presumably have the same number of forebears but consider ourselves a cut above others if we happen to know who for a handful of generations they were. Is it easier to start with a clean slate than with trunkloads of family history, at best half accurate?

Vera and I are the link between our European origins and the American future of our children and their offspring. I am the last one who can send them on their way with knowledge of who preceded them. I am loath always to discard anything and I'd be dispatching the generations before mine into oblivion if I had not written these pages. The past has navigated the Atlantic. Some record is here for George and Michael of earlier Eberstadts and Edingers, Flersheims and von Mayers — for them to use or to ignore.

Index